T5-DGK-509

Dictionary of international an

DICTIONARY

OF

INTERNATIONAL
&
COMPARATIVE LAW

JAMES R. FOX

Library of Congress Cataloging-in-Publication Data

Fox, James R.

Dictionary of international and comparative law.

1. International law—Dictionaries. 2 Comparative Law-
JX1226.F69 1992
341'.03—dc20

ISBN: 0-379-20430-4

©Copyright 1992 Oceana Publications, Inc.

Manufactured in the United States of America on acid-free paper.

DICTIONARY
OF
INTERNATIONAL
&
COMPARATIVE LAW

To Pat, Max,
and
The Dickinson School of Law Community

PREFACE

This work began out of the frustration of the author and The Dickinson School of Law Library staff in the early 1980's when research in international law became a major interest of our students and faculty. At that time, there was no source to consult to answer the basic questions we were constantly presented by novices in the field. Many commonly used international law terms are not in the standard law dictionaries and often international agreements are known by popular names; therefore, I set out to compile a dictionary of international law terms that would give the researcher a starting point.

Though far from comprehensive, the Dictionary as we have used it over the last couple of years answer many of the international law questions we confront. I hope it will prove as useful to you.

I would like to thank The Dickinson School of Law Library staff for all their patience while I slaved at my word processor, *incommunicado*. Much of the work of compiling, editing, and source checking has been done by a wonderful group of student research assistants. Thus, special thanks to Andi Dibble, Susan Duke, Richard Michael, Sawako Tachibana, Nancy Garner, Maria Czerniach, Ann Marie George, Rochelle Quiggle, and Blair McClenachan. Also, special thanks to Eileen Servos who typed and edited this manuscript till she must know it by heart.

Any bad cites or just plain wrong definitions are those of the author. I would appreciate receiving corrections and terms I may have left out. Please send them to:

James R. Fox
Law Librarian and Professor of Law
The Dickinson School of Law
150 S. College Street
Carlisle, PA 17013

INTRODUCTION

Terms have been selected for inclusion in this work from a number of sources. Indices of several hundred international law texts were consulted - yearbooks and journals of international law were perused. Many terms were brought to the author's attention by reference questions.

The inclusion of a term and the form in which it appears is somewhat idiosyncratic. Common variations have been included as cross references. Due to the fluid nature of language however, some of the responsibility must lie with the user to play with possible variations. If you do not find an entry for "Exploration and Use of Outer Space Treaty, " try "Outer Space Treaty."

Entries include a signal of the language if a term is not English, e.g., ACTIO INDICATI (L): the (L) indicates that the term is Latin. A definition or brief explanation of the term follows. Cross references are made using either law review style signals (*see also, but see,* etc.) or a parenthetical reference "q.v." (which see), or in the case of more than one reference, "qq.v." (both which see). The cross referenced entries are in all-capital letters.

KEY TO ABBREVIATIONS

A.C. ....Law Reports Appeals Cases (English)

A.D. ....Annual Digest of Public
                              International Law

All.E.R. ....All England Law Reports

Am.J.Comp.L. ....American Journal of Comparative Law

Am.J.Int.L. ....American Journal of International Law

Am. J. Int'l L. Supp. ....American Journal of International
                              Law Supplement

Am. Soc'y Int'l L. Proc. ......American Society of International
                              Law Proceedings

Am.U.L.Rev. ....American University Law Review

Am. Univ. J. Int'l L. & P. .....American University Journal of
                              International Law and Policy

Ann. Digest ....Annual Digest of Public International Law

App. Cas. ....The Law Reports, AppealsCases
                              (Great Britain)

Aust. Ybk. Int'l L. ....Australian Yearbook of International Law

Austl.L.J. ....Australian Law Journal

Avi. Cases ....Aviation Cases

Bevans...................................Bevans, Treaties and Other International
                              Agreements of the United States

Boston College Int'l & Comp.L.R.
....Boston College International and
                              Comparative Law Review

Brit.Y.B.Int'l.L. ....British Yearbook of International Law

Brooklyn J. Int'l L. ....Brooklyn Journal of International Law

Cal.West.Int'l.L.J. ....California Western International
                              Law Journal

Can.Y.B.Int'l L. ....Canadian Yearbook of International Law

Canada-U.S.L.J. .... Canada-U.S. Law Journal

Case W.Res.J.Int'l L. .... Case Western Reserv Journal
of International Law

C.F.R. .... Code of Federal Regulations
(United States)

Colum.J.Transnat'l.L. .... Columbia Journal of Transnational
Law

Colum. L. Rev..................... Columbia Law Review

C.T.S.................................... Parry, Consolidated Treaty Series
(Oceana)

Den. J. Int'l L.&Pol'y .... Denver Journal of International
Law and Policy

Dept. State Bull. .... Department of State Bulletin (United States)

Dick. J. Int'l L...................... Dickinson Journal International Law

Dick. L. Rev. .... Dickinson Law Review

E.C.R. .... European Court Reports

Eng.Rep............................... English Reports (Great Britian)

Eur.T.L................................. European Transport Law

F... French

F2d .... Federal Reporter 2d

Fed.R.Civ.P. .... Federal Rules of Civil Procedure

G... German

Ga.J.Int'l & Comp.L............ Georgia Journal of International and
Comparative Law

German Y.B. Int'l L............. German Yearbook of International Law

Harv. Int'l L.J...................... Harvard International Law Journal

Harv. L. Rev. .... Harvard Law Review

I.. Italian

I.A.L.M. .... Inter-American Legal Materials

KEY TO ABBREVIATIONS

I.C.J.............................International Court of Justice Reports

I.L.M............................International Legal Materials

I.L.R............................International Law Reports

Int'l.& Comp.L.Q. ....International and Comparative Law Quarterly

Int'l J. Legal Information....International Journal of Legal Information

Int'l.Lawyer ....International Lawyer

Int'l Org. ....International Organizations

Italian Y.B.Intl.L. ....Italian Yearbook of International Law

J. Air L. and Com. ....Journal of Air Law and Commerce

J.O..............................Journal Officiel (France)

J. Space L. ....Journal of Space Law

Jurid.Rev. ....Juridical Review (Edinburgh)

J.W.T.L. ....Journal of World Trade Law

K.B..............................English Law Reports, King's Bench

L................................Latin

Law. Am..........................Lawyers of the Americas

Lloyd's Mar. & Comm.L.Q.
...............................Lloyd's Maritime and Commercial Law Quarterly (Great Britain)

Loyola L.A.Int'l.& Comp.L.J
...............................Loyola of Los Angeles International and Comparative Law Journal

L.N.T.S..........................League of Nations Treaty Series

L.Q.Rev..........................Law Quarterly Review

Malaya L. Rev....................Malaya Law Review

McGill L.J. ....McGill Law Journal (Canada)

Mich.L.Rev.......................Michigan Law Review

N.Y. Times .... New York Times

Netherlands Y.B. Int'l L. .... Netherlands Yearbook of International Law

O.J. Eur. Comm. .... Official Journal of the European Community

P.C.I.J. .... Permanent Court of International Justice Reports

Q.B. .... Queen's Bench (Great Britian)

R .... Russian

Rev. Socialist L. .... Review of Socialist Law

R.I.A.A .... Reports of International Arbitral Awards

S .... Spanish

Sen. Res. .... Senate Resolutions (United States)

South. Univ.L.Rev. .... Southern University Law Review

Stanford J.Int'l L. .... Stanford Journal of International Law

Stanford L.Rev. .... Stanford Law Review

Stat. .... United States Statutes-at-Large

Toynbee, Treaties .... Toynbee, Major Peace Treaties of Modern History

T.S. .... Treaty Series

U.N. Doc. .... United Nations Documents

U.N. Rep .... United Nations Reports

UNGA .... United Nations General Assembly

U.N.T.S. .... United Nations Treaty Series

U.N. Yearbook .... United Nations Yearbook

U.S. .... United States Reports (U.S. Supreme Court

U.S.C. .... United States Code

U.S.T. .... United States Treaties and Other International Agreements

[A-B]

AALCC: ASIAN-AFRICAN LEGAL CONSULTATIVE COM-MITTEE (q.v.).

AALAND ISLANDS: Archipelago between Sweden and Finland. It was the subject of a treaty forbiding its fortification. *See* 114 C.T.S., 405 (1856). The League of Nations mediated the question of sovereignty over the islands between Sweden and Finland. *See* League of Nations Official Journal 1920 sp. Supp. 3.

AAPC: ALL-AFRICAN PEOPLES' CONFERENCE (q.v.).

AB INCONVEINENTI (L): out of inconvenience.

AB INITIO (L): from the start or beginning.

AB INITIO MUNDI (L): from the distant past.

ABANDONMENT OF A SHIP: formal relinquishing of property interest in a ship that is sunk or damaged. Marine insurance usually requires notice to the insurer of abandonment. Upon abandonment the right to SALVAGE (q.v.) arises. *See also* SCUTTLING.

ABANDONMENT OF TERRITORY: relinquishing of sovereignty over territory may be accomplished by withdrawing the sovereign's presence; giving up OCCUPATION (q.v.).

ABC MEDIATION: effort by Argentina, Brazil, and Chile to restore order in Mexico in 1914, and later to end the United States intervention. *See* 9 Am.J.Int.L. 147 (1915).

ABDICATION OF MONARCHS: abdication is the formally renouncing and resigning of one's position as the head of state of a monarchy or kingdom. *See* e.g., EDWARD VIII.

ABDUCTION OF CHILDREN: subject of a HAGUE CONFER-ENCE ON PRIVATE INTERNATIONAL LAW (q.v.); convention with provisions aimed at the prompt returning of children wrong-fully removed from a territory. *See* 19 I.L.M. 1501.

ABGRENZUNG (G): border; term specifically applied to the line separating East and West Germany. Also, applies to the East German policy of complete separation of the two Germanys.

ABIDJAN DECLARATION (1973): organization of African Union policy statement urging African economic cooperation and integration. *See* 12 I.L.M. 996.

ABLEGATUS (L): medieval designation for what became an ENVOY (q.v.).

ABM: ANTI-BALLISTIC MISSILE (q.v.).

ABOLITION OF FORCED LABOR CONVENTION (1957): treaty where the parties undertake not to use or to take measures to suppress the use of forced compulsory labor. *See* 320 U.N.T.S. 291.

ABOLITION OF SLAVERY CONVENTION (1956): international effort to outlaw slavery. *See* 18 U.S.T. 3201, 266 U.N.T.S. 3.

ABROGATIO LEGIS (L): law no longer in force.

ABROGATION: termination of a treaty; in general, this must be done by the mutual consent of the parties. Abrogation (abrogate) is often used to note a strong attempt at unilateral termination.

ABSENT DEFENDANT: generally the defendant's domicile, residence, or presence is required for a court to exercise jurisdiction over an action. English courts may grant leave to serve notice of a writ on an absent defendant and then assume jurisdiction. *See* TRIAL IN ABSENTIA.

ABSOLUTE RESPONSIBILITY: duty to act or indemnify without regard to fault.

ABSOLUTE RIGHT: right which continues to exist regardless of intervening circumstances, e.g., a state of war or competing claims of other rights.

ABSQUE INJURIA (L): without violating a legal right.

ABSTENTION: option of a state or a representative to decline to vote either for or against a particular measure. Abstentions are a common practice in international settings. The practice of abstention may pose a problem when calculating a majority.

ABSTINENTIA GUERRARUM (L): by treaty; agreement that a particular country will not be involved in a war, i.e., neither will it participate on one side nor the other, nor will it be attacked.

ABU DHABI OIL ARBITRATION: this decision interrupted the petroleum development concession by the Sheik of Abu Dhabi to a British Company. *See* 18 I.L.R. 144.

ABUS DE CONFIANCE (F): French penal law forbidding fraud.

ABUS DE DROIT (F): ABUSE OF RIGHTS (q.v.); use of legal process to harm another rather than to pursue a just claim.

ABUSE OF A MARITIME FLAG: sailing under a flag which the nation of the flag has not authorized, or while conducting some prohibited activity such as PIRACY or SLAVE TRADE (qq.v.).

ABUSE OF RIGHTS: state's liability for exercising a right unwarranted by the circumstances. *See* 24 I.L.R. 806-808.

ABUSO DE DERECHO (S): abusive exercise of a right. *See* 11 Cal.West.Int'l.L.J. 32 (1981).

ACADEMY OF INTERNATIONAL LAW: *see* HAGUE ACADEMY OF INTERNATIONAL LAW.

ACCESSIO CEDIT PRINCIPALI (L): an accessory when annexed to a thing becomes part of the thing.

ACCESSION: process of becoming a party to, or legally bound by a treaty without formal action, e.g., ratification and without substantial reservation. *See also* ADHERENCE.

ACCLAMATION: decision-making mechanism sometimes used in international conferences where approval of a proposal is shown by the participants' remarks, applause, etc.; without a formal vote.

ACCORD: agreement; usually referring to the settlement of a specific dispute or issue.

ACCRA DECLARATION (1973): policy statement by the Organization of African Unity's Liberation Committee giving priority to supporting the guerrillas fighting the Portuguese colonial rule and urging a united front against Portugal. *See* Z. Cernevka, *The Unfinished Quest for Unity* 58-59 (1977).

ACCREDITATION: act of presenting a diplomatic representative with credentials in the form of a LETTER OF CREDENCE or LETTRE D'INTRODUCTION (qq.v.).

ACCRETION: geological formation of new land mass, e.g., the building-up of islands at the mouth of a river which may affect borders and territorial seas.

ACDA: ARMS CONTROL AND DISARMAMENT AGENCY (q.v.).

ACHAIAN LEAGUE: confederation of Greek city-states in the 3rd century B.C., formerly cited as the ideal government. *See Federalist Papers* No.18 (Hamilton and Madison).

ACHESON-LILIENTHAL REPORT (1946): recommended that the United States propose a world authority to control all dangerous fissionable nuclear materials. *See* BARUCH PLAN.

ACHILLE LAURO INCIDENT (1985): Palestinians hijacked an Italian cruise ship, the *Achille Lauro,* and killed one passenger. *See* 26 Va.J.Int'l.L. 723, 745 (1986).

ACID RAIN: precipitation which has absorbed air pollutants and causes environmental damage, usually at some distance from the source of the pollution. Lakes and forests are the primary targets of the damage. *See* 25 I.L.M. 1022 and LONG-RANGE TRANSBOUNDARY AIR POLLUTION CONVENTION (1979) and the New York-Quebec Agreement on Acid Rain, 21 I.L.M. 721.

ACQUIESCENCE: passive agreement that a practice is legal or acceptable, usually proven by showing a lack of protest. *See Encyclopedia of Public International Law 5.*

ACQUIRED IMMUNE DEFICIENCY SYNDROME: action by the World Health Organization in their efforts against the world wide epidemic of AIDS are reported in N.Y. Times, Nov. 21, 1986, at 1.

ACQUIRED RIGHTS: property rights of all kinds which remain vested in individuals when sovereignty over territory changes hands, e.g., private land holdings were unchanged by the LOUISIANA PURCHASE (q.v.).

ACQUISITION OF NATIONALITY: subject of a protocol to the VIENNA CONVENTION ON CONSULAR RELATIONS (q.v.), *See* 596 U.N.T.S. 469.

ACQUISITIVE PRESCRIPTION: acquisition of title over territory by effective, continuous, and peaceful exercise of jurisdiction. *See* 27 Brit.Y.B.Int'l.L. 332.

ACT OF GOD: condition or occurrence beyond human control, e.g., a storm at sea. *See* FORCE MAJEURE.

ACT OF STATE: doctrine; acts carried-out as part of a nation's assertion of sovereign powers are not attributable to individuals. This doctrine is often followed by municipal courts to avoid ruling on the actions of states, e.g., nationalization of industries. *See* the Sabbatino Case, 376 U.S. 398 (1964).

ACT OF WAR: use of force or other action by one state against another. The state acted against recognizes this action as an act of war, either by use of retaliatory force or a declaration of war.

ACTA JURE GESTIONIS (L): act performed by a state which could have been performed by a private individual, e.g., the purchase of an office building.

ACTA IMPERII (L): act which is only within the power of a sovereign to commit, e.g., the conferring of citizenship.

ACTE AUTHENTIQUE (F): authentic or certified document.

ACTE D'ACCEPTATION (F): formal acknowledgement of the deposit of an INSTRUMENT OF RATIFICATION (q.v.), issued by the DEPOSITORY STATE (q.v.).

ACTE FINAL (F): FINAL ACT (q.v.).

ACTE DE GUERRE (F): ACT OF WAR (q.v.).

ACTES COMMIS (F): acts committed by states. The term usually contemplates only acts contrary to international law for which there is an obligation to make reparations.

ACTIO INDICATI (L): judgment from a foreign court being presented to a domestic court.

ACTIO PERSONALIS MORITUR CUM PERSONA (L): personal right of action dies with the person.

ACTOR FORUN REI SEQUITUR (L): person bringing suit cannot choose the court based on his convenience. He must sue in a court competent to take jurisdiction over the defendant, based on the defendant's presence, domicile, etc.

ACTORI IMCUMBIT PROBATIO (L): party which makes a claim has the burden of producing facts and legal doctrine to support the claim.

ACTUELLEMENT (F): now; at the present time. The term used in treaties has been interpreted as meaning on the day on which the treaty was signed.

AD HOC COMMITTEE ON THE INDIAN OCEAN: auxiliary body of the United Nations General Assembly established in 1972, to work toward a conference on the Indian Ocean. *See* 1973 U.N. Yearbook 35.

AD HOC COMMITTEE ON THE WORLD DISARMAMENT CONFERENCE: auxiliary body of the United Nations General Assembly appointed in 1977, to prepare a world disarmament conference. *See* 1978 U.N. Yearbook 17.

AD HOC JUDGE: judge appointed for a particular purpose, e.g., to hear one specific case.

AD HOMINEM (L): on an individual basis.

AD INSTANTIAM PARTIO (L): by request of one of the parties.

AD PERSONIAM (L): to the person, i.e. a right or duty pertaining specifically to an individual. *See* 80 I.L.R. 409.

AD INTERIM (L): during the intervening period of time; temporarily.

AD MODUM (L): in the manner of.

AD REFERENDUM (L): subject to further consideration. The signature of a treaty is subject to ratification before it constitutes a binding act. This is *ad referendum. See* Art. 12 of the VIENNA CONVENTION ON THE LAW OF TREATIES.

ADDIS ABABA CHARTER (1963): constitution of the ORGANIZATION OF AFRICAN UNITY (q.v.), 479 U.N.T.S. 39.

ADHERENCE: formal acceptance of the terms and obligations of a treaty by a state which was not a signatory state of the treaty. Signatory states give their formal acceptance by RATIFICATION (q.v.).

ADHESION: acceptance; with certain conditions or only partial acceptance of a treaty by a nation not originally a party to the treaty. *See* ACCESSION.

ADIZ: AIR DEFENSE IDENTIFICATION ZONE (q.v.)

ADMINISTRATIVE TRIBUNAL: judicial organ of an international organization to settle internal administrative disputes such as personnel complaints. The Administrative Tribunal of the United Nations was established by the General Assembly Nov. 24, 1949. *See* 1950 U.N. Yearbook 144.

ADMINISTRATIVE UNIONS: type of international organization usually dealing with a technical subject. May attempt to unify international efforts in the area of joining national technical organizations together. *See*, e.g., INTERNATIONAL TELE-COMMUNICATIONS UNION.

ADMISSIBILITY OF CLAIMS: question of the competence of a state to make a particular claim (either diplomatically or before an international judicial body) or question of the continued viability of the claim. Such a PRELIMINARY OBJECTION (q.v.) may be made before the merits of the case are presented.

ADMISSIONS CASE: two requests by the United Nations General Assembly for advisory opinions concerning the practices of and the need for Security Council approval, under Art. 4 of the UN Charter, for the admission of new members to the UN. *See* 1947/48 I.C.J. 57 and 1950 I.C.J. 4.

ADOPTION: process by which international law becomes part of municipal law by custom or statute, but is not automatically incorporated as it comes into existence.

ADOPTION OF CHILDREN: area of conflict between the laws of various jurisdictions; efforts have been made for international agreement to settle the conflicts problems. *See* e.g., EUROPEAN CONVENTION ON THE ADOPTION OF CHILDREN (1967).

ADR: EUROPEAN AGREEMENT CONCERNING THE INTERNATIONAL CARRIAGE OF DANGEROUS GOODS (1957) (q.v.).

ADVERSE DISTINCTION: the laws of war prohibit the differential treatment of PROTECTED PERSONS (q.v.) based on adverse distinctions such as race, color, social origin, wealth, language, sex, religion; or the nature or origin of an armed conflict. *See* Art. 16 of the Geneva Convention Protocol I (1977), 16 I.L.M. 1391.

ADVERSUS BONOS MORES (L): contrary to good morals.

ADVERSUS OMNI (L): against the interests of all.

ADVISORY OPINION: opinion rendered by the International Court of Justice on an administrative matter brought before it by an international organization. *See* the STATUTE OF THE INTER-

NATIONAL COURT OF JUSTICE, Arts. 65-68, 59 Stat. 1031, 3 Bevans 1191.

ADVOCATE: one who represents a party before a court or tribunal. An advocate appearing before the International Court of Justice is called an AGENT (q.v.).

AEGEAN SEA CONTINENTAL SHELF AGREEMENT: agreement between Greece and Turkey on procedures for negotiating a settlement of the border between the two, along the continental shelf in the Aegean Sea. *See* 16 I.L.M. 13.

AEQUO ET BONO: *see* EX AEQUO ET BONO.

AERIAL INCIDENT: any number of instances where the aircraft of one state have violated the airspace of another state. The most notable recent incident resulted in the shooting down of Korean Airlines Flight 007 by a Soviet fighter plane. *See* 88 Dick. L. Rev. 237 (1984); Israel v. Bulgaria, 1959 I.C.J. 127; and IRAN AIRBUS INCIDENT (1988).

AERIAL RECONNAISSANCE: form of spying; if a person on board an aircraft seeks to obtain information within a belligerent jurisdiction and intends to communicate the information to a hostile party. *See* Art. 27, Hague Rules of Aerial Warfare (1923) (never in force) *reproduced in,* 1 Friedman, *The Law of War* 437 (1972). Aerial reconnaissance is strictly controlled in most jurisdictions. *See also* Art. 36, CHICAGO CONVENTION (1945).

AFCAC: AFRICAN CIVIL AVIATION COMMISSION (q.v.).

AFFREIGHTMENT: contract by which a shipowner undertakes to carry goods by sea (by a BILL OF LADING or BOOKING-NOTE (qq.v.)) or put a vessel at the disposal of a shipper to carry goods in the form of a CHARTER-PARTY (q.v.).

AFFIRMATIO UNIS EST EXCLUSIO ALTERIUS (L): in civil law, the affirmation of one alternative to the exclusion of the other.

AFGHAN CONFLICT: civil war in Afghanistan between the communist government and Moslem rebels in which the Soviet Union intervened in 1979. *See* 82 Am.J.Int.L. 459 (1988).

AFRICAN CHARTER OF CASABLANCA (1961): adopted by Ghana, Guinea, Mali, Morocco, and the United Arab Republic establishing a short-lived organization to promote the "triumph of liberty all over Africa." *See* N.Y. Times, Jan. 8, 1961, at 1, col. 3.

AFRICAN CHARTER ON HUMAN AND PEOPLES' RIGHTS: *See* BANJUL CHARTER.

AFRICAN CIVIL AVIATION COMMISSION (AFCAC): regional organization to promote the development of civil aviation in cooperation with the INTERNATIONAL CIVIL AVIATION ORGANIZATION (q.v.). *See* 1001 U.N.T.S. 35.

AFRICAN COMMON MARKET: goal of the LAGOS PLAN FOR ACTION (1980) (q.v.) to establish a common market arrangement for Africa by the year 2000.

AFRICAN DECLARATION OF COOPERATION, DEVELOPMENT, AND ECONOMIC INDEPENDENCE (1973): calls for self-reliance by the summit meeting of the ORGANIZATION OF AFRICAN UNITY (q.v.). *See* N.Y. Times, May 31, 1973, at 6, col. 4.

AFRICAN DEFENSE FORCE: a multinational military force proposed by the ORGANIZATION OF AFRICAN UNITY (q.v.) for peacekeeping purposes but never established. *See* N.Y. Times, May 25, 1973, at 7, col. 1.

AFRICAN DEVELOPMENT BANK: international financial organization for cooperative economic development among African countries. *See* Agreement Establishing the African Development Bank, 510 U.N.T.S. 46.

AFRICAN DEVELOPMENT FUND: contributions made to the AFRICAN DEVELOPMENT BANK (q.v.) by wealthy nations. *See* 28 U.S.T. 4547.

AFRICAN ECONOMIC COMMUNITY TREATY (1991): organization of AFRICAN UNITY (A.V.) effort to, inter alia, establish an African customs union, promote human rights, and economic development. *See* 30 I.L.M. 1241.

AFRICAN NATIONAL CONGRESS (ANC): principal organization of the opponents to white-rule in South Africa. *See* 195 New Republic (Aug. 25, 1986), at 20.

AFRICAN PEACEKEEPING FORCE: *see* AFRICAN DEFENSE FORCE.

AFRICAN PETROLEUM PRODUCERS ASSOCIATION: group to foster consultation and cooperation among African petroleum producing countries. *See* 26 I.L.M. 1496.

AFRO-ARAB SUMMIT CONFERENCE (1977): meeting in Cairo of 60 nations to ratify efforts at African-Arab cooperation. *See* N.Y. Times, March 7, 1977, at 7, col. 1.

AGADIR INCIDENT (1957): alleged violation of Moroccan territorial waters by Spanish warships. *See* 4 Whiteman, *Digest of International Law* 406.

AGENCE POUR LA SECURITE DE LA NAVIGATION AERIENNE EN AFRIQUE ET MADAGASCAR (ASECNA): regional organization to promote air transport among the former African colonies of France. *See* 1965 Y.B. Air & Space L. 116 (treaty in French).

AGENCY: as in domestic law, one international party acting on behalf of and at the request of another. *See* HAGUE CONVENTION ON THE LAW APPLICABLE TO AGENCY.

AGENCY FOR INTERNATIONAL DEVELOPMENT: agency of the United States State Department in charge of U.S. foreign aid programs. For their regulations, *see* 22 C.F.R. sec. 200 et seq, and Valentine Petroleum v. A.I.D., 9 I.L.M. 889.

AGENCY OF NECESSITY: motivation of states to do that which is self-preserving. This is a strong factor in the formulation of rules of international law.

AGENT: one acting on behalf of a principal (*see* AGENCY). Specifically, a representative (the lawyer) of a party before the International Court of Justice or other international tribunal. *See* Art. 42 of the STATUTE OF THE INTERNATIONAL COURT OF JUSTICE.

AGENTS PROVOCATEURS (F): persons sent into another country to incite discontent or otherwise cause trouble in a covert manner on behalf of the government which employs them.

AGENTS REGNICOLES (F): diplomatic agents of foreign states who are nationals of the state to which they are accredited as representatives of other states.

AGGRAVATION OF SUFFERING: states engaged in armed conflict are prohibited from using methods of warfare designed to cause superfluous injury and unnecessary suffering. This is a long-standing principle of the law of war. *See, e.g.*, Preamble, SAINT PETERSBURG DECLARATION (1868) and Preamble, CONVENTIONAL WEAPONS CONVENTION (1980).

AGGRESSION: threat of force or use of force not sanctioned by the UNITED NATIONS CHARTER (q.v.). The international community has not been able to agree on a satisfactory definition. *See* U.N. Draft Definitions, 8 I.L.M. 661 and Convention Defining Aggression, 27 Am.J.Int.L. Supp. 192 (1933).

AGREATION (F): agreement between nations to appoint a certain individual to a diplomatic post. *See* PERSONA NON GRATA.

AGREED INTERPRETATION: subsidiary agreements regarding the specific meaning of terms or provisions of a treaty. *See, e.g.,* the Protocol to the ABM Treaty, 23 U.S.T. 3456, 11 I.L.M. 795.

AGREMENT (F): acquiescence of the host state to the appointment of the head of a diplomatic mission.

AGRICULTURAL DEVELOPMENT FUND: agreement for contributions to finance agricultural advancements in the developing world. *See* 28 U.S.T. 8435, 15 I.L.M. 922.

AID: AGENCY FOR INTERNATIONAL DEVELOPMENT (q.v.).

AID AND COMFORT TO THE ENEMY: in United States law, this includes providing money or supplies to a state or organization involved in armed conflict against the United States, or impeding the armed forces of the U.S. *See* 10 Whiteman, *Digest of International Law* 129.

AIDE-MEMOIRE (F): memorandum which may accompany a diplomatic message or note of protest explaining the state's point of view or action that is requested.

AIDS: ACQUIRED IMMUNE DEFICIENCY SYNDROME (q.v.).

AIFTA: ANGLO-IRISH FREE TRADE AGREEMENT (q.v.)

AIR CABOTAGE: carriage of passengers or cargo within the borders of one state by the airlines of another state. A commercial right carefully guarded in the system of bilateral air transport agreements. *See* Art. 7 of the CHICAGO CONVENTION (1944).

AIR CARRIER: business established to transport passengers, cargo, and mail by airplane or other flying apparatus. *See* Art. I of the WARSAW CONVENTION (1929).

AIR DEFENSE IDENTIFICATION ZONE (ADIZ): area beyond a nation's TERRITORIAL AIRSPACE (q.v.) in which identification of foreign aircraft is required. ADIZ refers in particular to the zone around the United States.

AIR IDENTIFICATION ZONE: *see* AIR DEFENSE IDENTIFICATION ZONE.

AIR-LAUNCHED CRUISE MISSILE (ALCM): CRUISE MISSILE (q.v.) capable of being launched from an airplane.

AIR LAW: *see* CHICAGO CONVENTION (1944) and WARSAW CONVENTION (1929).

AIR PIRACY: seizure of civilian aircraft for purposes of extracting ransom or promoting a political cause. Crimes against civil aviation are the subject of three widely adopted international conventions. *See* 20 U.S.T. 2941, 704 U.N.T.S. 219; 22 U.S.T. 1641; and 24 U.S.T. 565.

AIR POLLUTION: *see* TRANSFRONTIER POLLUTION and LONG RANGE TRANSBOUNDRY AIR POLLUTION CONVENTION (1979).

AIR SERVICE TRANSIT AGREEMENT: *see* INTERNATIONAL AIR SERVICE TRANSIT AGREEMENT.

AIRCRAFT: instruments capable of navigation through airspace. States have international responsibility for the aircraft on their registry. *See* Art.12 (and Art. 3 bis, not in force) of the CHICAGO CONVENTION (1944); STATE AIRCRAFT; and CIVIL AIRCRAFT.

AIRCRAFT SEIZURE: *see* AIR PIRACY.

AIRSPACE: area of atmosphere above the earth's surface capable of sustaining aerodynamic flight. The upper boundary of airspace has not been defined. *See also* TERRITORIAL AIRSPACE.

AIX-LA-CHAPPELLE CONGRESS (1818): meeting of the European powers which, *inter alia,* set about the codification of MARITIME HONORS (q.v.). *See* Satow, *A Guide to Diplomatic Practice* 45 (4th ed. 1957).

AL FATAH: main guerrilla group operating under the umbrella of the PALESTINE LIBERATION ORGANIZATION (q.v.).

ALABAMA ARBITRATION: dispute arising from United States' claim that Great Britain violated its obligation of neutrality during the United States Civil War by outfitting ships for the Confederacy. A sum of $15 million was awarded to the United States.*See* 1 Moore, *International Arbitrations* 653 (1898).

ALADI: LATIN AMERICAN INTEGRATION ASSOCIATION (q.v.).

ALASKA: example of CESSION OF TERRITORY (q.v.) wherein the transfer of sovereignty from the ceding state to the acquiring state was affected by sale. In 1867, Russia sold Alaska to the United States for $7,200,000. Many in the United States thought the purchase stupid and called it Seward's Folly after the then Secretary of State William Seward.

ALCM: AIR-LAUNCHED CRUISE MISSILE (q.v.).

ALEXANDRETTA DISPUTE (1921-1939): dispute between France and Turkey over the Treaty of Alexandretta setting the Syrian-Turkish border. *See* 39 Am.J.Int.L. 406 (1945).

ALFHEN INCIDENT (1954): the *S.S. Alfhem,* a Swedish flag ship, carrying a large supply of arms from the Soviet Bloc to Guatemala lead the United States to claim the right to detain and inspect ships in the area. This claim is not recognized in the GENEVA CONVENTION ON THE REGIME OF THE HIGH SEAS (1958) (in particular, Art. 22) (q.v.).

ALGECIRAS CONFERENCE (1906): meeting of 12 European states and the United States over the status of the Sultanate of Morocco. The results of the conference are found at 201 C.T.S. 39.

ALGERIA-MOROCCO CONFLICT (1963): military clash over disputed border areas was halted by the BAMAKO AGREEMENT (q.v.), but efforts by the ORGANIZATION OF AFRICAN UNITY (q.v.) failed to reach a definitive settlement.

ALGIERS ACCORD (1981): agreement between the United States and Iran ending the hostage crisis and setting up the UNITED STATES-IRAN CLAIMS TRIBUNAL (q.v.). *See* 20 I.L.M. 223.

ALGIERS DECLARATION (1975): nonaligned countries' declarations that urged, *inter alia*, the nations with veto power in the United Nations Security Council use that power with wisdom and moral integrity. *See* Rajan, *The Nonaligned and the United Nations* 305 (1987).

ALGIERS DECLARATION (1981): common name for the agreement which established The UNITED STATES-IRAN CLAIMS TRIBUNAL (q.v.).

ALIEN: individual residing in a country other than the country of his citizenship or nationality. *See* STATUS OF ALIENS CONVENTION (1928)

ALIOS ACTA (L): the act of another.

ALITER ET ALIUNDE (L): otherwise and from another source; beyond the competence of the evidence or discussion at hand.

ALL-AFRICAN PEOPLES' CONFERENCE (1958): nongovernmental meeting of African leaders which established a secretariat in Accra, Nigeria and sponsored subsequent meetings of private citizen activists. *See* Amate, *Inside the OAU* 42 (1986).

ALL-AFRICAN TRADE UNION FEDERATION: organization of African trade unions which has observer status with the OR-GANIZATION ON AFRICAN UNITY (a.v.) and favors African integration.

ALLEGIANCE: duties owed by an individual to a state, e.g., not committing SEDITION (q.v.). Allegiance may be owed to both the state of one's nationality and the state of one's residence. *See* 15 I.L.R. 78-107.

ALLIANCE: temporary or "permanent" union of two or more fully sovereign states for offensive or defensive purposes. The terms and conditions of the alliance are set forth by the states in a treaty of alliance. *See* 12 I.L.R. 285.

ALLIANCE FOR PROGRESS: United States initiative for Central and South American development to counter the influence of Castro's Cuban revolution. The efforts were made through the good offices of the ORGANIZATION OF AMERICAN STATES (q.v.). *See* Levinson, *The Alliance That Lost Its Way (1970).*

ALL-PARTICIPATION CLAUSE: treaty clause making acceptance of the treaty conditional on the ratification by all parties.

ALL-UNION FOREIGN TRADE ASSOCIATION (AUFTA): organization which administers the Soviet Union's state monopoly on all foreign trade. *See* 11 Rev. Socialist L. 215 (1985).

ALMA-ATA HEALTH DECLARATION (1978): product of a Conference on Primary Health Care sponsored jointly by the World Health Organization and UNICEF, calling, predictably, for greater efforts by nations to provide better primary health care. *See* 1978 U.N. Yearbook 1107.

ALTERNAT (F): practice of signing the copies of a treaty in an agreed rotation order to avoid questions of state hierarchy.

ALTUM MARE (L): HIGH SEAS (q.v.).

ALVEUS DERELICTUS (L): dry stream bed.

AMAZONIAN COOPERATION TREATY (1978): agreement by Bolivia, Brazil, Columbia, Ecuador, Guyana, Peru, Surinam, and Venezuela to promote harmonious development of the Amazon Basin and include the right of freedom of commercial navigation on the Amazon River. *See* 17 I.L.M. 1045.

AMBASSADOR: highest ranking diplomatic representative of a state. *See* 7 Whiteman, *Digest of International Law* 1930.

AMBASSADRESS: feminine form of the title AMBASSADOR (q.v.) or the wife of an ambassador.

AMBATIELOS CASE: strict application of the rule that local remedies must be exhausted before an international claim can be made. Arbitrators held that a Greek shipowner failed to exhaust his local remedies by failing to call a vital witness in his unsuccessful breach of contract action against Great Britain and by failing to appeal the adverse decision to the British Court of Appeals. *See* 1953 I.C.J. 10.

AMERASIAN CHILDREN: off-spring of American servicemen and Southeast Asian women conceived during the Vietnam War. They are subject to discrimination in some Asian countries. *See* 10 Brooklyn J.
Int'l L. 55 (1984).

AMERICAN CONVENTION ON HUMAN RIGHTS: *see* INTER-AMERICAN CONVENTION ON HUMAN RIGHTS.

AMERICAN DECLARATION OF THE RIGHTS AND DUTIES OF MAN: resolution of the Conference of American States in Bogota in 1948. *See* 43 Am.J.Int.L. Supp. 133 (1949).

AMERICAN FOREIGN TRADE DEFINITIONS: set of standardized trade terms developed in the United States in 1919 (revised in 1941), and published in an international pamphlet by the

United States Chamber of Commerce. They are superseded by INCOTERMS (q.v.).

AMERICAN INSTITUTE OF INTERNATIONAL LAW: organization founded in 1912, with members chosen by International Law Societies of the participating countries in the Western Hemisphere. Five members are chosen by each Society on the basis of merit. *See* 9 Am.J.Int.L. 923 (1915). For an example of their work, *see* 20 Am.J.Int.L. Special Supp. (1926).

AMERICAN JOINT RESOLUTION (1933): United States law which abrogated all GOLD CLAUSES (q.v.), declaring that it was against United States public policy to require payment in gold rather than legal tender. *See* 48 Stat. 113.

AMERICAN SELLING PRICE: value placed on goods for customs purposes; not based on the actual value of the goods, but upon the price of like products of United States origin. *See* 19 U.S.C. Sec. 1401 (a)(3).

AMERICAN STATES: *see* BOGOTA PACT (1948) and ORGANIZATION OF AMERICAN STATES.

AMERICAN SYSTEM: erstwhile international organization of the Western Hemisphere; the ORGANIZATION OF AMERICAN STATES (q.v.). *See* 19 Am.J.Int.L. 116 (1925).

AMIABLE COMPOSITEUR (F): CONCILIATOR (q.v.).

AMNESTY INTERNATIONAL: international, nongovernmental organization which seeks the unconditional release of persons imprisoned by reason of political, religious, or other conscientiously held beliefs; or by reason of their sex, race, or color. Amnesty International also seeks prompt trials for prisoners of conscience, and for the end of torture and executions. *See* Amnesty International Newsletter.

AMOCO CADIZ: oil supertanker which wrecked off the Breton coast on March 16, 1978, causing an ecological disaster and prompting action on the international scene resulting in the TANKER OWNERS VOLUNTARY AGREEMENT CONCERNING LIABILITY FOR OIL POLLUTION (q.v.).

AMPARO (S): writ or legal process used by the Mexican Judiciary to challenge the constitutionality of laws or administrative abuses. *See* 9 Cal.West.Int'l.L.J. 306 (1979).

ANARCHIES INTOLERANT (F): principle that when a state falls into a state of anarchy losing control over its population it ceases to be a state.

ANC: AFRICAN NATIONAL CONGRESS (q.v.).

ANCOM: ANDEAN COMMON MARKET (q.v.).

ANCON TREATY: agreement ending the WAR OF THE PACIFIC (q.v.). *See* 162 C.T.S. 453.

ANDEAN COMMON MARKET: South American steps toward regional integration and economic development. The principal instrument of the Andean Common Market is the Cartagena Agreement between Bolivia, Chile (withdrew 1976), Columbia, Ecuador, Peru, and Venezuela (adhered 1973), *reproduced in* 8 I.L.M. 910 (1969). *See* 16 Int'l. J. Legal Information 83 (1988).

ANDEAN DEVELOPMENT CORPORATION: international legal entity established by Ecuador, Bolivia, Chile, Colombia, Peru, and Venezuela in 1968, to further subregional integration by planning specialization and equitable distribution of investments. *See* 8 I.L.M. 940.

ANDEAN FOREIGN INVESTMENT CODE: effort by the countries of the Andean region to both control and promote foreign capital investment in their region. Foreign investment should contribute to capital formation and not create obstacles to regional integration according to the Code. *See* 16 I.L.M. 138.

ANDEAN RESERVE FUND: financial organization established by the Andean countries placing deposits in the Fund in order that members might draw on the Fund for balance of payments support. *See* 18 I.L.M. 1191.

ANGLO-AMERICAN LIQUOR TREATY (1924): attempt to deal with problems created by Prohibition in the United States including control of smuggling and nonapplication of anti-liquor laws to British ships in United States ports. *See* 43 Stat. 1761, 12 Bevans 414, and I'M ALONE CASE (1935).

ANGLO-ARGENTINE WAR (1982): Argentina took possession of the Falkland (Malvinas) Islands from Great Britain by military force, attempting to enforce their long standing claim of sovereignty over the islands located approximately 200 miles off the Argentine coast. Great Britain recaptured the Islands shortly thereafter, subjecting Argentina to an humiliating defeat leading to the fall of the Argentine Military Government. *See* R. Perl, *The Falkland Islands Dispute in International Law* and *Politics* (1983) and 76 Am.J.Int.L. 712 (1982).

ANGLO-IRISH FREE TRADE AGREEMENT: agreement for the elimination of customs duties on trade between the two countries and to establish other rules for free trade. *See* 5 I.L.M. 321 (in force July 1, 1966).

ANGLO-NORWEIGAN FISHERIES CASE: *see* NORWEIGAN FISHERIES CASE.

ANGOLA INVASION: continuous intervention (by South African troops stationed in Southwest Africa (Namibia)) into Angola to fight Namibian insurgents backed by the Angolan goverment. Also, to support the pro-Western guerrilla forces fighting the Angolan Government. *See* 17 I.L.M. 77Z0. *See also*, POPULAR MOVEMENT FOR THE LIBERATION OF ANGOLA.

ANGOLAN CIVIL WAR: continuing war between the Marxist government of Angola (established after independence from Portugal in 1976) and Western backed guerrillas, UNITA (q.v.). *See*

A.J. Klinghoffer, *The Angolan War* (1980). An agreement on the withdrawal of Cuban forces has been arranged. *See* 28 I.L.M. 957.

ANGUARY: right of a belligerent to use or destroy, in the case of necessity, property of neutrals. Originally, anguary also included the right to press neutral subjects into service. *See* HAGUE CONVENTION RESPECTING THE RIGHTS AND DUTIES OF NEUTRALS IN CASE OF WAR ON LAND (1907).

ANIMUS ADJUVANDI (L): intent to aid a belligerent to overpower his opponent; characterization of a neutral's aid to a belligerent. *See also* ANIMUS COMMERCIANDI.

ANIMUS AGGRESSIONIS (L): subjective intent of the attacking nation to commit an act of aggression.

ANIMUS BELLIGERENDI (L): subjective intent necessary to be in a formal state of war. *See also* STATUS MIXTUS.

ANIMUS COMMERCIANDI (L): intent to carry on normal trade and commerce; a characterization of a neutral's acts *vis-a-vis* a belligerent where neutral is not directly aiding the war effort of the belligerent.

ANIMUS DISPONENDI (L): element of intention in the effective renunciation of sovereignty over territory.

ANIMUS DOMINI (L): intention to hold territory for one's own use; an element of OCCUPATION (q.v.).

ANIMUS LUCRANDI (L): intention to gain something.

ANIMUS MANENDI (L): intention to remain, i.e., establish a residence.

ANIMUS OCCUPANDI (L): intention of a state to occupy territory. This is an essential element in a claim of sovereign title by occupation. *See* SOVEREIGNTY.

ANIMUS RELIQUENDI (L): intention to leave or give up resident status.

ANIMUS SIGNANDI (L): intention to sign a document.

ANNAHMEZWANG (G): legal tender.

ANNEXATION: unilateral inclusion of territory conquered or otherwise acquired; may or may not be recognized by other states. The United States requires that the territory be ceded before it will recognize the claim. *See* 2 Whiteman, *Digest of International Law* 1125.

ANSCHLUSS (G): literally, joining; the forced annexation of Austria by Germany in March 1938. *See* 38 Am.J.Int.L. 621 (1944).

ANTARCTIC MARINE LIVING RESOURCES CONVEN-TION: established a regime to conserve the Antarctic ecosystem. *See* 19 I.L.M. 841 and 38 Int'l.& Comp.L.Q. 104 (1989).

ANTARCTIC MINERAL RESOURCES: subject of treaty among claimants to Antarctic territory. *See* 27 I.L.M. L 859.

ANTARCTIC TREATY (1959): multilateral treaty establishing rules for the exploration of the Antarctic and suspending territorial claims. *See* 12 U.S.T. 794, 402 U.N.T.S. 71.

ANTI-BALLISTIC MISSILE SYSTEM (ABM): weapons system designed to track and destroy intercontinental ballistic missiles. Subject of a treaty between the United States and Soviet Union, 23 U.S.T. 3435.

ANTI-BALLISTIC MISSILE SYSTEM TREATY (1972): between the United States and the Soviet Union limiting the development and deployment of systems designed to defend against nuclear attack by intercontinental ballistic missiles. *See* 23 U.S.T. 3435 and 27 U.S.T. 1645.

ANTI-COLONIALISM: belief that industrialized or first world nations should not dominate other nations politically, economically, or socially. *See* SELF-DETERMINATION and NATIONAL LIBERATION MOVEMENT.

ANTI-DUMPING DUTY: tax or other fee on the import of specific goods placed on the goods because of evidence that foreign producers are "dumping" the goods on the local market, i.e., selling the goods below the cost of producing them. The European Community has placed such duty on Japanese roller bearings (*see* 16 I.L.M. 677), and the United States took similar measures against Japanese semiconductors in the Spring of 1987 (*see* 26 I.L.M. 1130.).

ANTI-DUMPING MEASURES: laws to prevent the importing of products at prices far below the fair market value. Such low prices usually result from subsidy of foreign industries by their governments. *See* 18 I.L.M. 621.

ANTI-SATELLITE WEAPON (A-SAT): system designed to destroy satellites while in orbit. A Soviet A-SAT weapon (currently deployed) homes in on the satellite and explodes. The U.S. version is fired from an F-15 fighter and destroys the satellite by impact alone.

ANTISUBMARINE WARFARE: attempts to track and destroy submarines, currently involving an extremely high level of technology, including tracking satellites and extremely sensitive sound detectors on the ocean floor. For the controversy over Japanese sale of milling machines capable of making quiet submarine propellers, *see* N.Y. Times , July 2, 1987, at D1.

ANZOATEGUI INCIDENT (1963): Venezuelan merchant ship, *Anzoategui*, was hijacked by Venezuelan dissidents. The dissidents were given political asylum by Brazil. *See* 4 Whiteman, *Digest of International Law* 666.

ANZUS: mutual defense agreement between the United States, Australia, and New Zealand. *See* 3 U.S.T. 3420, 131 U.N.T.S. 83.

AOUZOU STRIP: border area between Chad and Libya, claimed by both and occupied until recently by Libya; now partly controlled by Chad. *See* CHADIAN CIVIL WAR.

APARTHEID: system of racial separation applied in South Africa. This system excludes the Black majority from political participation and otherwise maintains their lower socio-economic status. *See* SUPPRESSION AND PUNISHMENT OF THE CRIME OF APARTHEID CONVENTION (1973).

APATRIDES (S): STATELESS PERSONS (q.v.).

APOLLO-SOYUZ MISSION (1975): rendezvous of manned spacecraft from the United States and the Soviet Union. *See* 4 J. Space L. 77 (1976).

APPAM CASE: in one of the last instances of PRIZE (q.v.); the German Navy in 1916, took charge of the British passenger ship *Appam* and brought it to the neutral port of Hampton Road, Virginia. There the legal battle ensued. *See* 11 Am.J.Int.L. 302 (1917).

APPEASEMENT: policy of acceding to the demands of an aggressor in the hope that by satisfying the demand conflict will be avoided. This policy was followed by the British *vis-a-vis* Hitler prior to World War II. Thought by some to be the underlying cause of the War. *See* MUNICH AGREEMENT (1938).

APPELATION D'ORIGINE (F): name given to product indicating its place of origin.

APPLICANT: party instigating a contentious proceeding in the INTERNATIONAL COURT OF JUSTICE (q.v.) *See* APPLICATION.

APPLICATION: adversarial form for bringing an action in the International Court of Justice which must indicate the subject of the dispute and the parties involved. *See* Art. 40 of the STATUTE OF

THE INTERNATIONAL COURT OF JUSTICE, 59 Stat. 1031, 3 Bevans 1191.

ARAB COMMON MARKET: efforts were made in the late 1950's and early 1960's to create an economic union of Arab states. On June 6, 1962, Jordan, Syria, U.A.R., Morocco, and Kuwait signed an agreement (*see* 8 Lazar, *Transnational Economic and Monetary Law* at 1.13.001 (1984)), but nothing has come of it.

ARAB EMIRATES FEDERATION: agreement between Abu Dhabi and Dubai formed this federation to maintain stability in their two small countries and unite their foreign policy and security efforts. *See* 7 I.L.M. 469.

ARAB INDUSTRIALIZATION ORGANIZATION: defunct effort of Egypt, Saudi Arabia, Qatar, and the United Arab Emirates to coordinate the development of their arms industry. *See* 80 I.L.R. 596.

ARAB LEAGUE: international organization of independent Arab nations primarily concerned with political cooperation. The League's Charter is found at 70 U.N.T.S. 237.

ARAB LEAGUE PACT (1945): precursor to the Arab League Charter. *See* 39 A.J.Int.L. Supp.266 (1945).

ARAB MAGHREB UNION: effort to establish close ties among Algeria, Morocco, and Tunisia. *See* 76 Foreign Policy 160.

ARAFAT VISA CASE (1988): United States refused to grant a visa to Yassir Arafat to allow him to speak to the United Nations in New York. The U.N. session was moved to Geneva. *See* 83 AM.J.Int.L. 253 and 519 (1989).

ARBITRAL AWARD: same as an ARBITRATION AWARD (q.v.).

ARBITRAL TRIBUNAL: ad hoc judicial body established to settle a dispute with members of the body chosen by the parties and with power to impose a resolution of the dispute. *See* PERMANENT COURT OF ARBITRATION and UNCITRAL ARBITRATION RULES.

ARBITRATION: process of dispute settlement where the parties choose an ad hoc judicial panel and give it power to impose a resolution on the parties. *See* PERMANENT COURT OF ARBITRATION and UNCITRAL ARBITRATION RULES.

ARBITRATION AWARD: decision of an arbitrator or arbitral tribunal. *See* REPORTS OF INTERNATIONAL ARBITRAL AWARDS.

ARBITRATION CLAUSE: clause in a treaty specifying arbitration as a means of settling disputes.

ARBITRATOR: individual or member of a panel which settles disputes through ARBITRATION (q.v.).

ARCHAEOLOGICAL, HISTORICAL, AND ARTISTIC HERITAGE OF THE AMERICAN NATIONS: subject of an agreement for their protection. *See* 15 I.L.M. 1350.

ARCHIPELAGO: a group of geographically related islands. *See* Arts. 46-54 of the LAW OF THE SEA CONVENTION (1982).

ARCHIPELAGO WATERS: waters between islands of an island chain (ARCHIPELAGO). *See* Arts. 46-54 of the LAW OF THE SEA CONVENTION (1982).

ARCHIVES: *see* CONSULAR ARCHIVES or DIPLOMATIC ARCHIVES.

ARCS-OF-CIRCLES: (or Courbe tangente) method of determining the baselines of the territorial sea of a coastal state. This was among the various methods discussed by the International Court in the NORWEGIAN FISHERIES CASE (1951) (q.v.).

ARGENTINA-BRAZILIAN INTEGRATION: *See* 27 I.L.M. 901.

ARGENTINA DIRTY WAR: *See* DIRTY WAR.

ARGUMENTUM A SIMILI (L): argument by analogy.

ARIAS PEACE PLAN (1987): attempt by the presidents of Central American countries to settle the insurgencies occurring there. The main author of the plan, President Oscar Arias of Costa Rica, won the Noble Peace Prize for his efforts. *See* 26 I.L.M. 573.

ARMED AGGRESSION: unprovoked use of force by one nation against another.

ARMED ATTACK: use of military force.

ARMED CONFLICT: hostile military engagement between nations which may or may not constitute a state of WAR (q.v.).

ARMED INTERVENTION: introduction of an armed force into one country by another, ostensibly for humanitarian purposes. *See* e.g., DOMINICAN CRISIS (1965) or GRENADA INTERVENTION (1985).

ARMISTICE: agreement to suspend military operations; *see* HAGUE CONVENTION IV (1907), Arts. 36-41, 36 Stat. 2277, 1 Bevans 631.

ARMOR PIERCING SHELL: munition designed to combine penetration, blast, and fragmentation effects. It is not considered an incendiary weapon. *See* GENEVA CONVENTION PROTOCOL III (1980).

ARMS CONTROL AND DISARMAMENT: efforts to reduce or eliminate armed forces and armaments of all kinds under international agreements. *See also* ARMS CONTROL AND DISARMAMENT AGENCY.

ARMS CONTROL AND DISARMAMENT AGENCY: United States government agency having primary responsibility for negotiating arms control agreements. *See* 22 U.S.C., sec. 2551 et seq (1982).

ARMS RACE: building-up of military weaponry by one country and the in-kind response of that country's adversaries. This armament-counterarmament is done with the aim of achieving greater security from attack. *See* CONVENTIONAL ARMS TRAFFIC.

ARMS TRANSFERS: sale of weapons from one country to another. Generally, developing countries which are unable to produce advanced weapons, procure sophisticated weapons from industrial states.

ARRANGEMENT: agreement; usually applied to less formal agreements.

ARRANGEMENTS ADMINISTRATIFS (F): agreements between the departments or agencies of two countries. Such agreements are not necessarily binding under international law.

ARREST: seizure of a person or a ship for committing an offense. A levy or fine may be placed on a ship. *See* EXTRADITION.

ARREST OF AIRCRAFT: subject of a convention which regulates the seizure of aircraft in private civil disputes. *See* 192 L.N.T.S. 289.

ARREST OF SEA-GOING VESSELS CONVENTION (1952): agreement concerning the jurisdictional attachment of vessels to satisfy maritime claims such as damages arising from a collision. *See* 53 Am.J.Int.L. 539 (1959), 439 U.N.T.S. 193.

ARRESTATIO NAVIUM (L): seizure of a vessel.

ARRESTUM AS FUNDANDUM IURISDICTIONEM (L): attachment of assets is necessary for the court to take jurisdiction. A maxim of Dutch and Scottish law.

ARRET DE PRINCE (F): embargo detaining foreign ships in order to prevent the spread of political information.

ART WORKS: *see* CULTURAL PROPERTY.

ARTHASASTRA: ancient rules for the conduct of affairs between states in India.

ARCTIC REGION: area around the North Pole; parts of which are subject to claims by both Canada and the Soviet Union. *See* 25 Can.Y.B.Int'l L. 325 (1987).

ARTISTIC HERITAGE: *See* ARCHAEOLOGICAL, HISTORICAL, AND ARTISTIC HERITAGE OF THE AMERICAN NATIONS.

ARTIFICIAL ISLANDS: man-made structure attached to the ocean floor and surrounded by ocean. The GENEVA CONVENTION ON THE TERRITORIAL SEAS AND CONTIGUOUS ZONE (1958) (q.v.), does not recognize artificial islands as having territorial seas of their own.

ARUSHA AGREEMENT: associated the East African Common Market with the EUROPEAN ECONOMIC COMMUNITY (q.v.) similar to the LAGOS AGREEMENT (1966) (q.v.). *See* 8 I.L.M. 741.

ASAMA MARU INCIDENT (1940): British sailors boarded a Japanese passenger ship and seized 21 German seamen of conscriptable age. The legality of the British action is unclear. *See* 34 Am.J.Int.L. 249 (1940).

A-SAT: ANTI-SATELLITE WEAPON (q.v.).

ASEAN: Association of South-East Asian Nations; organization to promote regional cooperation established by the ASEAN Declaration of 1967, and the Treaty of Amity and Cooperation in South-East Asia, 19 Malaya L. Rev. 407 (1977).

ASECNA: AGENCE POUR LA SECURITE DE LA NAVIGA-
TION AERIENNE EN AFRIQUE ET MADAGASCAR (q.v.).

ASIAN-AFRICAN CONFERENCE: *see* BANDUNG CONFER-
ENCE (1955).

ASIAN-AFRICAN LEGAL CONSULTATIVE COMMITTEE:
formed in 1956; group of legal experts from African and Asian
states reviewing proposals by the INTERNATIONAL LAW COM-
MISSION (q.v.), and making comments in the interest of the countries they represent. *See* 25 I.L.M. 920 and 17 Can.Y.B.Int'l L. 324.

ASIAN DEVELOPMENT BANK: international bank with membership from Asian and developed countries. *See* 17 U.S.T. 1418.

ASILADO (S): Latin American principle that political refugees
shall be accorded inviolable asylum. *See* Art. 20 of the MON-
TEVIDEO TREATY ON INTERNATIONAL PENAL LAW (1940).

ASSEMBLY: usually designates the body of an international organization in which each participating country is represented and
each has equal voting power. Smaller bodies, in an international
organization, are representative of the whole and are usually designated "councils."

ASSIENTO CONTRACT: contract resulting from the terms of
the UTRECHT TREATY (q.v.) giving the British South Seas Company the monopoly on the import of Negro slaves into the Spanish Colonies in South America. Problems over the Contract led to
the Anglo-Spanish War in 1739. *See* 4 Am.J.Int.L. 612 (1910).

ASSIGNED RESIDENCE: residence assigned to persons under
control of an enemy power. The placing of protected persons in
residences other than their usual place of abode may be ordered if
the security of the detaining power makes it absolutely necessary.
See Art. 42(1), GENEVA CONVENTION IV (1949).

ASSIGNMENT: transfer of treaty right or duty to a third party
without the consent of the other party or parties to the treaty.

ASSIST LETTER: in effect, a purchase order from the United Nations to a particular country requesting supplies. Purchase order acting as proof of the authorization of the expenditure.

ASSISTANCE IN THE CASE OF NUCLEAR ACCIDENTS CONVENTION (1986): to strengthen further international cooperation in safe development and use of nuclear energy. The parties granted to the INTERNATIONAL ATOMIC ENERGY AGENCY (q.v.) a greater role in cooperation and safety. *See* 25 I.L.M. 1377.

ASSURED RESISTANCE: strategy used by some governments to deter aggression against their territory, especially where the government announces that it will vehemently oppose any attack upon its territory in hopes that a potential aggressor will be deterred by the prospect of a long and costly war.

ASTRONAUT: outer space personnel, especially from a Western country. The Eastern bloc counterpart is cosmonaut. *See* RESCUE OF ASTRONAUTS CONVENTION (1968), 672 U.N.T.S. 119.

ASW: ANTI-SUBMARINE WARFARE (q.v.).

ASYLUM: refusal to deliver a person to another sovereign. *See* TERRITORIAL ASYLUM, POLITICAL ASYLUM, and EUROPEAN ASYLUM CONVENTION (1990).

ATHENS CONVENTION (1958): *see* INTER-GOVERNMENTAL MARITIME CONSULTATIVE ORGANIZATION.

ATHENS CONVENTIONS (1974): *see* CARRIAGE OF PASSENGERS AND LUGGAGE BY SEA CONVENTIONS (1954).

ATLANTIC CHARTER (1941): agreement between the United States and Great Britain on the prosecution of World War II. *See* 55 Stat. 1560 and 56 Stat. 1433, 1605.

ATTACHE: one of the most junior diplomatic ranks.

ATTACHMENT: judicial seizure of property in order to collect a judgment or gain jurisdiction over the property.

ATTENTAT CLAUSE: in an extradition treaty, a clause exempting the crime of attempted murder of a head of state from the general preclusion of extradition for political crimes.

ATTITUDE CORRECTE (F): foreign policy position by a lesser state which is subservient to the policy of a friendly great power.

AU PAIR (F): a live-in maid or nanny from a foreign country. *See* the EUROPEAN AGREEMENT ON AU PAIR PLACEMENT, 17 European Yearbook 241, Journal Officiel (France) 26 Sept. 1971.

AUDI ALTERAM PARTEM (L): to hear both sides.

AUDIATUR ET ALTERA PARS (L): one will not be condemned without being heard.

AUDIENCE: formal meeting with a head of state or a foreign minister where, e.g., an ambassador might present his credentials.

AUDIO VISUAL WORKS: subject of a treaty on international registration to facilitate enforcement of legal rights and protect against piracy. *See* 84 Am.J.Int.L. 738.

AUSTRIAN STATE TREATY (1955): agreement which ended Allied occupation of Austria after World War II and guaranteed Austria's neutrality. The Treaty is incorporated as part of Austria's Constitution. *See* 6 U.S.T. 2369, 217 U.N.T.S. 223.

AUTHENTIC INTERPRETATION: supplemental treaty or other agreement clarifying the meaning intended by the parties in the language of the treaty.

AUTHENTIC TEXT: version of a treaty in one or more languages, that is the official or correct version which was adopted by the parties, rather than a subsequent translation or version that was enacted by a legislature into municipal law. Where inconsistencies arise the authentic text governs. *See* Art. 33, VIENNA CONVENTION ON THE LAW OF TREATIES, 8 I.L.M. 679.

AUTOMATIC RESERVATION: reservation relating to a state's recognition of the International Court of Justice as having jurisdiction over all legal disputes in which the state may be involved (*see* OPTIONAL CLAUSE). The scope of automatic reservations is to be determined by the reserving state.

AUTONOMOUS NEUTRALIZATION: doctrine that a state may declare itself permanently neutral. *See* 11 Am.J.Int.L. 607 (1917).

AUTREFOIS ACQUIT (F): literally, already acquitted; principle that a person will not be subject to extradition for trial for a crime for which he has already been acquitted.

AUTREFOIS CONVICT (F): literally, already convicted; principle that a person will not be subject to extradition for trial for a crime for which he has already been convicted.

AVENANT (F): codicil or additional articles to an agreement.

AVERAGE: damage to a ship or its cargo during a voyage, *See* GENERAL AVERAGE and YORK-ANTWERP RULES.

AVULSION: sudden and violent shifting of a river-bed.*See also* ACCRETION.

AWARD: relief or damages provided the winning party in an adjudicated international dispute.

AYACUCHO DECLARATION (1974): eight South American nations hereby called for conditions to lead to disarmament. *See* N.Y. Times, Dec. 13, 1974 at 1, col. 1.

AYANT DROIT (F): those having rights; referring to the preservation of the rights of individuals in cases where territorial sovereignty changes hands. *See* 4 I.L.R. 291.

BACTERIOLOGICAL WARFARE CONVENTION (1972): use of disease producing microbes as a weapon. *See* Convention on the Prohibition of the Development, Production, and Stockpiling of Bacteriological and Toxin Weapons and Their Destruction, 26 U.S.T. 583, 11 I.L.M. 310.

BADGE: these identify rank and nationality and may not be taken from prisoners of war; moreover, prisoners of war are to be allowed to wear their badges of rank and nationality. *See* Art. 18(1)(3-6) and Art. 40 of the GENEVA CONVENTION III (1949).

BAGHDAD PACT (1955): defense and security pact signed by Iraq and Turkey, and adhered to in that same year by the United Kingdom, Pakistan, and Iran. In 1959, the Pact was redesignated the CENTRAL TREATY ORGANIZATION (CENTO) (q.v.) after Iraq withdrew. *See* 9 U.S.T. 1077, 335 U.N.T.S. 205.

BAHIA THETIS INCIDENT (1959): three Chilean military aircraft flew low over the Argentine training ship, *Bahia Thetis*. *See* 4 Whiteman, *Digest of International Law* 515.

BAILMENT BY SOVEREIGNS: legal doctrine under which a foreign sovereign serving as a bailor is considered to have sufficient possession of the bailed goods and can assert sovereign immunity if ownership of the goods comes into question.

BAILO (I): title of the diplomatic agent of Venice at Constantinople during the Renaissance.

BALANCE OF PAYMENTS: difference between what a nation owes and earns in international trade and other financial dealings between states. Either large deficits or surpluses can cause economic problems for a country.

BALANCE OF POWER: theory that peace can be maintained by a system of alliances in order to keep the military power of rival states approximately equal. In this way neither side could win a military victory.

BALFOUR DECLARATION (1917): statement of the British government favoring the establishment of a Jewish homeland in Palestine. This territory, then a British mandate, subsequently became Israel. *See* 1 Hackworth, *Digest of International Law* 113.

BALKAN ENTENTE (1934): political alliance of Greece, Turkey, Yugoslavia, and Romania. *See* 153 L.N.T.S. 153.

BALKANS ENTENTE PACT (1954): military alliance by Turkey, Greece, and Yugoslavia to contain Soviet encroachment. The Pact was never implemented.

BALLISTIC MISSILE: self-propelled, unmanned weapon which does not rely on areodynamics to produce lift. *See* STRATEGIC ARMS LIMITATIONS AGREEMENTS.

BALLOON INCIDENTS: instances where balloons have been released from one state and subsequently violated the airspace of another country; sometimes intentionally to spy or circulate propaganda leaflets. *See* T. Buergenthal, *Law-Making in the International Civil Aviation Organization* 131 (1969).

BALTIC CODE: set of conventions negotiated by the seven states on the Baltic Sea to protect the marine environment of that sea. *See* 13 I.L.M. 544.

BALTIC SEA: there is a Convention on the Protection of Marine Environment of the Baltic Sea Area, 13 I.L.M. 546.

BAMAKO AGREEMENT (1963): Organization of African Unity Arbitration Commission settled the ALGERIA-MOROCCO CON-

FLICT (1963) (q.v.) by negotiating this agreement. *See* Horne, *A Savage War of Peace (1977).*

BAMAKO CONVENTION (1991): *see* HAZARDOUS WASTE WITHIN AFRICA CONVENTION (1991).

BAMBOO CURTAIN: derived from the expression *"Iron Curtain."* It refers to the wall of isolation developed by the Communist Chinese prior to their opening to the West in the 1970's.

BANANAS: *See* UNION DE PAISES EXPORTORES DE BANANAS.

BANCROFT CONVENTIONS: concerning nationality questions during the nineteenth century; an agreements between the United States and several German states. *See* 8 *Encyclopedia of Public International Law* 46.

BANDUNG CONFERENCE (1955): conference of African and Asian nations at Bandung, Indonesia, which formed the basis for the nonaligned movement. *See* Poplai, *Asia and Africa in the Modern*
World (1955).

BANDUNG CONFERENCE (1985): second conference of African and Asian nations to review the progress of the NON-ALIGNED MOVEMENT (q.v.). *See* 105 Newsweek (May 6, 1985) at 44.

BANJUL CHARTER: organization of African unity sponsored convention on human rights. It is typical of regional human rights agreements except that it provides for individual duties as well. *See* 21 I.L.M. 58.

BANK FOR INTERNATIONAL SETTLEMENT: early attempt at a formal organization to deal with the problems of international payments arising out of German war REPARATIONS (q.v.). *See* 24 Am.J.Int.L. 665 and Am.J.Int.L.Supp. 81, 110 (1930).

This evolved into one of th most important international banking institutions. *See* 25 I.L.M. 978.

BANKRUPTCY: subject of a COUNCIL OF EUROPE (q.v.) agreement governing certain international aspects of bankruptcy. *See* 30 I.L.M. 165.

BARBARISM: condition of humankind prior to civilization and thought to be characterized by cruelty and bloodthirstiness. After World War II, the fascist states were said to have consciously reverted to a state of barbarism during the war.

BARCELONA CONFERENCE (1921): LEAGUE OF NATIONS (q.v.) meeting which formulated two conventions; one concerning free navigation for contracting states, and the other; concerning freedom of transit of persons or goods through states by rail or water without distinction of nationality. *See* 7 L.N.T.S. 11, 35, 65, and 73.

BARCELONA DECLARATION (1921): whereby states recognized the right of those states without access to the oceans to register ships under their flag. *See* 7 L.N.T.S. 73.

BARCELONA STATUTE: rules for the free navigation of international waterways formulated by the League of Nations, *See* 7 L.N.T.S. 35 (1921).

BARCELONA TRACTION COMPANY CASE (1964): ruled that the state of incorporation, rather than the state of the shareholders, had the standing to bring an action before the International Court of Justice where a third state had declared the corporation bankrupt. *See* 1970 I.C.J. 3.

BARE-BONES CHARTER: lease of a ship or airplane without crew or supplies. *See also* WET LEASE.

BAREBOAT CHARTER: lease of a vessel where the charterer supplies the crew and operates the vessel.

BARRATRY: crime of an intentional act (by the master or crew of a vessel) aimed at injuring the owner or charterer of a vessel.

BARRED WAR ZONE: area of water which a belligerent declares to be off-limits to all shipping (including neutral vessels). The exact measures a belligerent takes may vary, but all vessels may be subject to attack.

BARRING OF CLAIMS: time limitation on the ability of a state to make a claim. *See also*, EXTINCTION OF CLAIMS.

BARUCH PLAN: proposal for international control of atomic energy put forth by the United States in 1946. Controls were to be established after which the United States would turn over the technology. The GROMYKO PLAN (q.v.) proposed by the U.S.S.R would have reversed the steps; neither plan was implemented. *See* 14 Dept. State Bull. 1057 (June 28, 1946).

BASE-LINE: line drawn along a coast out from which is measured the territorial waters of the adjacent state.*See* GENEVA CONVENTION ON THE TERRITORIAL SEA AND CONTIGUOUS ZONE (1958) and the LAW OF THE SEA TREATY (1982).

BALES ACCORD: *See* BASEL AGREEMENT.

BASEL AGREEMENT: proposal for the international convergence of capital measurements and capital standards. *See* 27 I.L.M. 524 and 30 I.L.M. 967.

BASEL CLUB: regular meetings of the central bankers of the industrialized countries in Basel, Switzerland at the BANK FOR INTERNATIONAL SETTLEMENT (q.v.). *See* Coombs, *The Arena of International Finance* (1976).

BASEL COMMITTEE: Component of the BANK FOR INTERNATIONAL SETTLEMENT which makes recommendations on bank regulations. *See* 30 I.L.M. 967.

BASEL CONVENTION (1989): *see* TRANSPBOUNDARY MOVEMENT OF HARZARDOUS WASTE CONVENTION (1989).

BASEL PROGRAM: statement of purpose adopted by the First World Zionist Congress held in Basel, Switzerland in 1897. It was a cautious program of advancing Jewish settlement in what was then PALESTINE (q.v.). *See* Vital, *Zionism the Formation Years* 3, 4 (1982).

BASIC UNDERTAKINGS: essential element or elements of an agreement or project.

BASKET: theoretical selection of items grouped together to create an index or frame of reference, e.g., one dollar, 2 Deutsch marks, and 10 French francs might set the value for one "trade unit," which would act as the CURRENCY OF ACCOUNT (q.v.) for a particular transaction.

BAUXITE: ore from which aluminum is refined. Some producers are members of the International Bauxite Association. *See* 13 I.L.M. 1245.

BAY: a well-marked indentation on a coast line whose penetration is in such proportion to the width of its mouth, as to contain landlocked waters and constitute more than a mere curvature of the coast. *See* Art. 7 of the GENEVA CONVENTION ON THE TERRITORIAL SEA AND CONTIGUOUS ZONE (1958).

BAY OF PIGS INVASION: unsuccessful attempt by the United States to invade Cuba and overthrow the Castro government. The invasion was carried out by Cuban exiles, trained and equipped by the United States. Support of this group breached United States duty to prevent armed groups frm leaving its territory for the purpose of attacking the government of a presumably friendly state. *See* 5 Whiteman, *Digest of International Law 275.*

BEAGLE CHANNEL ARBITRATION (1971): dispute concerned the sovereignty over certain islands situated in the Beagle Channel on the border between Chile and Argentina. The case was submitted to arbitration to determine the territorial and maritime boundaries. *See* 17 I.L.M. 632.

BEARER OF DISPATCHES: individuals under commission to carry official communications between heads of state or diplomatic missions. They enjoy immunity and inviolability and the right of innocent passage through third states. *See* 4 Hackworth, *Digest of International Law* 621.

BEIRUT INVASION (1958): United States intervention in Lebanon, by invitation of the Lebanese Government, to quell civil unrest. *See* 52 Am.J.Int.L. 727.

BEIRUT RAID (1968): Israeli commando raid on the Beirut Airport which destroyed 12 planes. Raid was in retaliation for Arab attacks on an El-Al plane in Athens. *See* 63 Am.J.Int.L. 415.

BELGRADE CONVENTION (1948): *see* DANUBE COMMISSION.

BELGRADE DECLARATION (1964): policy statement of the first summit of the NONALIGNED MOVEMENT (q.v.) that urged, *inter alia*, the expansion of representative bodies in the United Nations organization to assure representative membership from nonaligned nations. *See* Rajan *The Nonaligned and the United Nations* at 302, 306 (1987).

BELGIAN CLAUSE: person who attempts to kill or injure a head of state shall not be granted asylum. *See also* ATTENTAT CLAUSE.

BELGIAN NEUTRALITY: Belgium was created an independent, permanently neutral state in 1839. *See* 18 British and Foreign State Papers 765. For a discussion of its status after World War I, *see* 26 *Am.J.Int.L. 514.*

BELIZE DISPUTE: questions involving the status of the territory of Belize (formerly British Honduras) between Great Britain and Guatemala. *See* 120 C.T.S. 371 and 52 Am.J.Int.L. 280.

BELLIGERENT: party to an armed conflict controlled by the LAWS OF WAR (q.v.).

BELLIGERENT COMMUNITY: community within a state; often representing a political movement aimed at independence and secession. In practice such communities may enter into legal relations and conclude internationally valid agreements with states and other belligerents. *See also* INSURGENT COMMUNITY.

BELLIGERENT OCCUPATION: condition arising when a state occupies territory and is not a sovereign of another nation or community. *See* e.g., ISRAELI-OCCUPIED TERRITORIES.

BELLUM JUSTUM (L): (morally) just war.

BEMBELISTA CLAIM (1903): Netherlands-Venezuelan Claims Commission rejected a claim for damage to Mr. Bembelista's real property which occurred as a consequence of a battle in his neighborhood. One should avoid owning property in a war zone. *See* 5 Hackworth, *Digest of International Law* at 695.

BENELUX ECONOMIC UNION: customs union between Belgium, Netherlands, and Luxembourg. *See* 381 U.N.T.S.165.

BENZENE CONVENTION (1971): INTERNATIONAL LABOR ORGANIZATION (q.v.) agreement to protect workers from the hazard arising from the use of benzene in the workplace. *See* 885 U.N.T.S. 45.

BERING SEA ARBITRATION (1892): settlement of dispute between the United States and Great Britain over fur-bearing seals. *See* 1 Moore, *International Arbitration 755 (1898)*.

BERLIN: former capital of Germany occupied by GREAT BRITAIN, FRANCE, THE UNITED STATES, AND THE SOVIET UNION after World War II. *See* QUADRIPARTITE AGREEMENT ON BERLIN and 30 I.L.M. 445. Allied occupation of Germany ended by treaty in 1990. *See* 29 I.L.M. 1186.

BERLIN AIRLIFT: in 1948, the Soviet Union cut-off land access to West Berlin. The Western allies responded by supplying the city by air transport. *See* 43 Am.J.Int.L. 92.

BERLIN CONFERENCE (1884-5): conference of European powers concerning occupied territories in Africa. An obligation to notify others of claims to territory and to maintain authority to protect acquired rights was affirmed. *See* GENERAL ACT OF THE BERLIN CONFERENCE (1885).

BERLIN CONFERENCE (1945): *see* POTSDAM CONFERENCE (1945).

BERLIN CONGRESS (1878): conference of European powers dealing with the affairs of Turkey and the Balkans. Historic precedent was made concerning the status of secured creditors in international law when it accorded priority to the secured bonds of Turkey, and also when adjusting debts that arose from the war between Turkey and Russia. *See* 153 C.T.S. 171 (in French).

BERLIN QUADRIPARTITE AGREEMENT (1971): attempt to normalize and facilitate day-to-day operations in areas such as communications and transport among the Four Powers who have continued to occupy and administer Berlin since World War II. *See* 10 I.L.M. 895 and 67 Am.J.Int.L. 44.

BERLIN TREATY (1921): peace treaty, between the United States and Germany, ending World War I as between these parties. *See* 42 Stat. 1939, 8 Bevans 145.

BERLIN WEST AFRICAN CONFERENCE (1884/5): final act of the conference provided that navigation of the Congo and Niger Rivers was to be free to merchant ships of all nations, *see* 165

C.T.S. 485. This act was abrogated by the convention for its revision signed at Saint-Germain-en-Laye on Sept. 19, 1919.

BERMUDA AGREEMENTS I AND II (1946 and 1977): agreements between Great Britain and the United States granting reciprocal commercial aviation rights. Bermuda I became the model for many so-called bilateral air transport agreements. *See* 3 U.N.T.S. 253 and 28 U.S.T. 5367.

BERNE CONVENTION (1886): Convention for the Protection of Literary and Artistic Works, established the BERNE UNION (q.v.), and provided for multinational recognition of copyrights. The United States is not a party. *See 77 British Foreign and State Papers* 22.

BERNE UNION: organization established in 1886, for the protection of authors' literary rights. For the latest revision of the union, *see* 828 U.N.T.S. 221.

BGB: BURGERLICHES GESETZBUCH (q.v.).

BHOPAL DISASTER: worst industrial accident on record. In December, 1984, a chemical cloud escaped from the Union Carbide plant in Bhopal, India. At least 2000 people were killed and up to 200,000 injured. *See* 25 I.L.M. 771.

BIAFRA: portion of Nigeria which attempted to secede from that country in 1967. The rebellion was crushed by the central government. *See* 6 I.L.M. 665, 7 I.L.M. 162, and 65 Am.J.Int.L. 551.

BIEN-FONDE (F): the merits of the case.

BIENS ET PROPRIETES (F): property and possessions including intangibles.

BIENS MEUBLES (F): moveable goods or property.

BIENS PRIVES DE LA FAMILLE (F): property of the family. This expression may include both the property of individual family members as well as property held by the family group as allowed in some legal systems.

BIENS VACANT (F): property which has no owner.

BILATERAL: between two parties or two groups of parties.

BILATERAL AIR TRANSPORT AGREEMENTS: the system of hundreds of bilateral agreements which control the scheduled commercial air services around the world. *See* BERMUDA AGREEMENTS I AND II.

BILATERAL INVESTMENTS TREATY: agreement between two countries providing rules to govern financial investments of one country's investments in the other country.. *See* 24 Int'l.Lawyer 655.

BILATERAL TREATY: formal international agreement between two countries.

BILBAO INCIDENT (1959): French warship seized the German freighter Bilbao suspected of running arms to Algerian rebels. The cargo was innocent and Germany protested the incident.

BILL OF LADING: document which evidences the loading (lading) of cargo aboard a transport vehicle. A bill of lading serves as a receipt for the goods, a document of title, and evidence of the contract for carriage of the goods. *See* HAGUE RULES, HAMBURG RULES, and International Convention for the Unification of Certain Rules Relating to Bills of Lading, 70 L.N.T.S. 157, 27 Am.J.Int.L. Supp. 18.

BILLS OF EXCHANGE: written documents signed by the maker or drawer containing an unconditional promise or order to pay a certain sum on demand or at a definite time. These documents are used by merchants in all countries. Generally, states follow one of two systems with respect to bills of exchange: the laws of the Geneva Convention on Bills of Exchange, 143 L.N.T.S. 257, 317, 337 (1930) or the ENGLISH BILLS OF EXCHANGE ACT (in the United States Art. 3 of the Uniform Commercial Code). *See also* 28 I.L.M. 170.

BIOLOGICAL WARFARE: use of living organisms or toxins manufactured by living organisms as a weapon. See Protocol, 94 L.N.T.S. 65 (1929) and BACTERIOLOGICAL WARFARE CONVENTION (1972).

BIPARTITE TREATY: treaty between two state parties; more commonly known now as BILATERAL TREATY (q.v.).

BIRDS PROTECTION CONVENTION (1950): regulating trade in birds and interference with nesting. *See* 638 U.N.T.S. 185.

BIRPI: UNITED INTERNATIONAL BUREAU FOR THE PROTECTION OF INTELLECTUAL PROPERTY (q.v.).

BIS: BANK FOR INTERNATIONAL SETTLEMENTS (q.v.).

BIS (F): indicates a second article with the same number in a convention.

BIT: BILATERAL INESTMENT TREATY (q.v.).

B/L: BILL OF LADING (q.v.).

BLACK LIST: list of enemies compiled by Britain and the United States in World War II. Including enemy nationals in neutral countries, as well as, neutrals attached to the enemy cause. Also, used generically for any list of enemies or persons with whom business is not done.

BLACK SEA: access to the Black Sea through the Dardanelles is governed by treaty. *See* 31 AM.J.Int.L.Supp. 1, 173 L.N.T.S. 213.

BLADING: international short form of BILL OF LADING (q.v.).

BLOCKADE: recognized limitation on the doctrine of freedom of the seas in that the rights of a belligerent includes the right to shut off a place or region from use by an adversary. *See* QUARAN-TINE.

BLOCKED ACCOUNT: money which cannot be removed from a country.

BLOCKED NATIONALS: term applied in 1941, to persons under United States proclamation prohibiting persons from exporting materials or munitions to Italy or Germany.

BOAT PEOPLE: generally refers to refugees who have fled their homeland on boats over the high seas. More particularly, it refers to people who after the collapse of the Saigon government fled South Vietnam by boat. A duty to rescue those in distress on the high seas is a well established principle of international law. *See* Art. 12 of the GENEVA CONVENTION ON THE REGIME OF THE HIGH SEAS (1958).

BOATRIGHT INCIDENT (1960): two U.S. sailors shipwrecked in the Bahamas swam out from land and boarded a passing vessel killing Capt. Boatright. They were subsequently found guilty of murder and theft and hanged in the Bahamas.

BOER WAR (1899-1902): fought between Dutch settlers and the British colonial army. The Dutch settlers capitulated in the Treaty of Vereeniging and left all of what became South Africa in the hands of the British, 191 C.T.S. 232. The British court-martialed several members of their own colonial forces for alleged violations of the laws of war.

BOFFOLO CASE (1903): arbitration involving a state's right to expel foreign nationals held. State's right should only be used in extreme cases and the state should be prepared to give reasons for the expulsion to an international tribunal.

BOGOTA DECLARATION (1948): AMERICAN DECLARATION OF THE RIGHTS AND DUTIES OF MAN (q.v.).

BOGOTA DECLARATION (1976): assertion by several equatorial states that their sovereignty extended above their territory to a height which would encompass the GEOSTATIONARY ORBIT (q.v.), approximately 223,000 miles. *See* C. Christol, *Modern International Law of Outer Space* 555 or 6 J. Space L. 193 (1978).

BOGOTA PACT (1948): political alliance of various Central and South American nations and the United States to promote economic, social, and cultural cooperation and to provide for common action against member states committing acts of aggression against fellow members. *See* 30 U.N.T.S. 55.

BOGOC: BOLIVIAN GULF OIL COMPANY (q.v.).

BOLIVIA-PARAGUAY BOUNDARY DISPUTE: *See* CHACO DISPUTE.

BOLIVIAN GULF OIL COMPANY: Bolivian government nationalized this company and paid compensation for the seized property. *See* 10 I.L.M. 173, 1201.

BOMBARDMENT: means of warfare employing weapons that strike at some distance such as artillery or bombs dropped from planes or missiles.

BONA FIDES (L): good faith or good intentions.

BONA VACANTIA (L): unclaimed property. Property without an owner usually escheats to the state. Among nations, unclaimed territory is RES NULLIUS (q.v.).

BONA MORES (L): good morals. A contract may be legal in a foreign jurisdiction where it was made, but not enforced in another jurisdiction because that jurisdiction considers its end to be contrary to good morals, e.g., a gambling debt.

BONN ECONOMIC SUMMIT CONFERENCE (1978): meeting of the leaders of Canada, West Germany, France, Italy, Japan,

Great Britain, and the United States to develop a comprehensive strategy for economic growth and development. *See*17 I.L.M. 1281.

BONS DE REQUISITION (F): receipt given by a commander of troops for provisions requisitioned from local populations. It acknowledges the quantity taken and may be used to pursue a claim against the responsible government or to prevent further requisitions.

BOOBY TRAP: any device or material which is designed, constructed, or adapted to kill or injure and which functions unexpectedly when a person disturbs or approaches an apparently harmless object or performs an apparently safe act. *See* Art. 2(2) of GENEVA CONVENTION PROTOCOL II (1980).

BOOKINGNOTE: document confirming the shipment of a cargo.

BOOKS OF MERCHANTS: in customary commercial law the records of merchants kept in the normal course of business and according to established practices of the particular trade are presumed to be accurate in a court of law. The presumption may be rebutted.

BOOTY: material that may be seized in the course of land warfare. *See* 1946 Brit.Y.B.Int'l.L. 236 and Arts. 4, 14 and 53 of the HAGUE REGULATIONS (1907). *See also D PRIZE.*

BORAH PLAN (1923): resolution sponsored by Sen. Borah, proposing that every nation undertake to punish their own war breeders and war profiteers. *See* Sen. Res. 441, 67th Cong. 4th Sess.

BORDER AND TRANSBORDER ARMED ACTIONS CASE (NICARAGUA V. HONDURAS): proceedings in the International Court of Justice relating to CONTRA (q.v.) activities along the border of the parties to the dispute. *See* 28 I.L.M. 338.

BORDER INCIDENT: unpleasant events along the frontiers of states which usually have long-standing disputes over territory. These incidents include shooting persons escaping over the frontier to all-out military invasions of short duration.

BORDERS: lines of demarcation between national territories or national territory and international waters. *See* TIMOR ISLAND ARBITRATION.

BOTTOMRY: contract to borrow money to fund a voyage, pledging the ship as security for the loan.

BOUNDARY: *see* BORDERS

BOUNDARY WATERS TREATY (1909): treaty between Canada and the United States creating a joint commission with jurisdiction over cases involving the use or diversion of water along their common border. *See* 36 Stat. 2448, 12 Bevans 319.

BOURSE: Paris Stock Exchange; colloquialism for a money market.

BOUT DE PAPIER (F): diplomatic note without heading, signature, or date to allow deniability.

BOYCOTT: form of sanction or reprisal in which a country or countries refuse to deal or associate with another country or countries.

BOXER INDEMNITY: payment for damage arising out of the BOXER REBELLION (q.v.). *See* 1904 *Foreign Relations of the United States* 177.

BOXER REBELLION (1900): outbreak of hostilities against foreigners by the Chinese in the northern provinces. *See* 4 Am.J.Int.L. Supp. 300.

BRACEROS (S): migrant workers.

BRAINWASHING: program of treatment of prisoners designed to alter their beliefs, attitudes, opinions, etc. Such treatment of prisoners of war is prohibited as are all other types of mandatory political instruction. *See* Art. 38 GENEVA CONVENTION III (1949).

BRAZZAVILLE CONFERENCE (1960): meeting of African nations to discuss, *inter alia*, the CONGO CRISIS (q.v.). *See* Amate, *Inside the OAU* 44-46 (1986).

BRAZZAVILLE GROUP: *See* UNION OF AFRICAN AND MALAGASY STATES (U.A.M.).

BREACH OF TREATY: any action or inaction by a party to a treaty which violates or denigrates the rights under the treaty of another party to the TREATY (q.v.).

BREAK IN DIPLOMATIC RELATIONS: suspension of formal diplomatic intercourse between two nations. The nations may continue other mutual activities such as CONSULAR RELATIONS (q.v.) or trade.

BREISACH TRIAL (1474): precursor to war crimes trials where one Peter von Hagenbach, administrator of Breisach for Charles of Burgundy, was tried by Austria for his brutal administration under Charles' orders.

BREST-LITOVSK TREATY (1918): formal end to World War I on the eastern front between Germany and her allies and Russia. *See* 223 CTS 15 (in German) or II Toynbee, *Treaties* 1235.

BRETTON WOODS CONFERENCE (1944): meeting of 44 governments at Bretton Woods, N.H., resulting agreements to create the INTER-NATIONAL MONETARY FUND and the INTERNATIONAL BANK FOR RECONSTRUCTION AND DEVELOPMENT (q.v.).

BREVET: instrument issued by a consul appointing a viceconsul or consular agent.

BREZHNEV DOCTRINE: the Soviet Union hereby claims the right to intervene militarily to maintain the Marxist governments of its bordering client states. Gorbachev renounced the Doctrine in 1989. *See* 66 Am.J.Int.L. 816.

BRIAND-KELLOGG TREATY (1928): treaty which declares the absolute illegality of war in the pursuit of national policy. It remains in force today because it is fully consistent with the UNITED NATIONS CHARTER (q.v.). It is also known as the Pact of Paris. *See* 46 Stat. 2343, 2 Bevans 732, 94 L.N.T.S. 57.

BRITISH COMMONWEALTH: association of sovereign states freely joining together and pledging allegiance to the British Crown. Included are the United Kingdom, Canada, Australia, New Zealand, India, Pakistan, Nigeria, Sierra Leone, Tanganyika, Jamaica, and Ghana among others. *See* W. Dale, *The Modern Commonwealth* (1983).

BRITISH SUBJECT: citizen of any country of the BRITISH COMMON-WEALTH (q.v.). This determination is particularly important under admiralty jurisdiction exercised in the Commonwealth.

BROADCAST CONVENTION (1936): effort to curb propaganda broadcasts. *See* 32 Am.J.Int.L. Supp. 113.

BROADCASTING: *see* PIRATE BROADCAST.

BRUSSELS CONVENTION ON SHIP COLLISION (1962): two agreements governing responsibility and jurisdiction over collisions of ocean-going vessels. *See* 439 U.N.T.S. 217 and 233, 53 AM.J.Int.L. 532 and 536.

BRUSSELS NOMENCLATURE: popular name for the HARMONIZED COMMODITY DESCRIPTION AND CODING SYSTEM (q.v.).

BRUSSELS SATELLITE CONVENTION (1974): DISTRIBU-
TION OF PROGRAM-CARRYING SIGNALS TRANSMITTED BY
SATELLITE CONVENTION (q.v.).

BRUSSELS TREATY (1948): agreement entered into by Belgium,
France, Luxembourg, the Netherlands, and the United Kingdom
for collective self-defense and economic, social, and cultural cooperation. When Italy and West Germany joined in 1954, the organization changed its name to the WESTERN EUROPEAN UNION
(q.v.). *See* 19 U.N.T.S. 51.

BRUTUM FULMEN (L): an empty threat.

BRYAN-CHAMORRO TREATY (1916): treaty between the
United States and Nicaragua. The former was granted an exclusive right to build a canal from the Atlantic to the Pacific Oceans.
The Inter-American Court, however, in 1917 declared that Nicaragua's signing violated its earlier treaty with Costa Rica not to
grant canal rights to a third state without consultation. *See* 39
Stat. 1661, 10 Bevans 379.

BRYAN TREATIES: several treaties designed to avert war. The
first was signed between the United States and Great Britain in
1914, under which the parties agreed to submit unsettled disputes
to a standing "Peace Commission." *See* 38 Stat. 1853, 12 Bevans
370 and 8 Am.J.Int.L. 565.

BUDAPEST TREATY (1978): *See* MICROORGANISMS DE-
POSIT FOR PATENTS TREATY (1978).

BUENOS AIRES TREATY (1915): treaty among Argentina, Brazil, and Chile establishing a permanent commission of enquiry.
The commissions function was to resolve conflicts arising among
the parties. *See* 221 C.T.S. 72.

BUFFER ZONE: strip of land separating hostile forces.

BULL (or BULLA): solemn papal writ. *See* e.g., INTER CAER-
ERA DIVINEA.

BULLIONISM: outmoded method of calculating a nation's wealth by the weight of the gold and silver in its treasury.

BUNDESGERICHTSHOF (G): the German Supreme Court. Its decisions are reported in *Entscheidungen des Bundesgerichtshof.*

BUNDESRATH CASE (1899): British cruiser seized the German mail steamer *Bundesrath* suspected of running ammunition to the Boers. The cargo was innocent, Germany protested and the British agreed to give compensation and to refrain from acting in similar instances *"on suspicion only."*

BUOYAGE: system for providing buoys or channel markers.

BUREAU DU PROTOCOLE (F): office in charge of the formalities of treaty drafting, formal correspondence, etc.

BURGERLICHES GESETZBUCH (BGB) (G): the Civil Code of Germany containing the basic law governing property rights and relations between people.

BURKINA FASO: formerly Upper Volta;, the name is formed from words found in the two predominate tribal languages meaning land of honorable men (though their recently deposed dictator was not one of them).

BURKINA FASO V. MALI: *see* FRONTIER DISPUTE.

BURUNDI-RWANDA DISPUTE (1963): Rwandi accused Burundi of supporting Batutai guerrillas and trying to overthrow their government. Burundi responded that Rwandi was slaughtering thousands of innocent Batutai tribesmen. The problems between these two small countries continue. *See* Amate, *Inside the OAU,* 425-7 (1986).

BURMA-INDIA MARITIME BOUNDARY: subject of an agreement dividing up the Andaman Sea, Coco Channel, and the Bay of Bengal. *See* 27 I.L.M. 1144.

BUS: international carriage of passengers by bus is the subject of a convention on general conditions for such carriage. *See* 802 U.N.T.S. 3.

BUSTAMANTE CODE (1928): code attached to the Convention on Private International Law, adopted at the Sixth International Conference of American States. *See* 86 L.N.T.S. 111.

BW CONVENTION (1972): BACTERIOLOGICAL WARFARE CONVENTION (1972) (q.v.).

BYEZHENTSY (R): refugee or fugitive.

C & F: cost and freight: an INCOTERM (q.v.), under which the seller is responsible for the cost of shipping but not for insurance.

CABOTAGE: navigation and trade along the coast of a country. Cabotage rights are the privilege of carrying traffic between two ports in one state. Also, used in international aviation for the right of a foreign airline to carry passengers and cargo between airports in the same country. *See* Art. 7 of the CHICAGO CONVENTION (1944).

CADUCITE, LA THEORIE DE LA, (F): the theory or doctrine that a treaty may lapse owing to a change in circumstances. *See* REBUS SIC STANDIBUS.

CACM: CENTRAL AMERICAN COMMON MARKET (q.v.).

CAETERIS PARIBUS (L): all other things being equal.

CAIRO DECLARATION (1943): allied policy statement that all Pacific islands, seized by Japan or occupied by aggression since 1914, would not be recognized and territory stolen from China would be returned. *See* 1 Whiteman, *Digest of International Law* 320.

CAIRO DECLARATION (1970): a NONALIGNED MOVEMENT (q.v.) declaration that urged changes in the UNITED NATIONS CHARTER (q.v.) in order to adapt it to the dynamic changes in international relations. *See* Rajan, *The Nonaligned and the United Nations* 304 (1987).

CAIRO SUMMIT (1977): *see* AFRO-ARAB SUMMIT CONFERENCE (1977).

CALLEY TRIAL: *see* MY LAI MASSACRE.

CALVO CLAUSE: contract provision used by some Central and South American governments. The contract provides that a foreign private contractor waives the right to be protected by its own state. Thus, when any claim or dispute arises under the contract, the contractor's only recourse is to the local courts of the contracting state. *See North American Dredging Co. Claim*, 4 R.I.A.A. 26 (1926).

CALVO DOCTRINE: basis for the CALVO CLAUSE (q.v.); an alien holding property has no greater right than others in the country where the property is located. Therefore, should not be allowed to call upon his own government to pursue his claim in an international forum when a citizen of the state could not pursue such a claim. *See* 40 Am.J.Int.L. 121.

CAMBODIAN INCURSIONS (1970): response to the use of bases in Cambodia (now Kampuchea) by the forces of North Vietnam and the VIET CONG (q.v.). The United States and South Vietnamese forces entered Cambodia to destroy the bases. The United States justified the act as one of collective self-defense.*See* 9 I.L.M. 840 and 65 Am.J.Int.L. 1.

CAMP DAVID AGREEMENTS (1978): agreements reached by President Sadat of Egypt and Prime Minister Begin of Israel at a meeting convened by President Carter at Camp David, Maryland. The two agreements, *"A Framework for Peace in the Middle East"* and *"Framework for the Conclusion of a Peace Treaty,"* established peaceful relations between Israel and Egypt. *See* 17 I.L.M. 1466, 1740.

CANADA-UNITED STATES FREE TRADE AGREEMENT (1988): treaty to eliminate barriers to trade, including tariffs between the United States and Canada. *See* 27 I.L.M. 281 and 83 Am.J.Int.L. 118.

CANADA-UNITED STATES FREE TRADE AGREEMENT BINATIONAL SECRETARIAT: organization to review dispute settlement procedures under the CANADA-UNITED STATES FREE TRADE AGREEMENT (1988). *See* 30 I.L.M. 181.

CANADIANIZATION: Canadian government program to preserve Canadian control of its economy by buying-up foreign interests and discouraging foreign investment a disastrous policy being dismantled by the current government. *See* 2 S. Lowenfeld, *International Private Investment* 66 (1982).

CANBERRA CONVENTION (1980): convention on the conservation of Antarctic marine living resources, *see* 19 I.L.M. 841.

CANCELLATION: termination of treaty obligation by agreement among the parties. *See* McNair, *The Law of Treaties* 506 (1961).

CANEVARO CASE (1911): arbitration of a dispute between Italy and Peru over debt owed Italian citizens by Peru. *See* 6 Am.J.Int.L. 709.

CANNON SHOT RULE: eighteenth century rule for establishing a states maritime jurisdiction, i.e., the littoral state exercises authority over the seas that its land-based arms can control. In the eighteenth century it was approximately three miles.

CAPACITY: status necessary for a state to make or enter into treaties or international agreements. Capacity may be limited by a states own constitution. *See* Arts. 6 *et seq* of the VIENNA CONVENTION ON THE LAW OF TREATIES.

CAPITULATION: 1) system of extraterritorial jurisdiction whereby treaties imposed on non-western countries gave citizens of western nations, who resided within a territory, subject to capitulation the right to judicial proceeding under the rules of their own state. 2) Agreement entered into by the commanders of belligerent forces to regulate the details of a surrender when continuation of battle is impossible and there is no means of receiving instructions from their superiors. Such agreements bind only the area under the commanders' authority.

CAPTURE: act of acquiring possession and assuming control over property of another with the intent to retain or destroy it as PRIZE or BOOTY (qq.v.).

CARACAS CONVENTIONS (1954) and CONVENTION ON DIPLOMATIC ASYLUM: convention on territorial asylum, 161 *British and Foreign State Papers* 566.

CARDENAS DOCTRINE: statement by a Mexican president that states should not have extraterritorial powers, e.g., one state could not act to protect its nationals in the territory of another state. *See* 34 Am.J.Int.L. 300.

CARDOZA DOCTRINE: when a government is not recognized by the United States, the U.S. courts will give cognizance to the laws and acts of that country only insofar as they are consistent with the laws and acts of the previous recognized government.

CARENCE DE SOUVERAINITE (F): a defective sovereign i.e., a government which due to lack of effective governance looses the cofidence of the population. *See* Crawford, *The Creation of States in International Law* 86 (1979).

CARIBBEAN BASIN INITIATIVE: Reagan Administration Economic Assistance Program for the countries in Central America and the Caribbean Sea (excluding Cuba and Nicaragua). *See* 14 Law. Am. (1983).

CARIBBEAN COMMISSION: treaty by a group of interested states for the purpose of conservation of Caribbean marine life. *See* 22 I.L.M. 227, and 14 Ga. J. Int'l and Comp. L. 201.

CARIBBEAN DEVELOPMENT BANK: financial institution to support Caribbean development efforts. *See* Command Papers 4254, Misc. No. 1 (1970).

CARIBBEAN ECONOMIC COMMUNITY (CARICOM): organization for Caribbean regional economic development which replaced and expanded the CARIBBEAN FREE TRADE ASSOCIATION (q.v.). *See* Caricom Treaty, 12 I.L.M. 1033, 12 Law. Am. 730 (1980), or Lazar, Transnational Economic and Monetary Law 4.10.001 (1984).

CARIBBEAN FREE TRADE ASSOCIATION: organization for regional economic cooperation. Created by agreement in 772 U.N.T.S. 2 (1975). *See also* 3 Lazar, Transnational Economic and Monetary Law 4.9.001 (1984).

CARICOM: CARIBBEAN ECONOMIC COMMUNITY, (q.v.).

CARIFTA: CARIBBEAN FREE TRADE ASSOCIATION,(q.v.).

CARNET: document issued for the temporary admission of goods under various customs conventions. *See* 20 U.S.T. 219 and 343 U.N.T.S. 129.

CAROLINE INCIDENT (1837): an American steamship was confiscated and sunk by the British in American waters because it had been used to supply Canada during the 1837 Rebellion. From this incident comes the doctrine that preventive self-defense could justify an act of intervention if absolutely necessary. *See* 32 Am.J.Int.L. 82.

CARRIAGE OF GOODS BY SEA CONVENTIONS: *See* HAGUE RULES and HAMBURG RULES.

CARRIAGE OF PASSENGERS AND LUGGAGE BY SEA CONVENTION (1974): establishes a liability regime for such carriage. *See* 14 I.L.M. 945.

CARTAGENA AGREEMENT (or Andean Subregional Agreement): subregional agreement by Bolivia, Chile, Colombia, Ecuador, Peru, and Venezuela (which later withdrew) forming the ANDEAN COMMON MARKET. Formed to improve the living standards of their peoples through economic integration. *See* 8 I.L.M. 910 (1969) as amended by 16 I.L.M. 235 (1976), and 78 Patent and Trademark Rev. 301 (1980).

CARTEL: 1) agreement entered into between belligerents for the exchange of prisoners. 2) Organization of producers of a commodity attempting to control price and production, *see eg.*, ORGANIZATION OF PETROLEUM EXPORTING COUNTRIES.

CARTEL SHIP: vessel specifically designated for the transport of exchanged prisoners. The ship is provided immunity from attack.

CARTER DOCTRINE: President Carter's declaration that the United States was prepared to use force to protect western interests in the Persian Gulf area. *See* Public *Papers of the Presidents: Jimmy Carter 1980-1* at 171 and 2479.

CASABLANCA GROUP: *See* AFRICAN CHARTER OF CASABLANCA.

CASSATION (or revisio in jure): used to describe a judicial body having the ability to review the decisions of the law of lower courts, but may not review their findings as to the facts in the case.

CASUS BELLI (L): act by one nation that offends another nation to the extent that the second nation is justified in declaring war.

CASUS FOEDERIS (L): occurrence which triggers the application of a mutual defense treaty, such as a third party attack against one of the parties to the treaty.

CATHAY PACIFIC INCIDENT (1954): shooting down of a Cathay Pacific passenger plane by the Communist Chinese and killing three American passengers, as well as others. This provoked an exchange of charges between several communist countries and the United States concerning interference with freedom of navigation on the high seas. *See* 4 Whiteman, *Digest of International Law* 534.

CAUSA CREDENDI (L): assumption of an obligation in exchange for the obligation of another.

CAUSA IMPOTENTIAE (L): because of impossibility.

CAUSA SOLVENDI (L): assumption of an obligation to cancel another obligation.

CAUTIO IUDICATUM SOLVI (L): security for costs, a requirement of the courts of some countries in order for a foreign plaintiff to bring an action.

CAVEAT: 1) a warning; 2) a request for action to be deterred.

CAYUGA INDIAN CASE: Great Britain pursued the claims of the Cayuga (who had moved to Canada after the American Revolution) under treaties between the tribe and the United States for compensation for the loss of land in New York. *See* 6 R.I.A.A. 173.

C.C.C.: CUSTOMS COOPERATION COUNCIL (q.v.).

C.C.I.R.: INTERNATIONAL RADIO CONSULTATIVE COMMITTEE (q.v.).

C.C.I.T.T.: INTERNATIONAL TELEGRAPH AND TELEPHONE CONSULTATIVE COMMITTEE (q.v.).

C.E.: COUNCIL OF EUROPE (q.v.).

C.E.A.O.: WEST AFRICAN ECONOMIC COMMUNITY (q.v.).

CECLA: SPECIAL LATIN AMERICAN COORDINATING COMMITTEE (q.v.).

CEDED TERRITORY: *see* CESSION OF TERRITORY.

C.E.E.: COMMUNAUTE ECONOMIQUE EUROPEANNE (F): French abbreviation for the EUROPEAN ECOMOMIC COMMUNITY (q.v.).

CELLAMARE CONSPIRACY: case standing for the proposition that a diplomatic agent may be detained or arrested as long as the detention is needed to preserve the security of the arresting state. *See* 1 Martens, *Causes Celebres* 139.

CENTO: CENTRAL TREATY ORGANIZATION (q.v.).

CENTRAL AFRICAN UNION: abortive attempt by the Central African Republic, the Congo, and Chad to coordinate development, plan transportation, telecommunications, and cooperate in cultural and security matters. *See* 7 I.L.M. 725.

CENTRAL AMERICAN COMMON MARKET (CACM): effort at economic integration by the five Central American countries. The name was changed to Central American Economic Union in 1976. *See* 455 U.N.T.S. 3 and 3 Lazar, Transnational Economic and Monetary Law 4.8.053 (1984).

CENTRAL AMERICAN COURT OF JUSTICE (1907-1918): regional international court with jurisdiction over cases between member states and questions of human rights. It decided 10 cases. *See* 5 Hackworth, *Digest of International Law* 161.

CENTRAL AMERICAN DEMOCRATIC COMMUNITY: countries in Central America with ostensibly democratic (i.e., not overtly anti- American) governments; Columbia, El Salvador, Costa Rica, and Honduras. *See* TEGUCIGULPA DECLARATION (1982).

CENTRAL AMERICAN DISARMAMENT CONVENTION (1923): five Central American countries agreed to limit their armed forces. *See* 1 Hackworth, *Digest of International Law* 188.

CENTRAL AMERICAN ECONOMIC UNION: new name adopted on March 23, 1976, for the CENTRAL AMERICAN COMMON MARKET (q.v.).

CENTRAL AMERICAN MEDIATION COMMISSION: in 1969,the foreign ministers of Guatemala, Nicaragua, and Costa Rica acted as a mediation commission for a controversy between El Salvador and Honduras. They proposed measures to facilitate the mediation process: that both governments enforce authority effectively, put aside warlike attitudes, and suppress media propaganda that might incite violence. *See* 8 I.L.M. 1080.

CENTRAL AMERICAN UNION (1921): a short-lived intergovern-mental organization of Costa Rica, El Salvador, Guatemala, and Honduras. *See* 5 L.N.T.S. 9.

CENTRAL INFORMATION AGENCY: during time of war, a clearinghouse for information about prisoners of war and civilian internees. This information usually was obtained under the auspices of the INTERNATIONAL COMMITTEE OF THE RED CROSS (q.v.). *See*, Art. 123 of the GENEVA CONVENTION III (1949) and Art. 140 of the GENEVA CONVENTION IV (1949).

CENTRAL TRACING AGENCY: clearinghouse for information about children separated from their families during war, operated by the INTERNATIONAL COMMITTEE OF THE RED CROSS (q.v.).

CENTRAL TREATY ORGANIZATION (CENTO)(1955): treaty by Turkey, Pakistan, Iran, Iraq (which subsequently withdrew), and the United Kingdom for security arrangements in the Middle East. Also, known as the BAGHDAD PACT (q.v.), the treaty had economic goals, as well. *See* 233 U.N.T.S. 199.

CERN: EUROPEAN ORGANIZATION FOR NUCLEAR RESEARCH (q.v.).

CERRUTI CLAIM (1885-1911): long-standing dispute between Italy and Columbia finally arbitrated by President Cleveland of the United States. *See* 6 Am.J.Int.L. 965 and 11 R.I.A.A. 377.

CERTIFICATE OF ORIGIN: document verifying the country from which particular goods have been exported.

CERTIFICATE OF REGISTRY: document evidencing the nationality and ownership of a vessel. The master of a vessel must have his name inscribed on the certificate before he can act as master.

CESSANTE RATIONE LEGIS, CESSAT IPSA LEX(L): principle that when the *raison d'etre* for a treaty has disappeared or changed substantially then there are grounds for recognizing the *ipso facto* termination of the treaty.

CESSATION OF HOSTILITIES: termination of belligerent action between two or more nations by, e.g., ARMISTICE, TRUCE, SURRENDER (qq.v.).

CESSIO LEGIS (L): involuntary assignment of a debt by law, e.g., where a surety pays a creditor, and thus, acquires the creditor's right to be paid by the debtor.

CESSION OF TERRITORY: passing of sovereignty over territory from one state to another. Cession can result from war or from peaceful negotiations; it can be either gratuitous or for some consideration. *See e.g.,* LOUISIANA PURCHASE.

CHACO DISPUTE (1933): boundary dispute between Bolivia and Paraguay. *See* 28 Am.J.Int.L. Supp. 137.

CHADIAN CIVIL WAR: fighting between the forces of Northern Chad led by Pres. Goukouni and aided by Libya, and those of Southern Chad led by Pres. Habre. The war has continued intermittently since the 1960's. *See* 34 Int'l. & Comp.L.Q. 593 (1985).

CHAMIZAL TRACT: area of land lying between the old and new beds of the Rio Grande River. Most of the tract is in the possession of Mexico. Dispute over ownership between the United States and Mexico was settled in 1963. *See* 15 U.S.T. 21, 505 U.N.T.S. 185.

CHANCELLERY: 1) term for the Foreign Office (in the United States, the State Department) used in many European countries. 2) The offices of an EMBASSY or CONSULATE (qq.v.).

CHAPULTEPEC CONFERENCE (1945): also known as the Inter-American Conference on Problems of War and Peace. The declaration of this conference is known as the Act of Chapultepec and lists basic principles of international law recognized in the Americas. *See* 39 Am.J.Int.L. Supp. 108.

CHARGE D'AFFAIRS (F): envoy from or to a minor country. One of three classes of "Heads of Mission" recognized in Art. 14 of the Vienna Convention on Diplomatic Relations, 23 U.S.T.3227, 500 U.N.T.S. 95 (1961).

CHARGE D'AFFAIRS AD INTERIM: temporary appointment as chief of a DIPLOMATIC MISSION (q.v.), either between permanent chiefs or when a mission is newly established, and the AMBASSADOR (q.v.) who has not yet arrived. *See* Art. 16 of the Vienna Convention of Diplomatic Relations, 23 U.S.T. 3227, T.I.A.S. 7502, 500 U.N.T.S. 95 (1961).

CHARGE D'AFFAIRS DE TITRE (F): envoy sent on a permanent basis to represent a government at the seat of another government.

CHARGES: restrictions on property resulting from special measures adopted against property owned by an ENEMY (q.v.) or by enemy nationals.

CHARTER OF ALGIERS: charted a common course of action for accelerated economic and social development; addressed com-

modities policy and problems; expansion of export manufactur-
ers, development, financing, and expansion of trade. The Charter
was adopted by a ministerial meeting of the GROUP OF 77 (q.v.).
See 7 I.L.M. 177.

**CHARTER OF ECONOMIC RIGHTS AND DUTIES OF
STATES (UNGA Res. 3281 (XXIX)):** recites the fundamental principles of international economic relations, e.g., permanent sovereignty over natural resources and the right to engage in trade. *See*
69 Am.J.Int.L. 484.

CHARTER OF PARIS FOR A NEW EUROPE: plan for cooperation in furthering the goals of the CONFERENCE ON SECURITY
AND COOPERATION IN EUROPE (q.v.). *See* 30 I.L.M. 190.

CHARTER OF THE INTERNATIONAL COURT OF JUSTICE:
see STATUTE OF THE INTERNATIONAL COURT OF JUSTICE.

CHARTER OF THE INTERNATIONAL TRIBUNAL: rules gov-
erning the proceedings of the INTERNATIONAL MILITARY TRI-
BUNAL FOR THE PROSECUTION OF WAR CRIMES (q.v.) after
World War II. *See* 59 Stat. 1544, 82 U.N.T.S. 279.

CHARTER OF THE UNITED NATIONS: organic document of
the UNITED NATIONS (q.v.) which forms the basis for the U.N.
organization and restates the most fundamental principles of international law. The Charter includes the STATUTE OF THE IN-
TERNATIONAL COURT OF JUSTICE (q.v.). *See* 59 Stat. 1031, 3
Bevans 1153.

CHARTER-PARTY: contract to lease a ship or airplane or part
thereof. *See also* WET LEASE and BARE-BONES CHARTER.

CHEMICAL WEAPONS: projectiles which diffuse asphyxiating
or deleterious gases. A declaration adopted by the First Hague
Conference (1899) prohibited their use during war as between parties to the Conference. Recently their use has been reported by

both sides in the IRAN-IRAQ WAR (q.v.). *See* 32 Stat. 1803, 1 Bevans 247.

CHERNOBYL INCIDENT (1986): fire at a Soviet nuclear power plant spread nuclear debris over a large part of Europe. The accident led to negotiation of two conventions at a meeting of the International Atomic Energy Agency in 1986. *See* 25 I.L.M. 1369.

CHICAGO CONVENTION (1944): International Convention on Civil Aviation, 61 Stat. 1180, 15 U.N.T.S. 295, which regulates many aspects of international civil aviation and established the INTERNATIONAL CIVIL AVIATION ORGANIZATION (ICAO) (q.v.).

CHICKEN WAR: trade dispute between the United States and the EUROPEAN ECONOMIC COMMUNITY (q.v.) over United States exports of chickens. *See* 58 Am.J.Int.L. 671.

CHILDREN'S RIGHTS DECLARATION (UNGA Res. 1386 (XIV)): states, *inter alia*, that a child has a right at birth to a name and nationality and to enjoy special protection. *See* 1959 U.N. Yearbook 192.

CHILEANIZATION: expropriation of the copper industry by the Chilean Government. *See* 9 .L.M. 921.

CHLOROFLUOROCARBONS: common propellant used in aerosol   containers, air conditioning, and refrigeration systems. The subject of an international agreement due to the harmful effects of such substances to the ozone layer which protects the Earth from ultraviolet radiation. *See* 26 I.L.M. 1541.

CHORZOW CASE: case standing for the proposition that a state may expropriate the property of foreign nationals as well as its own citizens, but may not do so without paying just compensation. 1928 P.C.I.J. (ser. A) No. 17.

CHRISTY COMMISSION (1930): League of Nations Commission to investigate charges of the existence of slavery and forced labor in Liberia. The Commission confirmed the charges and made recommendations. *See* International Commission of Inquiry in Liberia, League of Nations Pub. C.658.M272. 1930 VI.

C.I.F.: INCOTERM (q.v.) where seller pays the cost, insurance, and freight in transporting the goods to the buyer.

C.I.M.: See BERNE CONVENTION (1892).

CIPEC: CONSEIL INTERGOUVERNMANTAL DES PAYS EXPORTATEURS DE CUIRVE (q.v.).

CITES: convention on international trade in endangered species. *See* TRADE IN ENDANGERED SPECIES OF WILD FLORA & FAUNA CONVENTION (1975).

CIVIL AIRCRAFT: aircraft not conducting governmental or military functions. General subject of the CHICAGO CONVENTION (1944) (q.v.). In particular, *see* Art. 3 of the Convention.

CIVIL AVIATION CONVENTION (1944): *see* CHICAGO CONVENTION (1944).

CIVIL CAPACITY: in the LAWS OF WAR (q.v.), PRISONERS OF WAR (q.v.) are to be accorded the right to exercise their legal capacity to perform such acts as the making of a will or execution of a power of attorney. *See* Art. 14(3) of the GENEVA CONVENTION III (1949).

CIVIL DEFENSE: part of the general defense of a country. The aggregate of functions performed to protect the civilian population and to help in the recovery from the effects of hostilities or natural disasters, e.g., warnings, evacuation, rescue, and medical services.

CIVIL LAW: system of law based on Roman law as codified in the Napoleanic Code. Most of the countries of the world have a civil law system to some extent, with the exception of those following the British system or COMMON LAW (q.v.). The difference in approach of these two systems sometimes causes misunderstandings in international forums.

CIVIL LIABILITY FOR OIL POLLUTION DAMAGE CONVENTION (1970): agreement which places liability, for oil pollution damage occurring on territory or in territorial waters, on the owner of the ship that discharged the oil. In return, the owners liability is limited based on the tonnage of the ship. *See* 9 I.L.M. 45.

CIVIL STRIFE: conflict within a country which may be manifested in violence against the government, or between groups, or by a lack of civil authority approaching anarchy.

CIVIL WAR: war between rival groups within an existing state. *See* GENEVA CONVENTION PROTOCOL II (1977).

CIVILIAN: inhabitant of a territory not engaged or participating in the state's military operations. Civilian internees are protected persons (non-military) and sometimes taken into custody by a belligerent for their own safety or the security of the belligerent. *See* Art. 42 of the GENEVA CONVENTION IV (1949).

CIVILIAN OBJECT: all objects which by their nature, location, purpose, or use do not contribute to military action or ability, and whose capture or destruction do not contribute to a military advantage. *See* Art. 51 of GENEVA CONVENTION PROTOCOL I (1977).

CITIZENSHIP: status acquired by the inhabitants of a state either by birth within the territory of the state or by NATURALIZATION (q.v.).

CLAIM: allegation by an individual or state, that it is entitled to a remedy for an injury caused by the offending state. A state may take up a claim of its citizens or subjects, and in doing so, the claimant state asserts a right with respect to a wrong against itself.

CLARIS VERBIS (L): in clear, unambiguous language.

CLASSIFICATION OF GOODS AND SERVICES: subject of a multilateral treaty, 828 U.N.T.S. 191.

CLAUSA REBUS SIC STANDIBUS: *see* REBUS SIC STAN-DIBUS.

CLAUSE: smallest main subdivision of an international agreement.

CLAUSE COMPROMISSOIRE (F): arbitration clause within a treaty concerning a specific matter.

CLAUSULA REBUS SIC STANDIBUS: *see* REBUS SIC STANDIBUS.

CLAUSULAE INCONSUETAE SEMPER INDUCUNT SUSPI-CIONEM (L): terms which are unusual are always cause for suspicion.

CLAYTON-BULWER TREATY (1850): Great Britain and the United States agreed that neither party should obtain complete control over the proposed Panama Canal. *See* 9 Stat. 995, 12 Bevans 105. This agreement was superseded in 1901 by the HAY-PAUNCEFOTE TREATY (q.v.).

CLEAN BILL OF LADING: BILL OF LADING (q.v.), free of any qualifications as to the condition of the goods accepted for transport.

CLOSED TREATY: agreement between states which by its own terms limits the number of, or otherwise restricts those who may participate, e.g., the NORTH ATLANTIC TREATY ORGANIZA-TION (q.v.) is a closed treaty.

CLOSED SEA: a completely landlocked body of water or a partially enclosed body of water, such as a bay, which is recognized as part of the territory of the littoral state. *See* TERRITORIAL WATERS.

CMEA: COUNCIL FOR MUTUAL ECONOMIC ASSISTANCE (q.v.).

C.M.R.: GENEVA CONVENTION ON THE CARRIAGE OF GOODS BY ROAD (1955) (q.v.).

COALITION THEORY: alliances between states are formed only when the policymakers of those states rationally believe that the benefits of alliance outweigh the cost.

COASTAL TRADE: *see* CABOTAGE.

CO-BELLIGERENT: a state which provides limited assistance to a principal belligerent such as paying a subsidy or allowing troops or warships to pass through its territory.

COCESNA: CORPORACION CENTROAMERICANA DE SERVICIOS   NAVIGACION AEREA (q.v.).

COCOM: COORDINATING COMMITTEE FOR MULTILIATERAL EXPORT CONTROLS (q.v.).

CODES OF CONDUCT: recent coinage for written sets of rules which are intended to be followed by multinational business concerns. *See e.g.* Convention on the Code of Conduct for Liner Conferences, 13 I.L.M. 910, or Code of Conduct regarding Restrictive Business Practices, 72 Am.J.Int.L. 247.

CODIFICATION OF INTERNATIONAL LAW: process of reducing CUSTOMARY INTERNATIONAL LAW (q.v.) or other rules of international conduct to a written form which is then adopted as a treaty by the nations of the world. *See* HAGUE CODIFICATION CONFERENCE (1930).

CODIGO BUSTAMANTE (S): BUSTAMANTE CODE (q.v.).

COERCION: use of force or other pressure to gain control on the part of another against their will or interest. Treaties may be voided if their acceptance was gained by coercion against the state wishing to void the treaty. *See* VIENNA CONVENTION ON THE LAW OF TREATIES (1969), art. 52.

COEXISTENCE: recognition of a relationship of cooperation between states with different political and economic systems.

COFFEE AGREEMENT: *see* INTERNATIONAL COFFEE ORGANIZATION.

COGNITION: where the executive branch of a foreign state takes notice of the fact that a government authority has claimed competence over a territory and its people.

CO-IMPERIUM: mutual agreement between two states; that the right to administer state functions within a given territory shall be jointly held by the two states. Co-imperium gives neither state the right to cede the territory. *See also* CONDOMINIUM.

COLD WAR: state of hostilities between two countries (especially the United States and Soviet Union) conducted without resort to military engagement on any great scale, but includes arms buildup and unfriendly competition for world position.

COLLATERAL CONSTRAINTS: provisions of a treaty which attempt to close prospective loopholes and may negate the effectiveness of the agreement. *See e.g.,* STRATEGIC ARMS LIMITATION AGREEMENTS.

COLLECTIONS OF TREATIES: publications containing the treaties entered into by a particular country or group of countries, such as the United States Treaty Series or the United Nations Treaty Series. *See United Nations List of International Treaty Collections.*

COLLECTIVE GOODS THEORY (or PUBLIC GOODS THE-ORY): idea that there are benefits which can be shared noncompetitively; where consumption of the goods by individuals does not reduce the supply for others; and the use of the goods by some provides a benefit to all.

COLLECTIVE MEASURES: any steps taken by several states acting jointly to achieve an objective, *see e.g.*, COLLECTIVE SECURITY.

COLLECTIVE NATURALIZATION: conferring of citizenship on all the inhabitants of a newly acquired territory, as when the United States conferred citizenship on all Hawaiians (when Hawaii became a United States territory). *See* 10 I.L.R. 279.

COLLECTIVE PUNISHMENT: imposition of fines or other punishment on an entire population in an occupied area for the acts of individuals. One of the most extreme examples being the LIDICE MASSACRE (q.v.) by the Nazi occupation forces. Collective punishment is forbidden by Art. 50 of the HAGUE REGULATIONS OF 1907 (q.v.) and Art. 33 of the GENEVA CONVENTION IV (1949).

COLLECTIVE SECURITY: association of nations for the purpose of guaranteeing individual members (through the combined force of the association) against attack by an aggressor.

COLLECTIVE SELF-DEFENSE: modern concept that the common interest shared by certain states compels them to look at the security of another state as necessary to their own security. Thus, an attack on one state is a constructive attack on them all. Art. 51 of the UNITED NATIONS CHARTER (q.v.) governs collective self-defense.

COLLEGE ARBITRAL (F): group (such as a COMMISSION) acting as an arbitrator. *See* 22 I.L.R. 317.

COLLEGIUM FETIALIUM (L): body in the Roman government responsible for declaring war and conducting foreign relations.

COLLISION AT SEA: *See* LONDON CONVENTION ON THE INTERNATIONAL REGULATIONS FOR THE PREVENTION OF COLLISIONS AT SEA (1972) and the Brussels Conventions, 53 Am.J.Int.L. 532, 536.

COLOMBO DECLARATION (1979): NON-ALIGNED MOVEMENT (q.v.) declaration that urged, *inter alia*, that the Movement act as a collective force in the United Nations. *See* Rajan, *The Nonaligned and the United Nations* 304 (1987).

COLOMBO PLAN (1950): attempt at cooperation for development among commonwealth countries. *See* 9 Int'l Org. 1 (1955).

COLONIAL DOMINATION: because of the superior position of the Western powers *vis-a-vis* the third world, they are said to have repressed the economic, social, and cultural development of their former colonies. Also, used to describe repression of satellite states, e.g., Afghanistan by the Soviet Union.

COLONIAL POWER: nation which possesses territory held as colonies and which wields power because of the extent of its colonies. Great Britain and France were the major colonial powers in the first half of the 20th century.

COLONIAL RESERVATION: provision in a treaty modifying its application as to a party's colonies.

COLONIALISM: subjection of peoples to alien domination and exploitation. Fortunately this system fell out of favor after World War II. *See* FOURTH COMMITTEE OF THE UNITED NATIONS.

COLONY: dependent possession of a state, acquired by treaty of cessation, annexation, prescription, or conquest; not constitutionally under the state's own system of government.

COMBAT ZONE: *see* CONTACT ZONE.

COMBATANTS: persons authorized by their government to participate in the operations of WAR (q.v.). *See* Art. 43(2) of the Geneva Protocol I (1977).

COMBITERMS: standardized trade terms for use with consignments that are consolidated into containers for shipping. *See* ICC, Uniform Rules for a Combined Transport Document (1975).

COMECON: COUNCIL FOR MUTUAL ECONOMIC ASSISTANCE (q.v.).

COMITAS GENTIUM (L): COMITY OF NATIONS (q.v.).

COMITY OF NATIONS: acts or practices of nations based on good will and mutuality, rather than strict application and enforcement of rules of law.

COMMERCIA BELLI (L): special agreement between belligerents (usually during a truce) insuring the operation of certain non-hostile activities, such as provisioning civilian populations occasioned by necessity of convenience or humanity.

COMMERCIAL AGENT: person sent to another country to negotiate or arrange business dealings. Although sometimes sent by a state, these agents have no diplomatic status.

COMMERCIAL ATTACHE: person on the staff of an EMBASSY or LEGATION (qq.v.) charged with reporting upon the commerce and industry of the host state. *See* 24 Am.J.Int.L. 110.

COMMISSION (international): group appointed to investigate an international dispute and propose a settlement. Commissions may be established permanently for specific purposes such as the United States-Canadian Boundary Waters Commission. *See* BOUNDARY WATERS TREATY (1909).

COMMISSION AND CENTRE ON TRANSNATIONAL COR-PORATIONS: established by the UNITED NATIONS ECO-NOMIC AND SOCIAL COUNCIL (q.v.) in 1974, to draft a CODE OF CONDUCT (q.v.) for multinational businesses. *See* 22 German Y.B. Int'l L. 11 (1979).

COMMISSION ON HUMAN RIGHTS: body formed by the ECONOMIC AND SOCIAL COUNCIL OF THE UNITED NATIONS (q.v.) in 1946, to deal with questions of human rights. *See* 1946-1947 U.N. Yearbook 524.

COMMISSION ON NARCOTIC DRUGS: created under the authority of the ECONOMIC AND SOCIAL COUNCIL OF THE UNITED NATIONS (q.v.) to administer international drug suppression conventions. *See* 1946-1947 U.N. Yearbook 532.

COMMISSION ON THE STATUS OF WOMEN: created under the authority of the ECONOMIC AND SOCIAL COUNCIL OF THE UNITED NATIONS (q.v.) to establish equal rights for women in the national legal systems of member states. *See* 1946-1947 U.N. Yearbook 529.

COMMISSION ON TRANSNATIONAL CORPORATIONS: created to advise and assist the ECONOMIC AND SOCIAL COUNCIL OF THE UNITED NATIONS (q.v.) on the question of an international regime to control TRANSNATIONAL CORPO-RATIONS (q.v.). *See* 1974 U.N. Yearbook 480.

COMMISSIONER: diplomatic agent appointed to an international regulatory body, such as the INTERNATIONAL BOUND-ARY COMMISSION (q.v.).

COMMITTEE OF 20: Committee of the Board of Governors on Reform of the INTERNATIONAL MONETARY FUND (q.v.), one representative of the central bank from each country is represented on the Board of Governors and appointed to study reforms to be instituted. *See* Surr, "The Committee of 20," 11 Finance and Development No.2, p.24 (Jan. 1974).

COMMITTEE OF 24: established by United Nations General Assembly Res. 1810 (XVII); an enlarged version of the special committee on implementing the DECLARATION ON THE GRANTING OF IN
DEPENDENCE TO COLONIAL COUNTRIES AND PEOPLES (q.v.).

COMMITTEE ON HUMAN RIGHTS: created under Art. 28 of COVENANT ON CIVIL AND POLITICAL RIGHTS (q.v.), to promote and encourage the development of human rights and fundamental freedom. *See* 1976 U.N. Yearbook 611.

COMMITTEE ON PEACEFUL USES OF OUTER SPACE (COPUOS): Committee of the United Nations having had primary responsibility for the drafting of the several space law conventions. *See* OUTER SPACE TREATY (1967) and MOON TREATY (1979).

COMMITTEE ON PEACEFUL USES OF THE SEABED AND OCEAN FLOOR: United Nations Committee charged with the effort to prevent the extension of the arms race to the floor of the HIGH SEAS (q.v.), and to promote international cooperation in the development of its resources and use. *See* 8 I.L.M. 201.

COMMITTEE ON RELATIONS WITH THE HOST COUNTRY (1971): United Nations body to deal with questions of the security of United Nations missions and personnel, the size of missions, and problems with local arrangements. *See* 1971 U.N. Yearbook 622.

COMMITTEE ON THE LIQUIDATION OF RACIAL DISCRIMINATION (1969): *see* ELIMINATION OF ALL FORMS OF RACIAL DISCRIMINATION CONVENTION and 1969 U.N. Yearbook 484, 488.

COMMODITY AGREEMENTS: multilateral attempts to form cartels to control particular raw materials production. *See e.g.,* INTERNATIONAL BAUXITE ASSOCIATION, 13 I.L.M. 1245.

COMMODUM EX INJURIA NON ORBITUR (L): one cannot benefit from his breach of a legal right.

COMMON HERITAGE FUND: proposed by Nepal; countries with coastal resources would contribute part of their earnings from mineral resources in coastal waters to landlocked developing countries. *See* 10 Cal.West.Int'l.L.J. 25 (1989).

COMMON HERITAGE OF MANKIND: principle enshrined in the MOON TREATY (1979) and the LAW OF THE SEA CONVENTION (1983) (qq.v.) which holds that certain resources should be developed in such a way that they benefit all mankind, rather than just those who have the ability to exploit the resources.

COMMON LAW: legal system based on the rule of precedent in case decisions by courts, rather than a code as is found in CIVIL LAW (q.v.). The common law system was spread throughout the world by the British Empire.

COMMON MARKET: general term for a group of countries which has eliminated some or all trade barriers among themselves. Specifically, it is used to refer to the EUROPEAN ECONOMIC COMMUNITY (q.v.).

COMMONWEALTH OF NATIONS: *see* BRITISH COMMONWEALTH.

COMMORIENTES (L): (title of a lost play by Plautus), simultaneous death.

COMMUNE BONUM (L): common good; for the good of the community.

COMMUNIO INCIDENS (L): in Roman law a quasi-contract analogous to a contract arising out of a partnership.

COMMUNIQUE: official announcement concerning international negotiations or other formal diplomatic matters.

COMMUNIS SCRIPTURA (L): document of agreement; a TREATY (q.v.).

COMMUNIST INTERNATIONAL: world communist organization headquartered in Moscow, its goal is to promote and further worldwide Marxist/Communist revolution.

COMPARATIVE RESEARCH ON EVENTS OF NATIONS PROJECT (CREON): project (from 1959 to 1968) which studied the way states behave.

COMPENSATIO LUCRI CUM DAMNO (L): in measuring damages is the defendant entitled to "credit" for any benefit that may have accrued to the plaintiff by the injurious act.

COMPENSATION: payment of monetary damages to one whose rights have been violated by a breach of international law. *See also,* EX GRATIA.

COMPETENCE DE LA COMPETENCE (F): competent to determine competency; the ability of a court to determine its own jurisdiction or authority to hear a case. It is a generally accepted rule that courts are competent to decide the question of their own competence. *See* Shihata, *The Power of the International Court to Determine its Own Jurisdiction* (1965).

COMPETITION RULES IN THE EUROPEAN ECONOMIC COMMUNITY: rules for fair competition are part of the EUROPEAN ECONOMIC COMMUNITY (q.v.), Treaties, especially Art. 85 of the ROME TREATY (q.v.). Guidelines for their implementation are found at 7 I.L.M. 1150.

COMPOSITE INTERNATIONAL PERSONS: an actor (sovereign) in international affairs representing more than one state, e.g., a REAL UNION or FEDERATION (qq.v.).

COMPROMIS or COMPRIS D'ARBITRAGE (F): special agreement for the reference of a dispute to arbitration or judicial settlement. The compromise is a negotiated document setting forth precisely the issues to be determined. *See* Art. 40(1) of the STATUTE OF THE INTERNATIONAL COURT OF JUSTICE or Art. 52 of the HAGUE CONVENTION FOR THE PACIFIC SETTLEMENT OF DISPUTES (1907).

COMPULSORY JURISDICTION OF THE INTERNATIONAL COURT OF JUSTICE: *see* CONNALLY AMENDMENT.

COMPULSORY RULES: rules which must be followed within a legal system, but fall short of being principles of public order and must be followed even when considering questions that arise outside of the system, e.g., the necessity for consideration in contract formation that common law will not make a contract from a civil law country (which is enforceable in that country), but unenforceable in a common law court. However, fraud in the making of the contract (under the common law definition of fraud) would not though the act constitute fraud in the civil law country.

CONCENTRATION OF CIVILIANS: permanent or temporary inhabited parts of cities, villages, or camps by refugees, evacuees, or nomads. As a general rule of the Law of War, they are to be afforded protection. *See* Art. 1(2) of the GENEVA CONVENTION PROTOCAL III (1980)

CONCESSION: right granted to an individual or company to operate a business. The concession is limited by the terms of an agreement between the state and the CONCESSIONAIRE (q.v.).

CONCESSION AGREEMENT: grant of a commercial right to a foreign entity in order to develop a local resource or industry. *See e.g.,* Libyan Oil Concession to Occidental Petroleum, 14 I.L.M. 645.

CONCESSIONAIRE: individual or company party to a CONCESSION AGREEMENT (q.v.).

CONCILIATION: method of peaceful settlement of international disputes where the parties agree to refer the dispute to a COM-

MISSION (q.v.) for fact-finding and to make non-binding proposals for settlement.

CONCILIATION OF DISPUTES BETWEEN STATES: subject of United Nations draft rules. *See* 30 I.L.M. 229.

CONCILIATOR: person serving on a commission of CONCILIATION (q.v.).

CONCORDAT: agreement between the Pope and a head of state to protect the interests of the Roman Catholic Church in that particular state.

CONDITIO SINE QUA NON (L): condition that must be fulfilled before anything else can be done.

CONDOMINIUM: two states having both the right to perform state functions over a given territory as well as the right to cede that territory. *See also* CO-IMPERIUM.

CONFEDERATION: union of states under a central government that does not control all of the foreign relations of the member states.

CONFERENCE OF THE CMEA ON LEGAL MATTERS: permanent body established by the CMEA (q.v.) to improve legal relations in technical matters and matters of economic. *See* Butler, *A Sourcebook on Socialist International Organizations* 235 (1978).

CONFERENCE OF THE COMMITTEE ON DISARMAMENT (from 1961-69 the EIGHTEEN NATION DISARMAMENT COMMITTEE [q.v.]): though not a United Nations agency, this has become one of the principal forums for disarmament talks including nuclear and chemical weapons bans. *See* 1970 U.N. Yearbook 4 and 1982 U.N. Yearbook 151.

CONFERENCE ON SECURITY AND COOPERATION IN EUROPE: attempt to finally settle the questions of security and political arrangement still outstanding from the end of World War II. *See* 68 Am.J.Int.L. 181 and HELSINKI ACCORDS.

CONFIDENCE-BUILDING MEASURES: efforts to assure that adversaries are not preparing an attack. They include notification to the other side of troop movements and military exercises. *See* HELSINKI ACCORDS.

CONFISCATE: seizure of CONTRABAND (q.v.) carried by a vessel; or seizure of other property by a government under a claim that the property or title to it is somehow tainted. *See* 9 I.L.R. 19 and 35 I.L.R. 8.

CONFLICT OF LAWS: rules to help determine whether the courts of a given state will apply their own municipal law or the law of another state in adjudicating a case somehow involving that other state. *See* PRIVATE INTERNATIONAL LAW.

CONFLICTS BETWEEN AMERICAN STATES TREATY (1923): agreement to settle disputes by use of a commission, it is superseded by the BOGATA PACT (1948) (q.v.).

CONGO CRISIS (1960-64): civil unrest in the newly independent (formerly) Belgian Congo (now Zaire) led to intervention by United Nations forces. These forces were not very successful at doing anything. *See* Abi-Saab, *United Nations Operations in the Congo 1960-1964* (1978).

CONGO RIVER: GENERAL ACT OF THE BERLIN CONFERENCE (1885) (q.v.), internationalized the Congo though its status was subject to later dispute. *See* 1 Hackworth, *Digest of International Law* 608.

CONGRESS OF VIENNA (1815): conference of European nations attempting to restore a balance of power after the Napoleanic Wars. *See* VIENNA TREATY (1815).

C - D

CONNALLY AMENDMENT: reservation to the United States' acceptance of the COMPULSORY JURISDICTION OF THE INTERNATIONAL COURT OF JUSTICE (q.v.), in cases where the dispute is essentially within the jurisdiction of a United States national court. *See* 40 Am.J.Int.L. 699, 720, and 56 Am.J.Int.L. 357.

CONQUEST: forcefully taking possession of an enemy state's territory.

CONSEIL DE L'ENTENTE (F): association of the prime ministers of states formed from French West Africa, including Benin, Niger, Burkina Faso, Togo, and the Ivory Coast, to harmonize their relations. *See* ECONOMIC COMMUNITY OF WESTERN AFRICA.

CONSEIL INTERGOUVERNMENTAL DES PAYS EXPORTATEURS DE CUIRVE (CIPEC): cartel of copper producing countries, the original members were Chile, Peru, Zaire, and Zambia, Indonesia joined in 1975. *See generally,* CIPEC Quarterly.

CONSENSUS: making of a decision in which no party to the decision voices a substantial objection. The development of a solution to which all parties can agree has become a common working method of international organizations. *See* Art. 69 of the HELSINKI ACCORDS.

CONSENSUS OMNI (L): by agreement of all.

CONSENTIRE VIDETUR QUI TACET (L): if one remains silent he has consented; failure to object is tacit agreement.

CONSERVATION OF THE LIVING RESOURCES OF THE HIGH SEAS TREATY (1958): *see* FISHING AND CONSERVATION OF SEA RESOURCES.

CONSERVATION ZONE: areas of the oceans beyond and adjacent to a littoral state's territorial waters in which fishing is limited or controlled.

CONSOLATO DEL MARE (S): compilation of maritime laws from the 14th century in Barcelona, including rules of naval warfare and the rights of neutral ships in war. It is an important source for determining maritime custom.

CONSORITE (F): the obligation to make a joint defense with the defendants in the same proceedings. *See* 80 I.L.R. 619.

CONSTANTINOPLE CONVENTION (1888): agreement regulating the free navigation of the Suez Canal. *See* 171 C.T.S. 241.

CONSTANTINOPLE TREATY (1879): peace treaty between Russia and the Ottoman Empire, *see* 154 C.T.S. 477 (in French) or 2 Toynbee, *Treaties* 999.

CONSTITUTIVE THEORY OF RECOGNITION: theory that a community does not become a state merely by asserting its statehood, but is rather "constituted" by the willingness of other states to deal with it as a new state.

CONSTITUTIVE TREATY: agreement between two or more states acting in the public interest and designed to produce a permanent effect in the operation of relations with the entire world.

CONSTRUCTIVE POSSESSION: one who is in actual possession of part of a tract, claims it all under color of title, and extends his possession to the entirety in the absence of adverse possession on the part of another.

CONSTRUCTIVE PRESENCE: legal fiction deeming an act to have occurred within the jurisdiction of a state. Though it is performed outside the state's territory its effects are produced therein.

CONSUETUDO ANGLIAE (L): customary law of England; ancient common law, e.g., the law of primogeniture.

CONSUL: representative of a state dealing with commercial, as opposed to political, relations with another country.

CONSUL ELEVE (F): consular officer who is not the head of a consular post.

CONSUL GENERAL: head of a consular mission in residence in a foreign capitol; the highest ranking consular officer.

CONSULAR AGENT: *see* HONORARY CONSUL.

CONSULAR ARCHIVES: official records and papers kept at a consulate which are inviolable. *See* Art. 33 Vienna Convention on Consular Relations, 21 U.S.T. 77, 596 U.N.T.S. 261.

CONSULAR CONVENTION: agreement between two states formalizing the duties, immunities, etc., for an exchange of CONSULAR MISSIONS (q.v.).

CONSULAR IMMUNITY: protection from the jurisdiction of a foreign government for commercial representatives of that country. It is usually not as expansive as that afforded diplomats and is often defined by a BILATERAL TREATY (q.v.). *See* the Vienna Convention on Consular Relations, Chapter II, 21 U.S.T. 77, T.I.A.S. 6820, 596 U.N.T.S. 261.

CONSULAR INVOICE: invoice certified by the CONSUL (q.v.) of a country relating to goods shipped to that country.

CONSULAR MARRIAGE: marriage performed by a diplomatic officer which may, by the national law of that officer, have the same status and validity as if it were performed in that nation.

CONSULAR MISSION: diplomatic presence in a host country to protect the interests of the sending state and its nationals in the host country.

CONSULAR OFFICER: person appointed and commissioned by his government and recognized by the receiving country in his capacity as CONSUL (q.v.), and is there to protect the interests of the sending country. They notarize and authenticate official state documents.

CONSULAR PERSONNEL: officials of a consular post and their staff and families. Upon termination of the officers' functions or upon outbreak of armed conflict, the state in which the personnel are serving must grant them the time and facilities necessary for their safe departure. *See* Art. 26 Vienna Convention on Consular Relations, 21 U.S.T. 77, 596 U.N.T.S. 261.

CONSULAR RELATIONS: mutual maintenance of diplomatic presence between two countries whereby the interest of each country and its nationals are represented in the other country. The normal business of a CONSULAR MISSION (q.v.) is the issuance of visas, investigating the arrest of its nationals, and insuring their treatment, etc. *See* VIENNA CONVENTION ON CONSULAR RELATIONS.

CONSULATE: premises where a consular office and residence is located and is protected to some extent from local jurisdiction. *See* Art. 22, Vienna Convention on Diplomatic Relations, 23 U.S.T. 3227, 500 U.N.T.S. 95 (1961).

CONSULES DE CARRIERS (S): An HONORARY CONSUL (q.v.).

CONSULES ELECTI (S): An HONORARY CONSUL (q.v.).

CONSULES MISSI (S): a full-time career CONSUL (q.v.).

CONTACT ZONE: area (on land) in which opposing belligerent forces are fighting. *See* Art. 26(2) of the GENEVA CONVENTION PROTOCOL I (1977).

CONTADORA PROCESS: efforts by Mexico, Colombia, Panama, and Venezuela to stabilize Central America. *See* 85 Colum. L. Rev. 1445, 1471.

CONTAINMENT: policy or process of preventing the expansion or spread of a hostile power. *See* TRUMAN DOCTRINE (1947).

CONTEMPORANEA EXPOSITIO (L): interpretation based on the law as it existed at the time an agreement was concluded; rather than the law at the time the dispute arose.

CONTINENTAL SHELF: rim of land from the continental shores sloping gradually before the steep decline to the oceans depths. The seas here are relatively shallow, making the resources of the seabed accessible. Most fishing resources are located in these parts of the ocean, and so it is common for littoral states to claim control over their adjacent continental shelf. *See* 43 U.S.C. sec. 1331 *et seq.* and GENEVA CONVENTION ON THE CONTINENTAL SHELF (1958).

CONTIGUOUS ZONE: waters beyond a nation's territorial waters in which it claims some jurisdiction, particularly for purposes of customs, conservation, and exploitation of resources.

CONTINUITY OF STATES: principle that when there is a change of sovereignty the rights and obligations of the state remain unchanged.

CONTINUOUS VOYAGE: doctrine applied to CONTRABAND (q.v.) goods making them liable to seizure anytime after departing their port of origin, especially if they are destined for a neutral port where the goods may be used in further shipment to an enemy destination.

CONTRA BONOS MORES (L): against good morals; grounds upon which a court may refuse to enforce the law of another country, e.g., a court may refuse to enforce the payment of the price for an act of prostitution even though the contract was made and performed in a jurisdiction where prostitution was legal.

CONTRA LEGEM (L): an equitable solution which is not in accord with applicable law. *See* INFRA LEGEM.

CONTRA PACEM (L): act against peace.

CONTRA PROFERENTEM RULE: as in interpreting treaties; when the text has been prepared by only one party, the drafter is held liable for inaccuracies or ambiguities which are to be construed strictly against the drafter's interest. The rule is rarely applied for lack of treaties drafted solely by one party.

CONTRABAND: all goods destined for an enemy, whether carried in an enemy or neutral ship, airplane, or other vehicle; goods which are susceptible for use in war.

CONTRACT DEBTS: *See* LIMITATION OF EMPLOYMENT OF FORCE FOR RECOVERY OF CONTRACT DEBTS CONVENTION (1907).

CONTRAS: insurgency forces fighting against the Sandanista government of Nicaragua and supported from time to time by the United States government. *See* NICARAGUA V. UNITED STATES.

CONTRATOS-LEYES (S): contract laws; the laws governing contracts.

CONTRATS D'ADHESION (F): adhesion contract; an "agreement" where one party, because of their overwhelming position, can effectively dictate the terms of the contract.

CONTROL OF POPULATION: *see* ANARCHIES INTOLERANT.

CONVENTION: binding agreement between states on matters of vital importance but not of "high policy." The term is used synonymously with TREATY and PROTOCOL (qq.v.). For specific conventions go to the next important word in the title, e.g., for the Convention on the High Seas look under HIGH SEAS CONVENTION.

CONVENTIONAL ARMED FORCES IN EUROPE TREATY (1990): twenty-two nation agreement by the CONFERENCE ON SECURITY AND COOPERATION IN EUROPE (q.v.) to reduce and limit conventional forces such as tanks, artillery, and combat aircraft from Europe. *See* 30 I.L.M. 1.

CONVENTIONAL ARMS TRAFFIC: the sale or giving as "aid" of weapons of war especially from the developed countries to client states in the THIRD WORLD (q.v.).

CONVENTIONAL ARMS TRANSFER TALKS (1977-79): efforts by the Carter Administration to find ways of limiting arms sales by the United States and Soviet Union, particularly to developing countries. The talks broke off in 1979, without progress.

CONVENTIONAL WEAPONS CONVENTION (1980): attempt to ban certain excessively injurious non-nuclear weapons. *See* 1980 U.N. Yearbook 76 or 19 I.L.M. 1524.

CONVERTIBILITY: attribute of a particular country's currency noting the ability to freely exchange that currency for the currency of other countries.

CONVICTIO JURIS SIVE NECESSATATIS (L): belief that there is a legal obligation to act a certain way; an element of proof in the development of a customary rule of international law.

COOPERATION OF STATES: one of the purposes enshrined in the UNITED NATIONS CHARTER, Art. 1(3).

COORDINATING COMMITTEE FOR MULTINATIONAL EXPORT CONTROLS (COCOM): agreement among western countries to control the export of sophisticated, militarily-useful technology to the Soviet bloc. *See* 50 U.S.C. App. Sec. 2404.

COPIA VERA (L): a true copy.

COPUOS: COMMITTEE ON PEACEFUL USES OF OUTER SPACE (q.v.).

CORFU AFFAIR (1923): Italy bombarded then seized the Greek Island of Corfu, justifying the action as reprisal for the murder of an Italian General by Greek extremists. *See* 19 Am.J.Int.L. 303.

CORFU CHANNEL CASE (United Kingdom v. Albania): the International Court of Justice case involving the right of innocent passage for warships, and the duty of coastal states to warn such ships of danger, specifically in this case, the location of a minefield. *See* 1949 I.C.J. 4.

CORPORACION CENTROAMERICAN DE SERVICIOS NAVIGACION AEREA (COCESNA) (S): organization providing air navigation services in Central America. *See* 418 U.N.T.S. 171.

CORROBORATION: supplying evidence which adds weight or credibility to that already given. There are no rules in international litigation regarding corroboration.

CORRUPTION: illegal conduct on the part of officials of a government, particularly regarding the abuse of their office, such as taking bribes. Recently several Latin American governments have been accused of widespread corruption in their involvement with drug smuggling. *See* NORIEGA REGIME. A treaty is voidable if it was procured through the corrupt act of the representative of the state. *See* VIENNA CONVENTION ON THE LAW OF TREATIES (1969), Art. 50.

CORPS DIPLOMATIQUE (F): *see* DIPLOMATIC CORP.

CORPUS SEPARATUM (L): special status given to the City of Jerusalem by the United Nations General Assembly Resolution 303 (IV) in 1949. It never came into force as Jerusalem was first divided between Jordan and Israel and subsequently occupied by Israel.

COSMONAUT: Russian term for ASTRONAUT (q.v.); a number of non-Soviets have participated in the Soviet space program as cosmonauts including a Frenchman, an Indian, and several Eastern Europeans.

COSMOS 954: Soviet spacecraft which fell to earth landing in Northwestern Canada raising the possibility that the LIABILITY FOR DAMAGE CAUSED BY SPACE OBJECTS CONVENTION (q.v.) might be used. *See* 18 I.L.M. 899.

COUNCIL FOR MUTUAL ECONOMIC ASSISTANCE (CMEA or COMECON): specialized regional organization serving the communist states similar to the Common Market in Western Europe. *See* 368 U.N.T.S. 253.

COUNCIL FOR NAMIBIA: United Nations group charged with overseeing U.N. action regarding the territory of NAMIBIA (q.v.). *See* 13 I.L.M. 1513.

COUNCIL OF EUROPE: regional organization comprised of most of the non-communist countries of Europe. It is the umbrella organization for most regional cooperation and efforts at European integration. *See* 87 U.N.T.S. 103 or 43 Am.J.Int.L. Supp. 162. Note: the Council of Europe and the EUROPEAN ECONOMIC COMMUNITY (q.v.) are two very different organizations.

COUNSELOR: traditional title for the senior diplomatic secretary in an EMBASSY (q.v.)

COUNTER-MEMORIAL: written argument filed by the respondent to a suit in the International Court of Justice or other international forum. The counter-memorial admits or denies the assertions in the applicant's MEMORIAL (q.v.).

COUNTERTRADE: linkage of the sale of goods to another country with the purchase of goods from that country. Country A sells wheat to county B, but country B insists that A buy butter from B in order to support B's dairy industry. *See* 8 Dick. J. Int'l L. 269.

COUNTERVAILING DUTIES: tax on imported goods from a particular country in response to the subsidization of the goods by the exporting country. Generally trade is governed by the GENERAL AGREEMENT ON TARIFFS AND TRADE (q.v.). *See* 16 I.L.M. 520.

COUP D'ETAT (F): revolutionary or military overthrow of a government with the formation of a new government.

COURBE TANGENTE (F): ARCS-OF-CIRCLES (q.v.).

COURIER: person commissioned to handle the carriage of diplomatic mail.

COURIER LIST: document certifying the status of a COURIER (q.v.) and describing his cargo of diplomatic mail.

COURS FORCE (F): compulsory tender; paper money which is not convertible.

COURS LEGAL (F): legal tender (money).

COURTOISIE (F): COMITY OF NATIONS (q.v.).

COVENANT OF THE LEAGUE OF NATIONS: law-making treaty adopted by the League which, among other things, gave qualified guarantees to member states with respect to their independence and territorial integrity; provided for some mandatory arbitration of disputes; provided for the creation of the PERMANENT COURT OF INTERNATIONAL JUSTICE (q.v.); and made future world peace the collective responsibility of all members. *See* 225 C.T.S. 195 or II Toynbee, *Treaties* 1274 for covenant text which is part I of the VERSAILLES TREATY (q.v.).

COVENANT ON CIVIL AND POLITICAL RIGHTS (1966): convention which declares, *inter alia*, that all people have the right to self-determination and freedom to determine their political status and pursue their own development. *See* 6 I.L.M. 368

COVENANT ON ECONOMIC, SOCIAL AND CULTURAL RIGHTS (1986): parties to this convention promise, *inter alia*, to take steps to raise the standard of living of their people. *See* 6 I.L.M. 360.

COVENANTS ON HUMAN RIGHTS: COVENANT ON ECONOMIC SOCIAL, AND CULTURAL RIGHTS; the COVENANT ON CIVIL AND POLITICAL RIGHTS (qq.v.); and the optional protocol to the Covenant on Political and Civil Rights. *See* 6 I.L.M. 360.

CRAWLING PEG: frequent small (2-3%) devaluations of a currency to keep it in line with other currencies during a period of inflation. *See* EXCHANGE RATES.

CREDENTIALS: documents which certify the powers conferred by a state on its representatives. The documents are addressed to the sovereign to whom the representative is accredited.

CREON: COMPARATIVE RESEARCH ON EVENTS OF NATIONS (q.v.).

CRETAN QUESTION: dispute between Turkey and Greece over the status of the Island of Crete. *See* 4 Am.J.Int.L. 276.

CRIMEN LAESAE MAJESTATIS (L): encroachment on the dignity of the sovereign. *See* 8 I.L.R. 88.

CRIMES AGAINST HUMANITY: murder, extermination, enslavement, deportation, and other inhumane acts against any civilian population before or during war. *See* Art. 6 of the Charter of the International Military Tribunal, 59 Stat. 1544, 82 U.N.T.S. 279.

CRIMES AGAINST INTERNATIONAL LAW: serious violations of international law categorized as WAR CRIMES, CRIMES AGAINST PEACE, and CRIMES AGAINST HUMANITY (qq.v.) for which individuals may be held liable.

CRIMES AGAINST INTERNATIONALLY PROTECTED PERSONS CONVENTION: parties to this convention agree to punish crimes against PROTECTED PERSONS (q.v.). *See* 67 Am.J.Int.L. 383.

CRIMES AGAINST PEACE: planning, preparation, initiation, or waging of a war of aggression; or war in violation of international agreements; or participation in a conspiracy to commit war crimes or crimes against humanity. *See* Art. 6 of the Charter of the International Military Tribunal, 59 Stat 1544, 82 U.N.T.S. 279.

CRIMES AGAINST THE PEACE AND SECURITY OF MANKIND: subject of an International Law Commission draft code. *See* 84 Am.J.Int.L. 930.

CRIMES BY DIPLOMATIC AGENTS: diplomatic agents are immune from prosecution in their host country for ordinary crimes. They may be expelled or their recall may be demanded. *See* Satow, A Guide to Diplomatic Practice 181 (1957).

CRIMINAL JURISDICTION: *See* PASSIVE PERSONALITY PRINCIPLE.

CRISTAL: contract regarding an interim supplement to the Tanker Liability For Oil Pollution Agreement, a supplement

agreement to the TANKER OWNERS VOLUNTARY AGREE-
MENT CONCERNING LIABILITY FOR OIL POLLUTION
(TOVALOP) (q.v.). *See* 10 I.L.M. 137.

CRUISE MISSILE: pilotless aircraft distinguished from a ballistic missile in that its engines breath air and it has wings for aerodynamic lift. The design allows flight close to the ground to
avoid radar detection. Cruise missiles may be launched from the
ground, sea, or air.

CSCE: CONFERENCE ON SECURITY AND COOPERATION IN
EUROPE, *see* HELSINKI ACCORDS.

CSCE PARLIMENTARY ASSEMBLY: representative body established by the Madrid Conference of the CONFERENCE ON SE-
CURITY AND COOPERATION IN EUROPE (q.v.). *See* 30 I.L.M.
1344

CUBAN MISSILE CRISIS (1962): build-up of Soviet military
equipment, including medium-range missiles with nuclear war-
heads, in Cuba prompted the United States to impose a strict
quarantine on all offensive military equipment destined for Cuba.
The Soviets withdrew the missiles. *See* 57 Am.J.Int.L. 546.

CULTURAL CHARTER OF AFRICA: adopted by the Organization of African Unity in July 1976.

CULTURAL PROPERTY: works of art, monuments, and historical buildings. In the event of armed conflict, protective measures
against the harms of war are provided by the International Convention for the PROTECTION OF CULTURAL PROPERTY (q.v.)
and the European Convention on Cultural Property, 25 I.L.M. 44.

CULTURAL RELATIONS: agreements to carry on exchanges between countries in such areas as art, literature, and music. *See*
e.g., 12 I.L.M. 911.

CUM ONERE (L): all the burdens the law places on one invoking it.

CURRENCY OF ACCOUNT: monetary unit that will be used in a particular transaction or continuing economic relationship.

CURRENCY REGULATION: defines and regulates the coin and paper money circulation in a country. Often the regulations include restrictions on exchange of the money for that of another country and forbid or tightly regulate the export of the currency. This often poses a problem for multinational corporations who wish to take their profits elsewhere. See Title 31 of the United States Code for United States Law and 11 I.L.M. 648.

CUSTOM: principal source of international law,*see* Art. 42 of the STATUTE OF THE INTERNATIONAL COURT OF JUSTICE (q.v.); general practices which are accepted as legally binding (opinio juris) rules of conduct for civilized nations. *See The Paquete Habana,* 175 U.S. 677 (1900).

CUSTOMARY INTERNATIONAL LAW: body of international law comprised of CUSTOM (q.v.).

CUSTOMS COOPERATION COUNCIL (CCC): international governmental organization composed primarily of the heads of national customs administrations to promote harmony and uniformity in member countries' customs systems.

CUSTOMS COOPERATION COUNCIL NOMENCLATURE: *See* HARMONIZED COMMODITY PRESCRIPTION AND CODING SYSTEM.

CUSTOMS CONTROL: jurisdiction exercised by a state over goods transported across its borders.

CUSTOMS DUTIES: tax or fee levied against goods that are imported or exported.

CUSTOMS-FREE ZONE: area created by treaty and designated to be free from CUSTOMS DUTIES (q.v.).

CYPRUS CONFLICT: civil war between the Greek and Turkish populations on the Island of Cyprus led to a division of the territory and the stationing of a United Nations peacekeeping force (UNFICYP). *See* 13 I.L.M. 1275 and 12 Whiteman, *Digest of International Law* 55.

CYPRUS PEACEKEEPING FORCE (UNFICYP): international force stationed on Cyprus to separate the warring Greek and Turkish population. *See* 3 I.L.M. 545.

DAF: DELIVERED AT FRONTIER (q.v.).

DAIRY PRODUCTS: *see* INTERNATIONAL DAIRY AGREEMENT.

DAKAR CONFERENCE OF DEVELOPING COUNTRIES ON RAW MATERIALS (1975): attempt to promote cooperation among developing countries, in the field of raw materials export, by strengthening their negotiating position *vis-a-vis* the developed countries securing control over their natural resources and diversifying their economic structures. *See* 14 I.L.M. 520.

DAMAGES: wrongful international acts should be remedied by restitution in kind, or if this is not possible, payment of a sum corresponding to the value which a restitution in kind would have had. *See Chorzow Factory Case*, 1928 P.C.I.J., (Ser. A) No.17.

DAMME: *see* JUGEMENT DE DAMME.

DAMNUM EMERGENS (L): actual expenses and losses incurred.

DANGER ZONE: area where the risk of or exposure to the danger of hostilities is high. Now generally referred to as the CONTACT ZONE (q.v.). Also, areas designated as such for purposes of air navigation because of military activities or other circumstances that pose a threat to safety. *See* Art. 9 of the CHICAGO CONVENTION (1944).

DANISH SOUND DUES: heavy tolls charged by Denmark on ships passing through the straits between Denmark and Sweden. The Treaty of Copenhagen, 11 Stat. 719, 7 Bevans 11 (1857), exempted U.S. ships from the dues.

DANUBE COMMISSION: originally organized to maintain the Danube River for navigation at the Congress of Paris in 1856, and modified in 1921. The current commission - consisting of Bulgaria, Czechoslovakia, Hungary, Rumania, U.S.S.R, and Yugoslavia - was created by the Belgrade Convention of 1948, 33 U.N.T.S. 181, 197.

DANZIG: city on the Baltic Sea designated a free city by the VERSAILLES TREATY (q.v.) and under the protection of the League of Nations. It was transferred to Poland by the POTSDAM CONFERENCE (1945) (q.v.).

DATIO IN SOLUTUM (L): right to grant freedom.

DAWES PLAN: effort to regulate Germany's obligation under Art. 232 of the VERSAILLES TREATY (q.v,); to compensate individuals for damages suffered during World War I. It was replaced in 1930, by the YOUNG PLAN (q.v.).

DAYS OF GRACE: provision from the Second Hague Peace Conference which exempts, for an allotted time, from prize law merchant ships docked in an enemy port at the outbreak of war and ships which are at sea and unaware of the hostilities. The rule of days of grace is not one of customary international law. *See* 2 Am.J.Int.L. Supp. 127 (1908).

DBS: DIRECT BROADCASTING SERVICE (q.v.).

DDP: DELIVERED DUTY PAID (q.v.).

DE FACTO GOVERNMENT: the government actually exercising the powers of sovereignty over most of the state's territory as opposed to the lawful government established by the state's constitution. The possession of sovereign powers by the government *de facto* may be wrongful and liable to invalidation.

DE FACTO RECOGNITION: recognition of a government as being the government *de facto*. The term characterizes not the recognition but the entity recognized.

DE JURE GOVERNMENT: true and lawful government of the state. The government which ought to exercise sovereignty, but which may be deprived of this right by a government *de facto*.

DE JURE RECOGNITION: recognition of a government as the lawful government of the state. The term characterizes not the type of recognition but only the entity recognized.

DE LEGE FERENDA (L): from the standpoint of a new law or a law yet to be made. *See* LEX FERENDA.

DE LEGE LATA (L): on the basis of existing well established law. *See* LEX LATA.

DE RIGORE JURIS (L): by the exact letter of the law.

DEAN OF THE DIPLOMATIC CORP (or Doyen): senior of all foreign representatives in a foreign capital; the dean represents the diplomatic corps on ceremonial occasions.

DEATH MARCHES: transfer of prisoners of war, without regard to the prevailing conditions, which renders their transfer risky; usually without adequate food, water, and medical attention. *See* International Military Tribunal for the Far East 1043-5.

DEATH PENALTY: for offenses involving armed conflict the imposition of the death penalty is restricted by Arts. 76 and 77 of GENEVA PROTOCOL I (1977)(q.v.). The use of the death penalty is condemned by various United Nations actions, but is still widely practiced among most United Nations member states. *See* Art. 6 of the COVENANT ON POLITICAL AND CIVIL RIGHTS and 82 Am.J.Int.L. 601. *See* SOERING CASE (1989).

DEATH SQUADS: usually applied to right-wing paramilitary, or vigilante groups who murder their potential opposition, sometimes with covert approval of the sitting government. *See* 1983 Am. Soc'y Int'l L. Proc. 377.

DEBELLATIO (L): conquest of an enemy territory so total that it includes a devolution of sovereignty. Total occupation of an enemy state.

DECLARATION OF HUMAN RIGHTS: *see* UNIVERSIAL DECLARATION OF HUMAN RIGHTS (1948).

DECLARATION OF LONDON (1909): code signed by delegates of ten leading naval powers establishing rules governing, *inter alia*, blockades, contraband of war, and destruction of neutral prizes. *See* 3 Am.J.Int.L. Supp. 179 (1909).

DECLARATION OF PARIS (1856): agreement among the European powers declaring the abolition of privateering. Subsequent legal interpretation of the declaration gave rise to the principle that a breach of a multilateral treaty by one party does not free a wronged party from its obligation to other parties to the treaty. *See* 115 C.T.S. 1.

DECLARATION OF THE RIGHTS OF MAN AND OF CITIZENS: document adopted by the French Revolution in 1789, stating, *inter alia*, that the aim of all political association is the conservation of the rights of man including liberty, property, and security.

DECLARATION OF WAR: formal statement of the intention to commence hostilities required by international law under the Hague Convention III (1907) Arts. 1 and 2. *See* 5 I.L.M. 791.

DECLARATION ON FRIENDLY RELATIONS: *see* FRIENDLY RELATIONS DECLARATION.

DECLARATION ON INTERNATIONAL INVESTMENT AND MULTINATIONAL ENTERPRISES: OECD guidelines for the activities of multi- national enterprises. *See* 15 I.L.M. 967.

DECLARATION ON THE GRANTING OF INDEPENDENCE TO COLONIAL COUNTRIES AND PEOPLES (UNGA Res. 1514 (XV)): proclaimed the need to bring colonialism to a speedy end. *See* 1960 U.N. Yearbook 49.

DECLARATIVE THEORY OF RECOGNITION: legal position that legitimacy is achieved by a declaration by a new or trans- formed state that it is prepared to enter the international commu- nity. Thus it creates a new subject in international law, *contra* to the idea that new states only achieve international status by recog- nition of other states (*see* CONSTITUTIVE THEORY).

DECLARATORY JUDGEMENT: court determination that the act of the defendant state is illegal. The International Court of Jus- tice may give a declaratory judgment. *See* Rosenne, *The Law and Practice of the International Court* 621-28 (1965).

DECLARATORY THEORY OF RECOGNITION: see DECLA- RATIVE THEORY OF RECOGNITION.

DECOLONIZATION: the process of granting independence to a territory which has been governed as a COLONY (q.v.).

DEDUCTION (F): early version of a MEMORANDUM (q.v.).

DEEP SEABED MINING: retrieval of mineral nodules from the floor of the deep seabed. *See* INTERNATIONAL SEABED AUTHORITY and 26 I.L.M. 1502.

DEFECTIVE DRAFTING OF TREATIES: for a history of the treaties not saying what was meant by the parties *see* 11 Am.J.Int.L. 554.

DEFECTIVE SOVEREIGN: *see* CARENCE DE SOVERAINTITE.

DEFENSIVE WEAPONS: those weapons that have primarily a defensive rather than an offensive character; the distinction is often difficult, but perhaps the best illustration is military aircraft where the bombers are primarily to strike the opponents territory, and the fighters are primarily designed to defend one's own territory (though they can be used to support attacking ground troops as well).

DELEGATUS NON POTEST DELEGARE (L): right to appoint a diplomatic agent cannot be delegated by a sovereign. *See* Satow, *A Guide to Diplomatic Practice* 118 (1957).

DELICTS: in civil law; a wrong, injury or offense; a violation of a public or private duty. Under accepted principles of international law an injured party may not seek redress for delicts in an international forum before exhausting municipal law, and a state does not incur international responsibility until exhaustion of such local remedies results in a denial of justice.

DELICT COMPLEX (F): complex crimes; acts which are common crimes, but which are politically motivated so that their nature is questionable under such instruments as EXTRADITION (q.v.) treaties which have POLITICAL OFFENSE EXCEPTIONS (q.v.).

DELICTS MIXTES: crimes which are both common and political in nature. Thus posing a problem in terms of EXTRADITION (q.v.) where the POLITICAL OFFENSE EXCEPTION (q.v.) is invoked. *See* 3 I.L.R. 308-11.

DELIMITATION: fixing the boundaries of the TERRITORIAL WATER (q.v.) of a coastal state.

DELIVERED AT FRONTIER: an INCOTERM (q.v.); sales contract term where seller delivers goods to a buyer at the border.

DELIVERED DUTY PAID: an INCOTERM (q.v.); sales contract term where the seller bears all cost of delivering the goods to the buyer's place of business.

DEMARCATION LINES: borderlines established only until the political situation allows a final boundary to be set.

DEMARCHE: diplomatic act such as note from a head of state aimed at a foreign state to protect the interests of the acting state.

DEMILITARIZATION: by international agreement, or as a sanction. The prohibition of a state from maintaining particular military forces or any military force in some or all of its territory.

DEMILITARIZED ZONE (DMZ): geographical area in which a state is prohibited from stationing military forces or maintaining military installations. This term became particularly associated with the DMZ between North and South Vietnam.

DEMISE CHARTER: lease of a vessel where the charterer provides the crew and operates the vessel.

DEMURRAGE: damages, usually stipulated in the contract for carriage, for delay caused by the loading and unloading of the ship or for late return of a charter vessel.

DENATIONALIZATION: deprivation of nationality from persons by the unilateral act of the state of which they were nationals. *See* 24 I.L.R. 447.

DENIAL OF JUSTICE: term used in international law to include, *inter alia*, any treatment of an alien that violates international law; failure to afford treatment (of an alien), or failure of an adequate remedy, or failure to provide protection in the administration of justice, or failure to prosecute the perpetrator of a crime causing injury to an alien. American Law Institute, *Restatement (Second) of Foreign Relations* sec. 165 comment (c) (1965).

DENUNCIATION: declaration by a state that it no longer recognizes as binding the provision of a treaty to which it is a party. Unless the treaty contains a clause for unilateral termination, the denunciation must be agreed to by all parties before it is effective. *See* PACTA SUNT SERVANDA.

DEPENDENCY: relative position of individual countries with respect to their choices and capabilities in the system of international relations. Also, a quasi-independent territory which is under the sovereignty of another nation, e.g., a COLONY, PROTECTORATE, or TRUSTEESHIP (qq.v.).

DEPENS (F): court fees and any other cost. *See Richter and Sons v. Court of Appeals of Berne*, 8 I.L.R. 333, 334.

DEPLOYMENT: placing of a military force into a position where they will be able to execute effective military actions, e.g., to protect the right of neutral passage through straits a naval vessel would be positioned nearby.

DEPORTATION: moving of an alien away from the state after his exclusion or expulsion. Deportation procedures are implemented by following specific local laws.

DEPOSITORY: government entrusted to keep and register original text of the treaty and to prepare certified copies. The depository is usually named in the treaty and is now often the United Nations.

DERELICTION: loss of territory by actually withdrawing from the territory with the intent to abandon.

DESAPARECIDOS (S): "the disappeared," people seized by security forces during the ARGENTINE "DIRTY WAR" (q.v.) against left- and right-wing terrorists in the 1970's who then disappeared. Estimates of the number of desaparecidos range from 5,000 to 30,000.

DESERT STORM: designation for military actions, sanctioned by the UN Security Council in response to IRAQI AGGRESSION AGAINST KUWAIT (q.v.).

DESISTEMENT DOCTRINE: if, in a situation where the conflicts of law rules of country A led to the application of the substantive law of country B, but that law is not meant to apply to the case (even if it arose in Country B), then the court in Country A can apply its own laws.

DESUETUDE: discontinuation of a treaty or the agreement to discontinue a treaty. *See* McNair, *The Law of Treaties* 516 (1961).

DETENTE: 1) period of improved relations between the United States and Soviet Union in the 1970's, which ended with the Soviet invasion of Afghanistan and repression of Solidarity in Poland. *See* Helsinki Accords and 59 Am.J.Int.L. 1. 2) Any similar period of improved relations between adversaries.

DETENTION: deprivation of liberty by or under the authority of a foreign government. "The detention of an alien constitutes a denial of procedural justice if he is not, without unreasonable delay: (a) informed of the changes against him; (b) afforded access to a tribunal or other authority having jurisdiction to determine the lawfulness of his detention and to order his release, if such detention is unlawful; (c) permitted during detention to communicate with a representative of his government, (d) afforded access to counsel; or (e) granted a trial. *Restatement (Second) of Foreign Relations sec. 179 (2) (1965).*

DETERRENCE: policy of keeping such military force available to persuade an aggressor that an attack would be sufficiently costly as to be not worthwhile; some would say the opposite of APPEASEMENT (q.v.).

DETOURNEMENT DE POUVOIR (F): exercise of a right for a purpose different from that for which the right was created. Thus an ABUSE OF RIGHT (q.v.). *See* 25 I.L.R. 445.

DEVALUATION OF CURRENCY: official lowering in the value of a state's money and rate of exchange. An international claim may arise when a state manipulate its exchange rate in order to cause economic harm to another nation. *See* 70 L.Q.Rev. 186-87.

DEVELOPING COUNTRY: country in the process of developing an industrial infrastructure; a successful development process has eluded most of the Third World.

DEVELOPMENT STRATEGIES: various approaches used by developing countries to become industrialized and, therefore, less dependent on foreign economic ties. These strategies include heavy reliance on exporting (e.g., South Korea) and import substitution where a country attempts to fulfill its own domestic needs. Most development strategies have failed.

DEVOLUTION AGREEMENT: agreement in which a newly independent territory agrees with its mother country to remain bound by treaty rights and obligation. Such an arrangement may be included in the instrument of independence.

DICTORE (L): an ARBITRATOR (q.v.).

DIGNITY OF STATES: pseudo-right of a state to its good name and reputation, but there is no duty on the part of other states to uphold another state's reputation, which is the product of its own conduct. States are expected to give respect to each other's representatives and symbols. *See* 2 Hackworth, *Digest of International Law* 127.

DIKKO AFFAIR (1984): attempted kidnapping of an Israeli and a Nigerian diplomat and Alhaji Umaro Dikko. Britain and Nigeria expelled each other's diplomats as a result of the dispute over responsibility for the attempt. *See* 34 *Int'l & Comp.L.Q.* 602.

DIPLOMACY: formal state activity *vis-a-vis* its relations with other states including exchange of ambassadors or other diplomatic agents, correspondence between the heads of state, etc.

DIPLOMATIC AGENT: name given to class of persons including ministers, ambassadors, and envoys sent by their government to a foreign state for the purpose of being general representatives or to undertake special negotiations. *See* Art. 1(e) of the VIENNA CONVENTION ON DIPLOMATIC RELATIONS.

DIPLOMATIC ARCHIVES: records and official documents held in a diplomatic mission. Their inviolability is to be protected by the HOST STATE (q.v.). *See* 7 Whiteman, *Digest of International Law* 389.

DIPLOMATIC ASYLUM: a foreign embassy or legation granting refuge to individuals, guilty of political offenses, who have chosen to remain in their own country. Generally diplomatic asylum is granted only temporarily so as not to interfere in the internal affairs of the host state. Where recognized asylum constitutes an exemption from the territorial jurisdiction of the host state. *See* ASYLUM CASE.

DIPLOMATIC BAG: carrier containing documents or articles intended for official use by the ambassador. The VIENNA CONVENTION ON DIPLOMATIC RELATIONS (1961), Art. 27(4) provides that packages constituting the diplomatic bag must bear visible external marks of their character and may contain only diplomatic documents or articles intended for official use.

DIPLOMATIC COMMUNICATIONS: correspondence relating to the mission and its functions transmitted to or from the ambassadors either by courier, telephone, telegraph, or post. Art. 27(1) of the VIENNA CONVENTION ON DIPLOMATIC RELATIONS (q.v.) provides that the "receiving state shall permit and protect free communications on the part of the mission for all official purposes."

DIPLOMATIC CORP: group made up of the diplomatic representatives assigned by their governments to a foreign capitol. The DEAN or DOYEN (qq.v.) of the diplomatic corps represents the group at ceremonial occasions.

DIPLOMATIC COURIER: persons entrusted with carrying official dispatches or a DIPLOMATIC BAG. The courier is protected by the receiving state in the performance of his functions; he enjoys personal inviolability and is not liable to any form of arrest or detention. *See* Art. 27(5), VIENNA CONVENTION ON DIPLOMATIC RELATIONS (1961).

DIPLOMATIC IMMUNITY: the customary protection and benefits granted to members of a DIPLOMATIC MISSION by the host country. *See* VIENNA CONVENTION ON DIPLOMATIC RELATIONS, Arts. 29-32. *See also*, State Dept. Guidelines for Law Enforcement Officers, 27 I.L.M. 1617.

DIPLOMATIC LIST: the official roll of those persons holding diplomatic status in a particular place. *See Assurantie Compagnie Excelsior v. Smith*, 40 T.L.R. 105 (1923).

DIPLOMATIC MISSION: ambassador and his subordinates sent to the HOST STATE (q.v.) to protect, *inter alia*, the interests of the sending state in the receiving state, and to promote friendly relations between the sending state and receiving state. Art. 2 of the VIENNA CONVENTION ON DIPLOMATIC RELATIONS (1961) provides that the receiving state may require that the size of the mission be kept within limits considered by it to be "reasonable and normal". *See also* TERMINATION OF A MISSION.

DIPLOMATIC PASSPORT: PASSPORT (q.v.) issued to members of the foreign service (and their families) having diplomatic status.

DIPLOMATIC POUCH: *see* DIPLOMATIC BAG.

DIPLOMATIC PRIVILEGES AND IMMUNITIES: special status granted to diplomats including inviolability, diplomatic accommodations, freedom of movement and communications, etc. *See* VIENNA CONVENTION ON DIPLOMATIC RELATIONS (1961).

DIPLOMATIC RELATIONS: intercourse between nations through the use of representatives in order to keep peace and security among nations. *See* VIENNA CONVENTION ON DIPLOMATIC RELATIONS (1961), and RELATIONS OFFICIEVSES (F).

DIPLOMATIC SEAL: emblem of the sending government stamped in wax on official correspondence.

DIPLOMATIC USAGE: customary practices in the diplomatic community such as honorific titles, who sits where at dinner, etc. *See generally*, Satow, *A Guide to Diplomatic Practice* (1957).

DIPLOMATIST: any public servant employed in diplomatic affairs of a state.

DIPLOMACY: "[T]he application of intelligence and tact to the conduct of official relations . . . ." Satow, *A Guide to Diplomatic Practice* 1 (1957).

DIRECT BROADCASTING SERVICE (DBS): technology which allows small dish antenna to receive television signals directly from a satellite, bypassing ground stations and making government control of what is broadcast much more difficult. DBS has been the subject of continuous debate in COPUOS (q.v.), and a worry of the proponents of the NEW INTERNATIONAL INFORMATION ORDER (q.v.). *See* 9 J. Space L. 126 and 77 Am.J.Int.L. 733.

DIRTY WAR: anti-terrorist campaign by the Argentine military government in the 1970's featuring widespread human rights abuses. *See* DESAPARECIDOS and SECUESTRADOS.

DISARMAMENT: "[T]he identification, verification, inspection, limitation,control, reduction, or elimination of armed forces and armaments of all kinds under international agreement. This includes the necessary steps taken under such an agreement to establish an effective system of international control, or to create and strengthen international organizations for the maintenance of peace." Arms Control and Disarmament Act, 22 U.S.C. sec. 2552(a) (1982).

DISCONTINUANCE OF ACTION: INTERNATIONAL COURT OF JUSTICE (q.v.) may make an order of discontinuance upon learning from either the parties by agreement or from the applicant that if the respondent has taken no step in the proceedings that there will be no further action on the claim.

DISCOVERY: first claimant of newly discovered territory has title valid as against other claimants, but discovery is not the basis of title with respect to the inhabitants of the newly discovered territory. *See* PALMAS ISLAND ARBITRATION (1928) and 1931-32 A.D. 105.

DISCRETION: right (usually circumscribed by limits) to act in the way one thinks best or most appropriate. For cases regarding the discretion of the U.N. Secretary General, *see 18* I.L.R. 450-56.

DISEMBARKATION RESETTLEMENT ORDERS (DISERO): effort of international cooperation in the resettlement of BOAT PEOPLE (q.v.) by establishing a pool of offers to accept refugees, to alleviate the burden on countries near turmoil (especially in Southeast Asia), and on ships rescuing refugees on the high seas. See U.N. Doc. A/AC. 96/614, and EC/SCP/21 para. 18.

DISERO: DISEMBARKATION RESETTLEMENT ORDERS (q.v.).

DISINFORMATION: distribution of information by a government, usually through efforts of its intelligence community which is false or misleading in order to further a policy. In a recent incident the United States leaked information about a possible second attack on Libya to frighten Col. Qadaffi. See N.Y. Times, Oct. 26, 1986, sec. 6, at 10, col. 3.

DISPARITAS CULTUS (L): impediment to marriage in some legal system where persons of different religions may not marry.

DISPERSED FAMILIES: family members separated from each other due to the effects of war, through movement from the area of hostilities, military occupation, or forced transfer. They are to be provided assistance by the belligerents in locating and reuniting their families. See Art. 26 of the GENEVA CONVENTION IV (1949).

DISPLACED PERSON: REFUGEE (q.v.).

DISPOSITIVE TREATY: treaty which creates or affects territorial rights. The rights created by these treaties are permanent and are not affected by the outbreak of war between the parties to the treaty, nor by the extinction of a party to the treaty.

DISPUTE: disagreement on a point of law or fact; a conflict of legal views or of interests between two persons. See MAVROMATIS PALESTINE CONCESSIONS.

DISSENTING JUDGMENT: disagreement of one or more judges with the opinion of the majority upon the dispute before them. The statute of the International Court provides for the publication of dissents.

DISSOLUTION: termination of treaty obligations because the subject matter or *raison d'etre* of the treaty has been destroyed. See McNair, *Law of Treaties* 687 (1961).

DISTRESS: act of FORCE MAJEURE (q.v.) or other disaster which endangers the safety of a vessel or aircraft.

DISTRIBANCE OF AWARDS: the International Court of Justice may repudiate an award when its decision is treated as a nullity, i.e., where it lacked jurisdiction, or there was an essential or mani-fest error, fraud, or mistake.

DISTRIBUTION OF PROGRAM-CARRYING SIGNALS TRANSMITTED BY SATELLITE (1974): effort to protect the ownership of programs broadcast by satellite transmission. *See* 1144 U.N.T.S. 3, 13 I.L.M. 1444.

DIVORCE: subject of a convention sponsored by the HAGUE CONFERENCE ON PRIVATE INTERNATIONAL LAW (q.v.) on recognition of divorces and legal separations, 978 U.N.T.S. 393. An older convention on the same subject is found at 191 C.T.S. 259.

DIVORCE A FORFAIT (F): contractually arranged divorce settle-ment.

DJIBOUTI CODE OF INTERNATIONAL ARBITRATION: a fairly successful attempt to draft an ultra-modern set of rules for international arbitration which would encourage those seeking a site for such arbitrations to choose Djibouti. The Code may be found at 25 I.L.M. 2.

DMZ: *see* DEMILITARIZED ZONE.

DOL (F): civil law concept not directly translating into a common law meaning; roughly, to inflict damage intentionally and wrong-fully. The term poses problems for some adherents to the WAR-SAW CONVENTION (1929) (q.v.) where it appears in Art. 25. *See* 34 I.L.R. 201-10.

DOMICILE: place selected by an individual to be his or her prin-cipal residence. *See* 3 I.L.R. 376.

DOMICILIUM EX PROPIO MOTU (L): one's chosen place of residence.

DOMICILIUM NECESSARIUM (L): recognized domicile of dependents in a household.

DOMINICAN CRISIS (1965): unrest in the Dominican Republic prompted the dispatch of United States Marines to restore order. *See* 4 Can.Y.B.Int'l L. 178 (1966).

DOMINIUN: proprietary rights in the territory over which the state exercises its IMPERIUM (q.v.). In civil law systems, a state may exercise imperium without necessarily enjoying dominion over the asset concerned. In common law systems, sovereignty, and property are indistinguishable concepts.

DOMINIUM EMINENS (F): the paramount right of property that a state has *vis-a-vis* its territory, exercise of the right is governed by the laws of the state itself.

DOMINO THEORY: idea advanced during the VIETNAM WAR (q.v.) that if the communists won, the surrounding nations in Southeast Asia would fall like dominos. The "theory" has, also, been applied to Central America arguing against allowing any of the states there to fall to a communist government.

DOMMAGE MORAL (F): moral damages, a court award to a plaintiff to punish the bad act of the defendant.

DONAUVERSINKUNG (G): natural phenomenon where the Danube River between Baden and Wirttenberg appears to dry up at times, because the water flows into subterranean rivers and is diverted to the Rhine. This is the subject of a dispute reported at 4 I.L.R. 128.

DONNER ACTE (F): acknowledgement that another party has performed a necessary act.

DONNER LA MAIN (F): give the hand, i.e., place in the seat of honor or on the right or left side of the host.

DORPAT TREATY (1920): agreement between Russia and Finland limiting the territorial waters of the contracting parties in the Gulf of Finland to four nautical miles measured from the coast. It is also known as the Peace Treaty of Durpat, *see* 3 L.N.T.S. 5.

DOUBLE CRIMINALITY RULE: EXTRADITION (q.v.) of fugitives is available only when the act is considered to be criminal under the laws of both the requisitioned and requisitioning states. *See* 28 Am.J.Int.L. 274.

DOUBLE EFFECT RULE: moral theory of restraint on combatants over and above the LAW OF WAR (q.v.), which says an act of violence can only be justified if: 1) the intended effect is moral; 2) the positive effects outweigh the evil effects; 3) the evil effects are unintended; and 4) evil effects are not a means to an end.

DOYEN D'AGE (F): the most senior of the diplomatic representatives.

DOYEN OF THE DIPLOMATIC CORPS: the most senior diplomat in terms of rank and length of service in a particular place; also, called the dean of the diplomatic corps. This person has certain special duties according to diplomatic protocol including acting as intermediary between the diplomatic corps and the host country. In some Catholic countries this post is traditionally held by the papal NUNCIO (q.v.) regardless of time of service.

DOYENNE (F): wife of the senior diplomat (DOYEN). *See* Satow, *A Guide to Diplomatic Practice* 255 (1957).

DRAGO DOCTRINE: principle proposed by Latin-American jurists that force cannot be used to collect a public debt. *See* 1 Am.J.Int.L. 692.

DRESSING SHIP: the flying of certain flags, ensigns, and pennants on ceremonial occasions on a ship or yacht.

DRIFTNET FISHING: fishing with huge nets causes great environmental damage. Such fishing is to be prohibited in the South Pacific by a convention. *See* 29 I.L.M. 1449 and 1555.

DROIT D'AUBAINE (F): feudal law giving the sovereign the right to confiscate the property of a foreigner who dies in the sovereign's territory.

DROIT D'ENQUETE (F): see VERIFICATION DU PAVILLION.

DROIT D'EPAVE (F): see DROIT DE NAUFRAGE.

DROIT D'ETAPE (F): the right (because of a servitude) to send an armed force through the territory of another. *See e.g.*, 36 Am.J.Int.L.Supp. 153.

DROIT D'OUTRE-MER (F): legal regime governing French territories not part of mainland France; French Colonial Law. *See* 80 I.L.R. 473.

DROIT DE CHAPPELLE (F): diplomatic privilege of opening a chapel and conducting religious ceremonies for the diplomatic staff according to their own religious faith. It was an important development for the progress of diplomatic relations after the reformation but also subject to abuse.

DROIT DE DETRACTION (F): levy of taxes on the moveable property of a foreigner leaving a country. *See* GABELLA EMIGRATIONIS.

DROIT DE NAUFRAGE (F): ancient law giving all that floated up on shore, whether from a shipwreck or flotsam and jetsam, into the possession of the inhabitants of the shore or their sovereign.

DROIT DE PRESEANCE (F): right of precedent.

DROIT DE RENVOI (F): right of a state to exclude the citizens of another country.

DROIT DE RESCOUSSE (F): premium (per cent of the goods recovered) paid to those who capture goods stolen by pirates and return the goods to the rightful owners.

DROIT DE RETRAIT (F): *see* DROIT DE DETRACTION.

DROIT DES GENS (F): LAW OF NATIONS (q.v.).

DROIT DU CULTE (F): *see* DROIT DE CAPPELLE.

DROIT MORAL (F): moral law; rules of conduct based on moral principles rather than legal doctrine.

DROITS ET INTERETES LEGITIMES (F): similar to the concept of "legal or equitable interest" in American and English law.

DRUGS: subject of several international conventions including the OPIUM CONVENTIONS (q.v.), the United Nations Convention on Psychotropic Substances, 10 I.L.M. 261, the SINGLE CONVENTION ON NARCOTIC DRUGS (q.v.), and the Declaration of the United Nations Conference on Drug Abuse, 26 I.L.M. 1637.

DRYING ROCKS AND SHOALS: areas of land above water at low tide, but covered by water at high tide, also called "low tide elevations."

DUAL NATIONAL: person who is a national of two states. Every state has the right to disregard the fact that one of its nationals is also the national of another state. *See* 30 I.L.R. 366-74.

DUALISM: philosophy that international law is superior to municipal law in international disputes, and municipal law is superior to international law in municipal disputes. MONISM (q.v.) is the alternative school of thought. *See* Von Glahn, *Law Among Nations*, (1976).

DUBROVNIK RULES: preliminary work of the International Law Association which became the EUROPEAN CONVENTION ON FOREIGN MONEY LIABILITY (q.v.).

DUMBA AFFAIR (1915): recall of the Austro-Hungarian Ambassador to the United States for allegedly attempting to ferment strikes in U.S. munitions plants. *See* 9 Am.J.Int.L. 935.

DUMBARTON OAKS CONFERENCE (1944): preliminary meeting establishing the ground work for the establishment of the United Nations. *See* 39 Am.J.Int.L.Supp. 42.

DUMPING: placing of the products of one country into the commerce of another country at less than their normal value. *See* 26 I.L.R. 602 and Art. 34 of the HAVANA CHARTER (1946).

DURANTE BELLO (L): in the cause of war.

DURESS: employment of coercion against the persons signing a treaty on behalf of a state or against the persons engaged in ratifying or acceding to a treaty on behalf of a state. Art. 32, paragraph (a) of the Draft Convention of the Harvard Research on Treaties; 29 Am.J.Int.L.Supp. 657, 663.

DURPAT: *see* DORPAT.

DUTCH CLAUSE: Art. 22 of the MERGER CONTROL REGULATIONS (q.v.) of the European Community. It allows a state to request the European Community Commission to investigate a merger which does not directly effect competition in the Community.

DUTIES: *see* CUSTOMS DUTIES.

DZERZINSKY SQUARE: home address of the KGB (q.v.).

[E - F]

EAR: EXPORT ADMINISTRATION REGULATIONS (q.v.).

EARLY NOTIFICATION OF NUCLEAR ACCIDENTS CON-VENTION (1986): sponsored by the INTERNATIONAL ATOMIC ENERGY AGENCY (q.v.) as a result of the CHER-NOBYL INCIDENT (q.v.). It provides for the notification of states that may be physically affected in the event of a nuclear accident. *See* 25 I.L.M. 1370.

EARTH RESOURCES TECHNOLOGY SATELLITE: *see* RE-MOTE SENSING.

EASEMENT: right of a state arising through agreement or long continuing usage to enjoy a certain use of another state's territory without constituting a formal encroachment on the latter's sover-eignty. By doctrine, an easement may inure to the benefit of other nations not party to the initial creation of the easement. *See* 31 I.L.R. 23, 70.

EAST AFRICAN COOPERATION TREATY (1967): established by the East African Common Market - among Kenya, Tanzania and Uganda -eliminating customs duties and promoting bal-anced industrial development. *See* 6 I.L.M. 932.

EAST AFRICAN DEVELOPMENT BANK: part of the East Afri-can Common Market; this bank was to be established and funded by the member countries. *See* 6 I.L.M. 1003.

EASTERN GREENLAND CASE: disputed claim of sovereignty over Eastern Greenland between Norway and Denmark. The WORLD COURT (q.v.) declared Denmark sovereign over all of Greenland. This decision was based, in part, on the binding effect of a Norwegian diplomatic note. *See* 1933 P.C.I.J. (ser. A/B) No. 53, 3 Hudson, World Court Reports 151 (1969).

EASTERN QUESTION: problem of establishing nation-states in the Balkans, and the settlement of ethnic disputes which preoccupied Europe for the first half of the 20th century. *See* 6 Am.J.Int.L. 86, 659.

EC: *See* EUROPEAN ECONOMIC COMMUNITY.

ECA: ECONOMIC COMMISSION FOR AFRICA (q.v.).

ECAC: EUROPEAN CIVIL AVIATION COMMISSION (q.v.).

ECAFE: ECONOMIC COMMISSION FOR ASIA AND THE FAR EAST (q.v.).

ECHELLE MOBILE (F): sliding scale.

ECEA: ECONOMIC COMMUNITY OF EAST AFRICA (q.v.).

ECITO: EUROPEAN CENTRAL INLAND TRANSPORT ORGANIZATION (q.v.).

ECLA: ECONOMIC COMMISSION FOR LATIN AMERICA (q.v.).

ECONOMIC AID: assistance in the form of loans, outright grants, or technological assistance from one nation or organization to another to help improve the receiving nation's economy. Often the underlying motive for economic aid is the benefit the nation donating the aid will receive in sales of its machinery or in opening a market for its products.

ECONOMIC AND SOCIAL COUNCIL OF THE UNITED NATIONS (ECOSOC): council comprised of 54 members and concerned primarily with the field of population, economic development, human rights, criminal justice and narcotics control. *See* U.N. Documents numbered E/....

ECONOMIC CHARTER OF AFRICA: *See* AFRICAN DECLA-
RATION OF COOPERATION, DEVELOPMENT AND ECO-
NOMIC INDEPENDENCE.

ECONOMIC COMMISSION FOR AFRICA (ECA): United Nations body facilitating economic development in this region; established by the Economic and Social Council in 1947. *See* the latest
U.N. Yearbook for current activities. Regarding relations between ECA and the OAU, *see* Amate, Inside the OAU 546-49.

**ECONOMIC COMMISSION FOR ASIA AND THE FAR EAST
(ECAFE):** United Nations body facilitating economic development in this region; established by the Economic and Social Council in 1947. *See* the latest U.N. Yearbook for current activities.

ECONOMIC COMMISSION FOR LATIN AMERICA (ECLA):
United Nations body to facilitate economic development in Latin
America; established by the Economic and Social Council in 1948.
See latest U.N. Yearbook for current activities.

ECONOMIC COMMUNITY OF EAST AFRICA: created pursuant to a resolution by a meeting on East African Economic Cooperation in 1965. The membership consisted of Burundi, Ethiopia,
Kenya, Malawi, Mauritius, Tanzania, and Zambia. *See* 5 I.L.M.
633.

**ECONOMIC COMMUNITY OF WEST AFRICAN STATES
(ECOWAS):** organization for economic cooperation and develop-
ment of West Africa; established in 1975, after eight years of nego-
tiation and preliminary efforts by the states of Benin, Gambia,
Ghana, Liberia, Mali, Mauritania, Niger, Nigeria, Senegal, Sierra
Leone, Togo, and Upper Volta. *See* 14 I.L.M. 1200.

ECONOMIC COOPERATION AND ASSISTANCE: goal estab-
lished by various international organizations such as the GROUP
OF 7 (q.v.), (*see* Communique, 16 I.L.M. 724) and the UNITED
NATIONS INDUSTRIAL DEVELOPMENT ORGANIZATION

(q.v.). *See also* the INTERNATIONAL FUND FOR AGRICUL-TURAL DEVELOPMENT.

ECONOMIC INTERVENTION: use of sanctions against a state in the form of an economic blockade or formal interference with trade and shipping to influence the state's behavior.

ECONOMIC RIGHTS AND DUTIES OF STATES CHARTER: U.N. General Assembly Resolution 3281 (XXIX), declares that states have a right to determine their own economic system, have permanent sovereignty over their resources, and may regulate foreign economic activities within their borders. *See* 14 I.L.M. 251 and 15 I.L.M. 175.

ECONOMIC SANCTIONS: use of economic pressure tactics such as an embargo to enforce international law or national policy, *e.g.*, IRAQ-KUWAIT SANCTIONS.

ECONOMIC, SOCIAL AND CULTURAL RIGHTS: rights embodied in the United Nations COVENANT ON ECONOMIC, SOCIAL, AND CULTURAL RIGHTS (q.v.), including the right of self-determination, the right to work in just and favorable conditions, the right to education, and various rights associated with the family. *See* 6 I.L.M. 360.

ECONOMIC WARFARE: state of hostile relations between two or more nations in which one nation attempts to interfere with and damage the economy of another for military, political, or economic ends.

ECONOMIC ZONE: *see* EXCLUSIVE ECONOMIC ZONE.

ECOSOC: ECONOMIC AND SOCIAL COUNCIL OF THE UNITED NATIONS. (q.v.).

ECOWAS: ECONOMIC COMMUNITY OF WEST AFRICAN STATES (q.v.).

ECREHOS CASE: *see* MINQUIERS AND ECREHOS CASE.

ECSC: EUROPEAN COAL AND STEEL COMMUNITY (q.v.).

ECU: unit of currency of the European Community based on a market basket of member countries' currencies.

ECUADOREAN-PERUVIAN BORDER DISPUTE: long-standing dispute over a large tract of land between the two countries. *See* 63 Am.J.Int.L. 28.

EDEN PLAN (1955): proposal by British Prime Minister Anthony Eden for the reunification of Germany with a demilitarized zone on her eastern border.

EDWARD VIII: monarch of the British Empire who abdicated the throne to marry a divorced commoner, Wallace Simpson; the most notorious case of abdication in the 20th century. *See* 10 Austl.L.J. 393-98.

EEC: EUROPEAN ECONOMIC COMMUNITY (q.v.).

EEZ: EXCLUSIVE ECONOMIC ZONE (q.v.)

EFFECTIVE OCCUPATION: actual, continuous, and peaceful display of the functions of a state, as opposed to mere physical settlement, over newly found land or land over which sovereignty has been abandoned.

EFFECTIVENESS PRINCIPLE: measure for determining whether a new government should be recognized as legitimate by other governments based on its ability to exercise power in the territory in question.

EFFECTIVELY DOCTRINE: a nation should employ an effective and efficient force in order to enforce municipal and international law in its territorial waters. *See* 2 O'Connell, *The International Law of the Sea* 1063-65 (1984).

EFFECTIVITIES (F): effectiveness, *see* EFFECTIVENESS PRINCIPLE.

EFTA: EUROPEAN FREE TRADE ASSOCIATION (q.v.).

EGBGB (G): EINFUHRUNGSGESETZ ZUM BURGERLICH GESETZBUCH (q.v.).

EGYPT-ISRAEL BOUNDARY AGREEMENT: settlement on a permanent boundary between Egypt and Israel. *See* 28 I.L.M. 611.

EGYPT-ISRAELI PEACE AGREEMENT: *See* CAMP DAVID AGREEMENTS.

EICHMANN INCIDENT: in 1960, Adolph Eichmann, accused of being the commandant of a Nazi death camp, was abducted in Argentina by Israeli agents and taken to Israel where he was tried, convicted, and executed. He contended that the Israeli Court did not have jurisdiction because there was no extradition treaty between Israel and Argentina. *See* 6 Whiteman, *Digest of International Law* 1108, 1962 Brit.Y.B.Int'l.L. 181 and 55 Am.J.Int.L. 307.

EIGHTEEN NATIONS DISARMAMENT COMMITTEE: United Nations committee entrusted with seeking international agreement limiting all types of weapons systems and demilitarization. It was replaced by the UNITED NATIONS CONFERENCE ON DISARMAMENT (q.v.), in 1969. *See* 1961 U.N. Yearbook 16.

EINFUHRUNGSGESETZ ZUM BURGERLICH GESETZBUCH (EGBGB) (G): introductory law of the German Civil Code which contains conflict of laws rules. It is not itself part of the civil code. *See* Schonfelder, *Deutsch Gesetze* pt. 21.

EISENHOWER DOCTRINE (1957): initiative to strengthen United States influence in the Middle East with economic and military assistance including the right to send troops, if invited by a threatened government. *See* 5 Whiteman, *Digest of International Law* 1153 (1965).

EJUS EST INTERPRETARE LEGEM CUJUS CONDERE (L): one whohas the power to make a law has the power to interpret it. *See* 2 I.L.R. 384.

EJUSDEM GENERIS (L): of the same class, nature, or kind. Where a general term follows a specific enumeration, the general term is to be limited to persons or things of the same general class as those specifically mentioned. *See e.g.,* 1 I.L.R. 358.

ELECTROBILL: system for handling BILLS OF LADING (q.v.) or other transportation documents by means of computer record rather than a paper document. *See* Comite Maritime Internationale Doc. SWB 476.

ELEKTIVE KONKURRENZ (G): choice of law principle. The injured party may choose the legal system most favorable to his cause. *See* 80 I.L.R. 383.

ELIMINATION OF ALL FORMS OF RACIAL DISCRIMINATION CONVENTION (1965): to implement the U.N. resolution of the same name, the parties guarantee, *inter alia*, that they will not discriminate on the basis of race, color, or ethnic origin in the protection of civil rights. *See* 5 I.L.M. 352.

ELIMINATION OF ALL FORMS OF RACIAL DISCRIMINATION RESOLUTION (1963): UNGA Res.1904(XVIII). *See* 3 I.L.M. 164.

ELIMINATION OF DISCRIMINATION AGAINST WOMEN CONVENTION (1980): parties to this agreement promise, *inter alia*, to take measures to eliminate sex discrimination from their legal systems. *See* 19 I.L.M. 33, 34.

ELIMINATION OF INTERMEDIATE-RANGE AND SHORTER-RANGE NUCLEAR MISSILES CONVENTION: agreement between the United States and the Soviet Union to eliminate these classes of missiles from their arsenals. *See* 27 I.L.M. 84.

EMA: EUROPEAN MONETARY AGREEMENT (q.v.).

EMANCIPATIO TACTA (L): tacit emancipation; a child becoming independent of his parents without formal act of emancipation.

EMBARGO: state act prohibiting shipping from its territory to that of an enemy territory. *See* 6 I.L.R. 375.

EMBASSAGE: message or commission entrusted to an ambassador.

EMBASSY: residence of an ambassador. It is also an archaic term for EMBASSAGE (q.v.). *See also* CHANCELLERY.

EMBLEMS: symbol, figurative representations; the RED CROSS and RED CRESCENT (qq.v.) are the only internationally recognized distinctive emblems. They may not be deliberately misused in the same manner as a flag of truce may not be misused. *See* Art. 38 of the GENEVA CONVENTION PROTOCOL I (1977).

EMISSARY: special representative sent to another country on a specific mission, usually unofficially or in secret.

EMS: EUROPEAN MONETARY SYSTEM (q.v.).

EN CLAIR (F): clearly; a message sent in the normal course without coding.

EN POSTE (F): having assumed a diplomatic position; at one's desk.

EN PRINCIPE (F): 1) as a matter of principle (English usage); 2) generally speaking, as a rule (French usage).

ENCLAVES: detached portion of one state's territory completely surrounded by the territory of another state.

ENCLOSED SEA: " . . . a gulf, basin or sea surrounded by two or more states and connected to another sea or the ocean by a narrow outlet . . . ." *See* LAW OF THE SEA CONVENTION (1982), Art. 122, 21 I.L.M. 1261, 1291.

ENDANGERED SPECIES: *see* TRADE IN ENDANGERED SPECIES.

ENDC: EIGHTEEN NATION DISARMAMENT COMMITTEE (q.v.).

ENEMY: hostile state; citizen or subject of a hostile state; or one supporting a hostile state.

ENEMY AGENT: in time of war, a representative of a hostile state. When war is declared they may be granted safe conduct to return to their home state or may be treated as prisoners of war. *See* DUMBA AFFAIR (1915).

ENEMY PROPERTY: property engaged or used by a state's enemy whether belonging to an enemy, neutral, or ally tainted because the use, not the source, stamps it with its hostile character.

ENEMY SUBJECTS: individual, association, or corporation that is the subject or national of a state with which another state is at war.

ENFORCEABILITY OF UNITED NATIONS RESOLUTIONS: it seems that United Nations Resolutions are not enforceable laws (i.e. not self-executing), at least in United States Courts. *See Diggs v. Richardson*, 555 F.2d 848 (1976).

ENFORCEMENT MEASURES: collective acts authorized by the United Nations Security Council to counter a threat to peace. *See* Art. 41 of the UNITED NATIONS CHARTER.

ENFORCEMENT OF JUDGMENTS: *see* EUROPEAN CONVENTION ON THE ENFORCEMENT OF JUDGMENTS and GE-

NEVA CONVENTION ON THE EXECUTION OF FOREIGN AR-
BITRAL AWARDS.

ENGLISH BILLS OF EXCHANGE ACT (1882): English law of
commercial paper which has had much influence on the development of the law of commercial paper (checks, bills, etc.) around
the world. *See* 5 Halsbury's Statutes (4th ed.) at 334.

ENRICHISSEMENT SANS CAUSE (F): UNJUST ENRICH-
MENT (q.v.).

ENTEBBE RAID (1976): military action by Israel to rescue the
victims of the hijacking of an Air France plane by members of the
Popular Front for the Liberation of Palestine. They were holding
some of the passengers hostage at Entebbe Airport in Uganda
with the apparent cooperation of the Ugandan Government. The
raid led to the passage of a United Nations resolution. *See* 15
I.L.M. 1224.

ENTENTE CORDIALE (1903): treaty between Great Britain and
France and notable as the first agreement to call for anticipatory
reference of disputes to arbitration. *See* 194 C.T.S. 194.

ENTRY INTO FORCE: point in time at which a treaty becomes
binding, as between the parties that have ratified or acceded to it.
Multilateral treaties usually specify a certain number of ratifica-
tions or accessions for the agreement to come into force. All treaties recognized as being in force by the United States Department
of State (between the United States and other countries) are listed
each year in *Treaties in Force*.

ENVELOPE LINE: method of drawing a baseline on a coast for
purposes of defining the territorial sea based on a curve tangent
to each member of a set of curves forming the outline of the coast.

ENVIRONMENT: *see* TRANSFRONTIER POLLUTION and
STOCKHOLM DECLARATION ON HUMAN ENVIRONMENT.

ENVIRONMENTAL MODIFICATION CONVENTION: parties undertake not to engage in military or other hostile uses of environmental modification techniques which have widespread, long-lasting, or severe effects, i.e., the deliberate manipulation of natural processes changing the dynamics, composition, or structure of the earth, atmosphere, or outer space. *See* 16 I.L.M. 88.

ENVOI EN POSSESSION (F): court order granting possession of a residuary estate in French civil law.

ENVOY: class of diplomatic agent ranking below ambassador, but above minister and entitled to represent the sovereign in its affairs, but not its personal character.

ENVOYS EXTRAORDINARY: term implies a special character in the diplomatic employment of an envoy, but in current usage is honorific and has no special significance.

EPICONTINENTAL SEA: waters (and natural resources contained therein) which are adjacent to a state.

EPLF: ERITREAN PEOPLE'S LIBERATION FRONT (q.v.).

EQUALITY OF STATES: doctrine that all states are juridically equal and enjoy the same rights and capacity to exercise them. *See* Art. 4 of the MONTEVIDEO CONVENTION ON THE RIGHTS AND DUTIES OF STATES, 49 Stat. 3097, 3 Bevans 145, 165 L.N.T.S. 19 (1933), and Article 2(1) of the UNITED NATIONS CHARTER.

EQUALITY OF TREATMENT: prisoners of war are to be treated alike by the detaining power without adverse distinctions based on race, nationality, religion, or political beliefs, but subject to variations in treatment based on rank, sex, age, health, and professional qualifications. *See* Art. 16, GENEVA CONVENTION III (1949). Likewise equality of treatment is to be afforded to other PROTECTED PERSONS (q.v.). *See* Art. 27 (3) GENEVA CONVENTION IV (1949).

EQUIDISTANCE: concept applied in the delimitation of maritime boundaries of opposite (as opposed to adjacent) states establishing a median line between the states as a boundary.

EQUITABLE APPORTIONMENT: dividing of disputed property following principles of equity and justice rather than a strict application of a legal formula.

EQUITABLE DELIMITATION: doctrine that states negotiating continental shelf boundaries should employ equitable principles such as aspects of geology, geophysical configuration, and unity of resource deposits in delimiting such boundaries.

ERGA OMNES (L): against everyone.

ERITREAN PEOPLES' LIBERATION FRONT (EPLF): rebel group fighting for the independence of the Eritrean province of Ethiopia. *See* N.Y. Times , Jan.6, 1985 at 1.

ERREURS MATERIELLE (F): a material error, i.e. a mistate by a court which effects the outcome of the case. *See* 81 I.L.R. 431.

ERROR JURIS (L): error of law.

ERROR LAPSUS (L): error caused by negligence.

ERROR QUALITATIS (L): mistake as to a fact by a party which makes the conclusion of marriage voidable in some legal systems, e.g., impotency or mental defect.

ERTS: Earth Resources Technology Satellite, *see* REMOTE SENSING.

ESA: EUROPEAN SPACE AGENCY (q.v.).

ESPIONAGE: clandestine method of gathering information through disguise or false pretense. Formally applied to the passing of information about one enemy to another, but now everyone spies on everyone else.

ESTATE SUCCESSION: subject of a convention sponsored by the HAGUE CONFERENCE ON PRIVATE INTERNATIONAL LAW, *see* 28 I.L.M. 146.

ESTOPPEL: rule that states may not deny the truth of statements made or facts accepted by their accredited representatives.

ESTRADA DOCTRINE: declaration by Mexico's Foreign Minister Estrada recognizing governments involved in the passing of judgement on their legal capacity by other states invading the dignity of such governments. He urged that states merely maintain or recall diplomatic missions as they saw fit. The doctrine has not been widely accepted. *See* 25   Am.J.Int.L. 719 and Am.J.Int.L.Supp. 203.

ETABLISSEMENTS PUBLICS INTERNATIONAUX: legal person created by a multinational treaty, independent from the national laws of the treaty parties, possessing a considerable amount of delegated power and autonomy.

ETHICAL PRACTICES IN COMMERCIAL TRANSACTIONS: subject of an International Chamber of Commerce report urging governments to cooperate in the elimination of practices such as bribery and kickbacks. *See* 16 I.L.M. 686 and FOREIGN CORRUPT PRACTICES ACT.

ETHIOPIA V. SOUTH AFRICA: *see* SOUTH WEST AFRICA CASE.

ETHIOPIAN RESOLUTIONS: several United Nations General Assembly resolutions aimed at outlawing the use of nuclear weapons by, *inter alia*, declaring that their use is a violation, *per se*, of the United Nations Charter. *See* UNGA Res. 1653 (XVI) Nov. 24, 1961, UNGA Res. 1801 (XVII) Dec. 14, 1962, and UNGA Res. 1910 (XVIII) Nov. 27, 1963.

EURATOM: European Atomic Energy Community, created in 1957, promoting and developing the nuclear industry in Europe. *See 298* U.N.T.S. 3 and 16 I.L.M. 300.

EUREKA: EUROPEAN RESEARCH COORDINATING AGENCY (q.v.).

EUROCONTROL: organization unifying air traffic control in Western Europe outside the controlled air space around airports. The organization has also established uniform safety rules for aviation. *See* 523 U.N.T.S. 117.

EURODOLLAR: accounts held in European banks payable in United States dollars. *See* 13 Am.J.Comp.L. 30.

EUROPEAN AGREEMENT CONCERNING THE INTERNA-TIONAL CARRIAGE OF DANGEROUS GOODS BY ROAD (1957)(ADR): agreement on safety measures for the transport of dangerous goods which are enumerated in two annexes to the Agreement. *See* 1 Hill and Evans, *Transport Laws of the World* at I/A/2 (1983).

EUROPEAN ASYLUM CONVENTION (1990): agreement determining the state's responsibility for examining applications for ASYLUM (q.v.) lodged in one of the menber states of the EURO-PEAN COMMUNITY (q.v.). *See* 30 I.L.M. 425.

EUROPEAN ATOMIC ENERGY COMMUNITY: *See* EURA-TOM.

EUROPEAN BANK FOR RECONSTRUCTION AND DEVEL-OPMENT: international financial institution established to help revive the economics of Eastern Europe. *See* 29 I.L.M. 1077.

EUROPEAN CENTRAL INLAND TRANSPORT ORGANIZA-TION (ECITO): group established to rationalize inland transport in Europe   (*see* 5 U.N.T.S. 327, 40 Am.J.Int.L. Supp. 31); it was replaced by other organizations. *See* 2 European Yearbook 583.

EUROPEAN CIVIL AVIATION COMMISSION: organization promoting cooperation among European states. *See* 5 Annals of Air and Space Law 649 (1980).

EUROPEAN COAL AND STEEL COMMUNITY (ECSE): organization created in 1951 among France, West Germany, Italy, Belgium, Luxembourg, and the Netherlands to establish a common market for coal and steel and to harmonize their external tariffs on these products. The United Kingdom, Ireland, and Denmark joined in 1973, and Greece joined in 1981. *See* 261 U.N.T.S. 140

EUROPEAN COMMISSION OF THE DANUBE: body regulating commercial traffic on the Danube River. *See* 55 *British and Foreign State Papers* 93, and DANUBE COMMISSION.

EUROPEAN COMMISSION ON HUMAN RIGHTS: has authority under the EUROPEAN CONVENTION ON HUMAN RIGHTS (q.v.) to investigate grievances charged by private individuals against their governments and to bring charges of rights violations before the nineteen member governments. The Commission requires that local remedies be exhausted before taking a case, and does not rule on the case, but attempts to facilitate a settlement between the individual and the offending government.

EUROPEAN COMMUNITIES: several agreements among European governments; each centering on a part of the economy which attempted to unify the rules on marketing and production. These evolved into the EUROPEAN ECONOMIC COMMUNITY (q.v.) *See* EUROPEAN COAL AND STEEL COMMUNITY. *See also* 4 I.L.M. 776.

EUROPEAN COMMUNITY: goal of the process of integrating the governments of Western Europe; the structure had been established by the ROME TREATY (1958) (q.v.). *See* EUROPEAN ECONOMIC COMMUNITY and EUROPEAN PARLIAMENT. *See also*, 8 Legal Reference Service Quarterly 7 (1988).

EUROPEAN COMMUNITY COURT OF JUSTICE: court created in 1952, as part of the EUROPEAN COAL AND STEEL COMMUNITY (q.v.), it ensures observance of the European Economic Community Treaty and related treaties. *See* Arts. 164-188 of the ROME TREATY (1957), 298 U.N.T.S. 11.

EUROPEAN COMMUNITY LAW: regulation, directives, and jurisprudence developed by the EUROPEAN COMMUNITY (q.v.) pursuant to the ROME TREATY (1958) (q.v.).

EUROPEAN CONVENTION ON CRIMINAL MATTERS (1959): Council of Europe-sponsored treaty. *See* 472 U.N.T.S. 85.

EUROPEAN CONVENTION ON FOREIGN MONEY LIABILITY (1967): provisions govern the payment of debts in currency other than that of the place of payment. *See* 15 European Yearbook 285 or International Law Association 53rd Report at 663 (1968).

EUROPEAN CONVENTION ON HUMAN RIGHTS (1950): guarantees a list of human rights including the right to life, freedom from slavery, torture, and inhuman punishment. The European Convention, unlike the U.N. Convention, contains enforcement provisions. *See* 213 U.N.T.S. 221.

EUROPEAN CONVENTION ON PRODUCT LIABILITY (1977): sets out uniform rules for the liability of producers of products for the injury or death caused by defects in those products. It was adopted by the COUNCIL OF EUROPE (q.v.), *see* 16 I.L.M. 7.

EUROPEAN CONVENTION ON STATE IMMUNITY: rules for the applicability of sovereign immunity where state parties appear in the courts of other state parties. *See* 66 Am.J.Int.L. 923 (proceeding section).

EUROPEAN CONVENTION ON THE ADOPTION OF CHILDREN (1967): adopted by the COUNCIL OF EUROPE (q.v.), establishes certain uniform rules for the adoption laws of the member states, including appropriate cases for adoption and the rights and duties conferred. *See* 7 I.L.M. 211, 634 U.N.T.S. 255.

EUROPEAN CONVENTION ON THE ENFORCEMENT OF JUDGMENTS (1968): attempt to simplify the formalities governing mutual recognition and enforcement of judgment. It applies to civil and commercial matters regardless of the nature of the jurisdiction. *See* 8 I.L.M. 229.

EUROPEAN CONVENTION ON TERRORISM: parties promise to extradite persons accused of terrorist offenses. *See* 25 *European Yearbook* 289.

EUROPEAN COUNCIL: one of the four governing bodies of the EUROPEAN COMMUNITY (q.v.); it is composed of one representative from each member state. THE COUNCIL OF EUROPE (q.v.) is a different organization. *See* S. Bulmer and W. Wessels, *The European Council* (1987).

EUROPEAN COURT OF HUMAN RIGHTS: organ of the COUNCIL OF EUROPE (q.v.); the 22 member states have accepted the jurisdiction of this court which can issue binding rulings on whether a government has violated its obligations under the EUROPEAN CONVENTION ON HUMAN RIGHTS (q.v.). Governments may be required to pay compensation. *See e.g.*, 11 I.L.M. 1062.

EUROPEAN DANUBE COMMISSION: *see* DANUBE COMMISSION.

EUROPEAN ECONOMIC COMMUNITY (EEC): established in 1958 to develop a common market free of trade barriers and to promote the harmonization and approximation of member states economic policies. *See* 298 U.N.T.S. 11.

EUROPEAN ECONOMIC COMMUNITY TREATIES: *see* ROME TREATY (1957), MERGER TREATY (1967), and the SINGLE EUROPEAN ACT (1986).

EUROPEAN ECONOMIC COOPERATION CONVENTION (1948): precursor to the EUROPEAN ECONOMIC COMMUNITY (q.v.). *See* 43 Am.J.Int.L. Supp. 94.

EUROPEAN FISHERIES CONFERENCE (1964): agreement among 16 countries on control of coastal fishing. *See* 58 Am.J.Int.L. 1068.

EUROPEAN FREE TRADE ASSOCIATION (EFTA): organization formed in 1960, to establish a free trade area for industrial goods through the abolition of customs duties and quotas and the elimination of other indirect barriers. The original membership included Austria, Denmark (withdrew in 1973), Norway, Portugal, Sweden, Switzerland, and the United Kingdom (withdrew in 1973); joined by Finland (1961) and Iceland (1970). *See* 370 U.N.T.S. 3.

EUROPEAN HUMAN RIGHTS CONVENTION (1950): EUROPEAN CONVENTION FOR THE PROTECTION OF HUMAN RIGHTS AND FUNDAMENTAL FREEDOMS (1950) (q.v.). *See* EUROPEAN COURT OF HUMAN RIGHTS.

EUROPEAN INTEGRATION: process of breaking down the barriers created by national boundaries in Western Europe which has progressed to the point of the establishment of a limited European government the EUROPEAN COMMUNITY (q.v.). The process has also been facilitated by the COUNCIL OF EUROPE (q.v.).

EUROPEAN INVESTMENT BANK: established by the European Economic Community to provide loans to disadvantaged areas. *See* 298 U.N.T.S. 3.

EUROPEAN LAUNCHER DEVELOPMENT ORGANIZATION (ELDO): predecessor to the EUROPEAN SPACE AGENCY (q.v.) for the purpose of developing a European space launch capability. *See* 3 I.L.M. 234.

EUROPEAN MONETARY AGREEMENT (EMA): agreement that replaced the EUROPEAN PAYMENTS UNION (q.v.) and established the EUROPEAN MONETARY SYSTEM (q.v.) from which members could borrow to rectify temporary balance-of-payments difficulties. *See* B.Morris, Crane, and Boehm *The European Community* 96-99 (1981).

EUROPEAN MONETARY SYSTEM: procedures for rectifying temporary BALANCE OF PAYMENTS (q.v.) problems; established by the EUROPEAN MONETARY AGREEMENT (q.v.).

EUROPEAN ORGANIZATION FOR NUCLEAR RESEARCH: evolved from the Conseil Europeen pour la Recherche Nucleaire (and still retains the acronym CERN) this organization is involved exclusively in scientific and basic nonmilitary nuclear research. *See* 200 U.N.T.S. 149.

EUROPEAN PARLIAMENT: legislative body of the EUROPEAN COMMUNITY with limited power to make binding rules for the member countries. Representatives from each member country are elected by that country by popular elections. *See* Art. 137 *et seq.*, ROME TREATY, 298 U.N.T.S. 11.

EUROPEAN PAYMENTS UNION: multilateral clearinghouse system for financial settlement and a lending mechanism under the auspices of the Bank of International Settlements. *See* 14 Whiteman, Digest of International Law 566 (1970).

EUROPEAN RESEARCH COORDINATING AGENCY (EUREKA): 18 member organization designed to raise the productivity and competitiveness of European industries, through close cooperation among enterprises and research institutes in the area of civilian high-technology projects. *See* 25 I.L.M. 484,493.

EUROPEAN SOCIAL CHARTER: treaty promulgated by the Council of Europe outlining the rights of citizens and the social policy of the member states. *See* 529 U.N.T.S. 89.

EUROPEAN SPACE AGENCY (ESA): organization to create a long-term European space policy and carry out space-related activities including earth observation, communications, and scientific research. *See* 14 I.L.M. 855.

EUROPEAN SPACE RESEARCH ORGANIZATION: predecessor to the EUROPEAN SPACE AGENCY (q.v.); this organization coordinated the efforts of its member states in research in outer space. *See* 4 I.L.M. 306. See also EUROPEAN LAUNCHER DEVELOPMENT ORGANIZATION.

EUROPEAN TELECOMMUNICATIONS SATELLITE AGREEMENT (EUTELSAT): arrangement to operate the space segment of a European satellite telecommunications network. See 11 Annals of Air and Space Law 416 (1986).

EUROPEAN UNION: effort to transform the EUROPEAN COMMUNITY (q.v.) into a complete integrated political and economic unit. The current agreement being pursued is the SINGLE EUROPEAN ACT (q.v.)

EUTELSAT: EUROPEAN TELECOMMUNICATIONS SATELLITE AGREEMENT (q.v.).

EVACUATION: movement of persons, in particular prisoners of war, from areas of danger. In the case of prisoners of war, it is mandated by Arts. 19 and 20 of the GENEVA CONVENTION III (1949) (q.v.).

EVIDENCE: diplomatic agents cannot be compelled to testify in the courts of the host country, but may waive this right. See 4 Moore, Digest of International Law 644-45.

EVIDENCE CONVENTION: *see* HAGUE CONVENTION ON THE TAKING OF EVIDENCE ABROAD.

EX ABUNDANTE CAUTELA (L): by more abundant means.

EX ADVERSO (L): on the other hand; the contrary argument.

EX AEQUO ET BONO (L): equity principle in international law, deciding on the basis of justice and fairness rather than following the letter of the law. *See* STATUTE OF THE INTERNATIONAL COURT OF JUSTICE, Art. 38.

EX ARBITRIO JUDICIS (L): the discretion of a judge.

EX CONTRACTU (L): by reason of an agreement.

EX DELICTO ACTIO NON ORITUR (L): out of malfeasance no action arises.

EX FACTO JUS ORITUR (L): from the facts or actions the law arises. Principle holding that a rule of law remains in the theoretical abstract state until an act is done which the law can attach giving it body or shape.

EX GRATIA (L): payment of money damages without acknowledging fault or a legal obligation to pay. *See* 4 I.L.R. 376-77.

EX INJURIA JUS NON ORITUR (L): from the wrong or injury a right does not arise; legal maxim that normally a wrongful act cannot produce results beneficial to the wrongdoer. *See* 4 I.L.R. 281.

EX INJURIA JUS ORITUR (L): from a wrong or injury a right arises.

EX MAJORE CAUTELA (L): by more cautious means.

EX POST FACTO LAW: any law which creates and punishes as a criminal offense; an act which when committed was not a criminal offense; a law made after the fact.

EX PROPRIO MOTU (L): of his own accord. An act done spontaneously and not in response to a request.

EX QUAY: INCOTERM (q.v.); sales contract terms; seller delivers the goods to the buyer at the buyer's port.

EX SHIP : INCOTERM (q.v.); sales contract terms; seller makes the goods available on a ship in the buyer's port.

EX VI AUT METU (L): by fear or intimidation.

EX VI TERMINI (L): according to the meaning of the words.

EX WORKS: INCOTERM (q.v.); buyer takes goods to be delivered at the seller's place of manufacture.

EXCELLENCY: title of address used especially for ambassadors and ministers as in, "Good evening, Your Excellency."

EXCEPTIO EST STRICTISSIMAE APPLICATIONIS (L): an exception is of the strictest application, i.e., an exception made in a law should be narrowly construed. *See* 19 I.L.R. 481.

EXCEPTIO REI JUDICATAE (L): plea that a case should be dismissed because of a previous judicial decision settling the matter as between the parties.

EXCEPTION D'INCOMPETENCE (F): a challenge to the court's competence to decide a dispute. *See* 81 I.L.R. 468 and COMPETENCE DE LA COMPETENCE.

EXCES DE POUVOIR (F): beyond the powers of a tribunal.

EXCHANGE RATES: value of one currency in terms of another currency, e.g., one dollar will buy 1500 Lira. *See* FLOATING RATES and CRAWLING PEGS.

EXCHANGE OF NOTES: record of routine agreements between sovereign powers. *See* 6 I.L.R. 249-50.

EXCLUSION ZONE: zone declared by a belligerent in which all ships and/or aircraft entering the zone will be treated as hostile and liable to be fired upon and captured.

EXCLUSIVE ECONOMIC ZONE: coastal state's adjacent maritime area, usually 200 nautical miles in breadth, over which the state claims exclusive right to the economic resources, with powers relating to pollution control and freedom of passage and overflight. *See* the LAW OF THE SEA CONVENTION.

EXECUTION OF FOREIGN ARBITRAL AWARDS CONVENTION (1927): See GENEVA CONVENTION ON THE EXECUTION OF FOREIGN ARBITRAL AWARDS.

EXECUTIVE AGREEMENT: peculiarly American institution consisting of a binding international obligation entered into by the executive branch, made either on the basis of prior congressional authorization or within the powers vested in the Presidency. Unlike a treaty an executive agreement does not require Senate ratification. *See* 20 I.L.R. 412-17.

EXECUTIVE CERTIFICATE: document issued by the executive of a government certifying to a court that a particular person has diplomatic status. *See* 6 Halsbury's Statutes of England 1015, 1032 (3rd ed.).

EXECUTIVE DECREE: law made by declaration of the chief executive of a country, either under authorization of the state's constitution, or pursuant to a state of MARTIAL LAW. *See* 11 I.L.R. 17.

EXECUTIVE STATEMENT: communications by the executive branch of government (e.g., the President, Secretary of State) are relied upon because they indicate the policy that will be followed. *See e.g.*, 9 I.L.M. 1125.

EXEQUATUR: formal admission of a foreign consul by a head of state. *See* Satow, *A Guide to Diplomatic Practice* 406 (1957).

EXHAUSTION OF LOCAL REMEDIES: as a general rule, a person must seek to remedy a wrong in a foreign country under that country's legal system before his home state may pursue his claim in international forums. *See* 9 I.L.R. 314.

EXHIBITIONS: states holding or participating in international exhibitions are governed in part by the international convention relating to international exhibitions, 19 U.S.T. 5927, 111 L.N.T.S. 343.

EXILE GOVERNMENT: sovereign power banished from its territory by belligerent occupation, but continuing to act as the *de jure* government of the territory. *See* 19 I.L.R. 72-85.

EX-IM BANK: *see* EXPORT-IMPORT BANK.

EXPATRIATION: deprivation by a state of the rights of citizenship *vis-a-vis* certain groups or classes of its citizens. Although such citizens lose their rights under municipal law, they remain nationals of their home state for purposes of international law. *See e.g.*, 8 Am.J.Int.L. 665.

EXPERTS: skilled or learned person employed by the United Nations for a special mission and enjoying immunity while on that mission. *See* 1 U.N.T.S. 15, 26-28 (sec. 22 & 23).

EXPIRATION OF TREATIES: the termination of the obligations of the parties to a treaty due to the passage of time as specified in the treaty. *See also* LAPSED TREATY.

EXPORT ADMINISTRATION REGULATIONS: United States export licensing regulations. *See* 15 C.F.R. Sec. 768 *et seq.* and 24 Int'l.Lawyer 536.

EXPORT-IMPORT BANK: government subsidized bank to promote foreign trade by financing transactions. For the United States version, *see* 12 U.S.C. sec. 635 *et seq.* (1982).

EXPORT LICENSE: permit to sell goods abroad required by governments either to try to control their economics or to prevent the sale of arms or high tech goods to unfriendly states. *See* ISRAELI-SOVIET OIL ARBITRATION (1958).

EXPOSE DE MOTIFS (F): written explanation of the reason behind a certain course of conduct; a memorandum.

EXPRESSIO UNIUS NON EST EXCLUSIO ALTERIUS (L): expression of one thing implies the intention to exclude another. The fact that a statute or treaty specifies certain terms gives rise to the inference of an intention to exclude all others from its operation. *See* 18 I.L.R. 423-26.

EXPROPRIATION: either the taking of property by a state or its agent or the permanent transfer of the power of management or control in exchange for adequate and prompt compensation. *See* SABBATINO CASE (1960).

EXPULSION: action by a state ordering a foreigner (alien) to leave the country, and thereby terminating his legal right to enter and reside in the country. *See* 33 I.L.R. 255-96.

EXQ: EX QUAY (q.v.).

EXS: EX SHIP (q.v.).

EXTENSIVE INTERPRETATION: liberal or broad interpretation.

EXTERIOR COASTLINE: imprecise term for a line drawn along the coast of a country ignoring indentations. *See* TERRITORIAL WATERS.

EXTERMINATION OF PEOPLES: CRIME AGAINST HUMANITY (q.v.) punishable under international law. *See* GENOCIDE.

EXTERNAL DEBT CRISES: problem of massive amounts of debts in the Third World which the debtor nations are unable to pay. The possibility of default keep the creditors at bay. *See* 4 I.A.L.M. 846.

EXTINCTION OF CLAIMS: loss of the right to pursue a claim through the lapse of time.

EXTINCTIVE PRESCRIPTION: loss of a right through the lapse of time.

EXTORTION: holding or threatening persons to extract money. Subject of an Organization of American States Convention. *See* 65 Am.J.Int.L. 898 (proceedings).

EXTRA JUS (L): beyond the jurisdiction of.

EXTRA LEGUM (L): outside the protection afforded by law.

EXTRA TERRITORIUM (L): beyond the territorial boundaries.

EXTRADITION: process by which one state requests and obtains from another state the surrender of a suspected or convicted criminal who has fled from the requesting state. *See* ATTENTAT CLAUSE, DELICTS COMPLEX, and POLITICAL OFFENSE EXCEPTION.

EXTRADITION TREATY: agreement between countries on the rules governing the EXTRADITION (q.v.) of suspected or convicted criminals from one of the countries to the other. *See e.g.,* 28 U.S.T. 227 (United Kingdom and the United States).

EXTRATERRITORIAL CRIMES: act committed by a national in foreign territory which violates the criminal code of the national's home state and subjects the national to the home state's criminal jurisdiction.

EXTRATERRITORIAL JURISDICTION: exercise of authority over activities or persons outside the boundaries of the territory in which the acting body sits. *See e.g.*, 18 U.S.C. sec. 7, giving United States federal courts jurisdiction over crimes committed on United States space vehicles while in outer space, and the LO-TUS CASE (U.K. v. Turkey).

EXTRATERRITORIAL LEGISLATION: laws passed by legislative bodies purporting to have force and effect outside the boundaries of the territory in which the legislature sits. *See* 3 I.L.R. 136-48.

EXTRATERRITORIAL PROPERTY: property owned by the national of one country, but situated in another country, and thus questions of the choice of laws to apply to the property may arise.

EXTRATERRITORIALITY: 1) operation of laws upon persons or rights existing beyond the territorial limits of the state enacting such laws; 2) removal of diplomatic premises from the control of the state in which they are situated. *See* 1 I.L.R. 118-19 and 290-91.

EXW: EX WORKS (q.v.).

FAC: FREE CARRIER (q.v.).

FACT FINDING: process used by a tribunal to determine the facts (who did what) as opposed to the determination of the law applicable to the situation. Fact finding is sometimes separated from adjudication, e.g., by the appointment of a fact finding mission. *See* UNGA Res. 1967 (XVIII), Dec. 16, 1963.

FACT FINDING COMMISSION: generally, a group appointed to establish a record of facts in a case, but not to decide legal issues. Specifically, under the Geneva Conventions (1949) a group of 15 persons to inquire into the facts of an alleged serious breach of the GENEVA CONVENTIONS (1949) (q.v.). *See* Art. 90 to the GENEVA CONVENTIONS PROTOCOL I (1977).

FACTORING: contracts involving the sale or collection of accounts receivable. Factoring is the subject of a UNIDROIT (q.v.) sponsored convention, 27 I.L.M. 943.

FACULTY OF LAW: on occasion, the professors at a law school have been asked to render an opinion on questions of international law. *See e.g.,* 4 I.L.R. 33.

FAIT ACCOMPLI (F): established fact; formerly a method of establishing possession of territory, though the territory was claimed by another, by occupation with such presence that the claim could only be pursued by use of force, "a treacherous usurpation."

FAIT DU PRINCE (F): ACT OF STATE (q.v.).

FALKE AFFAIR (1924): German steamship *Falke* attempted to aid a COUP D'ETAT (q.v.) in Venezuela but failed. *See* 6 I.L.R. 31-32.

FALKLANDS ISLANDS CRISIS (1982): *see* ANGLO-ARGENTINE WAR.

FALSA DEMONSTRATIO NON NOCET (L): a false description does not vitiate. Maxim that an inaccuracy in the description of a beneficiary will not effect the bequest.

FALSE IMPRISONMENT: when aliens are detained by immigration officials and not allowed to proceed to another country; they may have a cause of action for false imprisonment. *See* 26 I.L.R. 466-74.

FAMILY OF NATIONS: obsolete term for the states in the world recognized as having rights and duties under international law. *See* 1 L. Oppenheim, *International Law* 234-37 (1948).

FAMILY RECORD: international effort to standardize the civil status information records of families is found at 23 European Yearbook 546.

FAO: *see* FOOD AND AGRICULTURE ORGANIZATION.

FAS: free alongside, price of goods including delivery to the quay from which they will be shipped; an INCOTERM (q.v.).

FASHODA INCIDENT (1894): attempt by the French to occupy the Sudan and repulsed by the British.

FATHOM: unit of measure equaling six feet used for measuring the depth of water.

FAUCES TERRAE (L): arm of the sea narrow enough for a man to see across from headland to headland.

FAUNA AND FLORA PROTECTION CONVENTION (1933): encourages the establishment of national parks, particularly in Africa. *See* 172 L.N.T.S. 241. *See also* TRADE IN ENDANGERED SPECIES OF WILD FLORA AND FAUNA CONVENTION (1973).

FAVOR NEGOTII (L): in favor of the agreement; an agreement should be interpreted in a way that makes it valid rather than adopting an interpretation that would make it invalid.

FAVOR TESTAMENTI (L): in favor of the maker of a will. In interpreting a will the interpretation that makes it valid should be preferred over one that would invalidate it.

FCN: FRIENDSHIP, COMMERCE AND NAVIGATION TREATIES (q.v.).

FEDERAL UNION GOVERNMENT OF AFRICA: dream of Kwame Nkrumah, the first President of Ghana, for a union of all African states under one government. It was also called the Federal African Union.

FEDERATION (or federal state): system of government where authority over domestic affairs is divided between a federal government and member states of the federation. The United States is a federation. *See* 10 I.L.R. 48-70.

FERNANDO POO: formerly a colony of Spain, now part of Equitorial Guinea.

FEZ DECLARATION (1982): principles for achieving peace in the Middle East according to the summit of 12 heads of Arab states. *See* 21 I.L.M. 1144.

FIAT EXECUTIO DECREE: court order to pay a judgment. *See* 11 I.L.R. 221.

FIFTH COMMITTEE OF THE UNITED NATIONS: one of the six Main Committees of the UN General Assembly which prepares items for the attention of the plenary meetings of the Assembly, the Fifth Committee is charged with administrative and budgetary matters.

FIN DE NOM RECEVOIR (F): an evasive reply, a complaint or accusation is thus rejected without examination of its merits.

FINAL ACT: document that sums up the work of an international meeting often including a treaty or other agreement or principles that the meeting has drafted.

FINAL ARTICLES: provision usually placed at the end of a convention such as the procedure for RATIFICATION (q.v.) and amendment of the convention. *See e.g.*, Art. 81 *et seq.* of the VIENNA CONVENTION ON THE LAW OF TREATIES (1969).

FINAL PROTOCOL: observations, declarations, and agreements attached to an international agreement elucidating the text. *See e.g.,* the Final Protocol to the SALT AGREEMENT I.

FINANCIAL LEASING: international lease financing contracts are the subject of a UNIDROIT (q.v.) sponsored convention, 27 I.L.M. 931.

FINLANDIZATION: from the position of Finland *vis-a-vis* the Soviet Union, the domination of a small country by a superpower without a physical presence in the country.

FIRST ASYLUM PRINCIPLE: a country does not have to grant ASYLUM (q.v.) to a refugee who has found asylum elsewhere, or who has spent a long period in transit to the country where the application for asylum is made.

FIRST COMMITTEE OF THE UNITED NATIONS: one of the six main committees of the U.N. General Assembly which prepare items for the attention of the plenary meetings of the Assembly. It is charged with political and security matters including the regulation of armaments and shares this work with the SPECIAL POLITICAL COMMITTEE (q.v.).

FIRST SECRETARY: the highest ranking diplomatic secretary of a legation or embassy.

FIRST WORLD: industrial nations enjoying a high standard of living. *See* GROUP OF TEN.

FISHERIES: fishing grounds where the industry of catching fish is practiced. *See e.g.,* EUROPEAN FISHERIES CONVENTION and ANGLO-NORWEGIAN FISHERIES CASE.

FISHERIES JURISDICTION CASE (*Federal Republic of Germany v. Iceland and U.K. v. Iceland*): International Court of Justice decided that Iceland could not unilaterally declare an exclusive fifty-mile fishing zone after it had previously negotiated a 12-mile zone with Germany and the United Kingdom. *See* 1974 I.C.J. 3, 175.

FISHERMEN'S ACCOMMODATIONS CONVENTION (1966): INTERNATIONAL LABOR ORGANIZATION (q.v.) convention providing for adequate living accommodations aboard fishing vessels. *See* 649 U.N.T.S. 229.

FISHERMEN'S COMPETENCY CERTIFICATES: INTERNATIONAL LABOR ORGANIZATION (q.v.) system for licensing shippers, mates, and engineers on fishing vessels. *See* 684 U.N.T.S. 81.

FISHING AND CONSERVATION OF SEA RESOURCES: maintenance of the productivity of the living resources of the sea. *See* Art. 7 of the Convention on Fishing and Conservation of the Living Resources of the High Seas , 17 U.S.T. 138, T.I.A.S. 5969, 559 U.N.T.S. 285.

FISHING VESSELS: boats or ships that are employed in the catching and bringing to shore of fish or other seafood products. Fishing vessels are traditionally exempt from capture as prize of war. *See* PACQUETE HABANA.

FIVE FREEDOMS: *see* FREEDOMS OF AERIAL NAVIGATION.

FLAG: a cloth banner or ensign. In admiralty a flag is displayed by a vessel to establish its NATIONALITY or REGISTRY (qq.v.). Flags are displayed as symbols of countries represented at an international event. *See* Satow, *A Guide to Diplomatic Practice* 46 (1957) and 55 Am.J.Int.L. 264.

FLAG OF CONVENIENCE: registry of commercial ships in nations (also, flying the flags of these nations) that provide legal advantages to the shipowner such as lax safety standards or low taxes. *See* 2 D. O'Connell, *The International Law of the Sea* 757-61 (1984).

FLAG OF TRUCE: white flag carried by an authorized agent of a belligerent in order to communicate with the enemy. The bearer of a truce flag is inviolable unless he abuses his protected status. *See* 10 Whiteman, *Digest of International Law* 509 and 205 C.T.S. 277 (in French).

FLAG STATE: state under whose flag a ship can lawfully sail. *See* FLAG OF CONVENIENCE, ABUSE OF A MARITIME FLAG, and BARCELONA DECLARATION (1921)..

FLAGRANTE BELLO (L): in time of warfare.

FLCS: Somali-backed group which fought for the independence of Djibouti, a rival of the MLD (q.v.).

FLOATING EXCHANGE RATE: by eliminating the fixed gold value for various currencies (especially the United States dollar) exchange rates in 1971 became essentially the rates set by the market - currencies floated or sank. *See* A. Lowenfeld, *The International Monetary System* sec. 8.2 (1977).

FLORA AND FAUNA: *see* FAUNA AND FLORA PROTECTION CONVENTION (1937).

F.O.B.: free onboard; price for goods which includes loading onto a ship; an INCOTERM (q.v.).

FOEDERA (L): treaty; class of treaties in Roman law where one party became subservient to the other, and the parties were tightly allied.

FOGGY BOTTOM: nickname for the United States State Department which is located in a foggy, low-lying area in Washington, D.C.

FOOD AND AGRICULTURE ORGANIZATION (FAO): United Nations specialized agency for the purpose of combatting world hunger and the promotion of agriculture. It performs research and provides information on food, nutrition, agriculture, and conservation of the world's natural resources. *See* 60 Stat. 1886, 3 Bevans 1288.

F.O.R.: INCOTERM (q.v.); same terms as F.O.B. (q.v.), except rail transport is used rather than a ship.

FORCE: aggressive policy involving coercion through acts or threats of action by economic, military or political means against the political independence or territorial integrity of a state. *See* Art. 2(4) of the United Nations Charter , 59 Stat. 1031, 3 Bevans 1153 (1945).

FORCE MAJEURE: acts of God; events generally uncontrollable by man either as storms, hurricanes, or other natural disasters. *See* 27 I.L.R. 631-37.

FORCED LABOR: *see* ABOLITION OF FORCED LABOR CONVENTION (1957).

FORCED LANDING: landing caused by peril or misfortune, affecting civilian or military persons on a vessel or aircraft, *See* SHIPWRECKED. A plane may be required (under threat) to land if it has violated the sovereign airspace of a state. *See* Art. 9 of the CHICAGO CONVENTION (1944), 61 Stat. 1180.

FORCLUSION (F): the loss of a right because it has not been used in a timely fashion or has been expressly or tacitly abandoned. *See* 80 I.L.R. 556.

FOREIGN CORRUPT PRACTICES ACT: United States law against bribery of foreign officials, paying kickbacks, etc. *See* 15 U.S.C. sec. 78 et seq.

FOREIGN ENLISTMENT ACT: statute which forbids the service by the nationals of a country in the military forces of another country. Such laws are designed to ensure the neutrality of the enacting country. *See* 3 Stat. 447, or the Foreign Enlistment Act of 1870 , 33 & 34 Vict. ch. 90.

FOREIGN LEGAL CONSULTANTS: lawyers from foreign countries who aid in the preparation of cases involving their country. *See* 80 Am.J.Int.L. 197.

FOREIGN MINISTER: cabinet member in a parliamentary system of government designated as the principal person conducting the state's international affairs.

FOREIGN OFFICE CERTIFICATE: document transmitted to a court evidencing a fact as recognized by a foreign office, such as the recognition of government as legitimate or that a particular state is considered to be a party to a treaty by the government.

FOREIGN OFFICE LIST: English method of establishing the diplomatic status of a foreign representative. The list may be consulted by the courts to determine if a defendant has diplomatic immunity.

FOREIGN POLICY: guiding principles under which a state conducts its relations with other countries. *See e.g.*, MONROE DOCTRINE, BREZHNEV DOCTRINE, or REAGAN DOCTRINE.

FOREIGN PROPERTY: *see* PROTECTION OF FOREIGN PROPERTY CONVENTION.

FOREIGN SECRETARY: state's principal spokesman in international affairs.

FOREIGN SOVEREIGN IMMUNITY: *see* SOVEREIGN IMMUNITY.

FORMAL SOURCES OF INTERNATIONAL LAW: listed in Art. 38 of the STATUTE OF THE INTERNATIONAL COURT OF JUSTICE (q.v.), they are: 1) TREATY; 2) CUSTOMARY INTERNATIONAL LAW; 3) GENERAL PRINCIPLES OF LAW RECOG-

NIZED BY CIVILIZED NATIONS; and 4) JUDICIAL DECISIONS AND WRITINGS OF PUBLICISTS (qq.v.).

FORUM CONNEXITATIS (L): rule allowing an English court to take jurisdiction over a party outside its territorial jurisdiction (if the party is a necessary party and jurisdiction is already had over another party). *See Massey v. Heynes*, 21 Q.B.D. 330, 338 (1888).

FORUM CONTRACTUS (L): court assuming jurisdiction over a dispute because it is in the place where the contract was signed. This formalistic rule is seldom used today.

FORUM LOCI CELEBRATIONIS (L): court of the place where the formal agreement was made; outdated rule which applied the law of the jurisdiction where the formal agreement took place despite its irrelevance to the transaction otherwise.

FORUM LOCI CONTRACTUS (L): court of the place of the contract; rule for applying the law of the jurisdiction in which the agreement was made or which was specified by the contract.

FORUM LOCI DELICTI (L): court of the place of the wrong; jurisdiction based on the physical location in which the injury or wrongful act occurred.

FORUM LOCI SOLUTIONIS (L): court of the place where the contract ought to have been performed.

FORUM PATRIMONIS (L): court of the place of the property; taking jurisdiction on the basis of the defendant holding property within the jurisdiction of the court despite the defendants absence from the forum.

FORUM PROROGATUM (L): where there is no formally expressed consent to a court's jurisdiction and the parties acquiesce,pleading the merits of the case, such action constitutes forum prorogatum, the equivalent of a COMPROMISE (q.v.).

FORUM SITUS (L): court of the place; rule that the court with jurisdiction over the place where real property is located has jurisdiction over questions that arise concerning that real property despite the absence of the owner.

F.O.T.: free on truck; INCOTERM (q.v.); same terms as F.O.B., except truck transport is used instead of a ship.

FOUL BILL OF LADING: BILL OF LADING (q.v.) which contains a note that the condition of the goods loaded could not be termed "good" or "in order." This causes it to be "foul" rather than "clean."

FOUR CORNERS DOCTRINE: interpretation of a document should be based on the entirety of the document and not just a small portion thereof. One should not read only one article of a treaty without consulting the whole document for its context.

FOUR FREEDOMS: 1) coined by President Roosevelt in a speech to congress in 1941, "We look forward to a world founded on four essential human freedoms . . . freedom of speech and of expression, freedom of worship, freedom from want, and freedom from fear; each of them to be enjoyed everywhere in the world." 2) European Community term for the free movement of goods, persons, services, and capital within the community as mandated by Art. 3 of the ROME TREATY (1957) (q.v.).

FOUR-POWER TREATY (1921): after World War I, this agreement between the United States, Great Britain, France, and Japan confirmed the status quo in the Pacific. *See 16* Am.J.Int.L. 193.

FOURTEEN POINTS: United States President Woodrow Wilson's proposal for the settlement of issues confronting Europe after World War I, including dividing up the Austro-Hungarian Empire, restoration of Belgium, and reestablishing an independent Poland. *See 13* Am.J.Int.L. 161.

FOURTH COMMITTEE OF THE UNITED NATION GEN-ERAL ASSEMBLY: one of the six main committees of the U.N. General Assembly which prepares items for the plenary meetings of the Assembly, the Fourth Committee is charged with DECOLO-NIZATION (q.v.).

FOURTH WORLD: see LEAST DEVELOPED COUNTRIES.

FRANCHISE DE L'HOTEL (F): privilege of diplomatic envoys which is essentially an immunity of their domicile from intrusion by the host state. The concept developed when official diplomatic residences were considered completely outside the territory of the host state.

FRANCHISE DU QUARTIER (F): also called jus quarteriorum, the extraterritoriality of diplomatic residences (*see* FRANCHISE DE L'HOTEL) which were often located in a particular quarter of the town which led to the designation of a diplomatic area having an extraterritorial character. This concept became outmoded in the 18th century.

FRANCS TIREURS (F): war traitor.

FRAUS LEGI FACTA (L): in contravention of the law; attempt of parties to circumvent the law, e.g., by making the contract in a country where its purpose is legal though the transaction is actually occurring in a place where it would not be allowed.

FRAUS OMNIA CORRUMPIT (L): fraud corrupts all; a statute or judgment should not be used for a fraudulent purpose.

FRAUS MERETUR FRAUDEM (L): one fraud leads to another.

FREE ALONG SIDE: *see* F.A.S.

FREE CARRIER: INCOTERM (q.v.); buyer takes delivery of goods at a specific point and provides transport.

FREE ON BOARD: *see* F.O.B.

FREE ON RAIL: *see* F.O.R.

FREE ON TRUCK: *see* F.O.T.

FREE CITIES: medieval concept of an independent city-state which was resurrected in the aftermath of World War I in an attempt to solve boundary disputes due to nationalism, the traditional heritage, strategic, or economic importance of a city. Examples include DANZIG and TRIESTE (qq.v.).

FREE PASSAGE WARRANT: document usually issued to diplomatic personnel relieving them of customs controls at a foreign border and requesting the assistance of customs officers to speed their transit.

FREE PORT: transport terminal and surrounding area where goods may be processed without clearing customs.

FREE TRADE: right to engage in commercial activity in a country or between countries. The term now implies a lack of trade barriers such as duties or quotas. *See* OSCAR CHINN CASE.

FREE TRADE AREA: zone established by a country or countries where customs duties are not levied.

FREE ZONE: *see* TERRITET AWARD.

FREEDOM OF AERIAL NAVIGATION: though the PARIS CONVENTION (1919) provided for a limited right to freedom of aerial navigation, the CHICAGO CONVENTION (1944) completely abrogated any freedom of aerial navigation by affirming the sovereignty of states over their airspace and providing for limited international regulation of flight over the high seas. Some form of permission is required to fly almost anywhere.

FREEDOM OF ASSOCIATION: subject of an INTERNA-
TIONAL LABOR ORGANIZATION (q.v.) sponsored convention
to protect trade union rights. *See* 68 U.N.T.S. 17.

FREEDOM OF INFORMATION: right to the exchange of infor-
mation and opinion without governmental interference. *See*
UNITED NATIONS CONFERENCE ON FREEDOM OF INFOR-
MATION (1948) and the NEW INTERNATIONAL INFORMA-
TION ORDER.

FREEDOM OF NAVIGATION: FREEDOM OF THE HIGH
SEAS plus the right to INNOCENT PASSAGE (qq.v.), the rather
expansive right of ships to sail about the earth. *See* 2 O'Connell,
The International Law of the Sea 792-830 (1984).

FREEDOM OF THE HIGH SEAS (or freedom of the open seas):
all ocean areas not part of some state's territorial or internal waters, may be freely used by the vessels of all nations for navigation. Generally, vessels on the high seas are bound only by
international law and the law of the flag state.

FREEDOM OF TRANSIT: right to move across the territory of
another, but may be distinguished from the right of transport or
the right to carry cargo or passengers for a fee across another's territory.

FREEDOMS OF AERIAL NAVIGATION: rights granted by
states to the air carriers of other states. The first and second freedoms are the right to pass through territorial airspace and to
make landings for technical purposes, e.g., to refuel. The other
"freedoms" are grants of various rights to pick up and discharge
passengers and cargo. *See* INTERNATIONAL AIR SERVICE
TRANSIT AGREEMENT (1945), and the INTERNATIONAL AIR
SERVICE TRANSPORT AGREEMENT (1945).

FREIBEWEISVERFAHREN (G): rule of evidence in Germinal
civil procedure allowing the court broad power to gather evi-

dence about collateral issues such as facts necessary as procedural perquisites. *See* 80 I.L.R. 412.

FREIGHT FORWARDER'S CONVENTION: agreement being drafted by the United Nations Commission on International Trade Law to establish uniform rules for the liability of freight forwarders (agents who facilitate the transhipment of cargos). *See* 1984 Revue de Droit Uniforme 160.

FREIGHT IN PRIZE: award of compensation to the carrier of cargo which is condemned as PRIZE (q.v.). *See* 11 Whiteman, *Digest of International Law* 131.

FREMILO: national liberation movement in Mozambique which fought the Portuguese colonial administration and eventually took over the government of the country. *See* Amato, *Inside the OAU* 275-7 (1986).

FRENCH COMMUNITY (or French Union): established in 1959, it resembles a confederation consisting of the French Republic, overseas departments, overseas territories, and autonomous member states which all adhere to a common policy set forth by the President of the French Republic in matters of foreign policy, defense, and economic affairs.

FRENCH COMPANY OF VENEZUELA RAILROAD CASE: dispute between a French company which built a railroad in Venezuela and the Venezuelan government. The former claiming that the latter caused its financial ruin. The arbitrators found in favor of Venezuela. *See* 10 R.I.A.A. 285.

FRENCH EQUITORIAL AFRICA: former autonomous member of the FRENCH COMMUNITY (q.v.) which became four independent sovereign states in 1960, i.e., Central African Republic, Chad, Congo, and Gabon.

FRENCH NUCLEAR TESTING: *see* NUCLEAR TEST CASE.

FRENCH UNION: *see* FRENCH COMMUNITY.

FRIENDLY RELATIONS DECLARATION: UNGA Res. 2625 (XXV) declared that states should, *inter alia*, refrain from the use of force or threat of force, act in good faith, and cooperate. *See* 65 Am.J.Int.L. 243.

FRIENDSHIP, COMMERCE AND NAVIGATION TREATIES (FNC): a series of bilateral agreements to promote trade. *See e.g.,* 196 L.N.T.S. 303 and 24 Int'l.Lawyer 461.

FROLINAT: FRONT DE LIBERATION NATIONAL DU TCHAD (q.v.). FRONT DE LIBERATION NATIONAL DU TCHAD: guerrilla movement based in northern Chad and led by Hissene Habre which eventually won the CHADIAN CIVIL WAR (q.v.) and is currently in power.

FRONTIER DISPUTE (Burkina Faso v. Mali): International Court of Justice issued an order for provisional measures to be taken in the border dispute between the parties, including withdrawal of troops and the temporary use of the boundary determined by an Organization of African Unity Mediation Commission. *See* 25 I.L.M. 147.

FRONTIERS: boundaries which separate a nation's territory from that of its neighbors. The boundaries can be in diverse form such as water, a mountain range, desert, or most usually an artificial line.

FRONTLINE STATES: nations bordering South Africa (and Rhodesia before it became Zimbabwe) and given special responsibility for fighting APARTHEID (q.v.).

FUGITIVE OFFENDER: criminal who flees the territory in which the criminal act was committed in order to avoid trial, prosecution, or imprisonment. *See* 6 Whiteman, *Digest of International Law* 808, or sec. 26 of the British Extradition Act of 1870 , 17 Halsbury's Statutes (4th ed.) 475.

FULL POWERS: document that provides evidence of the authority that diplomats involved in treaty negotiations have customarily been required to show before signing the treaty. *See* Art. 2 of the VIENNA CONVENTION ON THE LAW OF TREATIES, 8 I.L.M. 679.

FUNCTIONAL IMMUNITY: immunity extending to all acts relating to the particular function of the person holding the immunity, e.g., a Congressman's statements on the floor of Congress are immune no matter what the content of the statement.

FUNCTIONAL PROTECTION: rights similar to those of diplomats extended to the staff members of international organizations which may be enforced by those organizations. *See* DIPLOMATIC IMMUNITY.

FUNCTIONAL THEORY OF INTERNATIONAL LAW: theory that relates the development of principles of international law to the "social needs" of the international community. *See* Friedmann, *The Changing Structure of International Law* 175-77 (1964).

FUNDAMENTAL RIGHTS AND DUTIES OF STATES: important rights and duties of a state which are subject to international law such as independence, sovereignty, self-defense, and the duty to carry out its international obligations. *See* 1947-48 U.N. Yearbook 215.

[G - H]

G 5: *See* GROUP OF FIVE.

G 7: *See* GROUP OF SEVEN.

G 10: *See* GROUP OF TEN.

G 18: *See* GROUP OF EIGHTEEN.

G 20: *See* GROUP OF TWENTY.

G 24: *See* GROUP OF TWENTY-FOUR.

G 77: *See* GROUP OF SEVENTY-SEVEN.

GABELLA EMIGRATIONIS (L): emigration tax; under international law, aliens leaving a country should be treated the same as the country's nationals in respect to a tax or fee to leave the country or a tax on personal property the emigrant is taking along. *See* Convention on the Status of Aliens, 22 Am.J.Int.L. Supp. 136 (1928).

GAOR: GENERAL ASSEMBLY OFFICIAL RECORD (q.v.).

GARNISHEE PROCEEDINGS: attachment of property (particularly a salary) by a court to satisfy a judgment. Many international organizations including the United Nations are immune by treaty from judicial process unless they consent. For proceedings against individuals employed by international organizations, *See* In Re Poncet, 15 I.L.R. 346.

GASTARBEITER (G): quest worker; foreign laborers. *See* PROTECTION OF THE RIGHTS OF MIGRANT WORKERS AND THEIR FAMILIES CONVENTION (1979).

G.A.T.T.: GENERAL AGREEMENT ON TARIFFS AND TRADE (q.v.).

GATT - 12: dispute between the United States and Japan over 12 agricultural import quotas. *See* 27 I.L.M. 1539.

GAZA STRIP: area along Israel's southwest border and the Mediterranean Sea controlled by Israel, but of uncertain legal status. The population of Gaza is substantially Palestinian, and a source of security problems for Israel. *See* CAMP DAVID AGREEMENTS.

GENERAL ACT FOR PACIFIC SETTLEMENT OF INTERNATIONAL DISPUTES (1928): convention adopted by the League of Nations to compel the referral of all legal disputes to the International Court or to arbitration. *See* 25 Am.J.Int.L. Supp. 204.

GENERAL ACT FOR THE REPRESSION OF AFRICAN SLAVE TRADE (1890): treaty which sought, *inter alia*, to prevent the transportation of slaves on vessels owned by the signatory powers and to free any slaves taking refuge on a ship bearing the flag of the signatories. *See* 27 Stat. 886 (1890). The Act was abrogated by a convention for its revision signed at Saint-Germain-en-Laye on Sept 10, 1919. *See* 8 L.N.T.S. 11.

GENERAL ACT OF BRUSSELS (1890): *see* GENERAL ACT FOR THE REPRESSION OF AFRICAN SLAVE TRADE (1890).

GENERAL ACT OF GENEVA (1928): *see* GENERAL ACT FOR PACIFIC SETTLEMENT OF DISPUTES (1928).

GENERAL ACT OF THE BERLIN CONFERENCE (1885): provided that navigation of the Congo and Niger rivers was to be free to merchant ships of all nations. *See* 165 C.T.S. 485, 3 Am.J.Int.L. Supp. 7. The Act was abrogated by a convention for its revision signed at Saint-Germain-en-Laye on Sept. 10, 1919, 8 L.N.T.S. 25.

GENERAL AGREEMENT ON TARIFFS AND TRADE (GATT) (1947): provides for an organization of committees to work to reduce tariffs and other trade barriers, to raise standards of living, and to ensure full employment. The GATT is affixed to the final act of the United Nations Conference on Trade and Employment, it was not signed as a separate document. The text of the original agreement is found at 61 Stat. parts 5 and 6, T.I.A.S. 1700, 4 Bevans 639. It has been updated several times. *See* KENNEDY ROUND, TOKYO ROUND, NIXON ROUND, and URUGUAY ROUND.

GENERAL AND COMPLETE DISARMAMENT RESOLUTION (UNGA Res. 31/189): called for member states to respect NUCLEAR FREE ZONES (q.v.), condemned the United States and Soviet Union for the arms race, and called for a special session of the United Nations General Assembly to discuss disarmament. *See* 16 I.L.M. 451.

GENERAL ARRANGEMENT TO BORROW: agreement by the GROUP OF TEN (q.v.) and Switzerland to preapproved terms and conditions for the lending of their currencies to the INTERNATIONAL MONETARY FUND (q.v.) for emergencies. *See* IMF Dec. No. 1289-(62/1) Jan. 5, 1962.

GENERAL ASSEMBLY (United Nations): one of the principal organs of the U.N. consisting of representatives of all the member states. Although it has no general legislative power, the Assembly can act with legal effect when competent under the UNITED NATIONS CHARTER (q.v.), especially in matters relating to the overall operations of the U.N. The General Assembly initiates studies and makes recommendations in order to promote intertional cooperation in politics, economics, and various other fields.

GENERAL ASSEMBLY OFFICIAL RECORD: the formal published minutes of the proceedings of the United Nations General Assembly after they have been expurgated in an appropriate fashion.

GENERAL AVERAGE: equitable system which provides for contribution to be given by all interested parties when an accidental loss of ship, cargo, or freight arises as a result of an extraordinary sacrifice, reasonably and voluntarily incurred, in time of peril for the safety of the common adventure.

GENERAL COMMITTEE OF THE GENERAL ASSEMBLY (United Nations): composed of the president and vice-presidents of the Assembly and the chairmen of the main committees, this committee proposes the agenda for the General Assembly and the organization of its work.

GENERAL CONDITIONS FOR THE DELIVERY OF MERCHANDISE: standardized trade terms used by the COMECON (q.v.) countries. *See* Butler, *A Source Book of Socialist Organizations*, 925 (1978).

GENERAL LIST OF COURT: compilation of cases prepared and updated by the registrar, submitted to the International Court of Justice for decision or advisory opinion. Cases are entered on the General List when the registrar receives the document which institutes the proceedings. Art. 20 of the Rules of Court govern the maintenance of the General List.

GENERAL PARTICIPATION CLAUSE: provision in a multilateral treaty that the terms of the agreement shall be effective between all parties to the treaty and also between parties and non-parties who abide by the provisions of the treaty. *See e.g.*, Art. 2 (3) of the GENEVA CONVENTIONS (1949).

GENERAL PRINCIPLES OF LAW: legal doctrine intermediate between international and municipal law, i.e., principles common to various systems of municipal law such as the commonality of law against homicide. One of the sources of international law enshrined in Art. 38 of the STATUTE OF THE INTERNATIONAL COURT OF JUSTICE (q.v.).

GENERAL TERMS OF DELIVERY OF THE CMEA: unified substantive rules governing the sale of goods among CMEA (q.v.)

member states, adopted in 1968. *See* W. Butler, *A Sourcebook on Socialist International Organizations* 925 (1978).

GENERAL TREATY FOR THE RENUNCIATION OF WAR (1928): *see* KELLOGG-BRIAND PACT (1928).

GENERAL TRUCE: an agreement to discontinue military operations on all fronts or in all theaters of operation.

GENERALIS CLAUSULA NON PORRIGITUR AD EA QUAE ANTEA SPECIALITER SUNT COMPREHENSIA (L): a general clause does not include that which is specifically dealt with elsewhere.

GENERALIS SPECIALIBUS NON DEROGANT (L): general terms do not derogate from specific terms; maxim used when treaties are in conflict or are incompatible with one another. If the provisions of the earlier treaty are general and the provisions of a subsequent treaty are specific, this indicates that the parties intended the latter one to prevail.

GENET'S RECALL: recall of the French minister to the United States for outfitting PRIVATEERS (q.v.). *See* 4 Moore, *Digest of International Law* 489.

GENEVA CONFERENCE (1954): effort by the FOUR POWERS (q.v.) to settle the conflicts in Southeast Asia, especially Vietnam, it is important to the background of the VIETNAM WAR (q.v.). *See* XIII *Foreign Relations of the United States 1952-1954.*

GENEVA CONFERENCE ON PRIVATE INTERNATIONAL LAW: meeting of 32 nations under the auspices of the League of Nations to draft PRIVATE INTERNATIONAL LAW (q.v.) Conventions. *See* 44 Harv. L. Rev. 333 (1931).

GENEVA CONFERENCE ON THE LAW OF THE SEA (1958): conference of representatives of 86 nations who drafted the GENEVA CONVENTION ON THE REGIME OF THE HIGH SEAS

(1958) (q.v.) and the GENEVA CONVENTION ON THE TERRI-
TORIAL SEA AND CONTIGUOUS ZONE (q.v.).

GENEVA CONFERENCE ON THE LAW OF THE SEA (1960):
failed attempt by the representatives of 87 nations to resolve the
question of the breadth of the territorial sea and limitations on
fisheries. *See* 1960 U.N. Yearbook 542.

GENEVA CONVENTION (1864): Convention for the Amelioration of the Condition of Wounded Soldiers in Armies in the Field,
(also known as the Red Cross Convention)it was replaced by the
GENEVA CONVENTION I (1949) (q.v.). *See* 22 Stat. 940, 1
Bevans 7.

GENEVA CONVENTION I (1949): rules to ameliorate the conditions of sick and wounded members of the armed forces in the
field including the protection of medical personnel. *See* 6 U.S.T.
3114, 75 U.N.T.S. 31.

GENEVA CONVENTION II (1949): rules to ameliorate the conditions of sick, wounded, and shipwrecked members of the
armed forces at sea including those pilots of aircraft who end up
in the sea. *See* 6 U.S.T. 3217, 75 U.N.T.S. 85.

GENEVA CONVENTION III (1949): established a more complete set of rules for the treatment of prisoners of war. *See* 6
U.S.T. 3316, 75 U.N.T.S. 135.

GENEVA CONVENTION IV (1949): established rules for the
protection of civilian populations during time of war, a problem
that had become particularly evident with prosecution of World
War II as a "TOTAL WAR" (q.v.). *See* 6 U.S.T. 3516, 75 U.N.T.S.
287.

GENEVA CONVENTION ON ARBITRATION CLAUSES: established basic provisions for the inclusion of arbitration clauses
in international agreements. *See* 56 Harv. L. Rev. 219 (1942).

GENEVA CONVENTION ON BILLS OF EXCHANGE (1930): established uniform rules for the law of BILLS OF EXCHANGE (q.v.) among twenty-one European countries. *See* 44 Harv. L. Rev. 333, 370.

GENEVA CONVENTION ON CHEQUES (1931): a product of the GENEVA CONFERENCE ON PRIVATE INTERNATIONAL LAW (q.v.), it provided uniform rules regarding the law of cheques for twenty-one European countries. *See* 44 Harv. L. Rev. 333, 370.

GENEVA CONVENTION ON FISHING AND CONSERVA-TION OF THE LIVING OF SEA RESOURCES OF THE SEAS (1958): *See* FISHING AND CONSERVATION SEA RESOURCES. *See* 17 U.S.T. 138, 559 U.N.T.S. 285.

GENEVA CONVENTION ON TERRORISM (1937): defined terrorism as criminal acts against states designed to create a state of terror among certain groups or the general public, and provided for stronger municipal laws and extradition provisions. *See* 19 Brit.Y.B.Int'l.L. 214.

GENEVA CONVENTION ON THE CARRIAGE OF GOODS BY ROAD (C.M.R): agreement establishing uniform provisions for contracts for carriage of goods by road transport vehicles. *See* 399 U.N.T.S. 189.

GENEVA CONVENTION ON THE CONTINENTAL SHELF (1958): defined the CONTINENTAL SHELF (q.v.) and gave coastal states certain rights therein. *See* 15 U.S.T. 471, 499 U.N.T.S. 311.

GENEVA CONVENTION ON THE EXECUTION OF FOR-EIGN ARBITRAL AWARDS (1927): under certain conditions this convention made arbitral awards enforceable by the courts of the member states. *See* Russell, *Arbitration and Awards* (1931) 525 and 27 Am.J.Int.L. Supp. 1.

GENEVA CONVENTION ON THE HIGH SEAS (1958): law-making treaty declaring the high seas to be open to all nations and that freedom of the sea includes freedom of navigation, freedom to fish, freedom to lay submarine cables and pipelines, and freedom to fly over the high seas. *See* 13 U.S.T. 2312, 450 U.N.T.S. 82, 54 Am.J.Int.L. 751.

GENEVA CONVENTION ON THE TERRITORIAL SEA AND THE CONTIGUOUS ZONE (1958): provides, *inter alia*, that a coastal state may exercise control needed to prevent infringement of its customs, immigration, and sanitary regulations in a zone of the high seas contiguous to its territorial waters. The contiguous zone is limited to an area not more than 12 miles from the baseline from which the breadth of the territorial sea is measured. *See* 15 U.S.T. 1606, 516 U.N.T.S. 205.

GENEVA CONVENTION ON THE TERRITORIAL SEAS AND CONTIGUOUS ZONE (1960): second United Nations attempt at settling the breadth of the territorial sea. *See* 1960 U.N. Yearbook 542.

GENEVA CONVENTION PROTOCOL I (1977): established additional rules for the protection of members of the armed forces involved in war and for the protection of medical facilities and civilian populations. *See* 16 I.L.M. 1391.

GENEVA CONVENTION PROTOCOL II (1977): effort to protect those involved in armed conflicts that are not international in scope such as civil wars, affording them similar protection as that extended in war. *See* 16 I.L.M. 1442.

GENEVA CONVENTION PROTOCOL I (1980): banned the use of bullets which splinter into fragments designed to elude detection by X-ray. *See* 19 I.L.M. 1524.

GENEVA CONVENTION PROTOCOL II (1980): restricts the use of mines, booby traps, and similar devises designed to kill indiscriminately. *See* 19 I.L.M. 1529.

GENEVA CONVENTION PROTOCOL III (1980): furthers the restrictions on the use of INCENDIARY WEAPONS (q.v.). *See* 19 I.L.M. 1534.

GENEVA CONVENTIONS (1949): the four conventions negotiated at Geneva for the improvement of the laws of war in light of the practices experienced during World War II. The treatises are: Convention For The Amelioration Of The Conditions Of The Wounded And Sick In Armed Forces In The Field, 6 U.S.T. 3114, 75 U.N.T.S. 31; The Convention For The Amelioration Of The Condition Of Wounded, Sick And Shipwrecked Members Of Armed Forces At Sea, 6 U.S.T. 3217, 75 U.N.T.S. 85; Convention Related to the Treatment of Prisoners Of War, 6 U.S.T. 3316, 75 U.N.T.S. 135; Convention Relative To The Protection Of Civilian Persons In Time Of War, 6 U.S.T. 3516, 75 U.N.T.S. 287. They are also referred to as the Red Cross Conventions.

GENEVA OFFICE OF THE UNITED NATIONS: the former headquarters of the League of Nations taken over by the United Nations and housing the offices of the WORLD HEALTH OR-GANIZATION, WORLD INTELLECTUAL PROPERTY ORGANI-ZATION, UNCTAD, and the INTERNATIONAL LABOUR ORGANIZATION (qq.v.) among others. It is an anomaly that the second largest U.N. office is located in Switzerland, which is not a member of the United Nations.

GENEVA PASSPORT REGULATIONS (1926): *see* 24 Revue Generale du Droit International Public 242.

GENEVA PROTOCOL (1925): banned poisonous gas and bacteriological warfare. *See* 94 L.N.T.S. 65, 25 Am.J.Int.L. Supp. 94 and 64 Am.J.Int.L. 853.

GENOCIDE: the acts, "committed with intent to destroy, in whole or in part, a national, ethnical, racial, or religious group, as such, of: (a) killing members of the group; (b) causing serious bodily or mental harm to members of the group; (c) deliberately inflicting on the group conditions calculated to bring about the physical destruction, in whole or in part; (d) imposing measures intended to prevent birth within the group; (e) forcibly transfer-ring children of the group to another group." Art. II of the Convention on the Prevention and Punishment of the Crime of Genocide (1948), 78 U.N.T.S.277,280.

GENTLEMEN'S AGREEMENT: an agreement (not legally binding) between statesmen or diplomats, who are to perform the obligation on the basis of good faith. Because the commitment is only a political or a moral one, there is no legal or legally enforceable claim to specific performance.

GENUINE LINK PRINCIPLE: erstwhile rule that there must be a substantial connection between a state and the ships which fly that state's flag. *See* FLAG OF CONVENIENCE.

GEOSTATIONARY ORBIT: path of a satellite at a height of 223,000 miles where it travels at the speed of the earth's rotation which allows it to remain over the same point in the earth's surface. This orbit is essential for the operation of communications satellites. *See* INTELSAT, WARC (1985), and the BOGOTA DE-CLARATION (1976).

GERMAN CLAUSE: Art. 9 of the MERGER CONTROL REGU-LATIONS (q.v.) of the European Community. It allows the European Community Commission to authorize a member state to investigate a merger.

GERMAN EXTERNAL DEBT ARBITRATION (*Greece v. Federal Republic of Germany*): after World War II, Germany refused to settle claims held by Greek nationals arising out of decisions of the Mixed Graeco-German Arbitral Tribunal established after World War I. Greece instituted arbitration proceedings under the Agreement on German External Debts, March 21, 1968, which was ratified by Greece and Germany among others. The Arbitral Tribunal decided that Greece and Germany were obligated to negotiate with regard to the dispute between them. *See* Arbitral Tribunal and Mixed Commission for the Agreement on German External Debts, Reports of Decisions and Advisory Opinions, No.5, (1970/72).

GERMAN FINAL SETTLEMENT TREATY (1990): agreement among the Four Powers occupying Germany since World War II, and the two post-war German States for reuniting Germany and ending the occupation. *See* 29 I.L.M. 1184.

GERMAN-MEXICAN CLAIMS COMMISSION: established to settle claims by German citizens arising out of the Mexican Revolution. *See* 27 Am.J.Int.L. 62.

GERMAN REUNIFICATION TREATY (1990): agreement between the Federal Republic of Germany and the German Democratic Republic to become one state. *See* 29 I.L.M. 1108 and Am.J.Int.L. 160.

GERMAN SECULAR PROPERTY IN ISRAEL CASE: Israel and the Federal Republic of Germany agreed that Israel would pay compensation for German property left in Israel (345 U.N.T.S. 91). The F.R.G. represented German nationals as well as former German nationals (now Austrian nationals). The F.R.G agreed with the Austrian Government to divide the compensation received from Israel. Thus, when consent is given, the interests of a state and its citizens may be represented and protected by another state. *See* 16 R.I.A.A. 1 (1959).

GERMAN SETTLERS IN POLAND ADVISORY OPINION: German farmers entered into contracts with the Prussian Government, whereby the farmers were granted ownership of land in Western Prussia and Posen, Poland (if certain conditions were met). After World War I, the land was ceded to Poland, and Poland tried to evict the farmers. In an advisory opinion requested by the League of Nations, the Permanent Court of International Justice declared that the farmers had a right to the land by virtue of the laws in effect in those territories and that Poland had to recognize and honor the contracts. *See* 1923 P.C.I.J. (ser. B) No. 6.

GERMAN-SOVIET NON-AGGRESSION PACT (1939): agreement between the Soviet Union and Germany, just prior to the beginning of World War II, which secretly divided Poland and gave

Hitler the last assurance he needed before invading Poland. *See 1989 Internation Affairs (Moscow)* No. 10, at 81

GERMANY-LITHUANIA NATIONALITY ARBITRATION: the Memel territory was ceded to Lithuania in 1924. Inhabitants of the territory had the option of declaring either German or Lithuanian nationality. In 1935, the governor of the territory annulled the Option Commission's decision to affirm the choice of six Germans who chose Lithuanian nationality. An arbitrator denied Lithuania the right to unilaterally annul the Commission's decision and declared Lithuania to be bound to recognize the Lithuanian nationality of the six Germans. *See* 3 R.I.A.A. 1719 (1949) (in French).

GEWO (G): GEWERBEORDNUNG (q.v.).

GEWERBEORDNUNG (GEWO) (G): the German Industrial Code which contains rules concerning safety at work, protection of minor employees, and business licensing.

GHANA-GUINEA UNION: failed first step in the creation of the Union of Independent African States. *See* 1 Whiteman, *Digest of International Law* 428.

GIFT OF TERRITORY: a cession of territory by a sovereign in a similar manner as a gift made by an individual, i.e., the intention is to pass the territory to another sovereign gratis, so the territory is delivered into the hands of the other sovereign.

GLOBAL SYSTEM OF ENVIRONMENTAL MONITORING: part of the United Nations' Environmental Program providing for worldwide sharing of environmental information. It was adopted as part of the STOCKHOLM DECLARATION ON THE HUMAN ENVIRONMENT (1972) (q.v.).

GLOBAL SYSTEM OF TRADE PREFERENCES AMONG DE-VELOPING COUNTRIES: *See* 27 I.L.M. 1204 (1988).

GLOSSATORS: medieval scholars of Roman law who penned commentaries on a particular law in the margins of their manuscripts.

GOA GUIDELINES ON INTERGENERATIONAL EQUITY: *See* INTERGENERATIONAL EQUITY.

GOA INCIDENT (1961): invasion of the Portuguese enclave of Goa on the coast of India by Indian forces, ostensibly to allow the people of Goa self-determination. *See* 2 Whiteman, *Digest of International Law* 1140 and 56 Am.J.Int.L. 617.

GOLD BLOCK: declaration by several European countries between 1933 and 1976, to maintain the free function of the gold standard. *See* 6 Hudson, *International Legislation* No.396, at 945 (1937).

GOLD CLAUSE: term in many early commercial agreements specifying the amounts owed under the contract were payable in currency struck in gold. References to gold are found in many international agreements. *See e.g.,* Art. 262 of the VERSAILLES PEACE TREATY (1919).

GOLD POOL: agreement among several Western countries including the United States to maintain the official price of gold. The agreement was abrogated in 1971. *See* 7 I.L.M. 461.

GOLPE DE ESTADO (S): attack on the state, *see* COUP D'ETAT (F).

GOMULKA PLAN (1963): proposal to freeze nuclear weapons in Central Europe under the joint supervision and control made by Polish Communist Party Chief Gomulka. *See* SIPRI, *World Disarmament Yearbook* 408 (1969).

GONDRA TREATY (1923): *see* CONFLICTS BETWEEN AMERICAN STATES TREATY (1923).

GOOD FAITH: parties to a treaty are subject to the obligation to perform with honest and true intentions.

GOOD OFFICES: friendly efforts on the part of a third state or international organization to try to encourage disputing states to enter into or resume negotiations. There is no obligation to offer the service or to accept the tender of good offices. The technique of good offices may be exercised only with the consent of both parties to the dispute and the role of the third state ends when negotiations begin. *See* Arts. 2-8, HAGUE CONVENTION FOR THE PACIFIC SETTLEMENT OF DISPUTES (1899 & 1907).

GOODS AND SERVICES: *see* CLASSIFICATION OF GOODS AND SERVICES.

GOVERNMENT DE FACTO: *see* DE FACTO GOVERNMENT.

GOVERNMENT DE JURE: *see* DE JURE GOVERNMENT.

GOVERNMENT-IN-EXILE (also refugee government or absentee government): the chief executive and other members of a government flee their homeland in the face of hostile armed forces; generally this government remains the DE JURE GOVERNMENT (q.v.) of the state and can speak, in most respects, in the name of the state.

GOVERNMENT SUCCESSION: a change in government, not merely a change in sovereign, by REVOLUTION, RESTORATION, CONQUEST, or RECONQUEST (qq.v.). The successor government is bound by international law to perform the duties and obligations of the state which had been undertaken by the previous government.

GOVERNMENTAL CONTRACTS: negotiated promise of performance between a private person and a state or between two states.

GRADUAL AND RECIPROCATED INITIATIVES IN TENSION REDUCTION (GRIT): plan for arms reduction where each side reduces by a small amount, and urges the other side to do likewise. *See* Osgood, *An Alternative to War and Surrender* (1962).

GRAE: Governo Revolucionario de Angola no Exile, one faction which fought for the independence of Angola from Portugal, but lost out to the MPLA (q.v.).

GRAF SPEE: German battleship which used the neutral port of Montevideo, Uruguay for repairs during World War II. The British tried to hold the ship captive by invoking the rule that ships of belligerents may not leave a neutral port within 24 hours of each other (*see* Art. 16, Hague XII (1907)). Uruguay would not be a party to this and the *Graf Spee* was ordered out of port where it was scuttled by its crew. *See* 7 Hackworth, *Digest of International Law* 450.

GRAN CHACO DISPUTE: both Bolivia and Paraguay claimed the Chaco Boreal, a 115,000-square mile strip of undeveloped land through which Bolivia gained access to the Atlantic Ocean. To halt hostilities thirty states imposed an arms embargo which was ineffective. After seven years of hostilities, the two countries agreed to negotiate and, subsequently, the problem was placed before an eight-nation peace conference. The territory was divided between the two countries with Bolivia retaining transit rights. *See* 3 R.I.A.A. 1817 (1949).

GRATIS DICTUM (L): an unsupported assertion.

GRAVES REGISTRATION SERVICE: belligerents are to organize a group to keep records of graves so that bodies may be exhumed and identified for return to their homelands. *See* Art. 177 (3) & (4), of the GENEVA CONVENTION I (1949).

GREEK QUESTION: problems surrounding the establishment of a Greek nation-state in the 19th century, Greece formerly being part of the Ottoman Empire. *See* 6 Moore, *Digest of International Law* 4.

GRENADA INTERVENTION (1983): United States troops were landed on the island of Grenada, at the request of other Carribean nations, to restore order after a coup toppled the Marxist Government. *See* 78 Am.J.Int.L. 661 and 20 Stanford J. Int'l L. 173.

GRISBADARNA CASE: an international arbitral tribunal resolved a maritime boundary dispute between Norway and Sweden utilizing principles of law applicable in 1661, the year the boundary was set. The settlement follows international law in that a state of things that existed for a long time should be changed as little as possible. *See* 11 R.I.A.A. 147 (1961).

GRIT: GRADUAL AND RECIPROCATED INITIATIVES IN TENSION REDUCTION (q.v.).

GROMYKO PLAN: proposal by the Soviet Union, for international control of atomic energy, presented to the U.N. Atomic Energy Commission in 1946. *See also,* BARUCH PLAN.

GROTIAN RULE: when the boundary between two states is a river, the frontier should be located in the middle of the river.

GROUP OF EIGHTEEN: consultative group of the GENERAL AGREEMENT ON TARIFFS AND TRADE (q.v.) established to identify types of discrimination in foreign trade. *See* N.Y. Times, Sept. 28, 1986, at 27.

GROUP OF FIVE: the leading industrial countries: the United States, Great Britain, France, West Germany and Japan. *See* 24 I.L.M. 1731, and N.Y. Times, Ap. 9, 1987, at D7.

GROUP OF SEVEN: GROUP OF FIVE (q.v.) plus Canada and Italy.

GROUP OF SEVENTY-SEVEN: lobby group of the lesser developed countries which now numbers more than seventy-seven members. These states are the proponents of changes in the international order (*see* NEW INTERNATIONAL ECONOMIC ORDER and NEW INTERNATIONAL INFORMATION ORDER) and carry much weight in international organizations because of their overwhelming voting majority even though they lack the economic and political power to be effective elsewhere. *See* 26 Journal of African Law 12 (1982).

GROUP OF TEN: Belgium, Canada, France, West Germany, Italy, Japan, Netherlands, Sweden, United Kingdom, and United States; who meet to discuss international monetary arrangements.*See* 7 I.L.M. 709, 24 I.L.M. 1685.

GROUP OF TWENTY: the GROUP OF TEN plus Argentina, Australia, Brazil, India, Indonesia, Iraq, Morocco, Mexico, Switzerland, and Zaire; established by the INTERNATIONAL MONETARY FUND (q.v.) to suggest reforms. *See* 13 I.L.M. 1000.

GROUP OF TWENTY-FOUR: group of deputies appointed to study the functions and recommend improvements to the operations of the International Monetary Fund. *See* 24 I.L.M. 1699.

GROUP Q, S, T, V, W, Y, OR Z COUNTRY: United State export licensing classification system designations. *See* 15 C.F.R. 770 (1989).

GRU: Glaunoe Razdevyratelnoe Uprarlemic, Chief Military Directorate of the Soviet Armed Forces.

GRUNDNORM (G): basic law, positive law.

GRUPO ANDINO (S): the ANDEAN COMMON MARKET (q.v.).

GSTP: GLOBAL SYSTEM OF TRADE PREFERENCES (q.v.).

GUADELOPE HIDALGO TREATY (1848): treaty designating the Rio Grande River as the international frontier between Mexico and the United States. Thus confirming the loss of a large portion of Mexico's territory. *See* 9 Stat. 922, 9 Bevans 791.

GUANTANAMO NAVAL BASE: located in Cuba by agreement for the lease to the United States of lands in Cuba for coaling and naval stations. The United States agreed to recognize that the ultimate sovereignty over the land and water of Guantanamo Naval Base would remain in Cuba. *See* 6 Bevans 1113 or 193 C.T.S. 314 (1903).

GUARANTEE: act whereby a state takes upon itself the duty to safeguard the rights or status of another state, e.g., the four powers guarantee of the neutrality of Austria by treaty in 1955, *see* 6 U.S.T. 2369.

GUARANTEE OF TREATY: agreement entered into to ensure the observance of an existing treaty. Conditions of guarantee are detailed in the body of the treaty.

GUARANTEES OF PERMANENT NEUTRALITY: obligation undertaken by the great powers to observe as inviolable the territory of certain countries, e.g., Switzerland, Congo (*see* GENERAL ACT OF BERLIN (1885). *See* PERMANENT NEUTRALITY.

GUARDIANSHIP OF INFANTS CONVENTION CASE: an infant of Dutch citizenship was placed, pursuant to Swedish law, into the home of her maternal grandmother upon the death of her mother. The Dutch father appealed to the International Court of Justice alleging violation of a Convention of 1902 governing guardianship which provides, *inter alia*, that the guardianship of an infant should be governed by the law of the state of its nationality. The I.C.J. rejected the Dutch claim. *See* 1958 I.C.J. 55, and also the HAGUE CONVENTION ON THE GUARDIANSHIP OF INFANTS.

GUATEMALA CITY PROTOCOLS (1971): amendments to the WARSAW CONVENTION (1929)(q.v.). *See* 65 Am.J.Int.L. 670 (not in force).

GUATEMALA-HONDURAS BOUNDARY DISPUTE: 100-year dispute about the location of their border finally settled by arbitration. *See* 27 Am.J.Int.L. 403.

GUERRILLAS: combatants engaged against forces occupying a territory from within the territory or from clandestine bases nearby, fighting in an unconventional manner, e.g., from behind enemy lines, by ambush, etc.

GUIDON DE LA MER (F): French compilation of customary maritime laws from the late 16th century; it formed the basis for the French Commercial Code.

GULAG ARCHIPELAGO: chain of Soviet labor camps in Siberia.Russian soldiers who had fought for or were prisoners of the Germans in World War II were among the inmates sent to the Gulag, which was made famous by Aleksandr I. Solzhenitzn's book by the same name.

GULF: indentation in a coastline with a wide entrance (generally greater than six miles).

GULF COOPERATION COUNCIL: organization of Saudi Arabia, Kuwait, Oman, Qatar, Bahrain, and the United Arab Emirates. *See* 26 I.L.M. 1131.

GULF OF MAINE CASE (*U.S. v. Canada***):** International Court of Justice decision on claims to fishing rights in the Gulf. *See* 23 I.L.M 1197.

GULF OF SIDRA INCIDENT (1981): United States and Libyan fighters engaged in a dogfight over the Gulf of Sidra which Libya claims as internal waters, but which is widely regarded as high seas. *See* 10 Yale J. Int'l L. 59

GULF OF TONKIN RESOLUTION: *see* TONKIN GULF RESOLUTION.

GUNT: TRANSNATIONAL GOVERNMENT OF NATIONAL UNITY (q.v.).

GUT DAM CLAIMS: in 1952, property owners on the southern shore of Lake Ontario claimed that their property was damaged by the Gut Dam built by Canada on U.S. territory in 1903-04. At that time, Canada had assumed liability for future property damage. The two countries subsequently agreed to a lump sum settlement. *See* 8 I.L.M. 118 (1969).

HABITAT: human settlement; the subject of a United Nations program and the subject of a U.N. Conference held in Vancouver, Canada. *See* 1976 U.N. Yearbook 441.

HAEC EST CONVENTIO (L): that is the agreement.

HAGUE ACADEMY OF INTERNATIONAL LAW: prestigious organization which conducts classes in international law each summer and publishes the proceedings in *Receuil des Cours. See* 8 Am.J.Int.L. 351.

HAGUE CODIFICATION CONFERENCE (1930): meeting to codify certain subjects of international law including questions of nationality and territorial waters. Though thoroughly prepared by a committee of experts few points were agreed upon and only a few states ratified those. For documents *see* 24 Am.J.Int.L.Supp. 1 and 169.

HAGUE CONFERENCE ON PRIVATE INTERNATIONAL LAW: organized in 1892 and resurrected in 1951, member states send experts to sessions which prepare conventions on questions of private international law. *See e.g.*, HAGUE CONVENTION ON THE TAKING OF EVIDENCE ABROAD. For U.S. participation *see* 15 U.S.T. 2228.

HAGUE CONFERENCE ON REPARATIONS (1930): attempt to settle the problem of payment of reparations imposed after World War I. *See* 25 Am.J.Int.L.Supp. 7.

HAGUE CONVENTION I (1899): HAGUE CONVENTION FOR THE PACIFIC SETTLEMENT OF DISPUTES (1899 & 1907) (q.v.).

HAGUE CONVENTION I (1907): HAGUE CONVENTION FOR THE PACIFIC SETTLEMENT OF DISPUTES (1899 & 1907) (q.v.).

HAGUE CONVENTION II (1899): HAGUE CONVENTION RESPECTING THE LAWS AND CUSTOMS OF LAND WARFARE (1899 & 1907) (q.v.).

HAGUE CONVENTION II (1907): LIMITATION OF EMPLOYMENT OF FORCE FOR RECOVERY OF CONTRACT DEBTS CONVENTION (1907) (q.v.).

HAGUE CONVENTION III (1899): HAGUE CONVENTION FOR THE ADOPTION TO MARITIME WARFARE OF THE PRINCIPLES OF THE GENEVA CONVENTION (1899) (q.v.).

HAGUE CONVENTION III (1907): HAGUE CONVENTION RELATIVE TO THE OPENING OF HOSTILITIES (1907) (q.v.).

HAGUE CONVENTION IV (1899), Part 1: HAGUE DECLARATION PROHIBITING THE LAUNCHING OF PROJECTILES AND EXPLOSIVES FROM BALLOONS (1899) (q.v.).

HAGUE CONVENTION IV (1899), Part 2: HAGUE DECLARATION CONCERNING ASPHYXIATING GASES (q.v.).

HAGUE CONVENTION IV (1899), Part 3: HAGUE DECLARATION CONCERNING EXPANDING BULLETS (q.v.).

HAGUE CONVENTION IV (1907): HAGUE CONVENTION RESPECTING THE LAWS AND CUSTOMS OF WAR ON LAND (1899 & 1907) (q.v.).

HAGUE CONVENTION V (1907): HAGUE CONVENTION RESPECTING THE RIGHTS AND DUTIES OF NEUTRAL POWERS AND PERSONS IN WAR ON LAND (1907) (q.v.).

HAGUE CONVENTION VI (1907): HAGUE CONVENTION RELATIVE TO THE STATUS OF ENEMY MERCHANT SHIPS AT THE OUTBREAK OF HOSTILITIES (1907) (q.v.).

HAGUE CONVENTION VII (1907): HAGUE CONVENTION RELATIVE TO THE CONVERSION OF MERCHANT SHIPS INTO WARSHIPS (1907) (q.v.).

HAGUE CONVENTION VIII (1907): HAGUE CONVENTION ON SUBMARINE MINES (1907) (q.v.).

HAGUE CONVENTION IX (1907): HAGUE CONVENTION RE-GARDING THE BOMBARDMENT OF NAVAL FORCES (1907) (q.v.).

HAGUE CONVENTION X (1907): HAGUE CONVENTION FOR THE ADOPTION TO MARITIME WARFARE OF THE PRINCIPLES OF THE GENEVA CONVENTION (1899) (q.v.).

HAGUE CONVENTION XI (1907): HAGUE CONVENTION ON THE RIGHT OF CAPTURE (1907) (q.v.).

HAGUE CONVENTION XII (1907): HAGUE CONVENTION RELATIVE TO THE ESTABLISHMENT OF AN INTERNA-TIONAL PRIZE COURT (1907) (q.v.).

HAGUE CONVENTION XIII (1907): HAGUE CONVENTION RESPECTING THE RIGHTS AND DUTIES OF NEUTRALS IN THE CASE OF NAVAL WARFARE (1907) (q.v.).

HAGUE CONVENTION XIV (1907): HAGUE CONVENTION PROHIBITING THE DISCHARGE OF PROJECTILES AND EX-PLOSIVES FROM BALLOONS (1907) (q.v.).

HAGUE CONVENTION FOR THE ADAPTION TO MARI-TIME WARFARE OF THE PRINCIPLES OF THE GENEVA CONVENTION OF 1899 (1907): *see* 36 Stat. 2371, 1 Bevans 694.

HAGUE CONVENTION FOR THE PACIFIC SETTLEMENT OF DISPUTES (1899 and 1907): adopted by the first Hague Conference convened on May 18, 1899; the first convention established the PERMANENT COURT OF ARBITRATION (q.v.); the second conference adopted summary procedures whereby reference of a case may be made to three tribunal members. The Convention is still in force though many of its provisions are inappropriate to modern conditions. *See* 32 Stat. 1779, 1 Bevans 230, and 36 Stat. 2199, T.S. 536, 1 Bevans 577.

HAGUE CONVENTION ON CONFLICT OF NATIONALITY LAW (1930): an attempt to solve the problem of dual nationality, it states, *inter alia*, that a person possessing two nationalities may be regarded as a national by each state and that the person may remove a nationality with the permission of the state whose nationality he wishes to give up. The United States is not a party. *See* 179 L.N.T.S. 89.

HAGUE CONVENTION ON SUBMARINE MINES (1907): *see* 36 Stat. 2332, 1 Bevans 669.

HAGUE CONVENTION ON THE GUARDIANSHIP OF INFANTS (1902): *See* 191 C.T.S. 264 (text in French).

HAGUE CONVENTION ON THE LAW APPLICABLE TO AGENCY: established uniform rules for the law of agency including the establishment of an agency relationship and dealings with third parties. *See* 16 I.L.M. 775.

HAGUE CONVENTION ON THE LAWS AND CUSTOMS OF LAND WARFARE (1899): *see* HAGUE CONVENTION RESPECTING THE LAWS AND CUSTOMS OF LAND WARFARE (1899 & 1907).

HAGUE CONVENTION ON THE RIGHT OF CAPTURE (1907): *see* 36 Stat. 2396, 1 Bevans 711.

HAGUE CONVENTION ON THE SERVICE OF JUDICIAL AND EXTRAJUDICIAL DOCUMENTS ABROAD (1965): rules for getting legal papers to those in other countries. *See* 20 U.S.T. 361, 658 U.N.T.S. 163, 59 Am.J.Int.L. 87.

HAGUE CONVENTION ON THE TAKING OF EVIDENCE ABROAD (1970): established method for acquiring evidence for the pursuit of legal actions from persons located in other countries including the use of diplomatic officers to take evidence and settle disputes. *See* 23 U.S.T. 2555, 8 I.L.M. 37.

HAGUE CONVENTION PROHIBITING THE DISCHARGE OF PROJECTILES AND EXPLOSIVES FROM BALLOONS (1907): *see* 36 Stat. 2439, 1 Bevans 739.

HAGUE CONVENTION REGARDING THE BOMBARD-MENT OF NAVAL FORCES (1907), *see* 36 Stat. 2351, 1 Bevans 681.

HAGUE CONVENTION RELATIVE TO THE CONVERSION OF MERCHANT SHIPS INTO WARSHIPS (1907): *see* 2 Am.J.Int.L.Supp. 133.

HAGUE CONVENTION RELATIVE TO THE ESTAB-LISHMENT OF AN INTERNATIONAL PRIZE COURT (1907): *see* 2 Am.J.Int.L.Supp. 174.

HAGUE CONVENTION RELATIVE TO THE OPENING OF HOSTILITIES (1907), *see* 36 Stat. 2259, 1 Bevans 619.

HAGUE CONVENTION RELATIVE TO THE STATUS OF EN-EMY MERCHANT SHIPS AT THE OUTBREAK OF HOSTILI-TIES (1907): *See* 2 Am.J.Int.L.Supp. 133.

HAGUE CONVENTION RESPECTING LAWS AND CUS-TOMS OF WAR ON LAND (1899): *see* 32 Stat. 1803, 1 Bevans 247.

HAGUE CONVENTION RESPECTING LAWS AND CUS-TOMS OF WAR ON LAND (1907): rules for determining lawful belligerents, treatment of prisoners, sick and wounded, and proper means of warfare. *See* 36 Stat. 2277, 1 Bevans 631.

HAGUE CONVENTION RESPECTING THE RIGHTS AND DUTIES OF NEUTRAL POWERS IN NAVAL WAR (1907): *see* 36 Stat. 2415, 1 Bevans 723.

HAGUE CONVENTION RESPECTING THE RIGHTS AND DUTIES OF NEUTRAL POWERS IN WAR ON LAND (1907): *see* 36 Stat. 2310, 1 Bevans 654.

HAGUE CONVENTIONS ON CONFLICTS OF LAW: series of conventions dealing with marriage, divorce, guardianship, and minor points of civil court procedure. *See* HAGUE CONFERENCE ON PRIVATE INTERNATIONAL LAW.

HAGUE EVIDENCE CONVENTION: *See* HAGUE CONVENTION ON THE TAKING OF EVIDENCE ABROAD (1970).

HAGUE PEACE CONFERENCE (1899): produced the HAGUE CONVENTION FOR THE PACIFIC SETTLEMENT OF DISPUTES (1899) (q.v.) and laid the basis for the Second Hague Peace Conference (1907) which further codified the laws of war. *See* 7 Moore, *Digest of International Law* 78.

HAGUE PROTOCOL (1955): amendments to the WARSAW CONVENTION (1929) (q.v.). *See* 478 U.N.T.S. 371.

HAGUE RADIO RULES: failed attempt to codify rules on the use of radio communications in the time of war. *See* 32 Am.J.Int.L.Supp. 2.

HAGUE REGULATIONS: used loosely to refer to all the Hague Conventions on the law of war, but especially, the HAGUE CONVENTION RESPECTING THE LAWS AND CUSTOMS OF WAR ON LAND (1907) (q.v.).

HAGUE RULES (1923): model rules promulgated by the International Law Association regulating BILLS OF LADING (q.v.) in international ocean transport. They are integrated into national laws on the subject. *See* British Carriage of Goods by Sea Act (1971) 39 *Halsbury's Statutes* (4 ed.) 831 and the American Carriage of Goods by Sea Act (1936) 49   Stat. 1207.

HAGUE RULES ON AERIAL WARFARE (1923): failed attempt to codify customary international law concerning air warfare. *See* 32 Am.J.Int.L.Supp. 12 or 1 Friedman, *The Law of War* 437 (1972).

HAMBURG RULES (Carriage of Goods by Sea Convention (1978)): convention drafted by the UNITED NATIONS COMMISSION FOR INTERNATIONAL TRADE LAW (q.v.), concerning international shipping. Seventy-eight states sent representatives to Hamburg in 1978, where the convention was adopted. *See* 17 I.L.M. 603.

HARBOR: a natural site for the anchorage of ships and for the construction of a port for the docking of ships. *See* 4 Whiteman, *Digest of International Law* 263.

HARMONIZED COMMODITY DESCRIPTION AND CODING SYSTEM: a standardized international nomenclature for commercial products developed by the CUSTOMS COOPERATION COUNCIL (q.v.). *See* 103 Stat. 1107.

HARVARD RESEARCH ON TREATIES (1975): an important and successful private effort at the codification of international law; it is an encyclopedic presentation noting current practice and suggestions for improvement.

HAVANA CHARTER (1948): the organic document of the INTERNATIONAL TRADE ORGANIZATION (q.v.) adopted in 1946 at a conference on trade and employment. The Charter tried to remove trade restrictions and discrimination. The International Trade Organization was not successful, but it provided a basis for the GENERAL AGREEMENT ON TARIFFS AND TRADE (GATT) (q.v.).

HAVANA CONVENTION (1928): general agreement on commercial aviation rights in force in the Western Hemisphere prior to the adoption of the CHICAGO CONVENTION (1944)(q.v.). *See* 129 L.N.T.S. 224.

HAVANA CONVENTION ON THE RIGHT OF ASYLUM (1928): inter-American agreement on the granting of POLITICAL ASYLUM (q.v.). *See* 22 Am.J.Int.L.Supp. 158.

HAVANA DECLARATION (1983): NON-ALIGNED MOVEMENT (q.v.) declaration that urged, *inter alia*, the hastening of the establishment of the NEW INTERNATIONAL ECONOMIC ORDER (q.v.). *See* Rajan, *The Non-aligned and the United Nations* 305 (1987).

HAY-BUNAU VARILLA CONVENTION (1903): agreement between the United States and Panama giving the United States rights, power, and authority over the Panama Canal Zone while the U.S. guaranteed Panama's independence. *See* 33 Stat. 2234, 10 Bevans 663.

HAY-PAUNCEFOTE TREATY (1901): superseded the CLAYTON-BULWER TREATY giving the Untied States the right to construct the Panama Canal. The United Kingdom was granted the right to pay the same tolls for its vessels as those paid by U.S. flag vessels. *See* 32 Stat. 1903, 12 Bevans. 258.

HAYA DE LA TORRE CASES: Haya de la Torre was the unsuccessful leader of a revolt in Peru in 1948. He obtained asylum in the Colombian Embassy three months after he became subject to criminal proceedings. The International Court of Justice was asked to determine if Colombia had the right to grant asylum. Three judgments were delivered with the conclusion that Colombia was not obliged to surrender Haya de la Torre, but the asylum was to terminate immediately. The parties were to reach a settlement based on "courtesy and good neighborliness." *See* 1950 I.C.J. 266.

HAZARDOUS WASTE: *see* TRANSBOUNDARY MOVEMENT OF HAZARDOUS WASTE CONVENTION (1989).

HAZARDOUS WASTE WITHIN AFRICA CONVENTION (1991): ORGANIZATION OF AFRICIAN UNITY (q.v.) effort to ban the import into Africa and control the transboundary movement and management of hazardous waste. *See* 30 I.L.M. 773.

HAZARDS OF WAR: civilian internees and other protected persons are to be protected from such hazards as bombardment. *See* Art. 89 GENEVA CONVENTION IV (1949).

HEAD OF STATE: the highest governmental official of a state as defined by its constitution. The office may be the actual center of political power or may be for the most part ceremonial as with the British Monarchy. *See also* ATTENTAT CLAUSE.

HEADLAND: a high point of land or cliff extending out into the sea. *See also* KING'S CHAMBER.

HEADQUARTERS AGREEMENT (United Nations)(1947): agreement between the United Nations and the United States for the establishment of the U.N. headquarters in New York City. *See* 11 U.N.T.S. 11.

HEC: Hague Evidence Convention. *See* HAGUE CONVENTION ON THE TAKING OF EVIDENCE.

HEGEMONY: the domination by one country of the other countries in a region. A popular accusation in Communist propaganda, especially that of the People's Republic of China.

HELMAND RIVER COMMISSION (1951): body to establish the apportionment of water between Iran and Afghanistan from the river which forms part of their common border. *See* 3 Whiteman, *Digest of International Law* 1031.

HELSINKI ACCORDS: declaration of principles by the CON-FERENCE ON SECURITY AND COOPERATION IN EUROPE (q.v.), guiding the relationship between state parties, *inter alia*, affirming sovereign equality, declaring the current borders in Europe inviolable and guaranteeing human rights. *See* 14 I.L.M. 1292 and 25 I.L.M. 331.

HELSINKI RULES ON THE USE OF WATERS OF INTERNA-TIONAL RIVERS (1966): *See* International Law Association Report of the 52nd Conference, Helsinki, 1966, p. 447, 477.

HEREDITAS JACENS (L): in Roman law, the legal personality attributed to the estate of a decedent from the time of death until the property was acquired by the successor.

HICKENLOOPER AMENDMENT: requirement that the United States Government suspend assistance to any country that expropriates U.S.-owned property, or repudiates its contracts, or has a discriminatory tax system working against U.S. business concerns located in the country. *See* 22 U.S.C. sec. 2370(e).

HIGH COMMISSIONER: highest ranking official designated with diplomatic or administrative authority in a dependent territory. Also, title given to representatives exchanged among member countries of the British Commonwealth. *See also* UNITED NATIONS HIGH COMMISSIONER FOR REFUGEES.

HIGH CONTRACTING PARTIES: the parties to an international agreement. *See* 35 Am.J.Int.L. 132.

HIGH SEAS: all those ocean waters outside the limits of the TER-RITORIAL WATERS (q.v.) of coastal states including contiguous zones and the CONTINENTAL SHELF (q.v.). The high seas have the status of RES COMMUNIS (q.v.). *See* the GENEVA CONVENTION ON THE REGIME OF THE HIGH SEAS (1958) and the LAW OF THE SEA CONVENTION (1982).

HIGH SEAS CONVENTION: *see* GENEVA CONVENTION ON THE HIGH SEAS (1958) and LAW OF THE SEA CONVENTION (1982).

HIGH TREASON: making war against one's own state. In England, an offense against the personal safety or honor of the monarch.

HIJACKING: see AIR PIRACY.

HISTORIC BAY: undulation in a coast line which falls outside the usual definition of a BAY (q.v.), but nevertheless is considered internal water of the coastal state because of a long standing unilateral claim, e.g., the Chesapeake Bay.

HISTORIC RIGHTS: title created by an assertion of jurisdiction over a long period in derogation of international law, but which is acquiesced in by other nations. *See* NORWEGIAN FISHERIES CASE.

HISTORIC WATERS: waters which are treated as internal waters of the coastal country because of historic claim rather than because they fit the usual definition of internal waters. The claim must be manifested by exercise of jurisdiction over a long period.

HOLY SEE: the international persona of the Roman Catholic Church having capacity in international law to conclude agreements and carry on relations with states. *See* LATERAN TREATY (1929) and VATICAN.

HONDURAS-NICARAGUA BOUNDARY DISPUTE: for several years the two neighboring states failed to agree on the demarcation of a common border. In 1912, Nicaragua challenged the validity of a 1906 arbitration award which favored Honduras. The disagreement with respect to the award was submitted to the International Court of Justice which found it valid and binding. In order to fully execute the judgment, a Honduran-Nicaraguan Mixed Commission was created. By 1962, the two states had complied with the judgment and decisions of the Commission. *See* 1960 I.C.J. 192, 11 R.I.A.A. 101 (1961) and 30 I.L.R. 76 (1966).

HONORARY CONSUL: person acting as a consular agent of a country on a part-time basis. The appointment may go to someone other than a national of the sending country, usually someone already in residence at the locale where the representation is desired. Honorary consuls usually do not collect a regular salary from the government they represent.

HORS DE COMBAT (F): a combatant who is in the power of an adversary and expresses an intent to surrender or is unconscious. An *hors de combat* is a protected person under the law of war. *See* Art. 41(2) of GENEVA CONVENTION PROTOCOL I (1977).

HOSPITAL SHIP: ships constructed or arranged exclusively for the purpose of assisting the sick, wounded, and shipwrecked without distinction of nationality. They are exempt from capture. *See* the HAGUE CONVENTION REGARDING BOMBARDMENT OF NAVAL FORCES (1907).

HOST COUNTRY: 1) the country to which a diplomatic or consular mission is sent. The host country is responsible for protecting their diplomatic privileges. 2) Country in which an international organization's premises are located, e.g., Canada (Montreal) is the host country of the International Civil Aviation Organization.

HOSTAGES: *see* TAKING OF HOSTAGES CONVENTION (1979).

HOSTES GENERIS HUMANIS (L): enemies of mankind.

HOSTILE ACT: an UNFRIENDLY ACT (q.v.), an action which is contrary to the interest of another party, but not necessarily an ACT OF WAR (q.v.).

HOSTILE INFECTION: French doctrine that the carriage of a hostile cargo renders also the ship itself liable for capture as PRIZE (q.v.).

HOSTILITIES: acts constituting a state of war or STATUS MIXTUS (q.v.). Before hostilities are commenced the instigating party should notify both adversaries and neutrals. *See* Arts. 1 and 2, HAGUE CONVENTION III (1907).

HOSTIS HUMANI GENERIS (L): an enemy of all mankind, status ascribed to pirates and slave traders. *See* 630 F 2d 890 (1980).

HOT PURSUIT: the right of a coastal state to pursue foreign private vessels suspected of violating the laws or regulations of that state within the territorial or national waters of that state. The pursuit must begin within the territorial waters or contiguous zone of the pursuer and cannot proceed into the waters of another state. *See* Art. 23 of the GENEVA CONVENTION ON THE HIGH SEAS (1958).

HOVERING ACTS: series of eighteenth century British laws authorizing the seizure of smugglers on the high seas at distances varying from two leagues to one hundred leagues. Great Britain thus assumed the right to capture ships far beyond the usual three-mile limit: no foreign powers objected. In 1850, in the case of Petit Jules the Queen's Advocate advised the government that such seizures were illegal under international law. In 1876, the Hovering Acts were repealed by the Customs Consolidation Act.

HULL DOCTRINE: position that nations have the right to expropriate property for public purposes, but in return must pay prompt, adequate, and effective compensation to the private owner. *See* 8 Whiteman, *Digest of International Law* 1020.

HUMAN DIMENSION: part of the HELSINKI ACCORD (g.v.) dealing with issues of HUMAN RIGHTS (q.v.) and fundamental freedom. *See* 29 I.L.M. 1305.

HUMAN ENVIRONMENT CONFERENCE (1972): United Nations' sponsored meeting to establish an international environmental regime, the meeting produced no convention but rather the STOCKHOLM DECLARATION ON THE HUMAN ENVIRONMENT (1972) (q.v.). The United States refused to sign the final document.

HUMAN RIGHTS: basic principles which are purported to protect people; agreement, on the substance of the principles and application of the principles, is subject to greatly divergent views. The West places emphasis on individual liberty while the Soviet bloc emphasizes the provision of food, shelter, etc. insuring the "common good" at the expense of individual freedoms. *See* UNIVERSAL DECLARATION OF HUMAN RIGHTS and COMMITTEE ON HUMAN RIGHTS.

HUMANE TREATMENT: prisoners of war are to be provided with adequate food, potable water, clothing, and medical attention and during evacuation precautions shall be taken for their safety. *See* Art. 20, GENEVA CONVENTION III (1949).

HUMANITARIAN INTERVENTION: actions by one or more third parties to attempt to mitigate or halt abuses of human rights, prevent the continued cruelty of a regime or conflict, e.g., England, France, and Russia intervened in 1827 in the war between Greece and Turkey because of the barbarous acts both sides were committing. *See also* GRENADA INTERVENTION (1983).

HUNGARIAN-ROMANIAN LAND REFORM DISPUTE: question of compensation for Hungarian nationals whose land was ceded by Hungary to Romania by the TRIANON PEACE TREATY (1920)(q.v.), eventually settled by treaty, 121 L.N.T.S. 69, in 1930.

HUNGARIAN UPRISING (1956): short-lived attempt by the Hungarian Government to remove itself from Soviet domination. The revolt was crushed and a more compliant government installed. The U.S.S.R. vetoed a U.N. Security Council Resolution calling for the withdrawal of Soviet troops. *See* 1956 U.N. Yearbook 67.

HUTUS MASSACRE (1972): revolt by Hutu tribesmen in Burundi was put down by the government in a particularly brutal fashion, approximately 150,000 were executed. *See* 18 African Report 32 (Jl/Aug. 1973), or N.Y. Times, Sept. 4, 1987 at A3.

HYDERABAD QUESTION (1949): dispute over the status of the territory of Hyderabad which attempted to remain independent at the time India was granted its independence. The territory was occupied by Indian troops and the occupation was briefly challenged in the U.N. Security Council. *See* 1948-9 United Nations Yearbook 298-303 and 43 Am.J.Int.L. 57

[I]

IADB: INTER-AMERICAN DEVELOPMENT BANK (q.v.).

IAEA: INTERNATIONAL ATOMIC ENERGY AGENCY (q.v.).

IAF: INTERNATIONAL ASTRONAUTICAL FEDERATION (q.v.).

IATA: INTERNATIONAL AIR TRANSPORT ASSOCIATION (q.v.).

IBEC: INTERNATIONAL BANK FOR ECONOMIC COOPERATION (q.v.).

IBRD: INTERNATIONAL BANK FOR RECONSTRUCTION AND DEVELOPMENT (q.v.).

ICAO: INTERNATIONAL CIVIL AVIATION ORGANIZATION (q.v.).

ICARA: INTERNATIONAL CONFERENCE ON ASSISTANCE TO REFUGEES IN AFRICA (q.v.).

ICC: INTERNATIONAL CHAMBER OF COMMERCE (q.v.).

ICC COURT OF ARBITRATION: INTERNATIONAL CHAMBER OF COMMERCE COURT OF ARBITRATION (q.v.).

ICJ: INTERNATIONAL COURT OF JUSTICE (q.v.).

ICRC: INTERNATIONAL COMMITTEE OF THE RED CROSS (q.v.).

ICSID: INTERNATIONAL CENTER FOR THE SETTLEMENT OF INVESTMENT DISPUTES (q.v.).

IDA: INTERNATIONAL DEVELOPMENT ASSOCIATION (q.v.).

IDENTIC NOTES: diplomatic messages to a single recipient from several countries relaying the same message through varying texts.

IDENTITY CARDS: cards which attest to the identity and status of the holder. They may be issued to civil defense personnel, journalists, military and civilian medical personnel, and religious personnel and combatants. *See* GENEVA CONVENTION PROTOCOL I (1977) Art. 79 (3) and Annex I, Art.1 for the information and symbols which the cards are to contain.

IDENTITY DISK: plate which provides general information about the person wearing it. Usually two are worn at one time. They are commonly referred to in the United States military as "dog tags."

IEA: INTERNATIONAL ENERGY AGENCY (q.v.)

IFAD: INTERNATIONAL FUND FOR AGRICULTURAL DEVELOPMENT (q.v.). p1

IFRB: INTERNATIONAL FREQUENCY REGISTRATION BOARD (q.v.).

IGY: INTERNATIONAL GEOPHYSICAL YEAR (q.v.).

IGNORANTIA JURIS NEMINEM EXCUSAT (L): ignorance of the law is no excuse.

IHLEN DECLARATION (1919): statement by the Norwegian Minister of Foreign Affairs that Norway would not dispute Danish claims of sovereignty over Greenland which was later used against Norway's claim to Eastern Greenland. *See* Case of Legal Status of Eastern Greenland, 1933 P.C.I.J. (series A/B) No. 53, at 22, 36.

IJC: INTERNATIONAL JOINT COMMISSION (q.v.).

ILA: INTERNATIONAL LAW ASSOCIATION (q.v.).

ILC: INTERNATIONAL LAW COMMISSION (q.v.).

ILLEGAL WAR: has replaced the concept of JUST WAR (q.v.), a war can only be "legal" in the sense that a nation is pursuing legitimate self-defense within the framework of the UNITED NATIONS charter (q.v.).

ILO: INTERNATIONAL LABOUR ORGANIZATION (q.v.)

I'M ALONE CASE (1955): the U.S. Coast Guard sank a Canadian rumrunner on the high seas. An international commission found the sinking not justified in international law. *See* 7 A.D. 203.

IMCO: INTER-GOVERNMENTAL MARITIME CONSULTATIVE ORGANIZATION (q.v.)

IMF: INTERNATIONAL MONETARY FUND (q.v.).

IMMIGRATION: nationals of one country moving into another country with the intent of establishing permanent residency. For United States immigration law, *see* Title 8 of the U.S.C..

IMMUNITY: independent from outside control; an alleged right of each sovereign state from judicial process or other aspects of TERRITORIAL JURISDICTION (q.v.). *See* SOVEREIGN IMMUNITY and IMMUNITY CASE.

IMMUNITY CASE: the West German Constitutional Court rejected Iran's claim of sovereign immunity relating to bank accounts attached in suits by British and American claimants. *See* 22 I.L.M. 1279.

IMMUNIZATION OF PLACES: areas in which military operations are not to be conducted because of the presence of civilians,

PROTECTED PERSONS, or PROTECTED OBJECTS (qq.v.), but a state is not to use this as a means of shielding military objectives. *See* Art. 28, GENEVA CONVENTION IV (1949).

IMO: INTERNATIONAL MARITIME ORGANIZATION (q.v.).

IMPERIAL CONFERENCE (1926): meeting which established the British Commonwealth out of the British Empire. *See* 21 Am.J.Int.L. 95.

IMPERIALISM: the domination by one nation over another. The domination may be social or economic as well as political.

IMPERIUM: the sovereign right of governance that a state exercises over its territory.

IMPOSED TREATY: a treaty to which at least one of the parties was forced to assent; generally regarded today as unenforceable. *See* 7 Cal.West.Int'l.L.J. 5 (1977) and S. Malawer, *Imposed Treaties and International Law* (1977).

IMPOSSIBILIUM NULLA OBLIGATIO EST (L): an impossible obligation is null and does not need to be fulfilled.

IN ABSENTIA (L): proceedings against a party who is not present.

IN-BOND COMPANY: under Mexican law, a company with special customs treatment allowing the duty-free import of everything used to carry out its business. *See* 4 I.A.L.M. 803.

IN CASU CONSIMILI (L): standing in the same or similar position.

IN DUBIO MITIUS (L): recognized rule of equitable construction in several systems of municipal law which reinforces the presumption against limitations on the independence of states.

IN FORCE: a treaty which is said to be in force is binding as between the parties to it. A treaty will come into force by its own terms usually after ratification or accession by the parties. *See* Art. 24 of the VIENNA CONVENTION ON THE LAW OF TREATIES and ENTRY INTO FORCE.

IN FAVOREM DEBTORIS (L): in favor of the debtor; a maxim for the interpretation of treaties in case of doubt.

IN MITIORI SENSU (L): not in the harsh sense.

IN PARI PASSU (L): on equal terms.

INABILITAZIONE (I): a partial incapacity or restricted ability to carry on one's own legal affairs.

INCENDIARY WEAPONS: a weapon or munition that is primarily designed to set fire to objects or to cause injury through flame, heat, or both upon impact with its target, e.g., flame throwers, napalm. Their use is restricted by GENEVA CONVENTION PROTOCOL III (1980).

INCHJURA INCIDENT (1955): two British ships were intercepted by Chinese Nationalist warships and warned not to enter Foochow. When the British ships attempted to enter despite the warning, they were fired upon by the Chinese Nationalists and held captive for seven hours. The British protested indicating their intent to "afford protection to British ships on their lawful occasions on the high seas." *See also* Art. 27, 1956 Report of the *International Commission on the Law of the Sea*, Part II.

INCIDENT: imprecise term for an event of conflict in international relations. It can apply to anything from name-calling to the slaughter of hundreds of innocent people (in the latter situation it is a handy euphemism).

INCOGNITO: status of a person who appears or travels without disclosing his or her true identity.

INCORPORATION DOCTRINE: principle that customary rules are to be considered as part of the municipal law. They are incorporated only so far as they are not inconsistent with legislative acts or prior judicial decisions of final authority. *See Barbuit's Case*, 25 Eng.Rep. 777 (1737).

INCOTERMS: standardized shipping terms defined by the International Chamber of Commerce, e.g., F.O.B., C.I.F., EX WORKS, (qq.v) etc. The terms divide the responsibility for the cost of carriage, and liability for the safety of the goods between the buyer and seller. *See Guide to Incoterms* published by the International Chamber of Commerce.

INDEMNIFICATION: act by one state compensating another state for damage caused by the acting state, e.g., paying reparations or restoring the original state of affairs.

INDEPENDENT: free from the control of an outside power. *See* 5 Whiteman, *Digest of International Law* 88.

INDIA-CHINA BORDER DISPUTE: the 2500-mile border between India and China remains a point of contention between the two states. *See* 59 Am.J.Int.L. 16.

INDIA-PAKISTAN QUESTION: *see* KASHMIR QUESTION.

INDIAN LIFE: *see* INTER-AMERICAN INDIAN INSTITUTE.

INDIAN PRINCELY STATES: several hundred small territories ruled by native sovereigns, who remained in that status after the British conquest of India, holding their position under the SUZERAINTY (q.v.) of the British Crown. *See* 1 Whiteman, *Digest of International Law* 492.

INDIGENOUS POPULATION: the people native to an area, the people in residence when "civilization" arrived, e.g., the Inuit and Eskimo population of Canada or the Maori of New Zealand. *See* 80 Am.J.Int.L. 369.

I

INDO-PAKISTANI WAR: series of hostilities between India and Pakistan along their borders. When Pakistan surrendered in December 1971, India refused to return 90,000 prisoners of war for over two years in violation of Art. 118 of the GENEVA CONVENTION III (1949). *See also* KASHMIR QUESTION.

INDISCRIMINATE ATTACK: bombardments, etc. which are not directed at specific military targets or which employ a method or means that cannot be directed at a specific military target, e.g, a floating mine that may hit a battle ship or a hospital ship. *See* Art. 51(4) GENEVA CONVENTION PROTOCOL I (1977).

INDIVIDUAL: traditionally individual persons were not subjects of international law (*see* STATES), but through the development of rules of international law, particularly the Law of War, individual persons are more frequently afforded protection. *See* GENEVA CONVENTION and HUMAN RIGHTS.

INDUS RIVER DISPUTE: arose between India and Pakistan regarding the use of the Indus River. A commission was established to handle the dispute which adopted the concept of EQUITABLE APPORTIONMENT (q.v.) and considered the general interests of each riparian involved, weighting the benefits and detriments to each state. *See* 419 U.N.T.S. 125.

INDUSTRIAL AND AGRICULTURAL USE OF INTERNATIONAL RIVERS DECLARATION (1933): resolution of the Seventh International Conference of American States containing the principles that riparian states may utilize the water of international rivers, but must do so as not to injure their fellow riparian states and so as not to interfere with free navigation. *See* 28 Am.J.Int.L. Supp. 59.

INF: INTERMEDIATE-RANGE NUCLEAR FORCES (q.v.).

INF TREATY: *See* ELIMINATION OF INTERMEDIATE-RANGE AND SHORTER-RANGE NUCLEAR MISSILES.

INFECTION DOCTRINE: neutral goods may be subject to PRIZE (q.v.) if "infected" by association with contraband goods, e.g., hiding explosives in otherwise harmless goods make the latter CONTRABAND (q.v.).

INFORMATEURS (F): practice designed to allow a noncommittal presence at an international conference by the appointment of an observer or "informateur." The United States frequently sent an informateur to the League of Nations (it was not a member).

INFORMATION EXCHANGE: provisions in a number of international agreements on diverse subjects that require the parties to provide information to the other parties. These include CONFIDENCE-BUILDING MEASURES (q.v.) and OECD recommendations on the use of restrictive business practices, 25 I.L.M. 1633.

INFRA LEGEM (L): interpretation and application of rules of law using principles of equity. *See* CONTRA LEGEM and 80 I.L.R. 472.

INGE TOFT CONTROVERSY: Egypt claimed the right to seize Israeli goods in transit through the Suez Canal. *See* 54 Am.J.Int.L. 398.

INITIALING: practice of the negotiators of treaties to authenticate the draft or final document produced and may constitute a binding signature according to the VIENNA CONVENTION ON THE LAW OF TREATIES, Art. 12 (q.v.).

INLAND SEA: large body of water not connected to the ocean.

INLAND WATER: same as INTERNAL WATERS (q.v.).

INMARSAT: organization which operates an international telecommunications satellite system for use by ships at sea. *See* 15 I.L.M. 219, 233, 1051.

INNOCENT PASSAGE: the passage of a vessel which is not prejudicial to the peace, order, or security of the coastal state. Ships of all nations, by the existence of the right of innocent passage, may traverse the territorial sea of another state. *See* CORFU CHANNEL CASE.

INQUEST: in the case of the death of a person with diplomatic immunity the question may arise as to the ability of the host country to carry out a coroner's investigation into the cause of death. *See* Satow, *A Guide to Diplomatic Practice* at 203 (1957).

INSTITUT DE DROIT INTERNATIONAL: international organization of legal scholars founded in 1873, in Brussels, Belgium, to promote the progressive development of international law and its codification.

INSTRUMENT OF ACCESSION: document which is deposited with the designated depository state to formally acknowledge the ACCESSION (q.v.) to a treaty by the issuing state.

INSTRUMENT OF RATIFICATION: document exchanged by the parties to a treaty or deposited with the designated depository state (or the United Nations) formally acknowledging RATIFICATION (q.v.) of a treaty by the issuing state. *See* VIENNA CONVENTION ON THE LAW OF TREATIES, Art. 16.

INSURGENCY: an internal uprising that is aimed against the existing government, usually with the goal of replacing or overthrowing the government.

INSURGENT COMMUNITY: the population that is supporting a rebel force usually located in the territory under the control of the rebels and supplying the logistical support necessary to continue the rebellion.

INTEGRATION: the process by which small neighboring states develop a common identity and move by peaceful processes to become more closely joined together. Western Europe is trying to achieve integration through the development of the EUROPEAN COMMUNITY (q.v.).

INTELLIGENCE AGREEMENT: an arrangement between two governments to share classified, national security information. *See* 3 Brooklyn J. Int'l L. 1.

INTELSAT: INTERNATIONAL TELECOMMUNICATIONS SATELLITE ORGANIZATION (q.v.).

INTER ALIA (L): among other things.

INTER CAETERA DIVINEA (1493) (L): papal bull dividing the Western Hemisphere between Spain and Portugal. The bull was codified in the TORDESILLAS TREATY (1494) (q.v.). A translation of the bull is found in Shiels, *King and Church, The Rise and Fall of the Patronato Real* at 80 (1961).

INTER SE DOCTRINE: defunct argument that international law did not apply to the relations between British Commonwealth nations which were governed by their own set of rules established by treaty. *See* 1953 Brit.Y.B.Int'l.L. 320.

INTER PACEM ET BELLUM NIHIL MEDIUM (L): between peace and war there is no middle ground; a statement by Cicero describing the continuum between peace and war.

INTER-AMERICAN COMMISSION ON HUMAN RIGHTS: an organ of the ORGANIZATION OF AMERICAN STATES (q.v.) with power to recommend measures to governments for the protection of human rights. The Commission also prepares studies and conducts investigations related to human rights issues. *See* Art. 112 of the Amendments to the OAS charter, 21 U.S.T. 691.

INTER-AMERICAN CONFERENCE ON PROBLEMS OF WAR AND PEACE: *See* CHAPULTEPEC CONFERENCE (1945).

I

INTER-AMERICAN CONVENTION ON HUMAN RIGHTS (1969): established the INTER-AMERICAN COMMISSION ON HUMAN RIGHTS and the INTER-AMERICAN COURT OF HUMAN RIGHTS (q.q.v.). *See* 65 Am.J.Int.L. 679.

INTER-AMERICAN COURT OF HUMAN RIGHTS: a seven member judicial body which hears cases brought against member governments concerning HUMAN RIGHTS (q.v.) abuses. It is an organ of the ORGANIZATION OF AMERICAN STATES (q.v.). *See* 25 I.L.M. 123, and 76 Am.J.Int.L. 231.

INTER-AMERICAN DEVELOPMENT BANK (IADB): regional institution created in the 1960's in response to inadequate development resources and the special needs of the area. The basic purpose was to finance projects essential to development by loans not readily available through other sources. *See* 389 U.N.T.S. 69.

INTER-AMERICAN ECONOMIC AND SOCIAL COUNCIL: organ of the Organization of American States to promote economic and social development. *See* Arts. 93-97 of the Amendments to the OAS charter, 21 U.S.T. 685 or 8 I.L.M. 1149.

INTER-AMERICAN INDIAN CONGRESS: meeting convened every four years by the INTER-AMERICAN INDIAN INSTITUTE (q.v.). *See* 80 Am.J.Int.L. 682 (1986).

INTER-AMERICAN INDIAN INSTITUTE: created in 1940 to act as the Permanent Committee of the Inter-American Conference on Indian Life; it is a specialized agency of the ORGANIZATION OF AMERICAN STATES (q.v.). headquartered in Mexico City, it implements O.A.S. resolutions, distributes information, and coordinates scientific investigation into facets of Indian life. *See* 56 Stat. 1303.

INTER-AMERICAN REGIONAL SYSTEM: the various manifestations of regional cooperation in the Western Hemisphere, e.g., ORGANIZATION OF AMERICAN STATES, PAN-AMERICAN UNION, and 50 Am.J.Int.L. 18.

INTER-AMERICAN SPECIALIZED CONFERENCE ON PRI-VATE INTERNATIONAL LAW: meeting of representatives from American nations to draft conventions for the unification of private law. They have produced several conventions, *see* 18 I.L.M. 1417.

INTER-AMERICAN TREATY OF RECIPROCAL ASSIS-TANCE OF RIO DE JANEIRO (1947) (or Rio Treaty): a post-World War II regional arrangement for the collective security of the Western Hemisphere. The treaty terms include a declaration "that an armed attack by any state against an American state shall be considered as an attack against all parties to the treaty." *See* 62 Stat. 1681, 21 U.N.T.S. 77 (1947), and 43 Am.J.Int.L. 329. Cuba withdrew in 1960.

INTERAMPOL: proposed international police force to be organized among the American States, however, the United States proposal was never accepted. There is an Inter-American Police Convention relating the work of some national police forces, *see* 127 L.N.T.S. 444.

INTERCOSMOS: established in 1976, this program encouraged the participation of other countries in the Soviet space effort by allowing cosmonauts from mainly socialist countries to fly on Soviet spacecraft. *See* 16 I.L.M. 1.

INTERDEPENDENCE: conditions which have a reciprocal impact among nations such as economic development and trade or the utilization of the radio spectrum for communications.

INTEREST SECTION: office established in a foreign country to represent the interests of a SOVEREIGN STATE (q.v.) and act in a semi-diplomatic capacity, but below the level of a consulate or embassy.

INTERGENERATIONAL EQUITY: idea that each generation has a right to benefit from past generations and a duty to pass on those benefits. *See* 27 I.L.M. 1108.

INTER-GOVERNMENTAL MARITIME CONSULTATIVE OR-GANIZATION (IMCO): established in 1958 to promote safety at sea. Its name was changed in 1982 to INTERNATIONAL MARITIME ORGANIZATION (q.v.). *See* 9 U.S.T. 621, 289 U.N.T.S. 48.

INTERHANDEL CASE (*Switzerland v. U.S.):* the International Court of Justice dismissed a Swiss claim involving the U.S confiscation of corporate shares that may have been held by a Swiss national in trust for German interests during World War II. The dismissal was based on a failure of the Swiss to exhaust all local remedies before pursuing the case in the I.C.J. and is often cited as authority for the EXHAUSTION OF LOCAL REMEDIES (q.v.) rule. *See* 1959 I.C.J. 6, and for the U.S. District Court Settlement, 3 I.L.M. 426.

INTERIM MEASURES: measures to try to stabilize a situation or insure the maintenance of the status quo while a dispute is being settled or litigated. *See* 79 Am.J.Int.L. 190.

INTERIM OFFENSIVE ARMS AGREEMENT (SALT I): first United States-Soviet limitation on strategic offensive weapons. *See* 24 U.S.T. 1472.

INTERMEDIATE RANGE NUCLEAR FORCES (INF): series of arms control talks between the U.S. and U.S.S.R. held in Geneva beginning in 1980 concerning strategic nuclear weapons of less than inter-continental range. *See* ELIMINATION OF INTERMEDIATE-RANGE AND SHORTER-RANGE NUCLEAR MISSILES.

INTERIOR WATERS: same as INTERNAL WATERS (q.v.).

INTERNAL WATERS: lakes, rivers, and other bodies of water located within the land territory of a state and the waters on the landward side of the baseline marking the territorial seas of that state. *See* Art. 5 of the GENEVA CONVENTION ON THE TERRITORIAL SEA AND CONTIGUOUS ZONE (1958).

INTERNATIONAL AIR SERVICE TRANSIT AGREEMENT (1945): multilateral agreement to allow overflight and technical landings (e.g., refueling) of airplanes engaged in international commercial air transport. *See* 59 Stat. 1693, 84 U.N.T.S. 389.

INTERNATIONAL AIR SERVICE TRANSPORT AGREE-MENT (1945): failed attempt to develop a system of liberal rights for airlines engaged in international commercial transport. Instead of this agreement a system of restrictive bilateral agreements developed. *See* BERMUDA AGREEMENTS I and II.

INTERNATIONAL AIR TRANSPORT ASSOCIATION (IATA): cartel of international air carriers with headquarters in Montreal, both national airlines and privately owned airlines are members. IATA has set prices and controlled capacity over most international passenger and cargo routes. *See* 32 J.Air L. & Com. 222 (1966).

INTERNATIONAL ASSOCIATION OF PENAL LAW: organization to promote the exchange of ideas and cooperation among persons involved in administering the criminal law in their respective countries. They publish *Revue Internationale de Droit Penal.*

INTERNATIONAL ASTRONAUTICAL FEDERATION (IAF): a private international organization made up of 59 national astronautical societies. The International Academy of Astronautics and the International Institute of Space Law are creatures of the IAF.

INTERNATIONAL ATOMIC ENERGY AGENCY (IAEA): specialized agency of the United Nations designed to encourage research into peaceful uses of atomic energy. It was organized in 1957 with headquarters in Vienna and recently played an important role in the exchange of information about the CHERNOBYL INCIDENT (1986) in the Soviet Union. *See* 276 U.N.T.S. 3.

INTERNATIONAL BANK FOR ECONOMIC COOPERATION (IBEC): bank for COUNCIL FOR MUTUAL ECONOMIC ASSISTANCE (q.v.) member states to provide capital for development. *See* 3 I.L.M. 324.

I

INTERNATIONAL BANK FOR RECONSTRUCTION AND DEVELOPMENT (or World Bank)(IBRD): an international agency which strives to aid the economic development of member states, and to raise the living standard of the world. It provides advisory assistance as well as loans to member states. *See* 60 Stat. 1440, 3 Bevans 1390, 2 U.N.T.S. 134.

INTERNATIONAL BAR ASSOCIATION: international organization of national bar associations concerned with the status and problems of the legal profession. They publish *International Business Lawyer* and the *International Bar Journal.*

INTERNATIONAL BOUNDARY COMMISSION (U.S.-Mexico): has jurisdiction to administer questions arising under the bilateral treaty governing rights in the Colorado and Rio Grande rivers. *See* 59 Stat. 1219, 3 U.N.T.S. 313.

INTERNATIONAL BUREAU FOR THE PROTECTION OF INDUSTRIAL PROPERTY: known as the Paris Union. *See* 7 Whiteman, *Digest of International Law* 999 or 23 Am.J.Int.L.Supp. 21.

INTERNATIONAL BUREAU FOR THE PROTECTION OF LITERARY AND ARTISTIC PROPERTY: *see* BERNE UNION.

INTERNATIONAL BUREAU OF WEIGHTS AND MEASURES: international organization established in 1875 to do research and work towards standardization of measuring units. Its headquarters is in Sevres, a suburb of Paris. *See* 149 C.T.S. 237, 1 Bevans 39.

INTERNATIONAL CARRIAGE: the transport of passengers, baggage, cargo, and/or mail across an international boundary. The term may have a more exacting definition when applied to a particular mode of transport by an international convention, *see* *e.g.*, Art. 1 of the WARSAW CONVENTION (1929).

INTERNATIONAL CENTER FOR THE SETTLEMENT OF INVESTMENT DISPUTES (ICSID): associated with the INTER-

NATIONAL BANK FOR RECONSTRUCTION AND DEVELOP-MENT (q.v.), this organization mediates disputes between investors and the governments of developing countries in order to provide a more favorable climate to encourage private investment. *See* 4 I.L.M. 524 and 77 Am.J.Int.L. 784.

INTERNATIONAL CHAMBER OF COMMERCE: organization which includes both representatives of states and of national chambers of commerce. It promotes world business and is influential in establishing standards of practice. *See e.g.,* INCOTERMS. Their headquarters is in Paris, France.

INTERNATIONAL CHAMBER OF COMMERCE COURT OF ARBITRATION: the leading body in international commercial arbitration since the 1920's. It settles business disputes of an international character. Also, the Court supervises arbitrations taking place around the world and in almost all economic settings in order to insure the security of international business transactions. *See* 15 I.L.M. 395.

INTERNATIONAL CIVIL AVIATION ORGANIZATION (ICAO): United Nations organization dealing primarily with technical questions involving international air navigation and safety. headquartered in Montreal, it was established by the Chicago Convention (1944), 61 Stat. 1180, 3 Bevans 944, 15U.N.T.S. 295.

INTERNATIONAL COFFEE ORGANIZATION: established by the International Coffee Agreement of 1959, 647 U.N.T.S. 3, tries to stabilize coffee prices by setting coffee reserve quotas of exportable coffee for each member country. *See also* 469 U.N.T.S. 169.

INTERNATIONAL COMMISSION FOR CONTROL AND SUPERVISION FOR LAOS: established by the International Conference on Vietnam in 1973, the commission was made up of Indian, Polish, and Canadian delegates to carry out the principles of the Geneva Accords of 1954 and 1962. *See* 12 I.L.M. 405.

INTERNATIONAL COMMISSION FOR CONTROL AND SU-PERVISION FOR VIETNAM: established by the Agreement on Ending War and Restoring Peace in Vietnam, 935 U.N.T.S. 6 (Paris, 1973). Members were Canada, Hungary, Indonesia, and Poland with headquarters in Saigon (Ho Chi Min City). It was to supervise and control the implementation of Art. 18 of the Agreement. *See* 12 I.L.M. 56.

INTERNATIONAL COMMITTEE OF THE RED CROSS: private international organization headquartered in Geneva, Switzerland, which has assumed responsibility for enforcing the humanitarian aspects of the LAW OF WAR (q.v.) and providing disaster relief. *See* 2 Am. Univ. J. Int'l L. & P. 415-538.

INTERNATIONAL CONFERENCE ON ASSISTANCE TO REFUGEES IN AFRICA: United Nations meeting held in Geneva in April 1981. *See* 1981 U.N. Yearbook 1039.

INTERNATIONAL COUNCIL FOR THE EXPLORATION OF THE SEA: established in 1902 (revised in 1950) to execute the program for the international exploration of the seas and adopted by the 1899 Stockholm and 1901 Christiania Conferences. Its functions is to "encourage all investigation for the study of the sea and to coordinate operations of participating governments." *See* 652 U.N.T.S. 237.

INTERNATIONAL COURT OF JUSTICE (ICJ): the sixth principal organ of the United Nations which is composed of fifteen judges elected by the General Assembly and Security Council. Only states may bring cases before the court, and there is no compulsory jurisdiction. The Court plays an important role in the development of the international legal system. The Statute of the International Court of Justice is found in the United Nations charter, 59 Stat. 1031, 3 Bevans 1153.

INTERNATIONAL COURT OF JUSTICE RULES OF COURT: *See* 73 Am.J.Int.L. 748.

INTERNATIONAL COVENANT ON CIVIL AND POLITICAL RIGHTS: *see* COVENANT ON CIVIL AND POLITICAL RIGHTS.

INTERNATIONAL COVENANT ON ECONOMIC, SOCIAL AND CULTURAL RIGHTS: United Nations Convention confirming the right of self-determination, sovereignty over resources, and the principle that peoples shall not be deprived of their means of subsistence. *See* 1966 U.N. Yearbook 406, 419 (text).

INTERNATIONAL DAIRY AGREEMENT (1979): GENERAL AGREEMENT ON TARIFFS AND TRADE (q.v.) provisions for fair trade in dairy products. *See* 32 U.S.T. 679.

INTERNATIONAL DEBT CRISIS: problem arising from a large number of poor nations which have borrowed vast sums of money (particularly with the crash of oil prices in the 1980's), amd have no prospect of being capable of repayment. The already troubled economics of these nations are on the verge of total collapse or default. *See* 4 Dick. J. Int'l. L. 275.

INTERNATIONAL DEMOCRATIC UNION: organization of leading right-wing and centrist figures from democratic countries to promote the spread of democracy.

INTERNATIONAL DEVELOPMENT ASSOCIATION (IDA): a specialized United Nations agency whose object is to promote economic development through long-term, low-interest loans. The IDA is associated with the INTERNATIONAL BANK FOR RECONSTRUCTION AND DEVELOPMENT (q.v.). *See* 439 U.N.T.S. 249 or 11 U.S.T 2284.

INTERNATIONAL DEVELOPMENT LAW INSTITUTE: international organization based in Rome which promotes the use of law as a tool for economic development. *See* 28 I.L.M. 870.

INTERNATIONAL DRAINAGE BASIN: geographical area extending to or over the territory of two or more states and is bounded by the watershed extremities of a system of water, in-

I

cluding the surface and underground waters, all of which flow into a common terminus. *See* Art. II, International Law Association Rules on the Uses of Waters of International Rivers, Report of the 52nd Conference of the I.L.A. (Helsinki, 1966).

INTERNATIONAL ENERGY AGENCY (IEA): organization which was part of the response of industrial nations to the cartelization of petroleum by the ORGANIZATION OF PETROLEUM EXPORTING COUNTRIES (q.v.). IEA has tried unsuccessfully to manage oil shortages and develop conservation measures. *See* 27 U.S.T. 1685.

INTERNATIONAL ENERGY PROGRAM: established in Paris in 1974 by sixteen industrialized countries. The program attempts to promote oil supplies on reasonable and equitable terms, to take common effective measures to meet oil supply emergencies, promote cooperative relations with oil producers, and reduce dependency on imported oil. *See* 14 I.L.M. 1.

INTERNATIONAL FINANCIAL CORPORATION (IFC): a specialized agency of the United Nations established in 1956 to stimulate investment in lesser developed countries by investing in private enterprise in those countries. *See* 7 U.S.T. 2197, 264 U.N.-T.S. 117.

INTERNATIONAL FREQUENCY REGISTRATION BOARD (IFRB): a subdivision of the INTERNATIONAL TELECOMMUNICATIONS UNION (q.v.) charged with registering all requests for radio frequency allocations and allocation of slots in the GEOSTATIONARY ORBIT (q.v.). *See* Arts. 10 and 57 of 28 U.S.T. 2495.

INTERNATIONAL FUND FOR AGRICULTURAL DEVELOPMENT (IFAD): a specialized agency of the United Nations founded in 1977 and headquartered in Rome. It receives funds from developed countries and OPEC (q.v.) nations to support projects to increase food production in developing countries. *See* 28 U.S.T. 8435, 15 I.L.M. 916.

INTERNATIONAL GEOPHYSICAL YEAR (IGY): July 1, 1957 to Dec. 31, 1958, during which scientists from 66 nations conducted research in the fields of space, weather, oceanography, and other earth related sciences. UNESCO and government financial support was obtained for many of the IGY projects.

INTERNATIONAL INSTITUTE FOR THE UNIFICATION OF PRIVATE LAW (UNIDROIT): organization of government representatives which studies the process of harmonization of the private laws of states and drafts proposed uniform laws.
UNIDROIT publishes *Uniform Law Review* and *Bulletin d'informations UNIDROIT. See* 15 U.S.T. 2494.

INTERNATIONAL INVESTMENT BANK: organ of the COUNCIL FOR MUTUAL ECONOMIC ASSISTANCE (q.v.) to provide long-term financing for member states for capital construction projects. *See* 801 U.N.T.S. 319.

INTERNATIONAL JOINT COMMISSION (IJC)(United States-Canada): exercises jurisdiction over all boundary and transboundary waters of Canada and the United States. It was established by the Boundary Water Treaty of 1909, 36 Stat. 2448, 12 Bevans 319, and consists of six members, three from each country. Sessions are held semiannually while the commission staff continuously studies and makes recommendations concerning problems referred by the two governments.

INTERNATIONAL LABOUR ORGANIZATION (ILO): established in 1919 as part of the VERSAILLES PEACE TREATY (q.v.) to improve working conditions and promote social justice. The ILO became a specialized agency of the United Nations in 1946. The current constitution of the ILO is found at 62 Stat. 3485, 15 U.N.T.S. 35. The United States withdrew in 1975, 14 I.L.M. 1582, and resumed membership in 1980.

INTERNATIONAL LABOUR CONVENTION CONCERNING THE PROTECTION OF INDIGENOUS AND TRIBAL POPULATIONS (1957): *see* 328 U.N.T.S. 247

I

INTERNATIONAL LAW: system of rules and customary practices which regulate the relations between nations. The sources of international law are set out in Art. 42 of the STATUTE OF THE INTERNATIONAL COURT OF JUSTICE (q.v.).

INTERNATIONAL LAW ASSOCIATION: nongovernmental international organization composed of international law experts to promote the development of international law. Its proposals are highly respected in international law circles. *See* I.L.A., *The Present State of International Law* (1973).

INTERNATIONAL LAW COMMISSION (ILC): established by UN General Assembly Resolution 174 (II) (21 Nov. 1947). It is composed of persons of recognized competence in international law to promote the progressive development of international law and its codification. Currently there are 34 members elected by the General Assembly. *See* 42 Am.J.Int.L.Supp. 2. Reports of the work of the Commission are found in the Am.J.Int.L. each year in the Official Documents Supplement.

INTERNATIONAL LAW SOURCES: *see* SOURCES OF INTERNATIONAL LAW.

INTERNATIONAL LEGAL COMMUNITY: persons and organizations involved in the making and enforcement of INTERNATIONAL LAW (q.v.).

INTERNATIONAL LEGISLATION: international agreements which establish norms of conduct for nations, LAW MAKING TREATIES(q.v.).

INTERNATIONAL MARITIME ORGANIZATION (IMO): specialized agency of the United Nation (formerly the INTERGOVRENMENTAL MARITIME CONSULTATIVE ORGANIZATION (q.v.) to promote maritime safety and work to reduce marine pollution. *See* 9 U.S.T. 621, 289 U.N.T.S. 48.

INTERNATIONAL MARITIME SATELLITE ORGANIZATION (IMMARSAT): organization which operates the communication and navigation satellites serving ocean-going ships. *See* 31 U.S.T. 135.

INTERNATIONAL MILITARY FORCE: armed force constituted by an international organization, usually composed of personnel from several countries. *See e.g.,* UNITED NATIONS INTERIM FORCES IN LEBANON.

INTERNATIONAL MILITARY TRIBUNAL: a judicial body established by agreement between states for some *ad hoc* purpose. *See* NUREMBERG TRIBUNAL and TOKYO INTERNATIONAL MILITARY TRIBUNAL which were established after World War II for the trial of enemy leaders for war crimes.

INTERNATIONAL MILITARY TRIBUNAL FOR THE PROSECUTION OF WAR CRIMES: *see* NUREMBURG TRIBUNAL and TOKYO TRIBUNAL.

INTERNATIONAL MONETARY FUND (IMF): specialized agency of the United Nations designed to provide temporary funds to help solve balance-of-payments problems of developing states. The IMF also provides technical assistance in matters of taxation, statistics, and banking and operates a training institute. *See* 60 Stat. 1401, 3 Bevans 1351, 2 U.N.T.S. 39.

INTERNATIONAL MONETARY SYSTEM: various international institutions which work to stablize the world currencies and promote development through loans and sharing of economic expertice. *See* INTERNATIONAL BANK FOR RECONSTRUCTION AND DEVELOPMENT and INTERNATIONAL MONETARY FUND.

INTERNATIONAL MINIMUM STANDARD: generally, the least a state can do and still be behaving acceptably in terms of its international responsibilities. In the human rights arena, the treatment that must be accorded aliens (irrespective of the nation's treatment of its own nationals) by all states. *See* UNIVERSAL DECLARATION OF HUMAN RIGHTS (1948) and *The Neer Case*, 3 I.L.R. 213 (1926).

INTERNATIONAL OBLIGATION: a requirement imposed on a nation by international law or previous agreement which is enforceable under international law.

INTERNATIONAL OFFICIAL: high level employee of an international organization, e.g., the Secretary-General of the United Nations.

INTERNATIONAL ORGANIZATION: can be classified as either a governmental or nongovernmental organization whose chief function is the promotion of cooperation among states by furnishing a forum where decisions or agreements can be reached and multinational tasks carried-on.

INTERNATIONAL PATENT COOPERATION UNION: the state parties to the PATENT COOPERATION TREATY (1970)(q.v.) constitute the union for cooperation in filing, searching, and examination of applications for the protection of inventions and for rendering special technical services. *See* 9 I.L.M. 978.

INTERNATIONAL PATENT BUREAU: established by Belgium, Luxembourg, Netherlands, and France in 1947, to provide member governments with reports on the novelty of inventions subject to patent applications. The original agreement, 46 U.N.T.S. 249 was replaced by 808 U.N.T.S. 87.

INTERNATIONAL PERSONALITY: an entity that has capacity to enter into international legal relations and have international legal rights and duties. *See* Montevideo Convention on the Rights and Duties of States (1933), 165 L.N.T.S. 19.

INTERNATIONAL POSTAL UNION: *see* UNIVERSIAL POSTAL UNION.

INTERNATIONAL PRIZE COURT: the Hague Conference (1907) attempted to establish this body to adjudicate PRIZE (q.v.) cases. *See* HAGUE CONVENTION RELATIVE TO THE ESTABLISHMENT OF AN INTERNATIONAL PRIZE COURT (1907).

INTERNATIONAL PROGRAMME FOR THE DEVELOP-MENT OF COMMUNICATIONS: UNESCO (q.v.) program to promote journalism and the mass media in the THIRD WORLD (q.v.). It is tied to the NEW INTERNATIONAL INFORMATION ORDER (q.v.). *See* N.Y. Times, Jan. 24, 1982, Sec. 4, at 4 col. 1.

INTERNATIONAL RADIO CONSULTATIVE COMMITTEE (CCIR): one of the permanent organs of the INTERNATIONAL TELECOMMUNICATIONS UNION (q.v.). *See* 9 Whiteman, *Digest of international Law* 694.

INTERNATIONAL RED CROSS: see INTERNATIONAL COMMITTEE OF THE RED CROSS.

INTERNATIONAL REFUGEE ORGANIZATION: founded in 1948, to solve the refugee problem created by World War II. *See* 189 U.N.T.S. 150, and protocol, 19 U.S.T. 6223, 606 U.N.T.S. 267.

INTERNATIONAL REGIME: a system of rules, duties, obligations, and rights established to promote better relations between nations, either on a specific subject or for general relations. *See e.g.*, NEW INTERNATIONAL ECONOMIC ORDER or LAW OF THE SEA CONVENTION (1982).

INTERNATIONAL RELATIONS: narrowly, the interaction among nations, but the term generally includes the activities of international organizations, nongovernmental organizations, and even individuals who have some international status.

INTERNATIONAL RICE COMMISSION: organization concerned with the production, distribution, and consumption of rice. *See* 13 U.S.T. 2403, 120 U.N.T.S. 13.

INTERNATIONAL RIVER: generally indicates a river affecting the territory and interests of two or more states. It may be a river that flows through the territory of more than one state (successive river) or one separating the territories of two states from one another (a boundary or contiguous river).

INTERNATIONAL SALE OF GOODS CONVENTION: *see* SALE OF GOODS.

INTERNATIONAL SANITARY CONVENTION (1926): widely adopted attempt to control the spread of cholera, yellow fever, etc. *See* 78 L.N.T.S. 229, amended 198 L.N.T.S. 205.

INTERNATIONAL SANITARY REGULATIONS (1951): rules adopted by the WORLD HEALTH ORGANIZATION (q.v.) to prevent the spread of disease. *See* 175 U.N.T.S. 215.

INTERNATIONAL SEA-BED AREA: the floor of the ocean and the subsoil thereof outside the limits of national jurisdiction. *See* Art. 1 of the LAW OF THE SEA CONVENTION (1982).

INTERNATIONAL SEA-BED AUTHORITY: established by Arts. 156 *et seq.* of the LAW OF THE SEA CONVENTION (1982) (q.v.) to regulate and distribute the profits from the mining of the floor of the high seas. *See* 26 I.L.M. 1725.

INTERNATIONAL STANDARD BOOK NUMBER: system established by book publishers in some 22 countries by which a unique eight-digit number is assigned to each book that is published.

INTERNATIONAL TELECOMMUNICATIONS CONVENTION (1973): current organic document of the INTERNATIONAL TELECOMMUNICATIONS UNION (q.v.). *See* 28 U.S.T. 2495.

INTERNATIONAL TELECOMMUNICATIONS CONVENTION (1932): one of several organic documents under which the INTERNATIONAL TELECOMMUNICATIONS UNION (q.v.) has operated. *See* 6 Hudson, *International Legislation* No.316, at 109 (1937).

INTERNATIONAL TELECOMMUNICATIONS SATELLITE ORGANIZATION (Intelsat): composed of both government representatives and representatives of national communications operator. INTELSAT operates the network of satellites that provide most of the world's international telecommunications including the relay of television signals. *See* 23 U.S.T. 3813, and 23 U.S.T. 4091.

INTERNATIONAL TELECOMMUNICATIONS UNION (ITU): the oldest of the United Nations specialized agencies (founded in 1865 with headquarters in Geneva). It promotes the development and improved efficiency of telecommunications, allocates radio frequencies, and provides technical standards and assistance. *See* 28 U.S.T. 2495 and 9 Whiteman, *Digest of International Law* 694.

INTERNATIONAL TELEPHONE AND TELEGRAPH NATIONALIZATION (Chile): *see* 14 I.L.M. 781.

INTERNATIONAL TELEPHONE AND TELEGRAPH CONSULTATIVE COMMITTEE: one of the permanent organs of the INTERNATIONAL TELECOMMUNICATIONS UNION (q.v.). *See* 9 Whiteman, *Digest of International Law* 694.

INTERNATIONAL TIN AGREEMENT (ITA): the original agreement in 1956 (though similar efforts date back to 1921) was replaced by subsequent agreements which have attempted to stabilize price and supply, and which have included both supplier and consumer nations. The system collapsed in 1985. *See* McFadden, *The Collapse of Tin*, 80 Am.J.Int.L. 811 (1986).

INTERNATIONAL TRACING SERVICE: operated by the International Red Cross; this organization attempts to locate persons missing due to the ravages of war. *See* 6 U.S.T. 6186, 219 U.N.T.S. 79.

INTERNATIONAL TRADE CENTRE: established in Geneva by the members of the GENERAL AGREEMENT ON TARIFFS AND TRADE (q.v.) to help expand the trade of developing countries. *See* 1964 U.N. Yearbook 571.

INTERNATIONAL TRADE COMMISSION: United States Government body with responsibility for the study of U.S. international trade practices such as the imposition of customs duties and advising the President and Congress on action that should be taken. *See* 19 U.S.C. sec. 1330 et seq. and 16 I.L.M. 542.

INTERNATIONAL TRADE ORGANIZATION: a charter for an organization by this name was drafted by a UN Conference on Trade and Employment held in Havana in 1948, but it never came into being. The charter did lay the groundwork for the establishment of the GENERAL AGREEMENT ON TARIFFS AND TRADE (q.v.).

INTERNATIONAL WATER COURSE REGULATIONS: *see* 24 Annuaire de L'Institut de Droit International (1981).

INTERNATIONAL WATERS: waters which are outside the exclusive control of a particular nation or through which international shipping has an unrestricted right of passage. *See* 4 Whiteman, *Digest of International Law* 233.

INTERNATIONAL WHALING COMMISSION: organ created by the International Convention on the Regulation of Whaling (1946) to make regulations to preserve the whale population. *See* 62 Stat. 1716, 161 U.N.T.S. 72, and Protocol, 10 U.S.T. 952, 338 U.N.T.S. 366.

INTERNATIONALIZATION: the process of removing something from the control of a particular nation and placing it under the control of an international organization. *See e.g.,* UNITED NATIONS TRUSTEESHIP.

INTERNEE: person subject to INTERNMENT (q.v.).

INTERNES LIBRES (F): "free internees," persons who do not pose a security risk and whose word of honor that they will not leave the territory or engage in hostilities is a substitute for INTERNMENT (q.v.).

INTERNMENT: (1) compulsory confinement without trial of certain classes of persons in order to remove them from actual or potential involvement in a conflict which may be undertaken by either belligerents or neutrals. Internees are held under guard and surveillance. Because of the deprivation of liberty, Art. 42 (1) of the GENEVA CONVENTION IV (1949), provides that internment of protected persons may be ordered only if the security of the detaining state makes it absolutely necessary. (2) the detention of ships by neutrals to protect their neutrality.

INTERNUNCIO: a second class diplomatic representative used by the Vatican and Austria. *See* Satow, *A Guide to Diplomatic Practice* 169 (1957).

INTER-PARLIAMENTARY UNION (I.P.U.): organized in 1889 with headquarters in Geneva, this nongovernmental organization promotes personal contacts between members of parliaments of different nations to strengthen and promote the development of parliamentary institutions. *See* 53 Am.J.Int.L. 426.

INTERPOL: acronym for the International Criminal Police Association which is composed of police authorities from 133 countries affiliated to fight international crime. Interpol is forbidden to intervene in any situation having a political, military, racial, or religious character. Interpol is considered a nongovernmental international organization because its membership is police authorities and not the government. Interpol headquarters is in Lyons, France. *See e.g.,* 10 I.L.M. 1290 and N.Y. Times, Feb. 22, 1990, at A4, col 3.

INTERPRETATIO AUTHENTICA (L): AUTHENTIC INTERPRETATION (q.v.).

INTERSPUTNIK: satellite communications network among eastern bloc countries established to compete with the tremendously more successful INTELSAT (q.v.) system. *See* 862 U.N.T.S. 5 and 7 I.L.M. 1365.

INTERTEMPORAL LAW: doctrine that the law applied to a case should be the current law, but with an eye to whether or not the rights in dispute existed at the outset of the dispute. *See* 74 Am.J.Int.L. 285.

INTERVENOR: person, country, or other legal entity not originally a party to a case who wishes to take part in the proceedings. *See* 26 I.L.R. 587.

INTERVENTION: acts of a state which interfere with the internal affairs of another state, intervention is generally forbidden by international law, but there are exceptions. *See* COLLECTIVE SELF-DEFENSE.

INTIFADAH (A): uprising of the Palestinian people in Israeli-occupied territory. *See* 27 I.L.M. 1680.

INVASION: the movement of a hostile military force across a frontier for the purpose of occupying the territory into which they are moving. *See* 10 Whiteman, *Digest of International Law* 540.

INVESTIGATIVE INTERNATIONAL COMMISSION: name for several groups established to investigate international trouble spots. Both the League of Nations and the United Nations have had such groups.

INVESTMENT CODE: body of rules regulating foreign investment in a country or the conduct of multinational corporations, particularly regarding their activities in less developed countries. *See* UNCTAD CODE OF CONDUCT FOR MULTINATIONAL CORPORATIONS.

INVIOLABILITY: complete protection from investigation or interference of any kind, the protection afforded diplomats and their communications. *See* VON IGEL CASE.

IPCD: INTERNATIONAL PROGRAMME FOR THE DEVELOPMENT OF COMMUNICATIONS (q.v.).

IPU: INTER-PARLIAMENTARY UNION (q.v.).

IRA: IRISH REPUBLICAN ARMY (q.v.).

IRAN AIRBUS INCIDENT (1988): the U.S.S. Vincennes shot down an Iranian passenger plane with two hundred ninety people on board mistaking the passenger plane for an attacking aircraft. *See* 83 Am.J.Int.L. 318 and 28 I.L.M. 842 and 896.

IRAN-CONTRA AFFAIR (1985): White House run covert operation to sell arms to Iran and use the money to support the CONTRAS (q.v.) in Nicaragua. *See* 14 Syracuse J. Int'l L. & Com. 291.

IRAN HOSTAGE CRISIS: United States Embassy personnel were taken hostage by the Iranian Revolutionary Guard and held for over a year with the complicity of the Iranian Government. *See* 75 Am.J.Int.L. 418.

IRAN-IRAQ WAR (1980-88): turmoil in Iran following the fall of the Shah induced Iraq to invade disputed border areas. Iraq was subsequently driven out and the war became stalemated roughly along their previous border. *See* 37 Int.& Comp.L.Q. 629.

IRAQ-KUWAIT SANCTIONS: the blocking of trade and freezing of assets after Iraq's invasion of Kuwait in 1990. *See* 25 Int'l.Lawyer 391.

IRAQ MANDATE: after World War I Iraq became a League of Nations mandate administered by Great Britain. *See* 25 Am.J.Int.L. 436.

IRAQI AGRESSION AGAINST KUWAIT: in August 1990, Iraq invaded and occupied Kuwait. The U.N. General Assembly voted sanctions against Iraq and permitted the use of force. *See* 29 I.L.M. 1560 and 30 I.L.M. 567 and 847.

IRAQI NUCLEAR PLANT INCIDENT: the plant was attacked and destroyed by the Israelis who claimed that Iraq was manufacturing nuclear weapons. The attack was condemned by the Security Council. *See* 75 Am.J.Int.L. 724.

IRELAND V. UNITED KINGDOM (European Court of Human Rights). Ireland accused Britain of violating Art. 24 of the EUROPEAN HUMAN RIGHTS CONVENTION (q.v.) in Britain's conduct of anti- terrorist activities in Northern Ireland. *See* 17 I.L.M. 680.

IRISH REPUBLICAN ARMY (I.R.A.): political movement in Northern Ireland whose members are struggling for independence from Great Britain. The more militant factions use terrorist activities to promote their cause. EXTRADITION (q.v.) of I.R.A. suspects from the United States to Great Britain has become something of a problem between the countries (one man's terrorist is another man's freedom fighter). *See* 80 Am.J.Int.L. 338.

IRISH RESOLUTIONS: several United Nations General Assembly Resolutions calling for the prevention of the further spread of nuclear weapons, *see e.g.*, 1961 U.N. Yearbook 20. They formed the basis for the NUCLEAR NON-PROLIFERATION TREATY (q.v.).

IRON CURTAIN: term coined by Winston Churchill to describe the border between Soviet dominated Eastern Europe and the West.

IRREDENTA (I): a territory which is ethnically or historically related to one state but is incorporated into another. *See e.g.*, SUDETENLAND.

ISBN: INTERNATIONAL STANDARD BOOK NUMBER (q.v.).

ISLAMIC CONFERENCE charter: *see* 914 U.N.T.S.

ISLAND: ". . . a naturally formed area of land which is above water at high tide," Art. 10 of the GENEVA CONVENTION ON THE TERRITORIAL SEAS.

ISOLATIONISM: foreign policy that avoids foreign entanglements particularly that followed by the United States through much of its history, especially the period between World Wars I and II.

ISRAEL V. BULGARIA: aerial incident involving the shooting down of an Israeli passenger plane over Bulgaria in which case the International Court of Justice heard only the preliminary objections of Bulgaria. *See* 1959 I.C.J. 127.

ISRAELI-OCCUPIED TERRITORIES: at the conclusion of the YOM KIPPUR WAR (q.v.) Israel was in control of the Golan Heights in Syria, the West Bank of the Jordan including all of Jerusalem, the Gaza Strip, and the Sinai Desert to the banks of the Suez Canal. Israel continues to occupy all this territory except the Sinai which was returned to Egypt as part of the CAMP DAVID AGREEMENTS (q.v.).

ISRAELI-SOVIET OIL ARBITRATION (1958): a dispute over contracts for the sale of oil by Soviet authorities to Israeli companies when export licenses were cancelled by the Soviet Government after the SUEZ CRISIS (q.v.). *See* 53 Am.J.Int.L. 787.

ITA: INTERNATIONAL TIN AGREEMENT (q.v.).

ITO: INTERNATIONAL TRADE ORGANIZATION (q.v.).

ITU: INTERNATIONAL TELECOMMUNICATIONS UNION (q.v.).

IURA IN REM: *see* JURA IN REM.

IUS: for terms beginning with ius, *see* JUS.

IUSTITIA ET PAX: *see* JUSTITIA ET PAX.

[J]

JACOB-SALOMON CASE (1935): dispute between Germany and Switzerland concerning the abduction of a political refugee from Switzerland by German officials. The case was submitted to arbitration, but before a decision was reached Germany admitted that its officials had acted in an inadmissible manner and surrendered the refugee (Jacob-Salomon) to Swiss authorities.*See* 29 Am.J.Int.L. 502.

JACTITATION: a false claim that leads to the injury of another.

JAMAICA SETTLEMENT: part of the restructuring of the INTERNATIONAL MONETARY SYSTEM (q.v.) worked out in 1976 specifically dealing with exchange rates. *See* 54 Foreign Affairs 577 (1976).

JAMESON RAID (1896): strife between insurgents under the direction of Dr. Jameson and the South African Republic. They were convicted under Great Britain's Foreign Enlistment Act in *Regina v. Jameson and Others*, [1896] 2 Q.B. 425.

JAMMING: the intentional use of interfering radio signals transmitted with the purpose of distorting legitimate transmissions and making their reception unintelligible. *See* 13 Whiteman, *Digest of International Law* 1030-40.

JAN MAYEN ISLAND: some of this island located northwest of Iceland was claimed by Norway in a note to Great Britain, *see* 27 Am.J.Int.L. Supp. 92. The Island also played a role in a dispute between Norway and Iceland over fishing rights. *See* 82 Am.J.Int.L. 443.

JANINA-CORFU AFFAIR: See CORFU AFFAIR (1923).

JAPANESE-AMERICAN EVACUATION CLAIMS: claims brought against the United States by U.S. citizens of Japanese ex-traction for their internment during World War II. *See* 102 Stat. 903.

JAPANESE HOUSE TAX ARBITRATION: dispute between Japan and three European countries where the arbitrators held that Japan could not levy taxes on buildings built by aliens on Japanese soil held under lease in perpetuity. *See* 11 R.I.A.A. 51.

JAPANESE MANDATED ISLANDS: former German colonies in the Pacific (Marshall, Caroline, and Mariana Islands) which were placed by the League of Nations under Japanese mandate after World War I. They were transferred to the United States under United Nations Trusteeship after World War II. *See,* 1 Whiteman, *Digest of International Law* 598-731.

JAWORZINA ADVISORY OPINION: the International Court of Justice stated that the decision of the Paris Conference of Ambassadors concerning the boundaries of three districts on the Polish-Czech borders was a definitive delimitation of the boundary and therefore binding on the Polish and Czechoslovakian governments. *See* P.C.I.J. (series B) No. 8, 1 Hudson, *World Court Reports* 254 (1969).

JAY TREATY (1794): treaty ending the American Revolution signed by Great Britain and the United States. It contained provisions which laid the basis for modern international arbitration of disputes. *See* 52 C.T.S. 243.

JERUSALEM: city on the Jordan River having religious significances for Jews, Christians, and Moslems and has been a battleground for a thousand years. Currently, it is held by Israel and poses a major stumbling block to Middle East peace. *See* 21 Harv. Int'l L.J. 784.

JEWISH QUESTION: euphemism of anti-Semitic political rhetoric. *See* ZIONISM.

JODHPUR TREATY (1818): example of a British colonial treaty later involved in disputes in India. *See* 68 C.T.S. 243 and 22 I.L.R. 127.

JOHNSON DOCTRINE: assertion made by President Johnson in 1965, that the United States had a unilateral right to intervene militarily in any state in the Western Hemisphere which in the opinion of the U.S. was about to have a communist government. *See* 59 Am.J.Int.L. 867 and BREZNEV DOCTRINE.

JOHNSON-MANN DOCTRINE: United States foreign policy to support friendly governments in Latin America regardless of their political system. *See contra*, KENNEDY DOCTRINE.

JOINDER OF CASES: under Art. 48 of the STATUTE OF THE INTER-NATIONAL COURT OF JUSTICE (q.v.); the Court has the power to join two or more cases into a single case if the subject matter or parties are the same.

JOINT UNDERTAKING: very broad term for any activities performed by two or more parties in concert, including anything from a contract to build a factory to the establishment of an international organization.

JOINT VENTURE: a more restrictive term than JOINT UNDER-TAKING (q.v.), usually applied to two businesses or a state and a business cooperating on a particular economic project.

JORDAN-NEGEV PROJECT: Israeli development project to provide water for the Negev desert by diverting water from the Jordan River. *See* 2 Can.Y.B.Int'l L. 184.

JOURNALIST INTERNATIONAL CODE OF ETHICS: erstwhile effort at freedom of information by the United Nations. *See* 1952 U.N. Yearbook 465.

JOYCE V. DIRECTOR OF PUBLIC PROSECUTIONS: Joyce, a native-born American citizen who resided in England, was found guilty of treason committed outside the realm by the House of

Lords. Because Joyce had obtained and used a British passport, the House of Lords held that he owed allegiance to the King just as he sought the protection of the King for himself while abroad. [1946] 1 All.E.R. 186.

JUDEA AND SAMARIA: Israeli name for the territory usually referred to as the WEST BANK of the Jordan (q.v.).

JUDEX IN SUA CAUSA (L): to be the judge of one's own case.

JUDGMENT OF UNITED NATIONS ADMINISTRATIVE TRIBUNAL: an advisory opinion by the International Court requested by the United Nations Commission on Application for Review of ADMINISTRATIVE TRIBUNAL (q.v.) Judgments, following application for such review by a UN staff member in an employment contract dispute. The decision is important in defining the procedural rights of international civil servants. *See* 1973 I.C.J. 166.

JUDGMENTS OF THE ILO ADMINISTRATIVE TRIBUNAL: advisory opinion dealing with four judgments of the INTERNATIONAL LABOUR ORGANIZATION (q.v.) tribunal relating to disputes between UNESCO and four of its officials. The court upheld the tribunal's judgments in favor of the officials. *See* 1956 I.C.J. 77.

JUDGMENTS OF THE INTERNATIONAL COURT OF JUSTICE: the final decisions of international legal disputes rendered by the Inter-national Court of Justice. *See* Art. 54 *et seq.,* of the STATUTE OF THE INTERNATIONAL COURT OF JUSTICE.

JUDICIAL ASSISTANCE: the aid given by the courts of one country in support of judicial proceedings being entertained in the courts of another country. Requests for such aid are usually entertained pursuant to treaty, *see e.g.,* HAGUE CONVENTION ON THE SERVICE OF JUDICIAL AND EXTRAJUCICIAL DOCUMENTS ABROAD.

J

JUDICIAL DECISION: the findings made by a court or other judicial body. Judicial decisions are generally accepted as a source of international law although described as a "subsidiary source" in Art. 38 of the STATUTE OF THE INTERNATIONAL COURT OF JUSTICE (q.v.).

JUDICIAL FUNCTIONARY: persons acting in a judicial capacity, they are usually immune from liability for their official acts; however, the question may arise as to the liability of the state for the act of its judges. *See* 1929 Brit.Y.B. Int'l.L. 181.

JUDICIAL PRECEDENT: international courts are not obligated to follow previous decisions as are courts in common law jurisdictions under the doctrine of precedent. Art. 59 of the STATUTE OF THE INTERNATIONAL COURT OF JUSTICE (q.v.) provides that "the decision of the court has no binding force except between the parties and in respect to the particular case."

JUDICIAL SETTLEMENT OF DISPUTES: the utilization of the judicial functions of international courts or other tribunals in order to resolve disputes between parties subject to international law.

JUDICIUM FINIUM REGUNDORUM (L): a judgment delimiting an obscure boundary dispute.

JUGE DE SA COMPETENCE (F): judge of its competence, a court usually has the power to decide the scope of its own power. *See also* MAITRE DE SA COMPETENCE and COMPETENCE DE LA COMPETENCE. *See* 1958 Y.B.Int'l.L., Comm'n 43.

JUGEMENTS DE DAMME (F): the system of laws in vogue in Northern Europe from the 12th to the 16th centuries.

JULIAN MARCH: mountainous region north of Trieste on the Austrian, Italian, and Yugoslavian borders, part of the VENEZIA GUILA (q.v.).

JUNTA (or JUNTA MILITAR)(S): a military government.

JURA COMMUNIS (L): *see* JURA UNIVERSALIA.

JURA IN REM (L): a right which is effective against everyone such as the ownership of property.

JURA NOVIT CURIA (L): the presumption that the court knows the law. This maxim controls the manner in which the International Court handles questions of international law. As a consequence, the Court is not restricted to the law presented by the parties, but is free to undertake its own research.

JURA PRIVATA (L): the rights of individuals.

JURA UNIVERSALIA (L): the rights of all; laws that apply to both individuals and nations.

JURE GESTIONIS (L): the activities of a state which are of the same nature of those carried on by individuals, e.g., operating a factory.

JURE IMPERII (L): the activities of a state which only a sovereign is capable of conducting, e.g., enforcing laws, levying taxes, conducting foreign policy.

JURE REPRESENTATIONES (L): by right of representation.

JURIDICAL PERSON: a corporation, commission, or other international organization having the capacity to contract, to acquire and dispose of property, and to institute judicial proceedings, e.g., Art. I, Sec. 1 of the Convention on Privileges and Immunities of the United Nations provides that the UN shall possess juridical personality. *See* 21 U.S.T. 1418, 1 U.N.T.S. 15.

JURIS TANTUM (L): a presumption which is based on the lack of contradictory evidence.

JURISDICTION: 1) the authority a state exercises over its nationals, property, and airspace; 2) the territory of a state; 3) the authority a court has to hear cases concerning particular persons, property, or events. *See* 11 Recueil des Cours 1.

JURISDICTION AND ENFORCEMENT OF JUDGMENTS IN CIVIL AND COMMERCIAL MATTERS CONVENTION (1989): agreement among the European Community and the European Free Trade Association (qq.v.). *See* 28 I.L.M. 620.

JURISDICTION OF THE COURTS OF DANZIG ADVISORY OPINION: advisory opinion of the PERMANENT COURT OF INTERNATIONAL JUSTICE (q.v.) in a dispute between Poland and the free city of Danzig. The Court recognized that a treaty could confer rights on individuals as well as governments. If the international agreement is one conferring rights on individuals then its provisions are applicable by municipal courts. *See* 1928 P.C.I.J. (series B) No.15, 2 Hudson, *World Court Reports* 236 (1969).

JURISDICTION OF THE EUROPEAN COMMISSION OF THE DANUBE ADVISORY OPINION: decision in a dispute between Romania and the EUROPEAN DANUBE COMMISSION (q.v.) over the extent of the Commission's powers. The Court found that the Commission was empowered to perform supervisory functions to the extent necessary to ensure freedom of navigation and equal treatment of ships of all flags on the Danube River. *See* 1927 P.C.I.J. (series B) No.14, 2 Hudson, *World Court Reports* 140 (1969).

JURISDICTION OF THE ICAO COUNCIL CASE: the INTERNATIONAL COURT OF JUSTICE held that the INTERNATIONAL CIVIL AVIATION ORGANIZATION (qq.v.) was competent to entertain a dispute between Pakistan and India concerning overflight of civilian aircraft. The Court noted that the unilateral suspension of a treaty does not render the jurisdictional provisions of that treaty inoperable since one of the objects of the provisions may be to enable the validity of the suspension to be tested. *See* 1972 I.C.J. 46.

JURISDICTION OF THE INTERNATIONAL COMMISSION OF THE ODER CASE: the VERSAILLES PEACE TREATY OF 1919 (q.v.) charged the Oder Commission with revising the existing international agreements concerning the Oder River. The PERMANENT COURT OF INTERNATIONAL JUSTICE was asked to decide whether the jurisdiction of the Oder Commission extended to two tributaries to the Oder. Basing its decision on the idea that all riparian states of a navigable river hold a community of interests, the Court held that the Commission's jurisdiction included the navigable portions of the tributaries. *See* 1929 P.C.I.J (series A) No. 23, 2 Hudson, *World Court Reports* 611 (1969).

JURISPRUDENCE CONSTANTE: the settled practices of a court.

JURISTS: academics who write about questions of law, the writings of jurists are a source of international law recognized in the STATUTE OF THE INTERNATIONAL COURT OF JUSTICE, Art. 43 (q.v.).

JUS AD BELLUM (L): a justification for going to war; the right to go to war is now only available to a state which is a victim of AGGRESSION (q.v.). *See* LEGAL WAR.

JUS AEQUUM (L): equitable law, i.e., principles that allow flexibility in applying exacting rules where such application would be contrary to a sense of fairness and justice.

JUS ALBINAGII (L): right of a state to confiscate the estate of a foreigner who died in its territory.

JUS ANGARIAE (L): ANGUARY LAW (q.v.)

JUS ASYLI: the law of ASYLUM (q.v.).

JUS BELLI (L): the law of WAR (q.v.).

JUS BELLUM DICENDI (L): the right to declare WAR (q.v.).

JUS CADUCUM (L): the law of escheat, i.e., property that cannot be distributed to heirs is taken by the state.

JUS CIVILE (L): civil law. 1) The body of law applying only to one state or people; 2) The system of law based upon Roman law as exemplified by the Napoleanic Code in France.

JUS COGENS (L): the notion that states may not abrogate any of the rules of customary international law. Art. 53 of the VIENNA CONVENTION ON THE LAW OF TREATIES (q.v.) recognizes *jus cogens* by declaring void all treaties which conflict with a pre-emptory norm of general international law.

JUS COMMUNE GENTIBUS (L): more frequently now but less precise, JUS GENTIUM (q.v.), the laws that are recognized and adopted by most civilized nations.

JUS CONSUETUDINARIUM (L): the body of international law found in customary practices that nations feel bound by law to follow. *See* OPINIO JURIS.

JUS CUDENDAE MONETAE (L): the right to create and circulate money, now widely recognized as a power of every state. *See* [1951] A.C. 201.

JUS DENEGATA (L): the right to refuse.

JUS DETRACTUS (L): principle which mitigates JUS ALBI-NAGII (q.v.). By *jus detractus* the estate of a deceased foreigner is not confiscated by the state, but is taxed when removed from the state by a foreign heir.

JUS DISPOSITIVUM (L): a law which may be changed with the consent of the group to which it applies, e.g., customary law which changes with the usage of those governed. *Contra*, JUS COGENS (q.v.).

JUS EGRA OMNES (L): an ABSOLUTE RIGHT (q.v.).

JUS FECIALE (L): archaic branch of international law providing religious formalities to various acts such as ratification of treaties or declarations of war.

JUS FETIALE (L): law applied by a group of twenty Roman priests, the Fetiale, charged with managing Rome's relations with foreign states.

JUS GENTIUM (L): the law of nations. Originally, the term described the body of law used in ancient Rome to settle disputes between Roman citizens and foreigners or between foreigners alone. The term is now used to describe the body of rules common to the legal systems of all civilized states.

JUS IN BELLO (L): the law of war which includes rules concerning the conduct of war and the protection of war victims.

JUS IN PERSONAM (L): a right available only against a particular person.

JUS IN RE (L): a right which is effective against all persons.

JUS INTER GENTES : law applicable to the relations between nations.

JUS LEGATIONIS (L): the right to send DIPLOMATIC AGENTS (q.v.) which is usually reserved to the sovereign, but which is sometimes exercised by the sovereign's most senior representative abroad. *See* Satow, *A Guide to Diplomatic Practice* 118 (1957).

JUS NATURALE (L): natural law, the laws of nature.

JUS NAVIGANDI (L): the right to navigate and carry on commerce by ship. *See* CABOTAGE.

JUS PERSONARUM (L): the municipal law that establishes the status of an individual, e.g., regarding birth, age of majority, and civil capacity.

JUS POSTERIORI DEROGAT PRIORI (L): a recently assumed obligation takes precedent over an older obligation. *See* 25 I.L.R. 279.

JUS POSTLIMINII (L): the right of POSTLIMINIUM (q.v.).

JUS PRAEMINENS (L): *See* DOMINIUM EMINENS.

JUS PRIMI OCCUPATIS (L): the right of the first settler.

JUS PROTECTIONIS (L): the right to shelter.

JUS PUBLICUM EUROPAEUM (L): the public law (laws between nations) of Europe.

JUS PUNIENDI (L): a state's right to punish criminal offenses under its law. The punishment of extraterritorial offenses is discussed in *Kaiser and Attenhofer v. Basle*, 17 I.L.R. 189.

JUS REPRESENTATIONIS OMNIMODAE (L): the right to stand in the place of another, to represent another in all respects.

JUS RESISTENDI (L): the right to offer resistance; to argue against.

JUS QUARTERIORUM (L): also called FRANCHISE DU QUARTIER (q.v.), the extraterritoriality of diplomatic residences (*see* FRANCHISE DE L'HOTEL) which were often located in a particular quarter in the town led to this designation of a diplomatic area having extraterritorial character. The concept became outmoded in the 18th century.

JUS SACRUM (L): law used in Rome to regulate religious matters.

JUS SANGUINIS (L): law of the blood; civil law principle whereby the nationality of children follows that of the parents without regard to the place of the child's birth. *See* JUS SOLI.

JUS SINGULARE (L): an unusual law; one applicable only in a single locale.

JUS SOLI (L): law of the soil; principle of common law whereby birth upon a state's soil confers nationality, irrespective of the nationality of the parents. *See Contra*, JUS SANGUINIS.

JUS STANDI (L): standing in law, having the capacity to act in international law, e.g., one must be party to a treaty before having JUS STANDI (q.v.) to bring an action before the Inter' national Court of Justice to interpret its terms.

JUS STRICTUM (L): strict law; the law is interpreted strictly without any modification or consideration of equity.

JUS TALIONIS (L): the right to compensation in kind rather than monetary damages.

JUS TRANSITUS INNOXII (L): the right of INNOCENT PASSAGE (q.v.).

JUS VITAE AC NECIS (L): the right of life or death; in Roman law the father had this right over his family.

JUST FRONTIER: attempt at drawing borders between states in an equitable and rational manner, an impossible task in almost every instance.

JUST WAR: the doctrine first set forth by St. Augustine in the early fifth century, that war is permissible if the cause is just, e.g., a war to defend a state against invasion by an enemy state is a just war.

J

JUSTICIABLE DISPUTE: a conflict which is capable of resolution through resort to judicial process.

JUSTITIA ET PAX (L): justice and peace.

JUSTUM BELLUM (L): JUST WAR (q.v.).

[K - L]

KAHAN COMMISSION: group led by Israeli Chief Justice Yitzhak Kahan appointed to investigate the massacre of civilians in the Palestinian camps of Sabra and Chatilla (in Beirut) in September 1982 by Lebanese Christian militia. It was found that the Israeli occupiers of that area of Beirut were indirectly responsible for allowing the massacre to take place. *See* 22 I.L.M. 473.

KAINARDJI TREATY (1774): peace treaty between Russia and Turkey giving Moldavia and Wallachia, two provinces not fully sovereign, the right to send CHARGE D'AFFAIRES (q.v.) to foreign powers. *See* 45 C.T.S. 349.

KAISER: derivative of Caesar, title assumed by the emperor of Germany after the unification of the German principalities in the latter part of the 19th century.

KAISER WILHELM CANAL: *see* KIEL CANAL.

KANAGAWA TREATY (1854): first peace treaty between the United States and Japan providing for aid to United States ships in peril and the establishment of a U.S. consulate. *See* 11 Stat. 597, 9 Bevans 351.

KANO CONFERENCE (1979): abortive attempt to end the CHADIAN CIVIL WAR (q.v.) including a plan to demilitarize the capitol, N'Djamena, with a Nigerian peacekeeping force.

KASENKINA AFFAIR (1948): defection of a Soviet consulate school   teacher led to a break in consular relations between the United States and the Soviet Union. *See* 43 Am.J.Int.L. 37.

KASHMIR QUESTION: dispute between India and Pakistan with respect to the states of Kashmir and Jannu, claimed by both since their independence in 1947. On several occasions the UN Security Council has been asked to mediate the dispute. They arranged a cease-fire but no political settlement. *See* 1947-8 U.N. Yearbook 387.

KATANGA: rebellious province of the Congo, it surrendered to the Central Congolese authorities in January of 1962 after two years of aggressive secessionist activities. *See* CONGO CRISIS.

KATTAGAT: river flowing into the Baltic subject to DANISH SOUND DUES (q.v.). *See* 4 Whiteman, *Digest of International Law* 423.

KATYN CASE (1943): the bodies of 10,000 Polish troops were discovered by the German Army in the Katyn Forest, Poland. For many years responsibility for the massacre was not established as both the Germans and the Russians had the opportunity to commit the atrocity. *See* 10 Whiteman, *Digest of International Law* 348. Recently the Soviet government has released documents proving the Soviet Secret Police were responsible. *See* N.Y. Times, Ap. 14, 1990, sec. 1, p. 1, col. 4.

KEHL KEHLER HAFEN CASE (1953): agreement between France and the State of Baden (a subdivision of the Federal Republic of Germany) concerning the administration of the Port of Kehl was reviewed by the Constitutional Court of the Federal Republic of Germany. *See* 20 I.L.R. 407

KEKKONEN PLAN (1963 & 1978): attempts by the President of Finland to establish a NUCLEAR FREE ZONE (q.v.) in Scandinavia and joint control of the armaments owned by the Scandinavian countries. *See* 1963 Facts on File at 197.

KELANTAN: the status as a sovereign state of this territory in the Malaysian Peninsular has been the subject of litigation in England. *See* [1924] App.Cas. 797.

KELLOGG-BRIAND PACT (1928): also called the Pact of Paris; originally intended to be a bilateral treaty between France and the United States. The Pact promoted specific means of dispute settlement and parties renounced war as an instrument of national policy. It was adhered to by 63 nations and its principles were incorporated into the U.N. Charter. *See General Pact for the Renunication of war*, 46 Stat. 2343, 2 Bevans 732, 94 L.N.T.S. 57.

KENNAN DOCTRINE: the idea of containing the spread of Soviet Communism put forth in an article by Mr. X (George F. Kennan). *See* Foreign Affairs (July 1947).

KENNAN PLAN (1957): proposal by George F. Kennan for terms to the reunification of Germany. *See* 43 U.S. News 68 (Dec. 13, 1957).

KENNECOTT COPPER EXPROPRIATION (1974): part of the nationalization of the copper mining industry by the Government of Chile. *See* 14 I.L.M. 135.

KENNEDY DOCTRINE: the United States policy to give aid only to those Latin American countries with democratically elected governments. *See* Simons, *The Kennedy Doctrine* (1974) and JOHNSON-MANN DOCTRINE.

KENNEDY ROUND: negotiations initiated by the administration of the United States President John Kennedy within the GENERAL AGREEMENT ON TARIFFS AND TRADE (q.v.). They were not completed until 1967, by an agreement to liberalize trade restrictions. *See* 62 Am.J.Int.L. 403.

KENYATTA COMMISSION: failed attempt to end the CONGO CRISIS (1964) (q.v.).

KGB: Kommissariat Gosudarstvennoi Begopastnotoi (Commissariat for State Security) Soviet Secret Police charged particularly with internal security.

KHABAROVSK TRIAL (1949): Soviet military tribunal tried and convicted Japanese military officers accused of developing BACTERIOLOGICAL WEAPONS (q.v.). *See* 10 Whiteman, *Digest of International Law* 457.

KHEDIVE OF EGYPT: this was the title held by the Pasha of Egypt. *See Abbas Himli Pasha v. Great Britain*, 4 Ann. Digest 434.

KIAOCHOW: territory leased to Germany by China in 1898. *See* 186 C.T.S. 187.

KIDNAPPING: at common law, the forcible abduction and carrying away of a person from their own country to another. Forcing a person to another state for the purpose of subjecting the person to that states laws is considered a violation of the former state's sovereignty. *See* EICHMANN INCIDENT.

KIEL CANAL: canal linking the North Sea with the Baltic Sea; became an international waterway by virtue of Art. 380 of the VERSAILLES PEACE TREATY (q.v.). Germany was to maintain the canal and charge a reasonable fee to cover maintenance and it was to be open on an equal basis to both commercial and war vessels of all nations at peace with Germany. Hitler denounced the treaty but the canal retains its international status. *See* 2 Ann. Digest 99.

KIEL TREATY (1814): agreement which ended the 400-year union of the Kingdoms of Norway and Denmark. *See* 6 Ann. Digest 95.

KING: title which may be bestowed on the male head of state of a MONARCHY (q.v.).

KING'S CHAMBER: portions of the sea between lines drawn from headland to HEADLAND (q.v.) which Great Britain claims as territorial waters.

KINGMAN REEF: Pacific island reserved by the United States as a naval defense area. *See* 4 Whiteman, *Digest of International Law* 380.

KINSHASA RESOLUTION (1967): reaffirmation, by the African heads of state, of principles of sovereignty and territorial integrity, and condemned secession in any member state. *See* Amate, *Inside the OAU* 440 (1986).

KISKA: harbor in the Aleutian Islands reserved for the exclusive use of the United States Navy. *See* 4 Whiteman, *Digest of Inter national Law* 408.

KISSINGER COMMISSION ON CENTRAL AMERICA: group led by former Secretary of State Henry Kissinger, appointed by President Reagan to study and make proposals (some would say rubber stamp) for United States policy in Central America. *See* 1984 *American Foreign Policy* 1008. *See also* CONTADORA PROCESS.

KISSINGER-SONNENFELDT DOCTRINE (1975): policy of the United States to support moves for independence from Moscow's control by communist governments. *See* II *Public Papers of the Presidents:* Gerald R. Ford 1124.

KOLLISSIONRECHT (G): CONFLICTS OF LAWS (q.v.).

KOREAN AIRLINE INCIDENT (1983): Soviet fighter shot down a Korean Airlines 747 which had violated Soviet airspace over Sakhalin Island. Two hundred sixty-nine passengers and crew were killed. *See* 88 Dick. L. R. 237.

KOREAN WAR: shortly after the Republic of Korea (South Korea) came into being, after years of Japanese occupation, it was invaded by North Korea. In 1950, the UN Security Council voted to engage forces to repel the invasion. Sixteen member nations supplied forces under the U.S. command and were engaged in "police action" until an armistice was signed on July 27, 1953. *See* 4 U.S.T. 230, 4 U.S.T. 346 or 47 Am.J.Int.L. Supp. 178.

KOSTEN (G): literally "costs," refers to fees, court costs or security costs, and is equivalent to the French "depens." *See* 1935-7 Ann. Digest case no. 156.

KOWLOON: territory attached to Hong Kong and under the jurisdiction of Hong Kong courts.

KREISKY PLAN (1984): proposal for the denuclearization of Europe made by the Austrian Chancellor Bruno Kreisky.

KRIEGSBRAUCH IM LANDKRIEGE (G): manual published by Germany in 1902 to guide its officers in the law and customs of land warfare.

KRIEGSGEBRIET (G): "war zone" or "military area," generally referring to an area at sea.

KRIEGSRASON GEHT VOR KRIEGSMANIER (G): "necessity in war overrules the manner of war." An ancient German proverb that takes exception to the international custom that the laws of war are binding on all belligerents. *See* 16 I.L.R. 543.

KRISTALLNACHT (G): crystal night; night of November 9-10, 1938, when the Nazis unleashed their terror against the Jewish people, including the burning synagogues all over Germany. *See* Thalmann and Feinermann, *Crystal Night* (1974).

KRUPP CASES: in one of the NUREMBERG TRIALS (q.v.) the chief executives of Krupp Heavy Industries were accused of war crimes including the use of slave labor and the planning of aggressive war. They were acquitted. *See* 11 Whiteman, *Digest of International Law* 913.

KUANG-CHU WAN: territory leased by France from China in 1898. *See* 186 C.T.S. 220.

KURILE ISLANDS: chain of Japanese islands placed under the sovereignty of the U.S.S.R. by virtue of the CAIRO DECLARATION (1943) (q.v.). *See* 32 I.L.R. 582.

KUTCHUK-KAINARDJI TREATY (1774): *see* KAINARDJI TREATY.

KUWAIT INCIDENT (1961): Iraqi attempt to occupy Kuwait was stymied by a British-backed coup after which the ARAB LEAGUE (q.v.) administered Kuwait until 1963. *See* 13 Middle Eastern Affairs 2-13 and 43-53.

KWAJALEIN: one of the Marshall Islands occupied by the United States in World War II; subsequently became a United Nations TRUST TERRITORY (q.v.) under the trusteeship of the United States. *See* 1 Whiteman, *Digest of International Law* 786.

LA PLATA RIVER REGIME: international agreements covering the status and utilization of the La Plata River and its tributaries.*See* 13 I.L.M. 251 and the La Plata River Basin Treaty, 875 U.N.T.S. 3.

LABOR ORGANIZATION: *see* INTERNATIONAL LABOUR ORGANIZATION.

LAC LANOUX ARBITRATION: dispute between France and Spain beginning in 1917, over the use of waters flowing from Lac Lanoux, a large lake in the French Pyrenees, which feeds the Carol River flowing into Spain. An arbitral tribunal concluded, on the basis of French-Spanish treaty law, that the French plan to divert the water was legal. *See* 12 R.I.A.A. 281 or 53 Am.J.Int.L. 156.

LACAC: LATIN AMERICAN CIVIL AVIATION COMMISSION (q.v.).

LACUNAE: questions for which no answer can be found in international law.

LAFTA: LATIN AMERICAN FREE TRADE ASSOCIATION (q.v.).

LAGOS ACCORD (1979): attempt to settle the CHADIAN CIVIL WAR (q.v.) which failed. *See* N.Y. Times, Aug. 19, 1979, at 14.

LAGOS AGREEMENT (1966): associated Nigeria with the EUROPEAN ECONOMIC COMMUNITY (q.v.). *See* 5 I.L.M. 828.

LAGOS PLAN OF ACTION (1980): Organization for African Unity's attempt to implement a plan for African economic development. *See* 1980 U.N. Yearbook 557.

LAISSEZ-PASSER: travel document analogous to an international passport issued by the United Nations to UN officials. These documents are to be recognized and accepted as valid by all members of the UN. *See* 1 U.N.T.S. 28.

LAISSEZ-SUIVRE (F): note memorializing the payment of freight or the fulfillment of other conditions necessary to release cargo from a ship.

LANCASTER HOUSE AGREEMENT (1979): conference held in London to agree on a constitutional arrangement for an independent RHODESIA (q.v.) (now Zimbabwe) with majority rule and British supervision of elections. *See* 19 I.L.M. 387.

LAND WARFARE: armed conflict taking place on land as opposed to on the sea or in the air. Most of the law of land warfare is customary, but some rules have been codified in international treaties. *See* HAGUE CONVENTION RESPECTING THE LAWS AND CUSTOMS OF LAND WARFARE (1907) and the GENEVA CONVENTIONS.

LANDKENNING DOCTRINE: Scottish doctrine to determine the part of the sea within the King of Scotland's jurisdiction, which included all the water that could be seen from the coast.

LANDLOCKED: a state having no sea coast. The GENEVA CONVENTION ON THE REGIME OF THE HIGH SEAS (1958) (q.v.) grants landlocked states free access to the high seas, but this must be negotiated with the states between the landlocked state and the sea.

LANGUAGE OF DIPLOMACY: formerly Latin, then French was preferred: currently French, English, Chinese, Russian, and Spanish are the languages most commonly used for diplomatic intercourse (*see* Art. 111 of the UNITED NATIONS CHARTER). The two preferred languages are English and French.

LANGUAGE OF TREATIES: formerly Latin but currently there is no specific rule on the subject. The parties to a treaty may freely select the language or languages in which the treaty will be drafted. *See* AUTHENTIC TEXT.

LANSING-ISHII AGREEMENT (1917): agreement between the United States and Japan, whereby Japan's "paramount interest" in China was recognized by the U.S. The agreement was terminated in 1923. *See* 9 Bevans 425.

LAOS NEUTRALITY DECLARATION (1962): statement by the Royal Laotian Government that they would be neutral, accompanied by promises by other international parties not to introduce troops or armaments into Laos. *See* 57 Am.J.Int.L. 300.

LAPSED TREATY: the agreement found in the treaty has been destroyed by a change in circumstances or facts which effectively terminate the treaty. *See* REBUS SIC STANDIBUS.

LATERAN TREATY (1929): agreement between the HOLY SEE (q.v.) and the Italian government. Italy recognized the Vatican as a sovereign and independent state. The Vatican agreed to return fugitives from justice to Italy, and Italy agreed to take jurisdiction over crimes committed in the Vatican state's territory. *See* H.E. Cardinale, *The Holy See and the International Order* (1976).

LATIN AMERICAN CIVIL AVIATION COMMISSION (LA-CAC): organization to coordinate and facilitate civil aviation in Latin America. *See* 11 Annals of Air and Space Law 362.

LATIN AMERICAN ECONOMIC SYSTEM CONVENTION (SELA): established a permanent system of interregional economic and social cooperation with a permanent organization composed of a council, action committees, and a secretariat. *See* 15 I.L.M. 1081.

LATIN AMERICAN FREE TRADE ASSOCIATION (LAFTA): superseded by the LATIN AMERICAN INTEGRATION ASSO-CIATION (q.v.). It attempted to establish a free trade zone in Latin America but failed. *See* MONTEVIDEO TREATY (1960).

LATIN AMERICAN INTEGRATION ASSOCIATION (ALAI): association of eleven countries which superseded the LATIN AMERICAN FREE TRADE ASSOCIATION (q.v.), it has a more flexible structure to promote trade than the former organization. *See* Treaty of Montevideo, 20 I.L.M. 672 (1981).

LATIN AMERICAN NUCLEAR FREE ZONE TREATY (1967): by a United Nations treaty Latin America is declared to be a nuclear free zone where atomic weapons are forbidden and are not to be used against the countries there. An agency was created to monitor compliance. *See* 6 I.L.M. 521 and 8 I.L.M. 990.

LATIN AMERICAN PARLIAMENT: meeting of parliamentary delegates from 12 Latin American countries. *See* 27 I.L.M. 430.

LATO SENSU (L): a broad interpretation.

LAUNCHING STATE: state that launches or procures the launch of an object into outer space. The launch state retains jurisdiction over the object and is liable for damages to other states caused by its space objects. *See* Arts. 7 & 8 of the *Outter Space Treaty*, 6 I.L.M. 386 and LIABILITY FOR DAMAGES CAUSED BY SPACE OBJECTS CONVENTION (1973).

LAUREL-LANGLEY TRADE AGREEMENT (1955): treaty concerning United States and Philippine economic relations. *See* 6 U.S.T.2981. For efforts to update it *see* 7 I.L.M. 87.

LAUSANNE TREATY (1912): peace treaty ending the Italo-Turkish War by which Italy acquired Tripoli. *See* 7 Am.J.Int.L. Supp. 58.

LAUSANNE PEACE TREATY (1923): signed by the Allied Powers and Turkey at the end of World War I; it ended the CAPITULATIONS (q.v.) in Turkey and Turkey renounced all rights and title over Egypt. *See* 28 L.N.T.S. 12.

LAUTERPACT DOCTRINE: states are obligated to recognize territories which have met the factual requirements for statehood. Named for Sir Hersh Lauterpact the doctrine has been rejected by most states except for Great Britain. *See* RECOGNITION.

LAW MAKING TREATY: a source of international law, i.e., an agreement between a substantial number of states acting in their own interest modifying, establishing, or abolishing rules of international law. Such treaties are only binding on the states that sign and ratify them but may quickly become evidence of customary rules of international law.

LAW OF DISCOVERY: discovery of a territory gave the state in whose service the discoverer worked an inchoate title to the territory which the state had to perfect by effective occupation of the territory. *See* 27 Am.J.Int.L. 130.

LAW OF NATIONS: synonymous with INTERNATIONAL LAW (q.v.); the body of customary and conventional rules which regulate the intercourse between and relations of sovereign nations.

LAW OF THE SEA: rules governing the three zones of the sea, i.e., INTERNAL WATERS, TERRITORIAL WATERS, and THE HIGH SEAS (qq.v.). Much of the traditional customary law was codified at Geneva in 1958. *See* GENEVA CONVENTION ON THE REGIME OF THE SEA (1958). In the longest (over ten years) negotiating process in the history of international law, a new Law of the Seas regime has been adopted by the United Nations Conference on the Law of the Sea. *See* LAW OF THE SEA CONVENTION (1982).

LAW OF THE SEA CONVENTION (1982): "Progressive" reworking of the International Law governing the HIGH SEAS and

TERRITORIAL WATERS (qq.v.) by the United Nations Conference on the Law of the Sea. This "new order" includes broadening the extent of the territorial sea and rules for DEEP SEABED MINING (q.v.). *See* 21 I.L.M. 1261.

LAWFUL BELLIGERENT: nation legally at war; traditionally only a fully sovereign state may be a lawful belligerent.

LAWS OF WAR: body of rules brought into operation during armed conflict between nations. Many of the customary rules have been codified through general treaties, *see e.g.*, HAGUE CONVENTION RESPECTING LAWS AND CUSTOMS OF LAND WARFARE (1907) and the GENEVA CONVENTIONS (1949).

LDC: LEAST DEVELOPED COUNTRIES (q.v.).

LEAGUE COUNCIL: executive body of the League of Nations originally having four permanent and four nonpermanent members. *See* Art. 4 of the COVENANT OF THE LEAGUE OF NATIONS.

LEAGUE OF ARAB STATES: *See* ARAB LEAGUE.

LEAGUE OF NATIONS: first comprehensive international organization; established by the Covenant of the League of Nations which is Part I of the VERSAILLES PEACE TREATY (q.v.) (1919). It voted itself out of existence on April 18, 1946, when many of its functions were turned over to the United Nations.

LEAGUE OF NATIONS CODIFICATION COMMITTEE: sixteen-member committee of experts whose task was to codify certain rules of international law concerning nationality, territorial waters, and responsibility of states for damage to aliens. *See* 24 Am.J.Int.L.Supp. 215, 234.

LEAGUE OF NATIONS TREATY SERIES: compilation of treaties deposited with and published by the League of Nations.

LEARNED WRITERS: by Art. 38 (1)(d) of the STATUTE OF THE INTERNATIONAL COURT OF JUSTICE (q.v.) the Court is to utilize the "teaching of the most highly qualified publicists" (learned writers) as a subsidiary source of international law.

LEASE OF TERRITORY: peaceful mode of acquiring territory by one nation from another, usually for transit, or commercial purposes, or for military bases. The lease does not confer title. *See also* CONCESSION.

LEAST DEVELOPED COUNTRIES (LDC): those countries with the most primitive economic development and low standards of living.

LEBANON INVASION (1958). *See* BEIRUT INVASION (1958).

LEGAL DISPUTE: justiciable matter for which a decision founded upon the application of existing law is sought, i.e., "a disagreement on a point of law or fact, a conflict of legal views or of interests between two persons." *Mavrommatis Case*, 1927 P.C.I.J. ser. A., No.2, at 11.

LEGAL INTEREST: although, the STATUTE OF THE INTERNATIONAL COURT OF JUSTICE (q.v.) does not require an applicant state to have a sufficient legal interest to justify the bringing of a case, international law requires that the applicant have a direct concern in the adjudication of the case. *See also* Art. 62 of the *Statute,* 59 Stat. 1031, 3 Bevans 1191.

LEGAL QUESTION: issue that invites the court to undertake an essentially judicial task. The I.C.J. has not defined "legal question," but has suggested that interpretations were necessarily and always legal questions. *See Admissions Cases,* 1947/48 I.C.J. 57, 61.

LEGAL WAR: the conduct of formal hostilities, among nations permitted by INTERNATIONAL LAW (q.v.) under the COVENANT OF THE LEAGUE OF NATIONS (Art. 12) (q.v.), to resort to war after complying with certain conditions. Under the

UNITED NATIONS CHARTER (q.v.) SELF-DEFENSE is the only justification for war. *See also* JUS AD BELLUM.

LEGATE: diplomatic emissary of the Roman Catholic Church.

LEGATI A LATERE (L): an ambassador representing the Holy See, or a first class Papal envoy who is also a Cardinal.

LEGATION: 1) The right of a recognized independent state to accredit envoys to other states and to receive envoys from foreign states. Only states that are fully sovereign can exercise the right of legation. 2) A second class diplomatic establishment ranking below an embassy.

LEGATION BUILDING: embassy premises.

LEGATION BUILDING CASE: an Austrian Supreme Court decision affirmed the general view that legation buildings are inviolable. 1 I.L.R. 291.

LEGATUS NATUS (L): a representative of the Vatican who does not have diplomatic status.

LEGEM ENIM CONTRACTUS DAT (L): an agreement makes law.

LEGES WISBUENSESL: an important collection of the maritime laws of Wisby on the Island of Gotland, Sweden, dating from the fourteenth century.

LEGITIMACY: when recognizing a new government this term is applied usually for ideological reasons. Though a communist regime may have uncontested control of a country the United State may only recognize it as the DE FACTO GOVERNMENT (q.v.) and not as the LEGITIMATE GOVERNMENT (q.v.).

LEGITIMATE DEFENSE (or self-defense): a defense is justified when a state is attacked. All states have the right to resist acts of aggression. *See* Art. 51 of the United Nations Charter, 59 Stat. 1031, 3 Bevans 1153.

LEGITIMATE GOVERNMENT: administrative organization controlling a STATE (q.v.) which is recognized by other governments as the legal government of that state under the rules of international law.

LEGITIMATE INTERESTS: a judicial interest not necessarily justified in both law and morals. Generally for a party to intervene in a case before a tribunal it must have a legitimate interest in the matter.

LEIPZIG TRIALS (1920-22): trials conducted by the Supreme Court of Leipzig of German officials accused of war crimes in the prosecution of World War I. *See* 8 Va.L. Rev. 1 (1921).

LEONTIEF REPORT (1977): United Nations study authored by Professor Wassily Leontief titled *The Future of the World Economy* (Oxford University Press, 1977). It emphasized the harmful effects of the superpower arms race.

LETELIER MURDER: Orlando Letelier and Ronni Moffitt were assassinated in Washington, D.C. in 1976, by agents of the Chilean Government. The dispute over compensation for the deaths between the United States and Chile was settled in 1990. *See* 30 I.L.M. 421.

LETICIA DISPUTE (1932-33): a boundary dispute between Colombia and Peru was aggravated when Peru supported a band of Colombian nationals who had forcibly occupied the Colombian district of Leticia. A report adopted by the League of Nations, 1933 League of Nations Official Journal 526, stated that the presence of Peruvian forces in Leticia was contrary to the principles of the KELLOGG-BRIAND PACT (q.v.). A three-member commission reaffirmed the treaty which established the Peru-Colombia boundary in 1922.

LETTER OF CREDENCE: this document is addressed by the head of one state to the head of a foreign state introducing a diplomatic agent. The letter identifies the diplomatic agent, designates his rank, and requests that the agent be favorably received. When a CHARGE D'AFFAIRES (q.v.) is sent the letter of credence is addressed by the foreign secretary to the foreign secretary.

LETTER OF INTRODUCTION: correspondence identifying the bearer and asking that the bearer be recognized by the addressee. *See e.g.*, LETTER OF CREDENCE.

LETTER OF NOTIFICATION: note from a head of state to his counterparts informing them of his election to the position and expressing friendly intentions.

LETTER OF RECALL: formal notice to a state that an ambassador (or envoy) is being recalled, often a form of protest against the state from which the ambassador is recalled. *See* 7 Whiteman, *Digest of International Law* 89.

LETTER OF RELEASE: note from a head of state "releasing" an envoy who is returning to his own country, and usually praising the positive role he has played in the relations of the two states.

LETTERS OF MARQUE: documents granted by a sovereign authorizing a merchant ship that had been pillaged to recover its losses by pillaging ships of the offending nation. A ship which practiced such retaliation was known as a PRIVATEERING (q.v.).

LETTERS PATENT: same as LETTERS OF MARQUE (q.v.).

LETTERS ROGATORY: instrument by which the court of one country requests a court of another country to assist in obtaining evidence, serving notice, or performing other judicial tasks. The method and procedure used in carrying out the request is exclusively within the control of the court receiving the request. *See* Fed.R.Civ.P. 28(b), and the Inter-American Convention on Letters Rogatory, 14 I.L.M. 339 and 18 I.L.M. 1238.

LETTRE DE CREANCE (F): LETTER OF CREDENCE (q.v.).

LETTRE D'INTRODUCTION (F): LETTER OF INTRODUC-TION (q.v.).

LETTRE DE MISSION (F): document supplied by the Secretary General of the League of Nations certifying the status of officials sent on missions.

LETTRE DE PROVISION (F): commission given to a newly appointed consul authorizing the consul to act on behalf of his state in administering the office to which he has been assigned. The consul is admitted by a grant of EXEQUATUR (q.v.).

LETTRE DE RAPPEL (F): LETTER OF RECALL (q.v.).

LETTRE DE RECREANCE (F): a letter acknowledging a recall. When an envoy's mission is terminated by recall, the envoy presents the letter of recall to the receiving state. The head of the receiving state acknowledges the recall with a *lettre de recreance*.

LETTRES DE CABINET (F): correspondence between sovereigns.

LETTRES DE CHANCELLERIE (F): correspondence from a sovereign to the president of a republic.

LETTRES REVERSALES (F): an obsolete term for an international agreement or understanding.

LEVY EN MASSE (F): an armed resistance by the citizenry in advance of an invading force. When the participating individuals organize in accord with the HAGUE REGULATIONS (1907) and the GENEVA CONVENTION III (1949) (qq.v.), they are considered combatants, and thus must be treated in accordance with the LAWS OF WAR (q.v.).

LEX ABROGATA (L): abrogated law; a law no longer in force.

LEX CAUSAE (L): the law governing the legal relationship which gave rise to the rights in issue.

LEX DILATIONES EXHORRET (L): the law will not tolerate delay.

LEX FERENDA (L): the law which would be the most desirable to establish.

LEX FORI (L): the law of the place (forum) where a court sits; the law of the court's own jurisdiction.

LEX IMPERFECTA (L): law which has not been perfected and which is not in force.

LEX LATA (L): the law that is in force or applicable to the jurisdiction or situation.

LEX LOCI CELEBRATIONIS (L): law of the jurisdiction where the contract is formally entered into.

LEX LOCI CONSIDERATIONIS (L): law of the jurisdiction where the consideration for the contract is located.

LEX LOCI SOLUTIONIS (L): law of the jurisdiction where the contract is to be performed.

LEX LOCUS ACTUS (L): the law of the place where an act occurred. *See* 15 I.L.R. 23.

LEX MONETAE (L): Currency law of the state issuing the currency. *See* 70 L.Q.Rev. 186, and F.A. Mann, *Legal Aspects of Money*.

LEX NON COGIT AD IMPOSSIBILIA (L): law will not force one to do the impossible.

LEX NON SCRIPTA (L): the law not written, i.e., customary law.

LEX POSTERIORI DEROGAT PRIORI (L): a law made later in time takes precedence over one made before.

LEX REI SITAE (L): law of the place where the thing is located. *See* 15 I.L.R. 24.

LEX RHODIA DE JACTU (L): *see* RHODIAN LAW.

LEX SITUS (L): law of the place, i.e., rule that in cases of the transfer of property the validity of the transfer is dependent upon the law in effect where the property is at the time of the transfer.

LEX SOCIETATIS (L): the law of the group, e.g., the United Nations Charter is *lex societatis* for members of the United Nations.

LEX SPECIALIS (L): a law with a specific application.

LEX SPECIALIS DEROGAT LEGI GENERALI (L): a specific rule of law overrules a general principle.

LIABILITY FOR DAMAGE CAUSED BY SPACE OBJECTS CONVENTION (1973): rules for determining the liability of LAUNCHING STATE (q.v.), for the damage which is caused by their space objects. *See* 24 U.S.T. 2389, 10 I.L.M. 965. *See also* COSMOS 954.

LIABILITY FOR OIL POLLUTION DAMAGE CONVENTION (1969): an effort to prevent oil pollution from bulk carriers of oil on the high seas. *See* 64 Am.J.Int.L. 481.

LIABILITY IN INTERNATIONAL LAW: as with individuals in domestic law, states may be liable for injury to other states caused by their wrongful acts. However, international law in general does not have the mechanism to exact payment from the culpable state. *See* CORFU CHANNEL CASE.

LIABILITY LIMITATIONS: in a number of areas international agreements have been struck to set limits on the liability of those

engaged in transnational activities. *See e.g.,* WARSAW CONVEN-
TION (1929) (civil air transport) or HAMBURG RULES (Carriage
of Goods by Sea).

LIBBY DAM: a dam on the Columbia River which is an international river as it flows through both the United States and Canada. *See* 8 McGill L.J. 212 (1961-62).

LIBEL OF HEADS OF STATE: all nations grant to each other the
right to demand that their head of state shall not be defamed.
Many nations have laws penalizing such acts. It is contrary to international law to use the image of a head of state for commercial
purposes. *See* 8 I.L.R. 24.

LIBERATION COMMITTEE: this organ of the ORGANIZA-
TION OF AFRICAN UNITY (q.v.) channeled aid to NATIONAL
LIBERATION MOVEMENTS (q.v.) in Africa when it could decide
which one to support. *See* Amate, *Inside the OAU* 213 (1986).

LIBERATION MOVEMENTS: organizations whose aim is the
political independence of a particular nation or ethic people.
They may be recognized by states and their representatives
granted full diplomatic status, e.g., the PALESTINE LIBERATION
ORGANIZATION (q.v.).

LIBERATION THEOLOGY: a mixture of Marxist and Roman
Catholic ideas supporting involvement by the Church in leftist
revolutions particularly in Central and South America. It has
been rejected by the Roman Catholic hierarchy. *See* 10 Fletcher
Forum 317 (1986).

LIBYA OIL COMPANY ARBITRATION: Libya was required to
compensate oil companies which held drilling CONCESSIONS
(q.v.) when their wells were nationalized. *See* 17 I.L.M. 1 and 18
Colum.J.Transnat'l.Law 259.

LIDICE MASSACRE: Nazi troops killed or deported the inhabitants of this Czech town in June of 1942, in retaliation for the as-

sassination of the Nazi Governor. *See* COLLECTIVE PUNISH-MENT.

LIEBER CODE (or Instructions for the Government Armies of the United States in the Field): book by Francis Lieber codifying most of the laws and customs of war as they existed at the time of the American Civil War. The Code was designated as binding on the U.S. Army by President Lincoln and helped initiate the HAGUE PEACE CONFERENCE (1899) (q.v.).

LIFE BOATS: life boats and other small rescue craft are protected from attack by Art. 27(1) of the GENEVA CONVENTION II (1949).

LIGA DE NACIONES (S): the LEAGUE OF NATIONS (q.v.).

LIGHT DUES: fees collected from ships that benefit from the establishment and maintenance of lighthouses. It is usually based on tonnage and collected by the state maintaining the navigation aid.

LIGHTHOUSE: if built on rocks in the high seas a lighthouse does not have territorial waters of its own and does not extend the territorial waters of the owner state. *See* BERING SEAS ARBITRATION.

LIGHTSHIP: unarmed ship anchored at sea and equipped with characteristic lights to aid navigation in the surrounding waters. A state may not claim sovereignty over a maritime belt around a lightship on the high seas.

LIMA CONFERENCE (1938): Eighth Conference of the American States; it strongly condemned territorial changes brought about by war and reaffirmed the MONTEVIDEO CONVENTION ON THE RIGHTS AND DUTIES OF STATES (1933) (q.v.). *See* 33 Am.J.Int.L. 269 and 34 Am.J.Int.L.Supp. 190.

LIMA DECLARATION (1975): declaration and plan of action on industrial development and cooperation adopted by the UNITED

NATIONS INDUSTRIAL DEVELOPMENT ORGANIZATION (q.v.). *See* U.N. Monthly Chronicle, April 1975, at 28.

LIMA TARGET: goal set by the Organization of African Unity that African countries should be producing 2% of the world's industrial output by the year 2000.

LIMITATION OF EMPLOYMENT OF FORCE FOR RECOVERY OF CONTRACT DEBTS CONVENTION: *see* 1 Bevans 607.

LIMITED NUCLEAR TEST BAN TREATY (1974): agreement between the United States and the Soviet Union that limits underground nuclear tests to those yielding less than 150 kilotons of explosive force. *See* 13 I.L.M. 906.

LINE OF WAR: fictitious demarcation of the land area occupied by an enemy. All land within the line of war is considered enemy territory.

LINER CONFERENCES: cartels of shipowners who set the rates they charge for ocean transport on regularly scheduled routes. *See* 13 I.L.M. 910 and 19 Eur.T.L. 451.

LINGGADJALI AGREEMENT (1947): arrangement between Indonesia and its parent state, the Netherlands. It implicitly recognized the sovereignty of the Republic of Indonesia. *See* A.M. Taylor, *Indonesian Independence and the United Nations* (1960).

LINGUA FRANCA (F): the usual language of diplomacy which was first Latin, then French, but now *see* OFFICIAL LANGUAGES.

LIQUOR TREATIES: special treaties made between the U.S. and Great Britain, e.g., ANGLO-AMERICAN LIQUOR TREATY (1924) (q.v.) and other states during the era of Prohibition. Under these treaties the U.S. had the right to board vessels of signatory states if they were within one hour sailing time of the U.S. shore and were suspected of carrying liquor to be smuggled into the United States. In return vessels of signatory states were allowed into U.S. ports with liquor on board if it was destined for foreign ports.

LITISPENDANCE: rule requiring an international tribunal to refrain from entertaining litigation while the issue is before another international tribunal. *See* 5 I.L.R. 446.

LITTLE ENTENTE: short-lived alliance of the newly created states of Czechoslovakia, Yugoslavia, and Romania to balance the expansionist threat of Hungary after World War I. *See* 15 Am.J.Int.L. 67 and 27 Am.J.Int.L.Supp. 117.

LITTORAL STATE: a country bordering on a body of water, e.g., Egypt and Israel are littoral states of the Red Sea.

LITVINOFF AGREEMENT: executive agreement whereby the United States fully recognized the Soviet Union in return for the promise to settle outstanding claims by U.S. nationals. *See* 28 Am.J.Int.L.Supp. 14, *U.S. v. Belmont,* 301 U.S. 324 (1937), and *U.S. v Pink,* 315 U.S. 203 (1942).

LIVING RESOURCES OF THE SEAS: fish, marine mammals, and other biological resources exploited by man. *See* FISHERIES, WHALING REGIME, PEARL FISHERIES, and LAW OF THE SEA CONVENTION (1982).

LLOYD'S OF LONDON: loose association of international insurance underwriters, most notably involved in international maritime insurance. *See* H.A.L. Cockerell, *Lloyd's of London* (1984).

LNTS: LEAGUE OF NATIONS TREATY SERIES (q.v.).

LOAD LINE (also plimsoll line): mark placed on a ship proceeding to sea which indicates the point beyond which the ship may not be safely submerged because of the weight of the cargo it carries.

LOAD LINE CONVENTION (1930): prescribed maximum loads for vessels carrying cargo in international transport. Those ships are required to be checked for safety and marked with a load line, *see* 47 Stat. 8, 135 L.N.T.S. 301. A considerable part of this convention was superseded by the LONDON CONVENTION (1966) (q.v.).

LOAN AGREEMENTS: instrument used where a government borrows money from another government or international organization. Loan agreements between governments are registered with the U.N. *See Serbian and Brazilian Loans Case*, 1929 P.C.I.J. (ser. A) No. 20-21, at 5-89.

LOCAL CUSTOM: a practice that has been clearly established between two or more states and accepted by those states as binding in matters arising between them. Custom will prevail over general rules of law, *Portugal v. India*, 1957 I.C.J. 125. A party relying on a custom must prove that it has become binding on the other party. *Columbia v. Peru*, 1950 I.C.J. 274.

LOCAL REMEDIES RULE: "[A] state may not . . . resort to any kind of international procedure of redress unless its subject has previously exhausted the legal remedies offered him by the state of whose action he complains." *Interhandler case*, 1959 I.C.J. 6, 46 and 50 Am.J.Int.L. 924.

LOCARNO TREATIES (1925): agreements between several European nations to settle disputes by arbitration and international adjudication and in particular to promote peace in Central Europe. *See* 54 L.N.T.S. 289-363 or 20 Am.J.Int.L.Supp. 21.

LOCUS DELECTI (L): the place of the wrong.

LOCUS REGIT ACTUM (L): the place rules the act.

LOCUS STANDI: the right to appear before a court, legislature, or other official body.

LODGE RESERVATION: a number of objections to the Covenant of the League of Nations proposed by Henry Cabot Lodge including the voting rules which gave the British Empire a lot of clout. This contributed to the United States's refusal to join the League. *See* 41 Am.J.Int.L. 531.

LOGAN ACT: United State's law forbidding its citizens from unauthorized communications with a foreign government concerning a dispute with the United States. *See* 18 U.S.C. sec. 953.

LOME CONVENTIONS (1975, 1980, 1985, AND 1990): agreements between the EUROPEAN ECONOMIC COMMUNITY (q.v.) and a number of developing countries granting favorable trade arrangements. *See* O.J.Eur.Comm. (No.125) (Jan. 30,1976) and Official Journal of the European Community (No.347) (Dec.22, 1980), 19 I.L.M. 327 and 29 I.L.M. 809.

LONDON AGREEMENT (1945): the four major allied powers established the INTERNATIONAL MILITARY TRIBUNAL (q.v.) with jurisdiction over existing international crimes, i.e., CRIMES AGAINST PEACE, CRIMES AGAINST HUMANITY, and WAR CRIMES (qq.v.).

LONDON AGREEMENT (1953): established procedure for settling the German external debt questions after World War II *vis-a-vis* West Germany. *See* 333 U.N.T.S 2.

LONDON CHARTER: see LONDON AGREEMENT (1945).

LONDON CLUB: conference of fifteen states that supply nuclear technology to other states. *See* 1976 Stockholm International Peace Research Institute Yearbook 3.

LONDON CONVENTION (1966): most recent version of the LOAD LINE CONVENTION (1930)(q.v.) which regulates the safe maximum load of about 98.5 % of the world's merchant fleet. *See* 18 U.S.T.1957, 640 U.N.T.S 133.

LONDON CONVENTION ON THE INTERNATIONAL REGULATIONS FOR THE PREVENTION OF COLLISION AT SEA (1972): international rules for ships governing safe speed, overtaking, right of way, conduct in low visibility, towing, etc. *See* 28

U.S.T. 3459. *See also* BRUSSELS CONVENTION ON SHIP COLLISION (1962).

LONDON DECLARATION (1871). In 1870 Russia attempted to withdraw from earlier treaty obligations neutralizing the Black Sea, and by this declaration Russia's move was agreed to by the other parties involved as abolishing the neutral status of the Black Sea. The Declaration further states that "It is a principle of the law of nations that no power can free itself from the engagements of a treaty, nor modify its terms except with the assent of the contracting parties by means of friendly understanding." *See* 143 C.J.S. 99 (in French).

LONDON DECLARATION (1909): conference of leading maritime powers codified the rules of PRIZE (q.v.), but the code was never ratified. *See* 3 Am. J. Int'l. L. 596.

LONDON DECLARATION OF INDUSTRIALIZED NATIONS (1977): directed at the relations between the industrialized Northern Hemisphere and the underdeveloped Southern Hemisphere. It set out the goal of expanded trade to help overcome the differences. *See* 16 I.L.M. 724.

LONDON DUMPING CONVENTION (1972): effort to control pollution at sea by prohibiting the dumping of certain wastes and controlling the dumping of others. *See* 11 I.L.M. 1291.

LONDON GOLD POOL: established in 1960 by the Federal Reserve Board, the Bank of England, and other central banks in a GENTLEMAN'S AGREEMENT (q.v.) to attempt to stabilize the price of gold by intervening in the market. *See* Bank of England Quarterly Bulletin 16 (1964).

LONDON NAVAL CONFERENCE (1908-9): ten leading sea powers convened to determine the generally recognized rules of international law respecting PRIZE (q.v.). The LONDON DECLARATION (1909) (q.v.) was drafted and signed by the powers, but never ratified.

LONDON NAVAL CONFERENCES (1930,1935 and 1936): three meetings of the naval powers to attempt naval arms control; they failed. *See* 31 Am.J.Int.L. 661.

LONDON REPARATIONS CONFERENCE (1924): an attempt to settle the question of payment by the losers for damage to the winners after World War I. *See* 19 Am.J.Int.L.Supp. 23.

LONDON PACT (1915): agreement in World War I between Great Britain, France, and Russia that after the war Italy would be given all the territory around the Mediterranean in exchange for a guarantee that Italy would protect Western European interests in Central and Southern Europe. *See* 15 Am.J.Int.L. 252.

LONDON SUBMARINE PROTOCOL: instrument concerning the use of submarines against merchant ships. It provides, *inter alia*, that with few exceptions a submarine may not sink a merchant ship without having first placed the passengers, crew, and ship's papers in a place of safety. *See* 31 Am.J.Int.L.Supp. 137, 46 Stat. 2858.

LONG-DISTANCE BLOCKADE: line of ships extending beyond an enemy coastline in a manner such that they interfere with shipping to ports which the blockading force has no right to blockade.

LONG RANGE THEATER NUCLEAR FORCES (LRTNF): same as INTERMEDIATE RANGE NUCLEAR FORCES (q.v.).

LONG RANGE TRANSBOUNDARY AIR POLLUTION CONVENTION (1979): attempt to control the international effects of air pollution. *See* 18 I.L.M. 1442. *See also* CHLOROFLUROCARBONS and ACID RAIN.

LOOT: wrongful confiscation of enemy private property by a belligerent. "The purpose of immunity of private property from confiscation is to avoid throwing the burdens of war upon private individuals and is instead to place those burdens upon the states which are the belligerents." *See Cession of Vessels and Tugs for Navi-*

gation on the Danube, 1 U.N. Rep. 97 (1921) and 39 Am J. Int'l L. 216

LORAN: acronym for "long range navigation," a system developed during World War II to assist ships in establishing their location by use of pulsed radio signals.

LOS: LAW OF THE SEA (q.v.).

LOSINGER CASE: dispute between Switzerland and Yugoslavia concerning the enforceability of an arbitration clause in a contract between a Swiss Company and the Yugoslav Government which passed a law abrogating the clause. *See* 1936 P.C.I.J. (ser. A/B) No. 67 at 15-25.

LOSS OF VOTE FOR FAILURE TO MAKE CONTRIBUTION TO THE UNITED NATIONS: the United Nations Secretariat has concluded that members who have failed to make their contributions to the regular UN budget will not be included in the roll call when votes are taken pursuant to the Secretariat's duty under Art. 19 of the UNITED NATIONS CHARTER (q.v.). *See* 7 I.L.M. 1187.

LOTUS CASE: in deciding whether Turkey could exercise criminal jurisdiction over a French sea captain who collided with a Turkish ship on the high seas, the Permanent Court of International Justice concluded that no provision of international law prohibited such jurisdiction and thus it was permissible. *See* 1927 P.C.I.J. (ser. A) No. 10.

LOUISIANA PURCHASE: cession of French sovereignty over the Mississippi River Basin to the United States in 1803, in return for payment of a sum of money. *See* 5 Moore, *International Law Digest* 614.

LOW TIDE ELEVATIONS: naturally formed areas of land which are completely surrounded at low tide but submerged at high tide. They may be used in determining the BASELINE (q.v.)

of the territorial sea in some instances. *See* 4 Whiteman, *Digest of International Law* 274, 277.

LRTNF: LONG RANGE THEATER NUCLEAR FORCES (q.v.).

LUBLIN COMMITTEE: *de facto* government of Poland after the withdrawal of Germany at the end of World War II which won out over the London government-in-exile of Poland in the struggle for recognition. *See Gdynia v. Boguslawski*, [1953] App. Cas. 11.

LUBYANKA (R): address of the KGB headquarters in the Soviet Union, thus slang for the Soviet secret police.

LUCRUM CESSANS (L): loss of expected profits, damages representing the loss of expected profits. In expropriation cases states must on occasion pay both the market value of the assets taken and *lucrum cessans*.

LUMP SUM AGREEMENTS: when a group of citizens of one state is injured by another state, the latter may agree to pay a lump sum as compensation. The state of the injured parties then divide it among the claimants usually by means of a national claims commission. *See* 82 Am.J.Int.L. 69.

LUSAKA AGREEMENT (1973): an agreement signed on March 17, between ZANU and ZAPU (qq.v.), the two main guerrilla groups fighting white rule in Rhodesia on a joint military command. These two groups were never able to reconcile their differences.

LUSAKA CONFERENCE OF FRONTLINE STATES (1974): meeting of the heads of state of the states surrounding white-ruled Southern Africa to develop a strategy to liberate these territories from racist colonialism.

LUSAKA DECLARATION OF PEACE, INDEPENDENCE, DEVELOPMENT COOPERATION AND DEMOCRATIZATION OF INTERNATIONAL RELATIONS: statement issued at the conclusion of the Third Conference of Nonaligned Nations (1970) and included among other topics was a statement on the use of the seabeds. *See* 10 I.L.M. 215.

LUSITANIA: British luxury liner torpedoed without warning by a German U-boat on May 7, 1915, with the loss of 1198 lives. This incident was instrumental in bringing to focus the issue of the legality of unrestricted submarine warfare. *See* 9 Am.J.Int.L.Supp. 129.

LUXEMBOURG AGREEMENT (1971): contained terms for the admission of the United Kingdom into the European Economic Community. *See* European Community, July-August 1971, at 10.

LYNCH CLAIM: decision supporting the proposition that a certificate of consular registration is sufficient proof of nationality for its holder. *See Great Britain v. Mexico,* 5 R.I.A.A. 15 (1929).

LYTTON REPORT (1932): report to the League of Nations on the dispute between China and Japan involving Japanese occupation of Manchuria. *See* 27 Am.J.Int.L.Supp. 119.

MCLEOD INCIDENT (1840): Alexander McLeod was brought to trial in New York for murder and arson, but was released after the British government made diplomatic protest that he was an agent of the British government. Subsequently, McLeod sued New York for false imprisonment. *See* 6 Moore, *Digest of International Law* 1014.

MAD: MUTUAL ASSURED DESTRUCTION (q.v.).

MADCHENHANDEL (G): white slavery, *see* WHITE SLAVERY TRAFFIC.

MAGALHAES DOCTRINE: statement by the Brazilian Foreign Minister to the effect that sovereignty was an anachronism, Jornal do Brazil, Feb. 21, 1966.

MAGDALENA BAY CASE: corollary to the MONROE DOCTRINE (q.v.); arising from a Senate resolution against the sale of a Mexican bay (owned by an American company) to a Japanese company. The United States will object to the acquisition of any coastal property in the Western Hemisphere by a non-Western Hemisphere country when such property has the potential of becoming a naval base. *See* 6 Am.J.Int.L. 937.

MAGNA CARTA: example of a PACTA CONVENTA (q.v.), in which King John of England agreed to limitations on his powers *vis-a-vis* his subjects. *See* 2 Holdsworth, *History of English Law* 207 (3rd ed).

MAIL: *see* UNIVERSAL POSTAL CONVENTION.

MAILCERT: clearance certificate for postal matters granted by a representative of a nation at war in a neutral state for the purpose of controlling contraband while allowing postal service to continue operations.

MAIN COMMITTEES OF THE UNITED NATIONS GENERAL ASSEMBLY: the seven committees charged with making recommendations for approval of the General Assembly. They are: First Committee, Political and Security; Second Committee, Economic and Financial; Third Committee, Social, Humanitarian and Cultural; Fourth Committee, Decolonization; Fifth Committee, Administrative and Budgetary; Sixth Committee, Legal; and the Special Political Committee which shares the work of the First Committee. *See Everyman's United Nations* at 10-13 (1979).

MAITRE DE SA COMPETENCE (F): master of its own competence; generally a court has the power to determine the scope of its own ability to decide cases, i.e., to decide that it has jurisdiction over the parties and the subject matter of the case. This phrase is a strong affirmation of such power. *See also,* JUGE DE SA COMPETENCE and COMPETENCE DE LA COMPETENCE.

MAJORITY RULE: principle of democratic government whereby the leadership is elected by vote of the entire adult populace. Lack of majority rule is a basic complaint of South Africa's black majority, *see* APARTHEID. *See also,* CONSENSUS and UNANIMITY RULE.

MALA FIDES (L): bad faith, absence of honest intentions in international relations.

MALTHUSIAN IDEA: hypothesis that the resources of the earth are limited and that the growth of human population strains these limits and causes strife. Thomas Malthus theorized that population tends to increase at a faster rate than its means of subsistence.

MALVINAS ISLANDS CRISIS (1982): *see* ANGLO-ARGENTINE WAR (1982).

MANCHURIA: *see* LYTTON REPORT (1932).

MANCHURIAN BOOTY: after World War II, the Soviet Army in Northwest China claimed almost all Japanese assets as war booty, the Chinese disagreed. *See* 40 Am.J.Int.L. 584.

MANDATE TERRITORIES: territory separated from the former central powers after World War I, and in accordance with Art. 22 of the COVENANT OF THE LEAGUE OF NATIONS (q.v.), placed under a tutelary regime. Other mandates were created at the end of World War II involving territories liberated from Japan. *See also*, TRUST TERRITORIES.

MANDATORY JUDGMENT: decision of an international tribunal requiring or prohibiting the execution of an act.

MANILA DECLARATION (1976): communique of the WORLD FOOD COUNCIL (q.v.) making recommendations to eradicate world hunger and malnutrition. *See* 16 I.L.M. 1554.

MANILA DECLARATION ON THE PEACEFUL SETTLE-MENT OF DISPUTES (1982): draft by the United Nations General Assembly Special Committee on the Charter of the UN and on strengthening the organization. *See* 21 I.L.M. 449.

MANILA PACT: *see* SOUTHEAST ASIA TREATY ORGANIZATION (1954).

MAPS: maps are sometimes used as evidence in boundary disputes or appended to treaties. *See* 57 Am.J.Int.L. 781.

MAQUILADORA (S): Mexican program allowing IN-BOND (q.v.) manufacturing business to be established. *See* 4 Inter-American Legal Materials 803.

MARCONA SETTLEMENT (1976): agreement between the United States and Peru on compensation for the Peruvian government's expropriation of the Marcona Mining Company. *See* 71 Am.J.Int.L. 474.

MARE ALTUM (L): HIGH SEAS (q.v.).

MARE APERTUM (L): open sea.

MARE CLAUSUM (L): closed sea; ancient doctrine which supported the claim of a state or states to ownership of the high seas or portions thereof. It was replaced in the nineteenth century by the principle of freedom of the HIGH SEAS (q.v.).

MARE LIBERUM: freedom of the seas; title of a book by Grotius espousing the idea of freedom of the high seas.

MARGINAL SEA: that narrow strip of the ocean or other body of water along the border of a country which traditionally makes up the TERRITORIAL WATERS (q.v.) of the country.

MARIEL CUBANS: group of Cuban refugees allowed by Castro to emigrate to the United States in 1980. *See* 27 I.L.M. 1420.

MARINE POLLUTION: *see* LONDON DUMPING CONVENTION (1972) and OSLO DUMPING CONVENTION (1972).

MARINE RESOURCES: all the useful things found in the sea, including LIVING RESOURCES OF THE SEA (q.v.), and mineral deposits on the seabed. *See* LAW OF THE SEA CONVENTION (1982).

MARITIME BOUNDARY: border or limits of the TERRITORIAL WATERS (q.v.) of a coastal state.

MARITIME DOMAINE: that area of the sea over which a coastal state exercises jurisdiction, i.e., TERRITORIAL WATERS (q.v.).

MARITIME ECONOMIC ZONE: *see* EXCLUSIVE ECONOMIC ZONE.

MARITIME FLAG: flag flown by a vessel which indicates its character (e.g., commerical or military), and its state of registry. Vessels must abide by the conditions set forth by the state under whose flag the vessel sails (see FLAGS OF CONVENIENCE). In the past, states without a sea coast could not have a maritime flag, but the right was extended to all states by the BARCELONIA DECLARATION (1921) (q.v.).

MARITIME FRONTIER: a coastal state's TERRITORIAL WATERS (q.v.).

MARITIME HONORS: the dressing of ships (flying a pattern of flags) and the giving of salutes for ceremonial purposes. *See* Satow, *A Guide to Diplomatic Practice* 46 (1957).

MARITIME SAFETY CONVENTION (1988): attempt to suppress unlawful acts against maritime safety such as the ACHILLE LAURO INCIDENT (1985). *See* 82 Am.J.Int.L. 269 and 27 I.L.M. 668.

MARPOL: POLLUTION FROM SHIPS CONVENTION (q.v.).

MARRIAGE VALIDITY CONVENTION: recommendation of the Hague Conference on Private International Law to unify the national laws of the parties regarding the recognition of a marriage. *See* 16 I.L.M. 18.

MARSAT: precursor to INMARSAT (q.v.).

MARSHALL PLAN: economic aid provided by the United States to Europe to repair the ravages of World War II. Named for General George Marshall, its sponsor. *See* 18 Dept. State Bul. 112.

MARTENS CLAUSE: first appearing in the preamble to the HAGUE CONVENTION RESPECTING THE LAWS AND CUSTOMS OF LAND WARFARE (1899) (q.v.). This is a general statement of the humanitarian nature of the law of war. It states that " ... inhabitants and belligerents remain under the protection ...

of international law established from custom, laws of humanity, and dictates of public conscience."

MARTIAL LAW: use of military forces to temporarily govern civilian population of a domestic territory, as necessity requires, often without constitutional authority. Synonymous terms are state of emergency and state of seige. *See* 1 Am. Univ. J. Int'l L. & P. 35.

MASICA INCIDENT (1910): affray between Honduran soldiers and British West Indian subjects which resulted in the death of one, and the disagreement over compensation was arbitrated. *See* 10 Am.J.Int.L.Supp. 98.

MASS INFORMATION CONTROLS: some efforts have been made in international circles to control the mass media (see NEW INTERNATIONAL INFORMATION ORDER). International law frowns on dissemination of WAR PROPAGANDA (q.v.) and racist slander. *See* Art. 20 of the INTERNATIONAL COVENANT ON CIVIL AND POLITICAL RIGHTS.

MASTER OF A SHIP: the person appointed by the owner of a ship to take charge of its navigation. The master hires the crew, supervises the loading (*see* BILLS OF LADING), and is responsible for the welfare of the ship and crew.

MATRIMONIAL PROPERTY REGIME CONVENTION (1977): product of the HAGUE CONFERENCE ON PRIVATE INTERNATIONAL LAW (q.v.) making uniform rules concerning maintenance obligations between spouses, succession rights of a surviving spouse, and capacity of the spouse to control property. *See* 16 I.L.M. 14.

MAU-MAU: National Liberation Army of Kenya; through military actions in the 1950's, this group fought to gain the independence of Kenya succeeding in 1963.

MAVROMATIS PALESTINE CONCESSION: dispute concerning a concessionary contract between a government and an individual. The individual was described in the concession as an Ottoman national and, in fact, was not. The issue before the Permanent Court of International Justice was whether the nationality was a condition of the grant of the concession. The Court found that the grant was not dependent on the nationality of the grantee. The mistake was not an essential one and the contract was not void *ab initio. See* 2 I.L.R. 27.

MAYAGUEZ INCIDENT (1975): seizure of a U.S. merchant vessel prompted a military response and rescue operation against Cambodia. *See* 4 Boston College Int'l and Comp. L.R. 61.

MBEYA PROTOCOL: agreement to unify the military commands of ZANU and ZAPU (qq.v.) in the struggle against Rhodesia. *See* Amate, *Inside the OAU* 265.

MBFR: MUTUAL AND BALANCED FORCE REDUCTIONS (q.v.) (or as William Safire says, "more better for the Russians").

MEASURES OF CONTROL: activities that a government can engage in to control PROTECTED PERSONS (q.v.), such as enemy aliens, within their territory. These may range from registration and periodic reporting to assigned residence or internment.

MEDIATION: method of achieving peaceful settlement of a dispute by the intervention of a third party which assists the parties in negotiating a settlement. The mediator may be a third state, a group of states, an individual, or an agency of an international organization.

MEDICAL ETHICS: subject of draft international code, *see* 21 I.L.M. 211.

MEDICAL PERSONNEL: any person assigned by a party to a conflict to perform work exclusively for medical purposes such as transport and treatment of wounded combatants or efforts to prevent disease. *See* GENEVA CONVENTION I (1949).

MEMEL: territory on the Polish-Lithuanian border given autonomous status after World War I. *See* 30 Am.J.Int.L. 204.

MEMOIRE (F): a MEMORANDUM (q.v.).

MEMORANDUM: an informal diplomatic correspondence providing details and arguments on the subject at hand. *See* Satow, *Guide to Diplomatic Practice* 64 (1957).

MEMORIAL: instrument (which begins a proceedings) filed by an applicant before the International Court of Justice. The memorial contains statements of law and fact supporting the claim of the applicant (i.e., it is similiar to a compliant in U.S. civil procedure), and it is answered by the opposing party with a counter-memorial.

MEN-OF-WAR: capital WARSHIPS (q.v.).

MENS REA (L): intention to do wrong or a guilty mind.

MERCANTORIAL CHART: map on which the meridians and parallels of latitude are projected in straignt lines. The former parallel and equidistant, the latter with distance increased from the equator to each Pole, thus producing a flat map of a round world.

MERCENARIES: foreign nationals hired for military service. *See* 16 I.L.M. 1391 and 72 Am.J.Int.L. 37.

MERCHANT SHIP: ocean going vessels designed to carry cargo. Merchant ships may be converted to war ships under certain circumstances. *See* 4 Whiteman 635 and 2 Am.J.Int.L.Supp. 133. *See also* PRIZE and MINIMUM STANDARDS IN MERCHANT SHIPS (LABOR) CONVENTION (1976)

MERGER CONTROL REGULATIONS (1990): EUROPEAN COMMUNITY (q.v.) rules governing the merger and acquisition of business to protect against concentration and monopolies. *See* 25 Int'l.Lawyer 375.

MERGER OF STATES: a state may merge into another state and thus cease to exist. A state loses its independence when it voluntarily merges with another state. *See* 22 I.L.R. 230.

MERGER TREATY (1965): EUROPEAN COMMUNITY (q.v.) agreement merging the EUROPEAN COAL and STEEL COMMUNITY, EURATOM and THE EUROPEAN ECONOMIC COMMUNITY (qq.v.). *See* 4 I.L.M. 776.

MFN: MOST FAVORED NATION (q.v.).

M.I.5: British Counter-Intelligence Agency (William Safire says, "it stands for five old boys from Cambridge protecting Moscow's interest").

MICROORGANISMS FOR PATENTS TREATY (1978): parties recognizing and agreeing to follow certain procedures relating to the deposit of sample cultures of microorganisms for patenting, 17 I.L.M. 285 and 28 I.L.M. 290.

MIGA: MULTILATERAL INVESTMENT GUARANTEE AGENCY (q.v.).

MIGRANT FOR EMPLOYMENT: "a person who migrates from one country to another with a view to being employed otherwise than on his own account. . . ." *See* Art. II of the Convention Concerning Migration for Employment, 120 U.N.T.S. 72.

MIGRANT WORKERS: *see* PROTECTION OF THE RIGHTS OF ALL MIGRANT WORKERS AND MEMBERS OF THEIR FAMILIES CONVENTION (1991) and the European Convention on the Legal Status of Migrant Workers, 25 European Yearbook 297.

MILITARY ATTACHE: an officer of the armed forces of a state assigned by the head of state as an ATTACHE (q.v.). Duties of the attache in this capacity include obtaining information about the military operations of the state in which the attache is assigned.

MILITARY BLOC OF CAPITALIST STATES: Soviet propaganda term for the NORTH ATLANTIC TREATY ORGANIZATION (q.v.).

MILITARY GOVERNMENT: 1) exercise of governmental authority by an occupying power over an occupied territory. This situation usually arises when the legitimate government is unable to exercise its functions because of the occupation. 2) Government of a country by its own military establishment rather than by a civilian regime.

MILITARY-INDUSTRIAL COMPLEX: group of entities that have a vested interest in maintaining the level and shape of defense spending in its current pattern, i.e., senior military personnel, and the large corporations who manufacture weapons. President Eisenhower warned against the tremendous power of this group at the end of his term in office (many would say to no avail). For the text of Eisenhower's speech, "Liberty is at stake," *see* Vital Speeches, 238 (Feb. 1, 1961).

MILITARY INTERVENTION: interference, using military forces with matters recognized by international law as being solely within the domestic jurisdiction of another state.

MILITARY LAW: legal system applicable to military personnel as distinguished form MARTIAL LAW (q.v.) where the military governs the civilian population.

MILITARY NECESSITY: a fundamental principle of warfare allowing the use of the legitimate amount of coercive power to achieve the desired end. The force used may not at any time exceed the necessity posed by the situation.

MILITARY OBJECTIVE: an object which by its "nature, location, purpose, or use makes an effective contribution to military action." GENEVA CONVENTION PROTOCOL I (1977) Art.52(2) (q.v.), during armed conflict only military objects, as opposed to civilian objects, may be damaged or destroyed.

MILITARY OCCUPATION: status of territory in the possession of an enemy army. The occupying army exercises temporary sovereignty over the territory occupied.

MILITARY PASSPORT: document issued by a military commander to persons within his lines permitting them travel within such area. *See* 10 Whiteman, *Digest of International Law* 507.

MILITARY RECONNAISSANCE: examination or survey conducted by uniformed members of the armed forces operating within enemy lines for the purpose of collecting information about troop positions, strengths, and purposes.

MILITARY TRIBUNAL INTERNATIONAL FOR GERMANY: *see* NUREMBURG TRIBUNAL.

MILITARY TRIBUNAL INTERNATIONAL FOR THE FAR EAST: *see* TOKYO INTERNATIONAL MILITARY TRIBUNAL.

MILITIAS: citizens of a state collectively who are members of military organizations other than the state's regular armed forces. In Great Britain, the militia is composed of the Territorial Army, the Army Emergency Reserves, and the Home Guard; in the United States, the militia is composed of the Reserves and the National Guard. Members of a militia, if captured by the enemy, are considered PRISONERS OF WAR (q.v.). *See* Art. 4A Geneva Convention III (1949).

MINES: explosive devices planted underground or underwater detonated by the proximity of or contact with a person or moving object. *See* Protocol II of the Conventional Weapons Convention (1980), 19 I.L.M. 1529 and the *Hague Convention on Submarine Mines*, 36 Stat. 2332, 1 Bevans 669.

MINIMUM STANDARDS IN MERCHANT SHIPS (LABOR) CONVENTION (1976): effort at improving working conditions for merchant seamen. *See* 15 I.L.M. 1288.

MINIMUM STANDARDS OF INTERNATIONAL LAW: conduct required to be observed according to standards customarily accepted and followed by civilized nations.

MINISTER: diplomatic agent conducting the relations of his country with other states.

MINISTER PLENIPOTENTIARY: a class of foreign envoy not regarded as personal representatives of their heads of state. Ministers plenipotentiary are addressed as "Excellency."

MINISTERS RESIDENT: a class of foreign envoy distinguished from ministers plenipotentiary by lacking the right to the title "Excellency."

MINORITIES: linguistic, ethnic, religious, or national groups which are different from the majority of the country's population. *See* COVENANT ON CIVIL AND POLITICIAL RIGHTS (1966).

MINQUIERS AND ECREHOS CASE *(France v. United Kingdom)*: dispute concerning the sovereignty over the islets and rocks of the Minquiers and Ecrehos groups. The court found that sovereignty belonged to the United Kingdom in so far as the islets and rocks were capable of appropriation. The decision was based on evidence that the Island of Jersey had exercised ordinary local administration over the islets. *See* 1953 I.C.J. 47.

MISSILE TECHNOLOGY CONTROL REGIME (1987): agreement among the United States, Canada, United Kingdom, France, West German, Italy, and Japan to limit the spread of nuclear capable missile technology to the third world. *See* 126 Aviation Week & Space Technology, Ap.20, 1987 at 28.

MISSION: 1) a diplomatic task. 2) a person or group sent to perform a diplomatic task, e.g., the group of persons sent by France to the United Nations to represent it is called the French mission at the United Nations.

MISSION CIVILISATRICE (F): duty of "civilized" nations to rule and civilize uncivilized territories, "the white man's burden."

MISSION EN PASSANT (F): a specific diplomatic task performed by someone as they travel, e.g. a businessman delivers a diplomatic note while on a trip to a remote country. *See* 80 I.L.R.-D 416.

MISTAKE: a treaty concluded as a result of a fundamental mistake induced by one party is voidable if the party is free from negligence or the mistake was induced by a fraud of the other party. The mistake must be essential to the agreement for it to be voidable.

MIXED ARBITRAL TRIBUNAL: tribunal composed of one national from each of the states involved, together with a neutral chairperson. Mixed arbitral tribunals are generally established by peace treaties and are empowered to settle disputes concerning the rights and claims of private individuals who were affected by the war between the states involved.

MIXED CLAIMS COMMISSION: organ established by treaty composed of a majority of the nationals of the state party to the treaty; to settle claims which have arisen between the citizens of the states or between the nationals of one state and the other state's government.

MIXED COMMISSION: bodies created by two or more states each of which designates an equal number of members. The commission may be designed to perform diplomatic, administrative, or dispute settlement functions.

MIXED MEDICAL COMMISSION: the GENEVA CONVENTION III (1949)(q.v.) provides for the establishment of a commission of medical personnel to oversee the health of prisoners of war. Prisoners of war have a right to appear before a mixed medical commission for examination.

MLD: MOUVEMENT DE LIBERATION DE DIJBOUTI, Ethiopian backed force fighting for the independence of Dijbouti, a rival of the FLCS (q.v.).

MLS: MOUVEMENT DE LIBERATION DU SAHARA: one of the guerrilla forces which fought against Spanish colonial rule in Spanish Morocco.

MOBILIA SEQUUNTUM PERSONAM (L): intangible property is usually said to be located in the same place as its owner.

MODUS PROCEDENDI (L): the order in which obligations or actions will be fulfilled according to a diplomatic agreement, e.g., by agreement country A will release an imprisoned news reporter after which country B will drop spy charges against a national of country A.

MODUS OPERANDI (L): the normal way in which a thing works.

MODUS VACANDI (L): the process for renouncing one's right.

MODUS VIVENDI (L): term used to indicate a temporary agreement between the parties. Although the agreement is provisional, the parties are expected to observe it.

MOGADISHU DECLARATION (1971): resolution by a summit meeting of African leaders stating that the only means of liberating southern Africa was by armed struggle.

MOMBASA AGREEMENT (1975): short-lived (if at all) agreement between factions in the effort to liberate Angola from Portugese rule. *See* Amate, *Inside the OAU* at 251.

MONARCH: a person who rules a MONARCHY (q.v.), a king or emperor.

MONARCHY: government by a single ruler (a monarch, usually chosen by heredity) who represents the sovereignty of the state and consequently becomes sovereign himself.

MONISM: theory that there is no real difference between international and municipal law.

MONROE DOCTRINE: a unilateral declaration made by U.S. President Monroe in a message to Congress in 1823, concerning nonintervention. It stated that any threat from abroad to the security of a nation in the Western Hemisphere is a threat to all the hemisphere. This doctrine has been envoked numerous times by the U.S. *See* 5 Whiteman, *Digest of International Law* at 409.

MONROVIA GROUP: twenty African states that attended a summit meeting in Monrovia, Nigeria in May of 1961, which affirmed the equality of all African states. This group formally the Inter-African and Malagasy States Organization formed the basis for the Organization of African Unity. *See* El-Ayouty, *The Organization of African Unity After Ten Years* at 112.

MONROVIA STRATEGY FOR ECONOMIC DEVELOPMENT OF AFRICA (1980): *see* LAGOS PLAN FOR ACTION (1980).

MONTEGO BAY CONVENTION: the LAW OF THE SEA CONVENTION (1982) (q.v.).

MONTEVIDEO CONVENTION ON CIVIL INTERNATIONAL LAW AND COMMERCIAL INTERNATIONAL LAW (1940): revised previously adopted conflict of laws rules adopted by Argentina, Bolivia, Paraguay, Peru, and Uruguay. *See* 39 Mich.L.Rev. 517.

MONTEVIDEO CONVENTION ON THE RIGHTS AND DUTIES OF STATES (1933): agreement subject to various qualifications stating, *inter alia*, that the political existence of the state was independent of recognition, that states were juridically equal, that disputes should be settled by peaceful methods, and that territorial acquisitions or special advantages obtained by force should not be recognized. *See* 28 Am.J.Int.L.Supp. 75 (1934).

MONTEVIDEO CONVENTION ON POLITICAL ASYLUM (1933): amends the HAVANA CONVENTION ON THE RIGHT OF ASYLUM (1928)(q.v.). *See* 28 Am.J.Int.L.Supp. 70 (1934).

MONTEVIDEO DECLARATION ON THE LAW OF THE SEA (signed May 8,1970, by nine Latin American states): the signatories declared that their claims of sovereignty over maritime zones adjacent to their coasts had been extended out to a distance of two hundred marine miles measured from a baseline of the territorial seas. *See* 9 I.L.M. 1081 (1970).

MONTEVIDEO GROUP: nine Latin American states that promulgated the MONTEVIDEO DECLARATION ON THE LAW OF THE SEA (q.v.).

MONTEVIDEO TREATIES: *see* SOUTH AMERICAN CONGRESS ON PRIVATE INTERNATIONAL LAW.

MONTEVIDEO TREATY (1960): established the LATIN AMERICAN FREE TRADE ASSOCIATION (q.v.). *See* Lawson, *International Regional Organizations* at 345.

MONTEVIDEO TREATY (1980): established the LATIN AMERICAN INTEGRATION ASSOCIATION (q.v.). *See* 20 I.L.M. 672.

MONTEVIDEO TREATY ON INTERNATIONAL PENAL LAW (1940): inter-American agreement on conflicts of law rules for criminal law. *See* 8 Hudson, *International Legislation* at 482.

MONTREAL AGREEMENT (1967): agreement between the United States Government and individual airlines serving international routes. The airlines wavered the limitation of liability under the WARSAW CONVENTION (1929)(q.v.) up to $75,000 for personal injury. *See* 49 U.S.C. sec. 1502 and CAB Agreement 18900.

MONTREAL PROTOCOLS (1976): proposed amendments to the WARSAW CONVENTION (1929) (q.v.) including the introduction of the SPECIAL DRAWING RIGHT (q.v.) as the currency of account. *See* 76 Am.J.Int.L. 412.

MOON TREATY (1979): or agreement governing the activities of states on the moon and other celestial bodies; latest in the series of UN sponsored treaties on outer space. It is the only one not ratified by the United States which objects to the principle that celestial objects are the "COMMON HERITAGE OF MANKIND" (q.v.), and to the prospect of an international regime for allocating these resources. *See* 18 I.L.M. 1434 or U.N. Doc. A/Res/34/68.

MORAL OBLIGATION: duty to act in a certain manner despite the fact that the law does not require such an act, e.g., the rescue of someone who is drowning. Nations sometimes feel that they have moral obligations.

MORATORIUM: postponement of the fulfillment of an obligation either by agreement or unilateral act.

MOREHOB: mouvement de resistance des hommes bleus; guerrilla force which fought against Spanish colonial rule in the Spanish Sahara.

MOSCOW DECLARATION (1943): agreement by the Allies that German war criminals should be returned to the countries in which their crimes had been committed, in order that they might be punished according to the laws of the particular country. Crimes with no particular geographical location would be punished by joint decision of the allies. *See* 22 I.L.R. 399.

MOSCOW SUMMIT (1988): meeting of President Reagan and General Secretary Gorbachev. *See* 88 Dept. State Bull. 1 (Aug.1988) and 27 I.L.M. 1176.

MOSER DOCTRINE: military personnel who have violated the laws of war should be treated as ordinary criminals. *See* Johann

Moser, *Versuch des Neuesten Europaischen Volkerrechts*, Stuttgart, 1752.

MOSQUITO REBELLION (1895): Great Britain demanded in-demnifi-cation for the arbitrary explusion of twelve of its citizens from Nicaragua during a rebellion by Mosquito Indians. *See* 5 Moore, *International Arbitration* at 4966.

MOST-FAVORED NATION CLAUSE: clause in a commercial treaty to ensure equality of treatment. If one state grants to a third state privileges not extended by the treaty, it must extend such privileges to the parties to the treaty. *See* 17 I.L.M.1518.

MOSUL DISPUTE (1924): question of Iraqi claim to 35,000 square miles of territory. *See* 20 Am.J.Int.L. 453.

MOTOR TRAFFIC CONVENTION (1926): multi-party conven-tion setting forth rules regarding the conditions to be fulfilled by all passenger and goods carrying vehicles and the drivers of such vehicles. *See* 108 L.N.T.S. 123.

MPLA: POPULAR MOVEMENT FOR THE LIBERATION OF ANGOLA (q.v.).

MULTILATERAL INVESTMENT GUARANTEE AGENCY (MIGA): an affiliate of the WORLD BANK (q.v.) established to guarantee private investments in developing countries. 24 I.L.M.-D1598 and 27 I.L.M. 1227.

MULTIMODAL TRANSPORT OF GOODS CONVENTION (1980): effort to clarify the coverage of international transport re-gimes (*see* WARSAW CONVENTION (1929)) where more than one mode of transport is used between the places of origin and destination. *See* 19 I.L.M. 938.

MULTINATIONAL CORPORATION: business enterprise owned by private investors which conducts activities and holds assets in more than one state. They are typically engaged in for-eign trade over large geographically diverse areas and have diverse business activities. *See* UNCTAD CODE OF CONDUCT FOR MULTINATIONAL CORPORATIONS and OCED GUIDELINES FOR MULTINATIONAL ENTERPRISES (1976).

MULTIPLE NATIONALITY REDUCTION CONVENTION (1963): European effort to reduce the number of cases of persons with dual nationality, and settle the question of the military service obligations of such persons. *See* 58 Am.J.Int.L. 573.

MUNICH AGREEMENT (signed September 30, 1938, by Hitler, Mussolini, Chamberlain, and Daladier): separated the Sudeten German areas of Czechoslovakia creating a new frontier between Germany and Czechoslovakia leaving the Czechs defenseless and leading to the invasion of the rest of the country by Germany. In 1942, the British and French denounced the agreement and in 1973, it was found to be void since it was achieved by duress against Czechoslovakia. For contemporaneous comment *see* 33 Am.J.Int.L. 12 (1939).

MUNICIPAL LAW: customs practiced by and statutes enacted by a state. Municipal law governs relations between persons within the jurisdiction of the state, as well as, relations between those persons and the state.

MUNITIONS DE GUERRE (F): WAR MATERIALS (q.v.).

MUTILATION: to cut off or permanently damage parts of the body; a practice prohibited by the Laws of War. *See* Art. 75(2) of the GENEVA CONVENTION PROTOCOL I (1977).

MUTINY: taking over the control of a ship from its rightful authority by members of its crew. For a case of modern mutiny by Polish sailors *see* 6 Whiteman, *Digest of International Law* 815.

MUTUAL ADMINISTRATIVE ASSISTANCE IN TAX MATTERS: subject of a Council of Europe/Organization for Economic Cooperation and Development Convention. *See* 27 I.L.M. 1160.

MUTUAL ASSURED DESTRUCTION (MAD): basic premise of nuclear arms strategy followed by the U.S. and Soviet Union for the past quarter century. It places reliance on offensive weapons and the balance struck when both powers have overwhelming capacity to destroy each other.

MUTUAL AND BALANCED FORCE REDUCTIONS (MBFR): continuing East-West negotiation (in conjunction with the CONFERENCE ON SECURITY AND COOPERATION IN EUROPE (q.v.)) to reduce the size of NATO and Warsaw Pact forces facing each other in Europe. *See* 87 Dept. State Bull. 19 (July 1987).

MY LAI MASSACRE (1968): killing of a number of civilians at the village of My Lai in Vietnam. The United States government tried Lt. William Calley for war crimes, and for leading the forces which committed the killings. *See* 10 South.Univ.L.Rev. 205.

NACIONES UNIPAS (S): the UNITED NATIONS (q.v.).

NACIONALIZACION PACTADA (S): nationalization by agreement. A negotiated process between a government and an industry to implement a government takeover of the industry.

NAIRIOBI DECLARATION (1982): product of a United Nations Conference on the Human Environment. The Declaration affirmed the STOCKHOLM DECLARATION ON THE HUMAN ENVIRONMENT (q.v.). *See* Moliter, *International Environmental Law* 85 (1991).

NAKED POWER: antecedent of the term "black power." Term was coined by a Canadian journalist in the 19th century to describe the tactic of the Doukhobors who protested the worldliness of their neighbors by peaceful nude marches through town.

NAM: NON-ALIGNED MOVEMENT (q.v.).

NAMIBIA: formerly the German colony of Southwest Africa. Despite years of effort for its independence by the United Nations it remained under the control of South Africa. Independence was finally achieved in 1989. *See* SOUTHWEST AFRICA CASE and for recent developments, 28 I.L.M. 944.

NANKING INCIDENT (1927): during a riot in this Chinese city United States and British ships fired on the crowd in order to rescue U.S. citizens who were under seige by a mob. *See* 22 Am.J.Int.L. 593.

NANSENPASS: League of Nations issued identity cards for stateless people.

NAPALM: gelatinous flammable substance dropped in the form of bombs as a weapon. Its use is restricted by GENEVA CONVENTION PROTOCOL III (1980).

NARCOTIC DRUG CONVENTION (1931): *see* OPIUM CONVENTIONS (1931).

NARCOTIC DRUG CONVENTION (1988): United Nations sponsored agreement against traffic in illicit drugs. *See* 28 I.L.M. 493.

NASA: NATIONAL AERONAUTICS AND SPACE ADMINISTRATION (q.v.).

NATION: a group of people who share a common identity, heritage, and aspirations. It is not necessary for the group to also possess a territorial base and government.

NATIONAL: one who has a personal relationship to a particular state. In international law, all persons subject to the personal jurisdiction of a state are considered to be nationals of that state. *See* PROTECTION OF NATIONALS.

NATIONAL AERONAUTICS AND SPACE ADMINISTRATION: United States Space Agency which has worked with the space agencies of other countries (including the EUROPEAN SPACE AGENCY (q.v.)) on international space projects. *See e.g.* APOLLO-SOYEZ MISSION.

NATIONAL CLAUSE: feature of many international agreements that the parties will treat the citizens, commodities, products, ships, etc. of the other parties in the same manner as they treat their own.

NATIONAL JUDGES: International Court of Justice judge who retains the right to sit in a case which involves his own country.

NATIONAL LIBERATION MOVEMENT: common name for a group fighting against an established government, particularly a colonial regime. *See e.g.,* VIETCONG or PALESTINE LIBERA-TION ORGANIZATION.

NATIONAL RESISTANCE MOVEMENT (RENAMO): insurgent force fighting the government of Mozambique. RENAMO has been accused of horrendous atrocities and may have even lost the support of South Africa, its major sponsor in the past. *See* 11 Fletcher Forum 331.

NATIONAL RESOURCES: the natural and manmade resources controlled by a sovereign. *See* SOVEREIGNTY OVER NATURAL RESOURCES.

NATIONAL TECHNICAL MEANS: euphorism for spying used in arms control agreements. The Soviet Union did not want to admit that they had spy satellites so verification in the STRATEGIC ARMS LITITATIONS AGREEMENTS (q.v.) was to be carried-out by national technical means.

NATIONALISM: devotion to the interests of one's country, often to the detriment of others.

NATIONAL WATERS: interior or inland waters which comprise all those waters lying within the BASE-LINE (q.v.) of the territorial waters, viz., ports and harbors, land-locked seas, lakes, straits, and rivers, bays and gulfs.

NATIONALITY: fundamental legal bond between an individual and a state giving rise to reciprocal rights and duties. *See* NEMO PROTEST EXUERE PATRIUM (L).

NATIONALITY OF AIRCRAFT: under the CHICAGO CONVENTION (1944) (q.v.) all aircraft are required to be registered in one (and only one) country and to bear the registration marks of that country. A country is responsible for the international activities of aircraft on its registry. *See* Arts. 17 to 20 of the CHICAGO CONVENTION (1944).

NATIONALITY OF MARRIED WOMEN CONVENTION (1957): attempt to separate the nationality status of spouses so that the parties, e.g., agree that marriage will not automatically change the nationality of a wife to that of her new husband. *See* 309 U.N.T.S. 66.

NATIONALIZE: the taking over of a privately held business by a government. *See* SABBATINO CASE, INTERNATIONAL TELEPHONE AND TELEGRAPH NATIONALIZATION, and HULL DOCTRINE.

NATIONS UNIES (F): the UNITED NATIONS (q.v.).

NATIVE COMMUNITY: the peoples and tribes residing in a territory before it is colonized.

NATO: NORTH ATLANTIC TREATY ORGANIZATION (q.v.).

NATURAL LAW: opposite of manmade law (or POSITIVISM (q.v.)) rules derived from God, reason, or nature.

NATURAL PROLONGATION: the claim of costal states that the continental shelf is originally part of their territory. *See* 84 Am.J.Int.L. 846.

NATURAL RESOURCES SHARED BY TWO OR MORE NATIONS: subject of concern to the UNITED NATIONS ENVIRONMENT PROGRAMME (q.v.). *See* 17 I.L.M. 1091.

NATURALIZATION: the act of obtaining nationality by a foreigner in compliance with the municipal law of the state concerned.

NAUFRAGE: *see* DROIT DE NAUFRAGE (F).

NAULILAA INCIDENT (1914): incident between Portugese and German colonials in Southwest Africa where a minor incident led to German reprisal which destroyed several forts and towns. In the subsequent arbitration, the principle was invoked that all other channels should be tried before resorting to force, and reprisals by force should be proportional to the offense. *See* 2 R.I.A.A. 1012.

NAUTICAL MILE: 1852 meters or 6076.115 feet, reckoned at sixty nautical miles for each degree of latitude. It is also known as an admiralty mile, and is used in both sea and air navigation.

NAVICERT: a pass obtained by a shipper from an allied agent (during World War II) at the port of loading which allowed the ship to pass through naval controls. The navicert system was devised to control the flow of goods to the enemy. *See* 12 I.L.R. 532.

NAVIGABLE WATERS: bodies of water having the potential to be useful in commerce by commercial crafts or vessels.

NE JUDEX ULTRA PETITA PARTIUM (L): a judge's award to a party must not exceed the party's claim.

NE VARIETUR (L): no variation or departure from the text. Term appended to the signatures of the plenipotentiaries in order to guarantee the authenticity of a treaty's text, whenever there is a lapse of time between the conclusion of the negotiations and the signature of the treaty.

NEC VI, NEC CLAM, NEC PRECARIO (L): in Roman Law, possession is corrupted if obtained by force, precariously, or secretly.

NECESSARY REPRESENTATION: the fact that corporate bodies and states must act through individuals.

NECESSITIES OF WAR: *see* MILITARY NECESSITY.

NEGATIVE PRESCRIPTION: a statute of limitations; the criminal liability for an act will only exist for a particular length of time.

NEGOTIATING RECORD: documents preliminary to agreement on a treaty and transcripts of discussions by the parties leading thereto. *See* TRAVAUX PREPARATOIRE.

NEGOTIATION: discussion of international questions through ordinary diplomatic channels which may lead to a settlement.

NEGOTIORUM GESTIO (L): action for another person's interest, but lacking his authority. *See* 5 I.L.R. 502.

NEMO DAT QUOD NON HABET (L): principle that when a state cedes a piece of territory with a defective title, the defect will be transferred to the title of the state which is accepting the ceded territory.

NEMO JUDEX IN RE SUA (L): in one's own cause, one ought not be the judge. *See* 3 I.L.R. 387.

NEMO PLUS JURIS TRANSFERRE PROTEST QUAM IPSE HABET (L): principle that when a state cedes a piece of territory over which it has granted another state a right of transit, or other right, the ceded territory is transfered to the new sovereign encumbered with those obligations.

NEMO PROTEST EXUERE PATRIUM (L): no one can renounce their country. Rule applied in some municipal legal systems that a person cannot change his nationality without the permission of his country.

NEOCOLONIALISM: the purported exploitation of under- developed newly independent countries by the developed nations through economic and political coercion which has supplanted formal colonial regimes.

NEUILLY TREATY (1919): treaty ending World War I between Bulgaria and the allies. *See* 226 C.T.S. 333.

NEUMEISTER CASE: appeal to the European Court of Human Rights alleging Austrian violation of the EUROPEAN HUMAN RIGHTS CONVENTION (q.v.). *See* 8 I.L.M. 547.

NEUTRAL FLAG: the flag of a neutral state; it is different from a TRUCE FLAG (q.v.).

NEUTRAL GOODS: cargo which does not belong to a belligerent during time of war. *See* INFECTION DOCTRINE.

NEUTRAL MERCHANT SHIP: a ship flying the flag of a neutral country during time of war. It may be required to submit to search by a belligerent warship, but if its cargo is innocent must be allowed to proceed on its voyage. *See* 11 Whiteman, *Digest of International Law* 30.

NEUTRAL OBSERVER: person placed aboard a hospital ship to insure that the ship does not misuse its protected status or come under attack. *See* Art. 31 of GENEVA CONVENTION II (1949).

NEUTRAL PERSONS: "... nationals of a state which is not taking part in the war are considered neutrals." Art. 16 of the HAGUE CONVENTION RESPECTING THE RIGHTS AND DUTIES OF NEUTRALS IN CASE OF WAR ON LAND (1907).

NEUTRAL STATE: a state which completely abstains from participating in an existing war and provides no aid to the belligerents.

NEUTRAL SUBJECTS: nationals of a country not participating in a war. The intricacies of sorting out the status of a corporation are the subject of the INTERHANDEL CASE (q.v.).

NEUTRAL TERRITORY: the territory of states not taking part in a war. Neutral territory is inviolable and belligerents are forbidden to move troops or supplies across neutral territory. *See* Arts. 1 and 2 of HAGUE CONVENTION RESPECTING THE RIGHTS AND DUTIES OF NEUTRAL POWERS IN CASE OF WAR ON LAND (1907).

NEUTRAL WATERS: the territorial waters of a neutral state which are inviolable by the belligerents. Belligerents' ships may put-in at neutral ports in emergencies, *see* GRAF SPEE.

NEUTRALITY: status of a state that completely abstains from participating in an existing war.

NEUTRALIZATION: act of excluding by treaty a designated area of a state's territory from an armed conflict. Any military operation in that area is illegal.

NEUTRON BOMB: atomic explosive device designed to produce much radiation with minimal explosive force. They are designed for use against large attacking ground forces (e.g., an invasion of Western Europe by an overwhelming armored force) in such a way that would kill combatants, but the surrounding territory would suffer minimal damage. *See* 1982 U.N. Yearbook 56.

NEW DELHI DECLARATION: NON-ALIGNED MOVEMENT (q.v.) declaration urging prompt and effective COLLECTIVE SECURITY (q.v.) measures by the United Nations. *See The Non-aligned Movement and the United Nations* at 305.

NEW INTERNATIONAL ECONOMIC ORDER (NIEO): effort by the lesser developed countries to restructure parts of the international economic system which they perceive as being biased in favor of the developed countries. *See* 1974 U.N. Yearbook 305.

NEW INTERNATIONAL INFORMATION ORDER: effort by many lesser developed countries to develop rules to restrict the gathering and use of information which is perceived as prejudicial to the interests of these countries. Most notably the rules would include licensing of journalists. *See* 14 Case W.Res.J.Int'l L. 387.

NEW YORK CONVENTION ON FOREIGN ARBITRAL AWARDS: *see* RECOGNITION AND ENFORCEMENT OF FOREIGN ARBITRAL AWARDS.

NEWLY EMERGING STATES: states which gained their independence from COLONIAL POWERS (q.v.) after World War II. They make up most of the membership of the GROUP OF 77 (q.v.).

NGO: NON-GOVERNMENTAL ORGANIZATION (q.v.).

NICARAGUA JURISDICTION CASE: question before the International Court of Justice as to the ability of Nicaragua to sue the United States over the C.I.A.'s mining of Nicaraguan waters. The U.S. lost. *See* 24 I.L.M. 59.

NICARAGUA MIXED CLAIMS COMMISSION: established in 1910 to settle the question of debts owed by the previous Nicaraguan Government. *See* 9 Am.J.Int.L. 858.

NICARAGUA V. HONDURAS: *see* BORDER AND TRANSBORDER ARMED ACTION CASE.

NICARAGUA V. UNITED STATES: International Court of Justice decision on the substance of Nicaragua's complaint that the United States mined her waters. The United States lost, but refused to recognize the judgment. *See* 25 I.L.M. 1023.

NICARAGUAN CEASEFIRE: agreement between the Sandinista Regime and the CONTRAS (q.v.). *See* 27 I.L.M. 954.

NICARAGUAN VERIFICATION CONVENTION (1988): effort to implement the NICARAGUAN CEASEFIRE (q.v.). *See* 27 I.L.M. 957.

NIEO: NEW INTERNATIONAL ECONOMIC ORDER (q.v.).

NIGERIAN CIVIL WAR (1967-70): secession of the eastern region of Nigeria forming the state of BIAFRA (q.v.) led to a civil war with the central government which eventually put down the rebellion. *See* 7 I.L.M. 162.

NICHOLSON INCIDENT (1985): United States intelligence officer, Major Nicholson, was shot by a Soviet sentry in East Berlin. *See* 11 Yale J. of Int'l L. 521.

NIXON DOCTRINE: President Nixon's call for a balance in United States foreign policy objectives and defense spending. For a critique *see* 49 Foreign Affairs 201.

NIXON ROUND: seventh in the series of negotiations within the GENERAL AGREEMENT ON TARIFFS AND TRADE (GATT) (q.v.) system held in 1973, at the request of President Nixon. *See* 7 J.W.T.L. 489.

NKVD: Soviet Peoples' Commissariat of Internal Affairs, a forerunner to the KGB (q.v.).

NO FIRST USE OF NUCLEAR WEAPONS TREATY: WARSAW PACT ORGANIZATION (q.v.) proposed addition to the HELSINKI ACCORDS (q.v.). *See* 16 I.L.M. 224.

NON-AGGRESSION PACT: treaty between two or more states agreeing not to engage in aggressive military operations against one another. *See e.g.,* the DAVIS OFFER (1933) or GERMAN-SOVIET NON-AGGRESSION PACT (1939).

NON-ALIGNED COUNTRIES: *See* GROUP OF 77.

NON-ALIGNED COUNTRIES DECLARATIONS: *see* BELGRADE DECLARATION (1964), CAIRO DECLARATION (1970), ALGIERS DECLARATION (1975), COLOMBO DECLARATION (1979), HAVANA DECLARATION (1983), and the NEW DELHI DECLARATION.

NON-ALIGNED MOVEMENT (NAM): effort to join together the forces of countries ostensibly aligned with neither superpower. The first meeting of the NAM was held in Belgrade, Yugoslavia, in September of 1961. *See* Lyon, "Non-alignment at the Summit," 41 Indian Journal of Political Science 1 (1980).

NON-BELLIGERENCY: usually denotes a false claim of neutrality by a country that is secretly aiding one side of a conflict.

NON-COMBATANT: inhabitant of a belligerent state who is not taking part in the war effort.

NON-COMMISSIONED VESSEL: a ship which is not part of a navy; a non-military ship.

NON-GOVERNMENTAL ORGANIZATION (NGO): an international organization that is not the creation of agreement among states, but rather is composed of private individuals or organizations.

NON-INTERVENTION: one country staying out of the internal affairs of other states. *See* UNGA Resolution 2131/XX.

NON-JUSTICIABLE DISPUTE: problem between two parties which is not appropriate for settlement by a judicial body.

NON LICET (L): situation where a tribunal is not capable of deciding a dispute because it lacks authority to make necessary finding. *See* 80 I.L.R. 308.

NON LIQUET (L): when in a hypothetical situation a court is not able to give a decision on law because it lacks legally relevant rules.

NON-MATERIAL DAMAGE: intangible harm such as offense to one's good name or pain and suffering. *See Lusitania Claims,* 7 R.I.A.A. 32 and Art. 2(7) of the UNITED NATIONS CHARTER.

NON-MEMBER: a state which has not joined a particular international organization, e.g., Switzerland has not joined the United Nations on the grounds that it would compromise its neutrality, though it does participate in some United Nations activities.

NON-PARTY: a state which has neither ratified, acceded to, nor adhered to a particular international agreement and, therefore, has neither rights nor duties under the agreement.

NON-PROLIFERATION TREATY (1968): *see* NUCLEAR NON-PROLIFERATION TREATY (1968).

NON-RECOGNITION: the refusal of one government to recognize the legitimacy of another government.

NON-REFOULEMENT: rule that a refugee should not be returned to a country where he faces a threat of persecution or danger to life or freedom.

NON-SCHEDULED INTERNATIONAL AIR SERVICE: air transport conducted in an irregular manner such as a charter service.

NON-SELF-EXECUTING TREATY: a treaty which requires legislation in order to operate, e.g., a treaty that requires the legislative adoption of uniform international traffic signs.

NON-SELF GOVERNING TERRITORY: a territory which is governed by another state, e.g., a TRUST TERRITORY or a COLONY (qq.v.).

NON-TARIFF BARRIER: regulations that burden international trade other than outright taxes on exports and imports. *See* TECHNICAL BARRIERS TO TRADE.

NON-USE OF FORCE: basic principle of international law enshrined in Art. 2(4) of the UNITED NATIONS CHARTER (q.v.).

NORDIC CONVENTION ON THE PROTECTION OF THE ENVIRONMENT: *see* 13 I.L.M. 591.

NORDIC COUNCIL: consultative body for cooperation among Norway, Denmark, Sweden, Finland, and Iceland. The Statute of the Nordic Council was adopted in 1957, 434 U.N.T.S. 145, 182.

NORIEGA REGIME: government of Panama was linked to drug dealings and became the subject of sanctions by the United States Government. In December 1989, the United States invaded Panama, arrested General Noriega, and "restored democracy." *See* 82 Am.J.Int.L. 571 and N.Y. Times, Dec. 24, 1989 at sec. 1, p.9, col. 1.

NORTH ATLANTIC ASSEMBLY: annual meeting of legislators from the 16 NORTH ATLANTIC TREATY ORGANIZATION (q.v.) member countries. Their resolutions are not binding on NATO.

NORTH ATLANTIC COUNCIL: established by Art.9 of the NORTH ATLANTIC TREATY (q.v.); it has authority to meet promptly to consider matters of collective self-defense. *See* 28 I.L.M. 1040.

NORTH ATLANTIC TREATY: collective self-defense treaty between the Western European states and the United States and Canada. *See* 34 U.N.T.S. 243.

NORTH ATLANTIC TREATY ORGANIZATION (NATO): regional organization of North American and European states headquartered in Brussels. The organization of NATO is governed by the NORTH ATLANTIC TREATY (q.v.) and subsequent treaties such as the Status of Forces Agreement, 199 U.N.T.S. 67.

NORTH-SOUTH RELATIONS: one way of looking at the relations between the developed (North) and underdeveloped (South) countries of the world.

NORWEGIAN FISHERIES CASE (*U.K. v. Norway)*: The International Court of Justice discussed the delimitation of TERRITORIAL WATERS (q.v.) and the setting aside of fisheries. *See* 1951 I.C.J. 116.

NOTARIAL FUNCTION: tasks such as registering births and deaths, authenticating signatures, issuing visas and passports may be included in the duties of a DIPLOMATIC ENVOY (q.v.). In CIVIL LAW (q.v.) jurisdictions notaries play an important role in authenticating documents.

NOTE: diplomatic letter usually delivered by a diplomatic representative to the state or organization to which he is accredited. Two types of notes in particular are NOTE COLLECTIVE and NOTE VERBAL (qq.v.). For the binding character of notes see the EASTERN GREENLAND CASE. The formalities of Diplomatic Notes are discussed in Satow, *A Guide to Diplomatic Practice* 70.

NOTE COLLECTIVE (F): note by the representatives of several states to the state or organization to which they are accredited.

NOTE VERBAL (F): an unsigned note or AIDE-MEMOIRE (q.v.).

NOTIFICATION: formal announcement of a legally relevant fact, action, or intent, e.g., notification of intent to withdraw from a treaty.

NOTTEBOHM CASE (Liechtenstein v. Guatemala). The International Court of Justice discussed what is necessary for a person to come under the protection of a particular state. *See* 1955 I.C.J. 4.

NOUVEAU VENU (F): newcomer; one recently arrived; especially a recent entrant into the community of recognized nations.

NOVATION: change in a treaty so that its terms conform with current reality and thus preserve its intent.

NUCLEAR ACCIDENT AGREEMENTS: bilateral agreements between the United States, United Kingdom, France, and the Soviet Union to reduce the risk of the outbreak of nuclear war by accident. *See* 22 U.S.T. 1590, 807 U.N.T.S. 57.

NUCLEAR ACCIDENTS CONVENTION: *see* EARLY NOTIFICATION OF NUCLEAR ACCIDENTS CONVENTION.

NUCLEAR CLUB: the countries possessing nuclear weapons; the United States, Soviet Union, Great Britain, France, China, India, and perhaps Pakistan, Israel, and South Africa.

NUCLEAR-FREE ZONE: areas designated by treaty in which there is to be a total absence of nuclear weapons. *See* TLATELOLCO TREATY (1967).

NUCLEAR NON-PROLIFERATION TREATY (1968): promoted by the United States and the Soviet Union with over 100 parties. They agree not to acquire nuclear weapons or, if they already possess these weapons, not to provide them to other states. It does not prevent the spread of nuclear technology for peaceful purposes. *See* 21 U.S.T. 483, 729 U.N.T.S. 161.

NUCLEAR POWERED SHIPS: subject of a convention signed in Brussels in 1966, but not accepted by the United States and the Soviet Union which are the primary operators of such ships. *See* 57 Am.J.Int.L. 100, 268.

NUCLEAR PROLIFERATION: expansion of the number of nations that have the capability to build and use nuclear weapons. *See* NUCLEAR NON-PROLIFERATION TREATY.

NUCLEAR RISK REDUCTION CENTER: a United States-Soviet arrangement to exchange information reducing the risk of a nuclear war. *See* 27 I.L.M. 76.

NUCLEAR SUPPLIERS GROUP: organization of countries selling nuclear technology. For their guidelines for nuclear transfer *see* 17 I.L.M. 220.

NUCLEAR TEST BAN TREATY: *see* TEST-BAN TREATY (1963).

NUCLEAR TEST CASES (*Australia and New Zealand v. France):* application by the Plaintiffs to the Court requested a ruling that France's above-ground nuclear testing in the Pacific were contrary to international law. France made a unilateral declaration that it would, henceforth, conduct its tests underground. The Court found the question to be moot. *See* [1974] I.C.J. 253.

NUCLEAR TRANSFERS: *see* 17 I.L.M. 220 and NUCLEAR NON-PROLIFERATION TREATY.

NUCLEAR WEAPONS: instruments of war which rely on the explosive power of nuclear fusion or fission for their destructive power. There is some question as to the status of weapons, such as the X-ray laser powered by a nuclear explosion which does not actually use the destructive force of the explosion. *See* NUCLEAR NON-PROLIFERATION TREATY, ETHIOPIAN RESOLUTION, and TEST-BAN TREATY.

NUDA PACTIO OBLIGATIONEM NON PARIT (L): a bare promise does not create a legal obligation.

NULLA LEX NULLA INIURA (L): no law then no wrong; maxim raised by the defendants in NUREMBURG TRIALS (q.v.) to the effect that the acts they were accused of were not illegal at the time under the existing international law.

NULLA POENA SINE LEGE (L): "no punishment without a rule;" a punishment cannot be inflicted unless a preexisting law matches that punishment to the crime.

NULLITY OF JUDGMENT: making an international judgment null and void through circumstances, such as excess of authority or decisive and manifest error.

DICTIONARY OF INTERNATIONAL & COMPARATIVE LAW

NULLUM CRIMEN SINE LEGE (L): "no crime without a rule;" maxim for the proposition that an act cannot be considered a crime unless a preexisting law designates such acts as criminal.

NULLUM CRIMEN SINE POENA (L): "no crime without punishment;" for any act that is made criminal there is created implicit and some appropriate punishment.

NULLUS COMMODUM CAPERE DE SUA INJURIA PROPRIA (L): "the state must not be allowed to benefit by its inconsistency when it is through its own wrong that the other party has been deprived of its rights...." 33 I.L.R. 48, 76 (1962).

NUNCIO (L): first class envoy representing the Holy See in its temporal authority. A *nuncio* is an ambassador of the Holy See who is not a Cardinal. If a Cardinal, the title would be *legati a latere*. In some Catholic countries the *nuncio* is by tradition the DOYEN OF THE DIPLOMATIC CORPS (q.v.).

NUREMBURG DECREES: anti-semitic laws of Hitler's Third Reich. *See* 1 *Nazi Conspiracy and Aggression* 296-305.

NUREMBURG PRINCIPLES: code of offenses against peace and the security of mankind drafted by the International Law Commission for use by the Nuremburg Tribunal. *See* [1950] II Y.B.Int'l.L., Comm'n 374.

NUREMBURG TRIALS: the trials of the major German war criminals held before the NUREMBURG TRIBUNAL (q.v.) following World War II.

NUREMBURG TRIBUNAL: international military tribunal established by the United Nations to try the major war criminals of the European axis (Germany and Italy). *See* 11 Whiteman, *Digest of International Law* 880. Reports of the Tribunal were published.

NYON AGREEMENT (1937): collective security agreement signed by eight states in response to attacks on trading vessels in the Mediterranean Sea by unidentified submarines during the

Spanish Civil War. The vessels attacked did not belong to either side of the conflict. *See* 181 L.N.T.S. 135 (1937). A supplement to the Nyon Agreement was signed in Geneva, Sept. 17, 1937, entitled the International Agreement for Collective Measures Against Piratical Acts in the Mediterranean by Surface Vessels and Aircraft. *See* 181 L.N.T.S. 149.

[O - P]

OAMCE: ORGANIZATION AFRICAINE ET MALGACHE DE COOPERATION ECONOMIQUE (q.v.).

OAPEC: ORGANIZATION OF ARAB PETROLEUM EXPORTING COUNTRIES (q.v.).

OAS: ORGANIZATION OF AMERICAN STATES (q.v.).

OATH: customary manner of securing performance of a treaty; formal promise made by a sovereign.

OATH OF ALLEGIANCE: attestation of the inhabitants of a territory to be faithful and obedient to their sovereign or government. When territory is occupied by a belligerent, the authority of the occupant is not sovereignty and the inhabitants do not owe it allegiance and may not be compelled to pledge allegiance to it. *See Jalbuena v. Dulles,* 26 I.L.R. 460.

OATH OF NEUTRALITY: inhabitants of a territory occupied by a belligerent authority swear to abstain from taking a hostile attitude against the authority and to willingly submit to its legitimate plans. The belligerent may compel the inhabitants to take this oath and punish them for breaking it.

OAU: ORGANIZATION OF AFRICAN UNITY (q.v.).

OBITER DICTA: observations and points of law discussed in a court's opinion that are not necessary for the conclusion in the judgment rendered.

OBJECT OF WAR: the only legitimate object of war is to weaken the enemy's military forces. This definition comes from the ST. PETERSBURG DECLARATION (1868) (q.v.), but seems to have had little effect on those conducting wars since that time. *See* TOTAL WAR.

OBJECTIVE LAW: a real political status created by a treaty or convention, the effects of which are left outside the immediate control of the contracting parties. Thus, every state interested though not a party has the right to insist upon compliance.

OBJECTIVE REGIMES: rights and duties created by treaty which are binding on third party states not a participant to the treaty, e.g., regimes for major waterways or treaties for the demilitarization of a territory.

OBJECTS INDISPENSABLE: items which are necessary for the survival of a civilian population. Attack or destruction of these are forbidden by GENEVA CONVENTION PROTOCOL I (1977) (q.v.).

OBSCENE PUBLICATIONS: subject of two multilateral treaties for its suppression. *See* 37 Stat. 1511, T.S. 559, 1 Bevans 748, and 27 L.N. T.S. 213 (1923).

OBSERVER: representative of a state or international organization attending international meetings where the state or organization is not a member of the meeting body. Observers usually do not vote or sign documents but may participate in discussions.

OBSERVATION SATELLITE: *see* RECONNAISSANCE SATELLITE.

OBSOLESCENCE: the conditions either political, economic, or social, which made a law-making treaty desirable have changed. Therefore, the treaty is not in harmony with the present, modern conditions.

OCAM: ORGANIZATION COMMUNE AFRICAINE ET MALAGACHE (q.v.).

OCAS: ORGANIZATION OF CENTRAL AMERICAN STATES (q.v.).

OCCUPATIO BELLICO (L): military occupation; control of territory gained by military force. Under Art.42 of the Regulations annexed to the HAGUE CONVENTION IV (1907) (q.v.), "territory is considered occupied when it is actually placed under the authority of the hostile army. The occupation extends only to the territory where such authority has been established and can be exercised." *See* 36 Stat. 2277, 2306, T.S. 539.

OCCUPATIO NON PROCEDIT NISI IN RE TERMINATA (L): occupation cannot occur unless there is a boundary to that occupied. Theoretical reason for the abandonment of the claim by states to sovereignty over portions of the high seas.

OCCUPATIO PACIFICA (L): peaceful occupation; territory occupied by a foreign armed force after the state to which the territory belongs has agreed to the occupation. Such presence is legal unless the agreement was made under duress. The agreement determines the rights and duties of the occupying force.

OCCUPATION: the assumption or holding of possession of foreign territory, either belligerently or with the consent of the state to be occupied. Also, assuming possession of unoccupied territory with the aim of establishing sovereign title to it.

OCCUPIED TERRITORY: territory of one belligerent held by another, *see e.g.,* WEST BANK OF JORDAN.

OCEANS: large bodies of salt water covering approximately two-thirds of the earth's surface. *See* HIGH SEAS.

ODECA: ORGANIZATION OF CENTRAL AMERICAN STATES (q.v.).

ODER ARBITRATION: decided the extent to which tributaries of the Oder River (declared an INTERNATIONAL RIVER (q.v.) by the VERSAILLES PEACE TREATY) were under the jurisdiction of the International Commission of the Oder. *See* 1938 P.C.I.J. (ser. A) No. 23.

OECD: ORGANIZATION FOR ECONOMIC COOPERATION AND DEVELOPMENT (q.v.).

OECD GUIDELINES FOR MULTINATIONAL ENTERPRISES (1976): set of voluntary rules governing the conduct of MULTI-NATIONAL CORPORATIONS (q.v.) especially in the THIRD WORLD (q.v.). *See* 15 I.L.M. 967.

OEEC: ORGANIZATION FOR EUROPEAN ECONOMIC COOPERATION AND DEVELOPMENT (q.v.).

OFFENSES ON BOARD AIRCRAFT: subject of an international agreement to control hijacking and other violence against international air transport. *See* 20 U.S.T. 2941, 704 U.N.T.S. 219. *See also* AIR PIRACY.

OFFENTLICH-RECHTLICHE ZUSAGE (G): usually an administrative promise either to carry out or refrain from an administrative act. *See* 24 Int'l. Lawyer 411.

OFFICE FRANCAISE DE PROTECTION DES REFUGIES ET APATRIDES (OFPRA): French authority which determines refugee status. *See* Journal Officiel 7642 (July 25, 1952).

OFFICE INTERNATIONAL D'HYGIENE PUBLIC: *See* PUBLIC HEALTH.

OFFICIAL LANGUAGE: a language or languages adopted by an international organization in which it conducts its business. The official languages of the United Nations are English, French, Russian, Spanish, Chinese, and Arabic.

OFFICIAL RECORDS: documents maintained and sometimes published by international organizations such as the UN General Assembly, containing the important documents and transcripts of proceedings.

OFFICIAL SECRETS ACT: British legislation outlawing espionage against the British government. *See* 12 Halsbury's Statutes 176, 191 (4th ed.).

OFF-SHORE POLLUTION LIABILITY AGREEMENT: agreement among off-shore oil platform operators to provide for compensation for damage to third parties caused by their operations. *See* 13 I.L.M. 1409 and TOVALOP.

OFPRA: OFFICE FRANCAIS DE PROTECTION DES REFUGIES ET APATRIDES (q.v.).

OGADEN: region of Southeastern Ethiopia bordering on Somalia and the site of an on-going rebellion against the authority of the Ethiopian government.

OIHP: Office International d'Hygiene Publique, *see* PUBLIC HEALTH.

OIL POLLUTION: *see* TORREY CANYON INCIDENT.

OIL POLLUTION CONVENTION (1959): agreement by more than seventy nations to prevent oil pollution of the seas by discharge of oil from ships. *See* 12 U.S.T. 2989, 327 U.N.T.S. 3.

OIL POLLUTION PREPAREDNESS CONVENTION (1990): proposed agreement among nations to require oil production and transport enterprises to prepare emergency plans. *See* 30 I.L.M. 733.

OLADE: Organizacion Latino-Americano de Energia, LATIN-AMERICAN ORGANIZATION FOR ENERGY (q.v.).

OLAS: ORGANIZACION LATIN-AMERICANO DE SOLIDARIDAD (q.v.).

OLERON'S LAWS: *see* LAW OF OLERON.

OLIVE OIL AGREEMENT: United Nations sponsored agreement to try to stabilize the international market in olive oil. *See* 495 U.N.T.S. 30.

OMEGA: an advanced radio navigation system for use on the high seas.

OMNI EXCEPTIONE MAJORES (L): all exceptions are important.

OMNIA REX IMPERIO POSSIDET, SINGULI DOMINIO (L): all the territory that a king controls is one domain.

ONUC: United Nations military force in the Congo, *see* CONGO CRISIS.

ONUS PROBANDI (L): the burden of proof, denotes the party who must prove a fact.

OPEC: ORGANIZATION OF PETROLEUM EXPORTING COUNTRIES (q.v.).

OPEN CITY (also UNDEFENDED LOCALITY): area which a belligerent unilaterally withdraws from and declares open. It may be occupied by an opposing force without resistance. The HAGUE CONVENTION RESPECTING LAWS AND CUSTOMS OF LAND WARFARE (1907) (q.v.) prohibits attacks on undefended localities.

OPEN DIPLOMACY: because secret treaties impose upon people commitments of which they have no knowledge, are contrary to the principles of democracy, and are a threat to international peace. Both the COVENANT OF THE LEAGUE OF NATIONS (Art. 18) and the CHARTER OF THE UNITED NATIONS (Art. 102) require that treaties or international agreements entered into by member states must be registered with the Secretariat and published by it. Until registered a treaty is not binding.

OPEN DOOR POLICY: the forced opening of trade with China by western powers (particularly the U.S. and Great Britain) in the nineteenth century. The process was extended to Japan and Africa as well. *See* BOXER REBELLION, OPIUM WARS (1839-60), and BERLIN CONGRESS (1885).

OPEN PLACES: locality not defended by fortifications or other means of resistance for immediate defense. *See Bembelista Claim*, 10 R.I.A.A. 717 (1903).

OPEN SEA: waters beyond the TERRITORIAL WATERS (q.v.) and contiguous zones of littoral states. No title to the HIGH SEAS (q.v.) can be claimed by any nation, and they may be used freely by the ships of all nations. *See* LAW OF THE SEA CONVENTION (1982).

OPENING OF HOSTILITIES CONVENTION (1907): *see* HAGUE CONVENTION RELATIVE TO THE OPENING OF HOSTILITIES (1907).

OPERATIONAL ZONE (also, sea defense zone): area within the vicinity of naval operations in which a belligerent may establish special regulations or prohibit shipping altogether. A neutral vessel which does not comply may be fired upon.

OPERATIONS OF NATURE: one way in which a nation can acquire territory, e.g., the emergence of volcanic islands in territorial waters or the shifting of a river boundary.

OPERATIONS OF WAR: all activities which further the military advantage of a belligerent. In some cases, prisoners of war are to be allowed their freedom in exchange for a promise not to participate in any operations of war. *See* Art. 6, HAGUE CONVENTION ON THE RIGHT TO CAPTURE (1907).

OPIC: OVERSEAS PRIVATE INVESTMENT CORPORATION (q.v.).

OPINIO JURIS (L): *see* OPINIO JURIS SIVE NECESSITATIS.

OPINIO JURIS GENTIUM (L): international law as defined by international opinion.

OPINIO JURIS SIVE NECESSITATIS (L): more usual is simply opinio juris; opinion that an act is necessary by rule of law. Psychological factor in the formulation of customary international law, i.e., a belief that a particular form of conduct is mandated by international law and not simply a moral obligation.

OPIUM CONVENTION (1931): agreement attempting to limit the production of narcotics to the level of legitimate medical and scientific need. *See* 139 L.N.T.S. 301.

OPIUM CONVENTIONS: a series of conventions have attempted to control the production and distribution of narcotic drugs. *See* 3 Am.J.Int.L. 253, 6 Am.J.Int.L.Supp. 177 and the SINGLE CONVENTION ON NARCOTIC DRUGS.

OPIUM WARS (1839-60): wars between Great Britain and China which forced the opening of China to western trade. *See* OPEN DOOR POLICY.

OPOL: OFF-SHORE POLLUTION LIABILITY AGREEMENT (q.v.).

OPPOSABILITY: the application of a principle of law *vis-a-vis* an argument to the contrary by a party to a dispute, i.e., legal arguments for both sides of a dispute. *See* 1968 Aust. Ybk. Int'l.L. 1.

OPTIMUS INTERPRES RERUM USUS (L): the best interpretation comes from examining usage.

OPTION OF NATIONALITY: grant of right by treaty of cession to the inhabitants of the territory ceded to chose as their own either one of the nationalities concerned.

OPTIONAL CLAUSE: provision of Art. 36 of the STATUTE OF THE INTERNATIONAL COURT OF JUSTICE (q.v.) concerning recognition of compulsory jurisdiction in the Court. The basis of the jurisdiction under the Optional Clause is reciprocity, therefore, both parties to a dispute must have made the same declaration of recognition in order for the court to have jurisdiction. *See* 40 Am.J.Int.L. 778.

OPTIONAL PROTOCOL: addendum to an international agreement which at the option of each party may or may not be agreed to by that party.

ORAL AGREEMENT: a binding arrangement based upon the spoken word of duly qualified representatives of the parties to the agreement. International law does not require interstate agreements to be in writing, but oral agreements are rare.

ORAL PLEADINGS: proceedings provided for in Art. 43 (I) of the STATUTE OF THE INTERNATIONAL COURT OF JUSTICE (q.v.). They include hearing by the court of witnesses, experts, agents, counselors and advocates (q.q.v.) of the parties to a dispute.

ORBITAL TRANSPORT UND RAKETEN AKTIENGESELL-SCHAFT (OTRAG): West German company which can claim to be the first private enterprise space launch company. Their history, which some might describe as checkered, has involved launch pads in Libya and Zaire.

ORDER OF MALTA: order of knights dating from the crusades and possessing qualities of international personality being able to negotiate with sovereigns, etc. *See Nanni v. Pace and the Sovereign Order of Malta,* 8 I.L.R. 2 and 48 Am.J.Int.L. 554.

ORDER OF THE GARTER: ancient order of British knighthood. *See* 35 *Halsbury's Laws of England* (4th ed.) 474.

ORDERS OF CHIVALRY: honorary knighthoods such as the ORDER OF THE GARTER (q.v.).

ORDINE PUBBLICO INTERNAZIONALE (I): international public policy. *See* 77 I.L.R. 586.

ORDONNANCE DE LA MARINE (1681): French maritime code promulgated by Louis XIV forming a systemic restatement of customary maritime law.

ORDRE PUBLIC: conflict of laws; rule which allows the court to refuse to apply foreign law where it is contrary to the public policy of the forum state. The rule has been rejected as a means for circumventing treaty obligations. *See* GUARDIANSHIP OF INFANTS CONVENTIONS CASE, 1958 I.C.J. 55.

OREGON BOUNDARY DISPUTE (1827): the United States in a dispute with Great Britain claimed that effective occupation of land at the mouth of a river runs up to the crest of the watershed under the sovereignty of the occupying state. The question of the Oregon boundary was left open until finally settled by the Oregon Treaty, 9 Stat. 869, 12 Bevans 95 (1846).

ORGANIZATION LATINO-AMERICANO DE ENERGIA (OLADE): organization of Latin American countries to, *inter alia*, protect, conserve, and assure the rational use of the region's energy resources. *See* 13 I.L.M. 377.

ORGANIZATION AFRICAINE ET MALAGACHE DE COOPERATION ECONOMIQUE (OAMCE): precursor to the ORGANIZATION COMMUNE AFRICAINE ET MALAGACHE (q.v.).

ORGANIZATION COMMUNE AFRICAINE ET MALAGACHE (OCAM): organization of independent French-speaking African states to promote economic cooperation and development. *See* 6 I.L.M. 53.

ORGANIZATION FOR ECONOMIC COOPERATION AND DEVELOPMENT (OECD): inter-governmental entity established by industrialized states in 1961 as a reconstituted ORGANIZATION FOR EUROPEAN ECONOMIC COOPERATION AND DE-

VELOPMENT. The OECD meets annually to promote policies designed to achieve the highest sustainable level of economic growth and employment in member countries. Therefore, it contributes to the development of the world economy. *See* 888 U.N.T.S. 179.

ORGANIZATION FOR EUROPEAN ECONOMIC COOPERATION AND DEVELOPMENT: replaced by the ORGANIZATION FOR ECONOMIC COOPERATION AND DEVELOPMENT (q.v.). For charter *see* 888 U.N.T.S. 179.

ORGANIZATION OF AFRICAN UNITY (OAU): organization of independent African states with the objective to provide unity and solidarity and to improve the quality of life for African people. The OAU Charter, 479 U.N.T.S. 39, 2 I.L.M. 766 (in force, 1963), encourages member states to coordinate their policies in nutrition, economics, defense, and security. *See* Amate, *Inside the OAU.*

ORGANIZATION OF AFRICIAN UNITY MEDIATION COMMISSION: one of the principal organs of the ORGANIZATION OF AFRICIAN UNITY (q.v.). It has been generally ineffective at settling disputes. *See* Amate, *Inside the OAU* 154-169.

ORGANIZATION OF AMERICAN STATES (OAS): regional organization of independent American states created to strengthen the peace and security of the region, ensure the specific settlement of regional disputes, and promote cooperation in economic, social, and cultural development. *See* Charter of the OAS, 119 U.N.T.S. 3 (1952).

ORGANIZATION OF ARAB PETROLEUM EXPORTING COUNTRIES (OAPEC): created in 1968, because of the importance of oil as the primary source of income for the member states. This organization tries to safeguard the petroleum industry. *See* 681 U.N.T.S. 235.

ORGANIZATION OF CENTRAL AMERICAN STATES (OCAS): Costa Rica, El Salvador, Guatemala, Honduras, and

Nicaragua established the OCAS to provide for concerted and co-operative action in economic, social, and cultural development. *See* the Charter of the OCAS (or the San Salvador Charter), 122 U.N.T.S. 3, replaced by 552 U.N.T.S. 15, 2 I.L.M. 235.

ORGANIZATION OF PETROLEUM EXPORTING COUNTRIES (OPEC): the oil producers' cartel; an organization aimed at unifying petroleum pricing and safeguarding the interests of the member countries individually and collectively. *See* 443 U.N.T.S. 247.

ORGANTHEORIE (G): an entity is liable for the acts of a person acting as it "organ" (agent). *See* 77 I.L.R. 472.

ORIGIN OF GOODS: false or deceptive indications of the place of origin of goods are the subject of several international agreements. *See* 175 C.T.S. 53, 828 U.N.T.S. 163.

ORIGINAL RESPONSIBILITY: the responsibility of a state for the actions of its government's neglect of international duties. A state is also responsible for actions of lower agents or private individuals who act or perform with the government's authorization. *See also* ACT OF STATE.

ORINOCO STEAMSHIP COMPANY ARBITRATION: an arbitral tribunal made up of three members of the Permanent Court of International Arbitration annulled the award of a mixed American-Venezuelan arbitral commission, 2 R.I.A.A. 237 (1961), because the commission had disregarded the terms of the 1903 protocol granting it jurisdiction over the matter and setting forth the law to be applied. *See* 5 Am.J.Int.L. 35.

ORTRAG: ORBITAL TRANSPORT UND RAKETEN AKTIENGESELLSCHAFT (q.v.).

OSCAR CHINN CASE: Britain sought damages on behalf of British companies driven out of business when Belgium created a de facto monopoly in a Belgium river transport company on the Congo River. The British alleged that the Belgium action violated the SAINT GERMAIN PEACE TREATY (1919) (q.v.). *See* 1934 P.C.I.J. (ser.A/B) No. 63.

OSLO DUMPING CONVENTION (1972): establishes rules for the control or prohibition of the dumping of certain substances into the sea. *See* 11 I.L.M. 262.

OSNABRUCK TREATY (1648): ended the Thirty Year War; this treaty was one of the first to grant certain religious rights to minorities. *See* 1 C.T.S. 119.

OSTPOLITIK (G): efforts to improve relations between West Germany and the Warsaw Pact countries. *See* 78 I.L.R. 164.

OTTAWA AGREEMENT (1932): charter which binds the members of the British Commonwealth as a customs union. *See* 26 Am.J.Int.L. 811 or 174 Law Times 349 (Nov.5, 1932).

OTTOMAN DEBT ARBITRATION: the Republic of Turkey was the successor to the Ottoman Empire, and the Ottoman debt was finally settled by the LAUSANNE PEACE TREATY (1923) (q.v.) which apportioned the debt among Turkey and those states which had acquired Ottoman territory. The apportionment made by the Council of the Ottoman Public Debt was not acceptable to some of the states. This arbitration basically affirmed the Council's apportionment. *See* 1 R.I.A.A. 529 (1925).

OUTBREAK OF WAR: a condition of war between states can be commenced by: 1) a declaration of war by one state to another; 2) a proclamation by a state that it considers itself at war with another state; or 3) through recourse to hostilities. *See* HAGUE CONVENTION RELATIVE TO THE OPENING OF HOSTILITIES (1907).

OUTER CONTINENTAL SHELF: United States position as defined by the Outer Continental Shelf Lands Act of 1953, 43 U.S.C. sec. 1331-1343. The outer continental shelf is all the submerged lands lying seaward from the United States territorial waters covered by no more than 100 fathoms (600 feet) of water. This is the

U.S. claim that led to the claim by other nations of a 200 mile territorial sea.

OUTER SPACE: everything above a line that demarks the upper reaches of AIR SPACE (q.v.). Unfortunately, such a line has never been agreed upon by the nations of the earth, but something around 100 miles above the earth's surface seems reasonable to most of the interested parties. *See* BOGATA DECLARATION (1976).

OUTER SPACE TREATY (1967): the basic international agreement on the exploration and use of outer space including the moon and other celestial bodies. The treaty expresses the intention of the parties to insure international cooperation in the exploration and use of outer space exclusively for peaceful purposes. *See* 18 U.S.T. 2410, 610 U.N.T.S. 205.

OVERFLIGHT: flight of aircraft over sovereign territory, territorial waters, or vessels at sea. *See* CHICAGO CONVENTION (1944).

OVERSEAS PRIVATE INVESTMENT CORPORATION (OPIC): congressional effort to mobilize private capital in the United States to participate in the economic development of the Third World. *See* 22 U.S.C. sec. 2191.

OZONE: *See* CHLOROFLUORCARBONS and PROTECTION OF THE OZONE LAYER CONVENTION (1986).

PAC: PAN-AFRICAN CONGRESS (q.v.).

PACEM IN MARIBUS (L): peace on the seas.

PACEM IN TERRIS (L): peace on earth; title of a Papal encyclical.

PACIFIC BASIN ECONOMIC COUNCIL: a private organization founded in 1967, made-up of senior business executives from twenty countries. It supports private efforts of development.

PACIFIC BLOCKADE: blockade set up during a time of peace. Such blockades are utilized as a coercive means of settling disputes. Because the blockade is a matter between the conflicting parties only, the principles of international law prohibit the seizure of vessels other than those of the blockaded state for attempting to break the blockade. *See e.g.*, CUBAN MISSILE CRISIS. *See also*, PAPER BLOCKADE.

PACIFIC CHARTER: signed at the time of the creation of the Southeast Asia Treaty Organization. It included terms for the defense of Southeast Asia. *See* 6 U.S.T. 91, 209 U.N.T.S. 23.

PACIFIC SALMON TREATY (1985): agreement on salmon fishing between the United States and Canada, *see* 81 Am.J.Int.L. 577.

PACIFIC SETTLEMENT ACT (1949): United Nations Treaty parties to which agree to settle disputes through peaceful means such as ARBITRATION or CONCILIATION (qq.v.). *See* 71 U.N.T.S. 101. *See also*, HAGUE CONVENTION FOR THE PACIFIC SETTLEMENT OF DISPUTES (1899).

PACIFIC SETTLEMENT OF DISPUTES (1928): *See* GENERAL ACT FOR THE PACIFIC SETTLEMENT OF INTERNATIONAL DISPUTES.

PACIFISM: belief that only nonmilitary, nonviolent means prevent war and that the function of the military, if any, should be self-defense.

PACQUETE HABANA: two unarmed vessels, fishing off the coast of Cuba, were captured by a U.S. blockading squadron as a PRIZE (q.v.). The U.S. Supreme Court held that both captures were unlawful. "By ancient usage among civilized nations . . . and gradually ripening into a rule of international law, fishing vessels, pursuing their vocation . . . , have been recognized as exempt with their cargo and crew from capture as a prize of war." *The Pacquete Habana*, 175 U.S. 677,686 (1899).

PACT OF PARIS (1928): *see* KELLOGG-BRIAND PACT.

PACT OF SAN JOSE: *see* INTER-AMERICAN CONVENTION ON HUMAN RIGHTS CONVENTION.

PACTA CONVENTA (L): agreement between a monarch and his people, limiting the power of the monarch. *See* MAGNA CARTA.

PACTA NON OBLIGANT NIS GENTES INTER QUAS INITA (L): treaties are only binding on those who sign them.

PACTA SUNT SERVANDA (L): one of the oldest principles of international law stating that treaties properly concluded are to be observed. It guarantees to states the right to conclude treaties with binding effect. The VIENNA CONVENTION ON THE LAW OF TREATIES, Art. 26 (q.v.) provides that, " Every treaty in force is binding upon the parties to it and must be performed by them in good faith."

PACTA TERTIIS NEC NOCENT NEC PROSUNT (L): general principle that a treaty binds only the contracting parties and neither rights, nor duties arise under a treaty for a state not a party to the treaty. *See* 4 I.L.R. 393-4.

PACTIONES(L): class of treaties in Roman law involving agreement against war between the two parties, and rules for the travel of their citizens on each others territory.

PACTUM DE CONTRAHENDO (L): clause in a treaty which obligates the parties concerned to conclude a further agreement on a specific problem. The parties to the pactum de contrahendo and those to the subsequent required agreement must be identical.

PACTUM DE NEGOTIANDO (L): clause of a treaty which creates for the parties concerned an obligation to negotiate with a view to concluding a subsequent agreement. The parties to the pactum de negotiando and those to the subsequent agreement must be identical. The mutual obligation to negotiate must be fulfilled in good faith in accordance with the principle of PACTA SUNT SERVANDA (q.v.).

PAGANI CASE: involved the effect of a bilateral treaty on the nationals of a third state. *See* 10 *Encyclopedia of Public International Law* 323.

PALESTINE: Roman name for the area which now comprises Israel for the most part. The area is subject to claims by both Jews and Arabs as their homeland. *See* PALESTINE LIBERATION ORGANIZATION and WEST BANK OF JORDAN.

PALESTINE LIBERATION ORGANIZATION (PLO): "government in exile" for the group of Arabs who claim PALESTINE (now Israel) as their homeland. The PLO includes guerrilla military groups and other factions. They are represented in many international settings including the United Nations. *See* 10 Den. J. Int'l L. & Pol'y 221.

PALESTINE LIBERATION ORGANIZATION EJECTION FROM BERUIT: *see* 21 I.L.M. 1193.

PALESTINE LIBERATION ORGANIZATION OFFICES IN THE UNITED STATES: in 1987 the United States Congress penned litigation (101 Stat. 1406) to force the closing of PLO offices in the U.S. United States courts found that the act did not require the closing of the PLO office at the United Nations, as that would conflict with the UNITED NATIONS HEADQUARTERS AGREEMENT (q.v.). *See* 35 Wayne L.Rev. 83.

PALLETS: devices to facilitate the loading of cargo and subject to a customs convention, 429 U.N.T.S. 211.

PALMAS ISLAND ARBITRATION (1928): dispute between the Netherlands and the U.S. concerning sovereignty over the Island of Palmas. The arbitrator found that the island "forms in its entirety a part of the Netherlands territory." The strength of the Netherlands title was based on its continuous display of state authority. *See* 2 R.I.A.A. 829 and 22 Am.J.Int.L. 735.

PAN-AFRICAN CONGRESSES: series of meetings in the 1940's to promote PAN-AFRICANISM (q.v.).

PAN-AFRICANISM: failed efforts to unite black Africa into a large nation which could act as a great power and improve the lives of its people. Pan-Africanism still has a following particularly in Liberia. *See* G. Padmore, *Pan-Africanism or Communism* (1956).

PANAMA CANAL: shipping canal running through the Isthmus of Panama, constructed in the early 1900's by the U.S. Government. The canal is open to the ships of all nations. *See* 17 I.L.M. 820

PANAMA CANAL TREATY (1977): between the United States and Panama. It reaffirmed the permanent neutrality of the canal and set a schedule for turning over the administration of the canal to Panama. *See* 16 I.L.M. 1022 and 72 Am.J.Int.L. 225.

PANAMA CONGRESS (1826): early meeting of the nations of the Western Hemisphere which discussed, *inter alia*, excluding further European colonial activities from the Hemisphere. *See* 6 Moore, *Digest of International Law* 416.

PANAMA INVASION (1989): United States forces invaded Panama "to protect the lives of U.S. citizens and restore democracy." *See* NORIEGA REGIME and 84 Am.J.Int.L. 494.

PANAMA SANCTIONS: *see* NORIEGA REGIME.

PAN-AMERICAN UNION: central and permanent organ of the ORGANIZATION OF AMERICAN STATES (q.v.). The Union existed prior to the adoption of the OAS Charter. The Charter did not substantially alter either the identity or the functions or the Pan-American Union, but rather made the Union one of the entities through which the OAS accomplishes its goals. *See* 119 U.N.T.S. 3, Art. 78.

PANAY INCIDENT (1937): Japanese aerial attack on the U.S.S. Panay, and eleven merchant vessels it was escorting on the Yangtse River which resulted in an apology and indemnification of $2.2 million. *See* 5 Hackworth, *Digest of International Law* 687

PANCH SHILA (Hindi for "five principles"): principles upon which state relations are based: 1) mutual respect for one another's territorial integrity and sovereignty; 2) non-aggression; 3) non-intervention in one another's domestic affairs on any economic, political, or ideological grounds whatsoever; 4) equality and mutual benefit; and 5) peaceful coexistence.

PANEVEZYS-SALDUTISKIS RAILWAY CASE: the PERMANENT COURT OF INTERNATIONAL JUSTICE discussed the ownership of a railroad in dispute after the independence of the Baltic States in 1919. Issues raised included STATE RESPONSIBILITY and EXHAUSTION OF LOCAL REMEDIES (qq.v.). *See* 9 I.L.R. 308.

PAPACY: official government of the Roman Catholic Church, represented by the HOLY SEE (q.v.).

PAPAL STATES: territories in central Italy over which the Pope exercised control. The territory prevented the church from being identified with any other state or its politics with the exception of the Vatican. Italy annexed the Papal states in 1870. The Italian Law of Guarantees (May 13, 1871) granted the Pope free use of the Vatican.

PAPER BLOCKADE: a BLOCKADE (q.v.) declared by a state, but not maintained with a force sufficient to prevent access to the coastline of the blockaded state. *See* PARIS DECLARATION (1856).

PAR IN PAREM NON HABET JURISDICTIONEM (L): rule that no state may claim jurisdiction over another. Thus, a state can sue in a foreign court, but absent its consent. It cannot be sued in that forum. *See* 28 I.L.R. 158,160.

PAR SUITE DE FAITS DE GUERRE (F): a consequence of an act of war. *See* 22 I.L.R. 626.

PARACHUTE: the rules of war provide that a combatant parachuting as part of an attack may be fired upon, but that a combatant who parachutes to escape a damaged aircraft is a "ship-wrecked" person, therefore, entitled to protection and may not be fired upon. *See* Art.42, GENEVA CONVENTION PROTOCOL I (1977).

PARAMOUNT INTEREST: a concern which is of greatest importance in the foreign affairs of a state. *See, e.g.,* LANSING-ISHII AGREEMENT (1917).

PARIS AGREEMENTS (1950-54): process of integrating West Germany into the Western European Defense structure. *See* NORTH ATLANTIC TREATY and PLEVEN PLAN.

PARIS CLUB: an informal organization of creditor nations which is created when a mutual debtor nation falls behind in paying its obligations. The "club's" purpose is to assure equal treatment of all the creditors.

PARIS CONVENTION (1919): predecessor to the CHICAGO CONVENTION (1944) (q.v.), which codified the basic international laws of aviation in Europe. *See* 11 L.N.T.S. 174.

PARIS DECLARATION (1856): declaration of basic principles governing aspects of warfare and capture at sea by the major European Powers including the abolition of privateering and requiring that blockades be maintained by force to be binding. *See* 115 C.T.S. 1, 7 Moore, *Digest of International Law* 561.

PARIS PEACE TREATY (1856): ended the Crimean War in which France, Great Britain, Piedmont-Sardinia, and Turkey had fought and defeated Russia. Russia met the demands of the victors by, among other things, conceding the free navigation of the Danube and demilitarizing the Black Sea. *See* 46 British and Foreign State Papers 8 or 114 C.T.S. 409.

PARIS TREATY (1763): treaty by which Great Britain resigned her claim to St. Lucia Island which became a French territory. *See* 42 C.T.S. 320.

PARIS TREATY (1814): agreement between Great Britain and France to cooperate in furthering the abolition of slave traffic. *See* 63 C.T.S. 172.

PARIS UNION: the INTERNATIONAL BUREAU FOR THE PROTECTION OF INDUSTRIAL PROPERTY (q.v.).

PARLEMENTAIRE (F): agents designated by commanders of belligerents in the field to go in person within the enemy lines for the purpose of communicating or negotiating directly with the enemy commander. They have the right to inviolability. *See U.S. Army Field Manual* (1956) Para. 459.

PAROLE: the promise of a prisoner of war to, e.g., not participate further in the hostilities in return for his release as a prisoner of war. *See* Art. 21, GENEVA CONVENTION III (1949).

PARTEIFAHIGES GEBILDE (G): an entity which has the power to sue and be sued. *See* 77 I.L.R. 450.

PARTICIPATION CLAUSE: article in a treaty that controls who may become a party to the treaty. *See* CLOSED TREATY.

PARTISAN: combatants participating in a guerrilla war against enemy forces occupying a territory. It is now recognized that as long as partisan groups abide by the HAGUE REGULATIONS (q.v.), they are entitled to the same treatment as conventional combatants. *See* Art. 44, GENEVA PROTOCOL I (1977).

PASSAGE: in the absence of rights secured by a convention or other treaty stipulation, internal waters, canals, and airspace above territory are subject to the sole control of the state, and vessels of other states have no right to traverse these. A coastal state's sovereignty over its territorial seas is subject to limitations imposed by the right of INNOCENT PASSAGE (q.v.).

PASSIVE EXTRADITION: provisional detention of a suspect at the request of another government pending a formal request for EXTRADITION (q.v.). *See* 30 I.L.R. 390.

PASSIVE NATIONALITY: criminal jurisdiction based on the nationality of the victims by the courts of the victims' country. *See* 15 I.L.R. 491.

PASSIVE PERSONALITY PRINCIPLE: one of the grounds used in granting criminal jurisdiction with respect to acts of aliens abroad. It gives a state jurisdiction over foreigners when the effect of the foreigner's act causes detriment to the nationals of the state asserting jurisdiction.

PASSPORT: document addressed to foreign governments requesting the safe passage of the bearer, and that the bearer be recognized as a citizen of the issuing state. *See Urtetiqui v. D'Arbel*, 34 U.S. 692 (1835).

PATENT COOPERATION TREATY (1970): established the INTER- NATIONAL PATENT COOPERATION UNION (q.v.), to facilitate the filing, searching, and examination of patents including provisions for an "international patent application." *See* 9 I.L.M. 978.

PATENTS: intangible rights recognized by law of the author of an invention or design to the exclusive use of his work for a limited period of time. Most nations have laws protecting the inventor's interests. International agreements have also been concluded to protect these rights. *See* WORLD INTELLECTUAL PROPERTY ORGANIZATION.

PAYMENTS AGREEMENTS: special kind of treaty which establishes mechanisms to settle debts between the nationals of two countries. *See* 30 I.L.R. 404.

P.C.: pour condolier (F), to offer condolences.

P.C.I.J.: PERMANENT COURT OF INTERNATIONAL JUSTICE (q.v.).

PEACE: more than the absence of war, peace includes cooperation and respect among states and the amicable settlements of disagreements. *See* UNGA Res. 377 (V) (3 November 1950), 1950 U.N. Yearbook 193, 203.

PEACE MOVEMENTS: effort of groups of people to rid the world of war. These efforts have been carried on since the middle ages and have led to the development of the Law of War to ameliorate the evil of war. *See* KELLOGG-BRIAND PACT (1928) and 26 McGill L.J. 135.

PEACE OF GOD: a series of decrees issued by the Roman Catholic Church proclaiming an unlimited state of peace.

PEACE PALACE: the seat of the INTERNATIONAL COURT OF JUSTICE (q.v.) at the Hague. Art. 22 of the STATUTE OF THE INTERNATIONAL COURT OF JUSTICE (q.v.) provides that the court's headquarters should be in the Hague. The rental payments for the premises are made by the United Nations. The Palace was erected and is maintained by the Carnegie Foundation.

PEACE TREATY: instrument ending a state of war. Though it is seldom achieved, the primary function of a peace treaty is to succeed in gaining lasting reconciliation between former enemies.

PEACEFUL COEXISTENCE: political, economic, and ideological competition between Marxism and capitalism by means of peaceful work and cultural activities. *See* 56 Am.J.Int.L. 951.

PEACEFUL SETTLEMENT OF DISPUTES: obligation imposed on the parties to various international instruments such as the UNITED NATIONS CHARTER and the HAGUE CONVENTION FOR THE PACIFIC SETTLEMENT OF DISPUTES (1899 & 1907) (q.q.v.). Such agreements generally contain provisions on diplomatic negotiation, mediation, conciliation, arbitration, and adjudication.

PEACEKEEPING FORCE: military force, usually consisting of troops from several neutral countries, which is deployed between warring factions or to keep order in a demilitarized area. *See* UNITED NATIONS FORCES.

PEACEKEEPING MACHINERY: institutions, such as UNITED NATIONS FORCES (q.v.), which are set up to enforce peace agreements between hostile forces.

PEACEKEEPING OPERATIONS: operations of a military, paramilitary, or nonmilitary character conducted by the United Nations in order to maintain international peace and security. The country on whose territory an operation is to take place must consent to the operation. If armed force is involved, the use of force is strictly limited to the requirements of self-defense. *See The Blue Helmets: A Review of United Nation's Peacekeeping* (1986).

PEARL FISHERIES: areas of seabed in the Persian Gulf containing pearl oysters which by long use have been appropriated by the littoral states. This is an example of littoral states acquiring exclusive rights to living resources of the seas. *See* 2 Hackworth, *Digest of International Law* 677-79.

PEKING CONVENTIONS: secured foreign indemnities on Chinese customs revenues. *See* 106 British and Foreign State Papers 73 (1913).

PELE-MELE (F): signing in no particular order. *See* PRECEDENCE.

PENDENTE BELLO (L): while a state of war exists. *See* 1 Whiteman *Digest of International Law* 275.

PER LEGEM TERRAE (L): according to municipal law.

PERDUELLIO (L): an offense against the authority of the State. *See* 8 I.L.R. 88.

PEREMPTORY NORMS: basic international law principles from which no derogation is permitted, e.g., a treaty is void if at the time of its conclusion it conflicts with the peremptory norms of international law according to Art. 53 of the VIENNA CONVENTION ON THE LAW OF TREATIES (q.v.). *See also* JUS COGENS.

PERESTROIKA (R): Soviet policy opening up their system to allow some freedom. *See* 82 Am.J.Int.L. 788.

PERFIDY: acts inviting the confidence of an adversary leading him to believe that he is entitled to, or is obliged to accord protection under the rules of international law. This is applicable in armed conflict with the intent to betray that confidence. *See* Art. 37 of GENEVA CONVENTION PROTOCOL I (1977) and 72 Am.J.Int.L. 457, 473.

PERMANENT CENTRAL OPIUM BOARD: created by the Opium Convention (1925) to police that agreement. *See* 81 L.N.T.S. 339.

PERMANENT COMMITTEE OF THE INTER-AMERICAN CONFERENCE ON INDIAN LIFE: *see* INTER-AMERICAN INDIAN INSTITUTE.

PERMANENT COURT OF ARBITRATION: panel created by the HAGUE CONVENTION FOR THE PACIFIC SETTLEMENT OF DISPUTES (1899) (q.v.), from which arbitrators may be selected by disputing parties. It is not a court, but only a list of approved arbitrators to facilitate "an immediate recourse to arbitration for international differences" (Art.20). The awards announced are to put an end to the dispute definitively and without appeal (Art. 54).

PERMANENT COURT OF INTERNATIONAL JUSTICE (P.C.I.J.): principal judicial organ of the League of Nations and vested with the competency to hear and determine any dispute of an international character which the parties thereto submit to it. The P.C.I.J. could also render advisory opinions upon the request of the League Council or Assembly. The P.C.I.J. was dissolved April 18, 1946, and replaced by the INTERNATIONAL COURT OF JUSTICE (q.v.). *See* Art. 14 of the COVENANT OF THE LEAGUE OF NATIONS.

PERMANENT MANDATES COMMISSION: under the League of Nations Charter, this body assisted the Council in supervising the administration of MANDATE TERRITORIES (q.v.).

PERMANENT MISSION: a diplomatic or consular representative sent to a foreign (host) country for an indefinite period of time, e.g., the typical embassy is a permanent mission.

PERMANENT NEUTRALITY: the neutrality of a state which has been neutralized by a special international treaty. Permanently neutral states are obligated to prevent a belligerent from using the neutral state's territory for military purposes and to refrain from other assistance to belligerents. *See* 21 Am.J.Int.L. 79.

PERMANENT SOVEREIGNTY: third world catch phrase to emphasize the states control over its territory, resources, and population.

PERMANENT SOVEREIGNTY OVER NATURAL RESOURCES: UNGA Res. 1803 (XVII), Dec. 19, 1962, declares that nations should have complete control over their products and the use of their own natural resources. *See* 2 I.L.M. 223.

PERMISSIVE ENFORCEMENT: COLLECTIVE MEASURES (q.v.), approved by the United Nations which are carried out by decentralized national efforts, e.g., the early phase of the KOREAN WAR (q.v.).

PERMISSIVE ENGAGEMENT: ability of the Secretary General of the United Nations to involve himself, and subsequently with approval the United Nations, in the settlement of international disputes. *See e.g.,* the SUEZ CRISIS (1956).

PERPETUAL NEUTRALITY: self-imposed permanent status as a nonparticipant in hostilities of any kind, e.g., Switzerland. *See* 21 Am.J.Int.L. 79, 87.

PERSONA NON GRATA: someone not welcome, in diplomatic usage; a person accredited as a diplomatic agent who is unacceptable to the host country.

PERSONA NON GRATA OF A DIPLOMATIC ENVOY: the refusal of a state to accept a particular individual as an envoy from another country. *See* AGREATION and 4 Moore, *Digest of International Law* 668.

PERSONA STANDI IN JUDICIO (L): a person who can pursue or defend a legal action in a court. Formerly, in time of war, an enemy subject had no persona standi in judicio.

PERSONAL BELONGINGS: prisoners of war are allowed to retain all of their personal belongings - except arms, military equipment, and documents. *See* Art. 18 of GENEVA CONVENTION III (1949). Similar rules apply to internees under GENEVA CONVENTION IV (1949) in Arts. 97 and 128.

PERSONAL UNION: two (or more) states which have entered into a constitutional relationship as a result of a monarch, through the internal laws of succession in each state, becoming the sovereign of both of those states. The union lasts only as long as the laws of succession coincide in the selection of the identical monarch.

PERSONS ACCOMPANYING THE ARMED FORCES: those persons who accompany military forces without being actual members of the military, such as, civilian maintenance crews for aircraft or laborers building barracks. If they are captured by the enemy they are to be considered prisoners of war, GENEVA CONVENTION III (1949), Art. 4A and Art. 13 of both the GENEVA CONVENTIONS I and II (1949).

PETITIONER: party instituting an appeal proceeding in a court or other judicial forum. The party beginning an action before the INTERNATIONAL COURT OF JUSTICE (q.v.) is referred to as the APPLICANT (q.v.).

PETITUS (L): the object of a claim.

PHILADELPHIA DECLARATION: redefined the INTERNA-TIONAL LABOUR ORGANIZATION's (q.v.) aims and purpose after World War II. *See* 1946-7 UN Yearbook 670.

PHOSPHATES IN MOROCCO CASE: in a dispute over expropriation of Morocco's phosphate resources, the Permanent Court of International Justice ruled that the claim made was outside its jurisdiction. *See* 1938 P.C.I.J. (ser A/B) No. 74.

PICAO: PROVISIONAL INTERNATIONAL CIVIL AVIATION ORGANIZATION (q.v.).

PILLAGE: unauthorized appropriation of property done through exploiting the circumstances of war. Pillage is expressly forbidden by Arts. 27 and 48 of the HAGUE REGULATIONS (q.v.).

PILOTAGE: service performed for vessels in transit through a canal, river, or other waters. Such services are generally rendered by a person duly licensed or appointed for such purposes. The state in which the passage lies may charge for pilotage.

PINSON CLAIMS ARBITRATION (*France v. Mexico*): first decision by the French-Mexican Claims Commission established to settle the claims of French citizens resulting from revolutionary events in Mexico. States were held to be liable for damages incurred by aliens, as a result of acts of revolution, only if the revolution was successful in overthrowing the government. Equal treatment of aliens and nationals with respect to state compensation programs was required. *See* 5 R.I.A.A. 327.

PIOUS FUND ARBITRATION (*U.S. v. Mexico*): moneys collected by Jesuit priests for missionaries in California (called "Pious fund for the Californias") were administered by Mexico while California was a Mexican territory . When California was acquired by the United States, an umpire awarded the United States the interest accrued on the fund. Again, in 1902, the U.S. demanded interest payments from Mexico. This arbitration found that the decisions of international tribunals can be res judicata, and that when the parties and the facts of a case are the same, a later tribunal is bound by an earlier decision. Accordingly, Mexico was required to pay the interest. Also, the tribunal found that rules on time limits for bringing claims are not applicable in cases of international financial obligations. *See* 9 R.I.A.A. 1.

PIPELINES: all states possess the right to lay cables and pipelines on the bed of the high seas. Coastal states may not impede the laying or maintenance of the pipelines of a foreign state subject to the right to take reasonable measures for the exploration and exploitation of the resources of the continental shelf. *See* 1956 Report of the International Law Commission on the Law of the Sea, Part II, Sec.I (C) and UNGAOR 11th Sess., Supp. No. 9 (A/3159), p.23, 38-39.

PIRACY: any illegal act of violence, detention, or any act of depredation committed for private ends by the crew or passengers of a private ship or aircraft, and directed; (1) on the high seas against a ship or aircraft, or persons or property thereon; or (2) against a ship, aircraft, or property in a place outside the jurisdiction of any state. *See* Art. 15 of the GENEVA CONVENTION ON THE REGIME OF THE HIGH SEAS (1958) (q.v.).

PIRATA NON MUTAT DOMINIUM (L): capture by pirates does not change ownership; the property recovered from pirates should be restored to its original owner. *See* DROIT DE RESCOUSSE.

PIRATE BROADCASTING: unauthorized transmission of radio or television signals; usually from outside the territory of the offended state. They may be politically motivated or simply commercial ventures playing rock and roll. *See* 45 Law and Contemporary Problems 71 and 59 Am.J.Int.L. 715.

PLAGUE CONVENTIONS: *see* SANITARY CONVENTION.

PLASTIC EXPLOSIVES DETECTION CONVENTION (1991): proposed international agreement to make plastic explosive detectable by airport security screens. *See* 30 I.L.M. 721.

PLATT AMENDMENT: provision insisted upon by the United States Senate in granting Cuba independence in 1903. *See* 2 Revised Stat. Supp. 1503 (1892-1901) and 17 Am.J.Int.L. 761.

PLAZA ACCORDS (1985): agreement by developed countries to help ease United States trade deficit. *See* N.Y. Times Sept. 23, 1985 at A1, col.6.

PLEADINGS: the presentation of each side of a judicial dispute by the parties thereto according to the rules of the body it is before. For the International Court of Justice the basic rules for pleading are found in Arts. 40 et seq. of the STATUTE OF THE INTERNATIONAL COURT OF JUSTICE (q.v.).

PLEBISCITE: an expression of the popular will of the people by voting. A treaty may stipulate that the validity of a cession of territory shall be depend upon the results of a plebiscite by the nationals of the ceding state who inhabit the territory. *See* SAAR REFERENDUM.

PLEDGE: former practice where a state turned over territory to a second state as a guarantee that it would compensate the second state for an undertaking such as the defense of the first state. *See* 10 *Encyclopedia of Public International Law* 326.

PLEIN DROIT (F): favorable treatment. *See* 4 I.L.R. 406.

PLEIN POUVOIRS (F): diplomatic credentials giving the accredited diplomat "FULL POWERS" (q.v.) to conduct a negotiation.

PLENITUDO POTESTATIS (L): fullness of power; papal claim to the ability to exercise temporal power when necessary for the God of Christendom.

PLEVEN PLAN: arrangement where West Germany was allowed to rearm and be integrated into the Western European defenses. *See* 47 Am.J.Int.L. 275.

PLIMSOLL CERTIFICATE: document issued after a ship has been found in compliance with the INTERNATIONAL LOAD LINE CONVENTION (q.v.), which is designed to prevent the overloading of ships.

PLIMSOLL LINE: *see* LOAD LINE.

PLO: PALESTINE LIBERATION ORGANIZATION (q.v.).

PLURINATIONAL ADMINISTRATIVE INSTITUTIONS: entities designed to perform transnational activities of an administrative nature where politically oriented international organizations and traditional international agreements are unsuitable. They may arise in any field where transnational arrangements are necessary, e.g., natural resource management, transportation, utilities, etc. They are highly diverse in structure and may be organized like international corporations, national agencies, or private corporations. *See, e.g.,* SCANDINAVIAN AIRLINES SYSTEM.

POISON: the use of poison or poisoned weapons as a means of injuring the enemy is forbidden. *See* Art. 23 (a), HAGUE REGULATIONS (1907).

POISON GAS: weapon used in World War I, but its ineffectiveness led to a ban. Recently some countries have revived its use as the "poor man's A-bomb." Notably Iran, Iran, and Libya have developed chemical weapon capabilities. *See* 28 I.L.M. 1018 and GENEVA PROTOCOL (1925).

POLAR REGIONS: *see* ANTARCTIC TREATY (1959) and ARCTIC REGION.

POLISARIO: People's Liberation Front for the Western Sahara; guerrilla force attempting to separate the Western Sahara from

Moroccan and Mauritanian rule. *See* SAHWARI ARAB DEMO-
CRATIC REPUBLIC.

POLISH CORRIDOR: strip of land (containing the free city of
DANZIG (q.v.)) given to Poland after World War I which divided
East Prussia from the rest of Germany. It provided one of the ex-
cuses Hitler used for his aggression against Poland to start World
War II. *See* 1 Hackworth, *Digest of International Law* 214.

POLITICAL ASYLUM: status granted to an alien who has fled
his country in fear of persecution for political activities or beliefs.
See MONTEVIDEO CONVENTION ON POLITICAL ASYLUM
(1933) and CARACAS CONVENTION (1954).

POLITICAL OFFENSE: any act which purports to overthrow the
domestic political order of a country. Consequently, even murder
may sometimes be regarded as a political offense. *See The Asylum
Case* , (1950) I.C.J. 266.

POLITICAL OFFENSE EXCEPTION: in extradition treaties, a
provision that crimes considered political in nature (e.g. acts of
revolution) are not extraditable offenses. *See* 6 Whiteman, *Digest
of International Law* 799.

POLITICAL RIGHTS OF WOMEN CONVENTION (1953): attempts to protect and extend the political rights of women. *See* 27
U.S.T. 1909, 193 U.N.T.S. 135.

POLITICAL TREATY: agreement between the two Germanys to
develop normal, good neighbor relations and respect each other's
territorial integrity. *See* 12 I.L.M. 16.

POLLUTER PAYS PRINCIPLE: European Communities Counsel recommendation to allocate costs of pollution and prevention
of pollution (pollution controls) to those causing it. *See* 14 I.L.M.
138.

POLLUTION: *see* TRANSFRONTIER POLLUTION and
TOVALOP.

POLLUTION CIVIL LIABILITY CONVENTION (1969): establishes rules for civil liability in instances where ships cause damage by the discharge of oil. *See* 9 I.L.M. 45.

POLLUTION FROM SHIPS CONVENTION (1973): attempt to control the discharge of harmful pollutants such as oil from ships at sea. *See* 12 I.L.M. 1319.

POLLUTION FUND CONVENTION (1971): a supplement to the POLLUTION CIVIL LIABILITY CONVENTION (1969) (q.v.) which provides for compensation in cases where those liable are excused from liability by the convention or are financially incapable of paying the damages. *See* 11 I.L.M. 284.

POLLUTION OF THE NORTH SEA BY OIL CONVENTION (1969): *see* 704 U.N.T.S. 3.

POLLUTION OF THE SEA BY OIL CONVENTION (1954): first multi-national agreement whose primary objective was the protection of the environment. *See* 327 U.N.T.S. 3.

PONSONBY RULE: British practice of tabling treaties subject to ratification in both houses of parliament for twenty-one days before the government proceeds to ratification. The object of this is to assure publicity of the treaty and to provide opportunity for their discussion in Parliament.

POPULAR MOVEMENT FOR THE LIBERATION OF ANGOLA (MPLA): LIBERATION MOVEMENT (q.v.) which took over the Angolan government from the Portuguese when the colonial regime fell. *See* ANGOLAN CIVIL WAR.

PORT D'ATTACHE (F): home port.

PORTEE DE VUE (F): distance out from the shore from which land could be discerned from the foremast top, roughly 14 miles, and early rule for determining the TERRITORIAL WATERS (q.v.) of a nation.

PORTEE DE CANON (F): CANNON SHOT RULE (q.v.), the effective range of guns on shore varying from three to nine miles and used as a measure of the states TERRITORIAL WATERS (q.v.).

PORTER CONVENTION: instrument adopted at the second Hague Peace Conference (1907) (*see* HAGUE PEACE CONFERENCE (1899)). The signatory states agreed that they would abstain from using force to recover "contract debts" claimed by one government as owed to its nationals by another government. This agreement not to use force is subject to the condition that the debtor state agrees to submit the dispute to arbitration; or if the debtor state fails to honor the judgment handed down by the arbitrator, the creditor state is not bound by its promise not to use force. *See* 1 Bevans 607 or 205 C.T.S. 250.

PORTS: part of the internal waters of a state (usually used for the docking of ships) and fully a portion of the state as the land itself.

PORTSMOUTH TREATY (1905): treaty negotiated by President Roosevelt between Russia and Japan ending the Russo-Japanese War. *See* 1 Am.J.Int.L.Supp. 17.

POSITIVISM: theory that the rules of international law are based on the consent of the states of the world. This consent may be given expressly, as in a treaty, or it may be implied by states acquiescing in customary rules. *See also* NATURAL LAW.

POSSESSIO LONGI TEMPORIS (L): a state's claim to territory based upon its exercise of jurisdiction for a long period of time without opposition from other states.

POSTAL COMMUNICATIONS: letters, postcards, and other small packages sent through the offices of the postal service of one or more countries. For a general description of the international postal system, *see* 9 Whiteman, *Digest of International Law* 1037.

POSTAL SHIP: a ship which is commissioned to carry mail. Because of this status it may have some immunity from attachment.

POSTLIMING: *See* POSTLIMINIUM (L).

POSTLIMINIUM (L): invalidation of all acts, which are contrary to the laws of nations, performed in time of war by a belligerent occupant and a revival when the occupation is ended of all legal relations illegitimately modified by the occupant in their former condition and without payment of compensation. *See Gold Looted by Germany from Rome in 1943*, 20 I.L.R. 441.

POSTLIMINY: *see* POSTLIMINIUM (L).

POTENTIS DEBET SEQUI JUSTIUM, NON ANTECEDERE (L): the use of force must follow justice, not go before it.

POTESTAS STRICTE INTERPRETATUR (L): powers are to be interpreted narrowly.

POTSDAM CONFERENCE (1945): decisions of the heads of government of the Soviet Union, United States, and United Kingdom with respect to Germany after its unconditional surrender May 8, 1945. The agreement is published in two separate documents: A report on the Conference, 13 Dept. State Bull. 153, and a protocol of the proceedings of the Berlin Conference, Dept. of State Press Release No. 238 of March 24, 1947. *See also* 40 Am.J.Int.L.Supp. 21.

POTSDAM PROCLAMATION (1945): agreement by U.S., Great Britain, and China which set forth the terms of surrender to be demanded of the Japanese, i.e., that the CAIRO DECLARATION (1943) (q.v.) be accepted and that Japanese sovereignty would be limited to the principal islands of Japan. These terms were accepted on August 14, 1945.

POURVOIR A SA REPRESENTATION EN JUSTICE (F): consular authorities may provide their nationals with legal counsel if local law permits them. *See* 77 I.L.R. 542.

POW: PRISONER OF WAR (q.v.).

POWER POLITICS: system of relations based on the relative economic and military strength of the participants. *See* 9 *Encyclopedia of Public International Law* 306.

POWER TRANSITION THEORY OF WAR: theory that wars begin when rival states draw close to each other in strength. *See* Chan, *International Relations in Perspective* (1984) at 124-5.

POWERS OF ATTORNEY TO BE USED ABROAD: subject of an inter-American agreement to accept Powers of Attorney executed in other member countries. *See* 14 I.L.M. 325.

P.P.: pour presenter (F), to present.

P.P.C.: pour prendre conge (F), to take leave, say good-bye.

P.R.: pour remercier (F), to express thanks.

PRAETOR PEREGRINUS(L): office developed in Rome which appointed judges to adjudicate disputes between Romans and aliens or between aliens alone.

PRACTICE: the usual or typical activities of a state. Practice is one element in proving that a particular act is customary. *See* CUSTOMARY INTERNATIONAL LAW.

PRAETER LEGEM (L): equitable ruling of a court based on a sense of justice or rules of NATURAL LAW (q.v).

PREAMBLE: the narrative introduction of a treaty. It is the portion of a treaty extending from the title to the text. The preamble often serves as an aid for interpretation of treaty provisions.

PREAMBLE PROPER: that part of the preamble which states the motives, objectives, and purpose of a treaty. *See* 26 I.L.R. 585.

PRECE PARTIUM (L): done at the request of the parties.

PRECEDENCE: order or rank of heads of state or diplomats, e.g., if walking in a procession at a ceremony or order in which a treaty is signed. Formerly it was established by the Pope, but now is decided by rank of title, length of service, alphabetical, or perhaps by lot.

PREDICATES OF TITLE: forms of address used with a person holding a title, e.g., a King is addressed as "Your Majesty."

PREFERENTIAL CLAIM AGAINST VENEZUELA ARBITRA-TION: in 1902-03 Great Britain, Germany, and Italy forced Venezuela to honor the claims that several countries had against her by blockading the Venezuelan coast. A tribunal of the Permanent Court of Arbitration determined that priority should be given to the demands of the blockading powers over those creditor states not participating in the blockade. *See* 9 R.I.A.A. 99 and PORTER CONVENTION.

PREFERENTIAL ZONE: area of the high seas adjacent to the territorial sea in which a coastal state claims preferential fishing and conservation rights.

PRELIMINARY OBJECTIONS: in an international adjudication, any objection which if upheld would make it impossible or unnecessary for the tribunal to decide the case. The object of a preliminary objection is not to avoid merely a decision on, but even any discussion of the merits. *Barcelona Traction Company Case*, (1964) I.C.J. 44. *See also, PANEVEZYS-SALDUTISKIS RAILWAY CASE.*

PRENDRE ACTE (F): to take note of the act of another party without acknowledging its truth or correctness.

PREPARATORY WORKS: the "legislative history" of a treaty, TRAVAUX PREPARATOIRE (q.v.).

PRESCRIPTION: *see* EXTINCTIVE PRESCRIPTION, ACQUISITIVE PRESCRIPTION, and RIGHT OF PRESCRIPTION.

PRESCRIPTION ACQUISITIVE (F): ACQUISITIVE PRESCRIPTION (q.v.).

PRESCRIPTION LIBERATOIRE (F): EXTINCTIVE PRESCRIPTION (q.v.).

PRESTATION: the payment of feudal dues.

PRESUMPTION OF FACT: in some instances the facts as pleaded are presumed to be true in order for the court to have a starting place to decide preliminary questions such as jurisdiction.

PRESUMPTION OF NON-DERELICTION: a state does not lose sovereignty over a territory unless the withdrawal from the territory is coupled with the intent to abandon. The intention to abandon must be unquestionable. There is a presumption against territory reverting back to the status of TERRA NULLIUS (q.v.).

PRESUMPTION OF TRUTH OF CLAIMS: if a claim is not formulated or prosecuted against a state within the available adjudicatory bodies it is presumed not to be honest, i.e., having no basis. The presumption becomes stronger the longer the delay. The justification for this presumption is that evidence which may oppose the claim is difficult to produce after the passage of a certain period of time.

PRESUMPTION OF TRUTH OF FACT AND CORRECTNESS OF LAW: every allegation of fact and contention of law set forth by a claimant in a suit against a state is presumed to be correct when determining whether the claimant has, in fact, exhausted the local remedies and thus has standing in international law. *See* AMBATIELOS CASE.

PRESS CASE (1962): interpreted the jurisdiction of the International Labour Organization Tribunal. *See* 32 I.L.R. 518 and 526.

PREVENTION OF COLLISIONS AT SEA: *see* LONDON CONVENTION ON THE INTERNATIONAL REGULATIONS FOR THE PREVENTION OF COLLISIONS AT SEA (1972).

PREVENTION OF POLLUTION FROM SHIPS CONVENTION (1973): *see* POLLUTION FROM SHIPS CONVENTION (1973).

PREVENTIVE MEASURES: COLLECTIVE MEASURES (q.v.) of self-defense by a nation threatened by a breach of the peace or AGGRESSION (q.v.).

PREVENTIVE SELF DEFENSE: *see* CAROLINE INCIDENT (1837).

PRIME MINISTER: leader of the government in a parliamentary system of government. The prime minister is usually not the HEAD OF STATE (q.v.).

PRIMUS INTER PARES (L): first among equals applied to the presidency of the PERMANENT COURT OF INTERNATIONAL JUSTICE (q.v.).

PRINCIPAL LEGAL ADVISOR: chief legal counsel to an international organization. *See* 9 I.L.M. 879.

PRISONER OF WAR: a person who has fallen by capture or surrender into the power of the enemy, and who belongs to one of eight enumerated categories listed in the Geneva Convention relative to the treatment of prisoners of war (1949), 6 U.S.T. 3516, 75 U.N.T.S. 135. Included are members of the armed forces and persons authorized to accompany the armed forces.

PRIVATE INTERNATIONAL LAW: rules which govern the choice of law in private matters (such as business contracts, marriage, etc.) when those questions arise in an international context, e.g., will country A enforce the divorce granted under the laws of country B.

PRIVATEER: private individuals permitted by LETTERS OF MARQUE (q.v.), issued by a state, to arm their merchant vessels for the purpose of attacking enemy trading ships. The practice of privateering was abolished by the PARIS DECLARATION (1856) (q.v.).

PRIVATOTUM CONVENTIO JURI PUBLICO NON DERO-GAT (L): a private agreement cannot denigrate the public law.

PRIVILEGE OF DOCUMENTS: the refusal and acquiescence of a court to the production of documentary evidence. Great Britain was allowed to withhold some secret documents in the CORFU CHANNEL CASE (q.v.).

PRIVILEGES AND IMMUNITIES OF THE UNITED NA-TIONS: by treaty the United Nations is given juridical personality so that it may make contracts, own property, etc. *See* 43 Am.J.Int.L.Supp. 1.

PRIZE: property, generally ships but also arms, munitions, and other cargo captured at sea during war. *See* APPAM CASE and the HAGUE CONVENTION ON THE RIGHT OF CAPTURE (1907).

PRIZE COURTS: the municipal court or administrative tribunal in which the validity of maritime capture (prize) is adjudicated. Title to the enemy vessel or goods in prize does not pass until adjudicated by a prize court. For the United States *see* 10 U.S.C. sec. 7652.

PRIZE LAW: domestic and international rules relating to the capture of enemy property in time of war. *See* HAGUE CONVENTION ON THE RIGHT OF CAPTURE.

PROCES-VERBAL (PROCES-VERBAUX) (F): documents of written facts recorded to provide proof of authenticity. Proces-verbaux form the official records of international conferences and are generally attested to by signature. They may be cast in whatever form the concerned states prefer. *See also*, TRAVAUX PRE-PARATOIRES.

PROCES-VERBAL OF RATIFICATION: record certifying the conclusion of the treaty-making process and the deposit of instruments of ratification.

PROCES-VERBAL OF SIGNATURE: official record of proceedings prepared when a treaty or multilateral convention is signed by a number of states. The proces-verbal of signature enumerates the states participating in the convention and reservations or declarations made by the states' representatives.

PROCONSUL: an officer with consular authority but lacking the formal title CONSUL (q.v.).

PRODUCERS' AGREEMENTS: *see* COMMODITY AGREE-MENTS.

PRODUCT LIABILITY CONVENTION (1977): treaty sponsored by the COUNCIL OF EUROPE (q.v.) to unify the law of liability for the manufacture of defective products among European countries. *See* 16 I.L.M. 7.

PROGRAM FOR SUSTAINED GROWTH (1985): proposal of United States Secretary of the Treasury, James Baker, for solving the international debt crisis. *See* Comment, 4 Dick. J. Int'l. L. 275.

PRO-MEMORIA: a MEMORANDUM (q.v.).

PROOF OF CUSTOM: establishing a principle of customary international law involves a showing of PRACTICE (q.v.) by most states whose actions are motivated by OPINIO JURIS (q.v.). *See* Art. 38 of the STATUTE OF THE INTERNATIONAL COURT OF JUSTICE.

PROPAGANDA: information used by a belligerent state to encourage its citizens to support the war effort, or information disseminated across enemy lines to cause dissension among the enemy's populace. *See* Art. 51 of the GENEVA CONVENTION IV (1949).

PROPORTIONALITY: bringing things into balanced order by avoiding excessive behavior. It is a principle of international law that the use of force should be proportional to the threat or grievance. *See* the NAULILAA INCIDENT (1914).

PROPOGATION AGREEMENT: established jurisdiction over certain disputes within the competency of the court or arbitral tribunal of a particular country.

PROPRIETE COMMERCIALE (F): a commercial property including a leased place of business. *See* 4 I.L.R. 454.

PROPRIO MOTU (L): acting on its own motion.

PROSTITUTION TREATIES: *see* WHITE SLAVERY.

PROTECTED OBJECTS: objects such as art treasures, religious icons, etc., which are shielded from destruction by the LAWS OF WAR (q.v.). *See* PROTECTION OF CULTURAL PROPERTY IN THE EVENT OF ARMED CONFLICT.

PROTECTED PERSONS: individuals who are protected by rules of international law such as PRISONERS OF WAR (q.v.). *See* HUMAN RIGHTS, GENEVA CONVENTION III (1949) and GENEVA CONVENTION IV (1949).

PROTECTED STATE: *see* PROTECTORATE.

PROTECTING POWERS: diplomatic representatives of a country who take responsibility for protection of the rights of the nationals of a third country in the country where the diplomats are stationed, e.g., Switzerland has acted as the protecting power for United States nationals in Iran since the suspension of United States/Iranian relations.

PROTECTIO TRAHIT SUBJECTIONEM ET SUBJECTIO PRO-TECTIONEM (L): those protected by the sovereign owe the sovereign allegiance. *See* 15 I.L.R. 84, 88.

PROTECTION OF CULTURAL PROPERTY IN THE EVENT OF ARMED CONFLICT: subject of a convention requiring the parties to safeguard property of cultural importance. *See* 249 U.N.T.S. 215.

PROTECTION OF FOREIGN PROPERTY CONVENTION (1967): attempt to insure the fair treatment of property owned by the nationals of the parties to the treaty. *See* 7 I.L.M. 117.

PROTECTION OF INDUSTRIAL PROPERTY CONVENTION (1883): *See* INTERNATIONAL BUREAU FOR THE PROTECTION OF INDUSTRIAL PROPERTY.

PROTECTION OF NATIONALS: an extension of the right of self- defense to justify the use of force outside ones territory. It was cited by the British during the SUEZ CRISIS (1956) (q.v.), and recently invoked as part of the justification for the United States GRENADA INTERVENTION (1983) (q.v.)., *see* 12 Whiteman, *Digest of International Law* 68, 197.

PROTECTION OF THE OZONE LAYER CONVENTION (1986): attempt to reduce the production and use of chemicals which deplete the ozone layer of the atmosphere. *See* 26 I.L.M. 1516 and 6 Dick. J. Int'l L. 87.

PROTECTION OF THE RIGHTS OF ALL MIGRANT WORK-ERS AND MEMBERS OF THEIR FAMILIES CONVENTION (1991): United Nations effort to protect the human rights of migrant workers. *See* 30 I.L.M. 1517.

PROTECTIVE PRINCIPLE: a basis for jurisdiction which relies on the need of the sovereign to protect itself. *See* 32 I.L.R. 112, 116.

PROTECTORATE (or protected state): a relationship of dependency is created when one state places itself by treaty under the protection of another more powerful state. "The extent of the powers of a protecting state depends first upon the treaties between the protecting and protected states, and secondly upon the conditions under which the protectorate has been recognized by third powers against whom there is an intention to rely on the provisions of these treaties." *Nationality Decrees in Tunis and Morocco Case*, 1923 P.C.I.J. (ser. B) No. 4 at 27.

PROTEGE: a person under the protection of a foreign state while residing in their own country.

PROTEGE SPECIAL (F): national of the host (receiving) state or a third state in the diplomatic service of a country and receiving customary diplomatic protection. The use of such persons has become obsolete for the most part.

PROTEST: a strong objection, either written or oral, to an action by another state which the state making the protest deems improper, wrongful, etc.

PROTOCOL: 1) An agreement less formal than a treaty. A protocol may be an independent agreement, or it may be supplemental to a convention drawn up by the same negotiators explaining or interpreting the provisions of the convention. 2) Diplomatic manners and courtesy. *See* Satow, *A Guide to Diplomatic Usage.*

PROTOCOL FINAL (F): FINAL PROTOCOL (q.v.).

PROTOCOLE DE CLOTURE (F): FINAL PROTOCOL (q.v.).

PROVISIONAL INTERNATIONAL CIVIL AVIATION ORGANIZATION (PICAO): organization established at the CHICAGO CONVENTION (1944) (q.v.) to begin the work envisioned for the INTERNATIONAL CIVIL AVIATION ORGANIZATION (q.v.) until that body could be formally convened. *See* 40 Am.J.Int.L.Supp. 63.

PROVISIONAL MEASURES: INTERIM MEASURES (q.v.).

PROXENAI: official in the Greek city-state responsible for the welfare of aliens residing in a given state. A predecessor to the modern CONSUL (q.v.).

PSYCHOTROPIC SUBSTANCES CONVENTION (1971): effort to control drugs, other than narcotics, which have a mind altering effect. *See* 10 I.L.M. 261.

PUBLIC GOODS THEORY: *see* COLLECTIVE GOODS THEORY.

PUBLIC HEALTH: subject of international cooperation including efforts to control the spread of disease. Early efforts included the establishment of the Office International d'Hygiene Publique (OIHP) (*see* 206 C.T.S. 31). Current efforts are under the auspices of the WORLD HEALTH ORGANIZATION (q.v.).

PUBLIC INTERNATIONAL LAW: law dealing with the relations between states. The other division of international law, which pairs with public international law, is PRIVATE INTERNATIONAL LAW (q.v.).

PUBLIC INTERNATIONAL UNIONS: permanent associations to administer technical aspects of activities which of necessity require international cooperation. *See* INTERNATIONAL POSTAL UNION or INTERNATIONAL TELECOMMUNICATIONS UNION.

PUBLIC ORDER: ORDRE PUBLIC (F) (q.v.).

PUBLIC VESSEL: ship used by a state for a public purpose. The ship's flag, along with the ships documents, provide proof of the ship's public character. A private vessel chartered by a state for a public purpose (e.g., as a troop transport) is a public vessel.

PUBLICISTS: scholars writing on the subject of international law; their work is a source which the International Court of Justice may consult in finding international law. *See* Art. 38, STATUTE OF THE INTERNATIONAL COURT OF JUSTICE.

PUEBLO CLAUSE: list of activities which, if done by a ship during its exercise of INNOCENT PASSAGE (q.v.), constitutes a prejudicial act against the coastal state and nullifies the right of innocent passage. *See* Art. 19, LAW OF THE SEA CONVENTION (1982).

PUEBLO INCIDENT: a United States ship and crew were taken prisoner by North Korea and held for 11 months on charges of spying. *See* 63 Am. J.Int.L. 682.

PUGWASH CONFERENCE: privately organized international conferences of scientists held at Pugwash, Nova Scotia, to promote peace and publicize the effects of nuclear war. Also, it is called the Conference on Science and World Affairs.

PUNS: Party for the National Unification of the Sahara; the pro-Spanish force in the struggle for the liberation of Spanish Morocco.

PUNTA DEL ESTE CHARTER (1961): principal document establishing the ALLIANCE FOR PROGRESS (q.v.), a United States sponsored effort at Latin American development through the ORGANIZATION OF AMERICAN STATES (q.v.).

PUNTA DEL ESTE DECLARATION (1967): made by the presidents of the Organization of American States; it supported development efforts and the establishment of a Latin American Common Market. *See* 6 I.L.M. 535.

PUPPET STATE: an ostensibly independent state which is, in fact, under the control of another state in important matters. Countries of Eastern Europe were often referred to as puppet states of the Soviet Union.

PURSUIT: the chasing of a foreign vessel or aircraft into international waters or airspace, after a violation of the enforcing state's laws. *See* the *Marianna Flora*, 24 U.S. 1 (1826).

PYRENEES TREATY (1659): formal end to the Thirty Years War between France and Spain; it established the Pyrenees Mountains as the natural boundary between France and Spain and marked the decline of Spain as a great power. *See* 5 C.T.S. 325 (in French) or 1 Toynbee, Major *Peace Treaties* 51 (English translation).

[Q - R]

QUADRIPARTITE AGREEMENT ON BERLIN: concluded by the United States, France, the Soviet Union, and the United Kingdom to facilitate the parties' exercise of governance over BERLIN (q.v.) which has been occupied by the four powers since the end of World War II. *See* 10 I.L.M. 895.

QUADRUPLE ALLIANCE: formed between Russia, Prussia, Austria, and Great Britain during the Napoleanic Wars. They pledged themselves to strive for peace and assumed some quasi-legislative powers to govern the alliance. *See* 65 C.T.S. 251.

QUADRUPLE PACIFIC TREATY (1921): treaty between Japan, Great Britain, France, and the United States to respect the status quo in the Region of the Pacific Ocean. *See* 25 L.N.T.S. 183.

QUAELIBET JURISDICTIO CAUCILLOS SUOS LABET (L): for every jurisdiction there are self-imposed limits.

QUAI D'ORSAY: street upon which the French Foreign Ministry is located, thus slang for this office.

QUALIFIED IMMUNITY: freedom from liability which is granted or exists only in respect to governmental acts (acts JURE IMPERII), but not with respect to commercial acts (acts JURE GESTIONIS).

QUALITY OF LIFE: psuedo-measurement of how well-off a population is in terms of food, education, life-expectancy, literacy, etc. It is usually related to the per capita income of the place being discussed.

QUALITY OF STATES: those characteristics that derive from statehood and, some would argue, define the relative status of a state, e.g., states are usually granted equal voting power in international organizations, sovereign equality, though efforts have been made from time to time to have weighted voting.

QUANTITATIVE RESTRICTIONS: in arms control agreements, provisions based on numbers of weapons rather than their quality (i.e., accuracy or destructive capabilities). *See* STRATEGIC ARMS LIMITATION TALKS or LONDON NAVAL CONFERENCE (1930).

QUANTUM MERUIT (L): "as much as he deserves," describes the extent of liability of a party to a contract which is implied by law. It is an equitable doctrine based on the concept that one should not be unjustly enriched by the benefit of another's labor and materials.

QUARANTINE: term coined by the Kennedy Administration during the CUBAN MISSILE CRISIS (q.v.) as a euphemism for a BLOCKAGE (q.v.). They stopped and searched ships for intercontinental ballistic missiles being sent to Cuba by the Soviet Union. *See* 57 Am.J.Int.L. 512, 515.

QUARTER: clemency in not killing an enemy who has surrendered or is rendered defenseless. The modern law of war prohibits an order to give no quarter, i.e., an order to leave no survivors. *See* Art. 40, GENEVA CONVENTION PROTOCOL I (1977).

QUARTERING OF SOLDIERS: the placing of soldiers in private homes for their shelter and feeding when the necessities of war require such. The home owner is to be reimbursed a fair value for the service. The United States Constitution, Amendment III deals with the United States Government's power to quarter soldiers.

QUASI-INTERNATIONAL LAW: law concerned with the relations between nations and other entities not the subject of public international law such as a multinational corporation. Municipal law generally applies to such relationships.

QUASI-LEGISLATIVE INTERNATIONAL ORGANIZATION: organization with international personality with the power to develop international guidelines or standards but not to make strictly enforceable rules. *See e.g.*, INTERNATIONAL LABOUR ORGANIZATION.

QUEBEC-LOUISANA CULTURAL AGREEMENT: *see* 30 Proceeding of the Louisiana Academy of Science 112 and 64 Am.J.Int.L. 380.

QUEMOY AND MATSU: islands near Formosa controlled by the Republic of China; the subject of a territorial dispute between the People's Republic of China and Taiwan. *See* 4 Whiteman, *Digest of International Law* 407.

QUESTIONS DE PRESEANCE (F) (or *droit de preseance*): discussion of the relative ranks of states which was hotly debated in the sixteenth and seventeenth centuries, but now has only ceremonial significance (if any) in the signing of treaties or at diplomatic occasions. States with royal honors came before those without, sovereigns came before protectorates, etc. *See* Satow, *A Guide to Diplomatic Practice*, (4th ed.), at 25.

QUI IN TERRITORIO MEO EST, ETIAM MEUS SUBDITUS EST (L): that which is in my territory is my subject; old rule of a states supreme authority over persons and things found within its territory.

QUI TACET CONSENTIRE VIDETUR (L): a particular practice will prevail over a general rule of law.

QUIDQUID EST IN TERRITORIO, EST ETIAM DE TERRITORIO (L): all individuals and property in the territory of a state are under its sovereign control.

QUIET DIPLOMACY: efforts to settle disputes without publicity.

QUIET REVOLUTION: the revision of the status of the province of Quebec within the Federation of Canada. *See* 7 Can.Y.B.Int'l L. 3.

QUIETA NON MOVERE (L): a peaceful state of affairs should not be disturbed.

QUISLING: one who collaborates with an occupying army; derived from the puppet head of the government of Nazi occupied Norway, Vadkin Quisling.

QUITO DECLARATION AND ACTION PLAN (1984): agreement among Latin American and Caribbean countries concerning their external debt payment which they linked to their export earning income. *See* U.N. Chronicle, March 1984, pp.13-17.

QUITTANCE D'USAGE (F): receipt of usage, acceptance of custom in international law.

QUORUM: the number of participants in attendance necessary in order to conduct business of approved measures, e.g., the United Nations General Assembly must have one-third of its members present for discussion, and a majority of members present to take a decision. *See* Rule 67, Rules of Procedure of the General Assembly, U.N. Doc. no. A/520.

RACE: a division of humankind possessing distinctive, hereditary characteristics, but often used more loosely to designate national, ethnic, or cultural groups. *See* Art. 1, ELIMINATION OF ALL FORMS OF RACIAL DISCRIMINATION CONVENTION (1965).

RACIAL DISCRIMINATION: *see* ELIMINATION OF ALL FORMS OF RACIAL DISCRIMINATION CONVENTION (1965).

RACIST REGIME: governments which practice racial discrimination or carry on campaigns against the members of a particular racial or ethnic group. *See* ELIMINATION OF ALL FORMS OF

RACIAL DISCRIMINATION CONVENTION (1965) and APART-
HEID.

RADIO BROADCASTS: the sending of information by use of radio signals; the broadcast of material calculated to incite distur-
bances was the subject of the BROADCAST CONVENTION
(1936) (q.v.).

RADIO FREE EUROPE: United States sponsored radio transmissions aimed at Eastern Europe. For an example of protest by the
target countries *see* 13 Whiteman, *Digest of International Law* 974.

RADIO LIBERTY: part of the United States Information Agency
aiming radio broadcasts at the third world, *see* 22 U.S.C. sec. 1463.

RADIO MARTI: part of the United States Information Agency
which broadcasts specifically to Cuba. It was authorized by Congress in 1983, after intense debate and remains controversial. *See*
N.Y. Times, Sept. 17, 1987, p.A8, and 22 U.S.C. sec. 1465(c).

RADIO-ORIENT ARBITRATION: dispute over the right of the
Egyptian Government to prohibit the operation of a French radio-
telegraph company in violation of the INTERNATIONAL TELE-
COMMUNICATIONS CONVENTION (1932) (q.v.). *See* 37
Am.J.Int.L. 341.

RADIO PIRATE: *see* PIRATE BROADCASTING.

RADIOACTIVE FALLOUT: debris from atmospheric nuclear explosions. Such explosions were condemned by the International
Court of Justice in the NUCLEAR TEST CASES (q.v.).

RADIOLOGICAL WEAPON: a weapon which does not use the
explosive force of an atomic reaction, but relies on the deadly effects of radiation alone to be effective.

RADIONAVIGATION: use of radio signals to determine the location of a ship or aircraft; now especially the use of satellite signals such as LORAN (q.v.). *See also* INMARSAT.

RAILWAY TRAFFIC BETWEEN LITHUANIA AND POLAND: subsequent to the VILNA DISPUTE (q.v.), Lithuania was advised that it had no obligation to repair or operate a section of railway on its border with Poland. *See* 1931 P.C.I.J. (ser A/B) No. 21.

RAILWAY TRANSPORT: subject of regional international law which attempts to unify the rules of liability and coordinate services provided. *See* 241 U.N.T.S. 336.

RAINBOW WARRIOR AFFAIR (1985): a Greenpeace vessel, which had been used to conduct protests against French nuclear testing, was sunk in New Zealand waters by French agents. *See* 26 I.L.M. 1346.

RAISON D'ETAT (F): for reasons of state; the intent of the state is supreme.

RAMADAN WAR: *see* YOM KIPPUR WAR.

RAMBOULLETT CONFERENCE (1975): summit meeting of the leaders of the United States, Great Britain, France, Japan, West Germany, and Italy where a dispute between the United States and France over fixed or floating exchange rates was resolved, at least temporarily. *See* 11 Weekly Comparative Presidential Documents 1292 (Nov. 24, 1975).

RAMSAR CONVENTION (1971): *see* WETLANDS OF INTERNATIONAL IMPORTANCE CONVENTION (1971)

RANK OF STATES: *see* QUESTION DE PRESEANCE.

RANN OF KUTCH ARBITRATION: after the 1968 border war between India and Pakistan, the parties agreed to settle the demarcation of the border by arbitration. The tribunal set the border as it lay when the two countries gained their independence from Great Britain in 1947. *See* 7 I.L.M. 633.

RANSOM BILL: instrument memorializing the repurchase of a captured vessel which serves as a safe conduct for the ransomed vessel.

RAPACKI PLAN (1957): Polish proposal to make Central Europe a nuclear free zone. *See* 2 *Documents on Disarmament 1945-1959* 944. *See also* GOMULKA PLAN.

RAPALLO TREATY (1922): agreement between Soviet Russia and Germany settling questions that remained at the close of World War I, including renouncing all claims for compensation arising from the War and resuming normal trade and diplomatic relations. *See* 19 L.N.T.S. 247 and 26 L.N.T.S. 387 or 20 Am.J.Int.L.Supp. 116.

RAPPORTEUR: person appointed to prepare a report of the work of a committee, conference, etc. *See* Satow, *A Guide to Diplomatic Practice* (4th ed.) at 310.

RARC: REGIONAL ADMINISTRATIVE RADIO CONFERENCE (q.v.).

RASSEMBLEMENT DEMOCRATIQUE AFRICAINE (F): meeting in 1948 of the national leaders of the French colonies in West Africa (then French West Africa).

RATIFICATION: constitutional process by which a legislature confirms the government's action in signing a treaty, and thus the government may submit an instrument of ratification to the depository government and become bound by the agreement.

RATING OF EMBASSIES: the setting of property values on real property used for diplomatic residences for purposes of local taxing, some of which covers the cost of municipal services (sewer, water, etc.) provided to the embassies. The problem is usually resolved through reciprocal arrangements between the national governments. *See* 10 I.L.R. 337.

RATIO DECIDENDI: the reason or principles leading to a judicial decision.

RATIO IMPERTINENS (L): an argument that is irrelevant to the subject under discussion.

RATIO LEGIS: the reason or principle behind a law.

RAUTER CASE: Hans Rauter, the Chief of Police for the Nazi occupation of the Netherlands, was found guilty of war crimes and sentenced to death. His appeal on various grounds was denied, and he was executed. *See* 12 Revue Belge de Droit International (1976).

RDA: RASSEMBLEMENT DEMOCRATIQUE AFRICAINE (F) (q.v.).

REAGAN DOCTRINE (1984): policy that the United States would support anticommunist guerrilla movements in such places as Afghanistan and Angola. *See* 13 Yale J. Int'l L. 171.

REAL UNION: a composite state consisting of two or more sovereign states joined by allegiance to one monarchy, e.g., the Austro-Hungarian Empire where the Hapsburgs ruled over the sovereign countries of Hungary and Austria.

REALPOLITIK (G): pragmatic view of international affairs, especially German acceptance (at least for the time being) of the division into East and West Germany and the development of relations with Eastern Europe.

REASON OF WAR: justification of an act that would otherwise be illegal, but which becomes necessary because of the exigencies of war.

REBEL: person who participates in a REBELLION (q.v.).

REBELLION: uprising against a government; attempting to change that government. If successful the new government may be recognized. *See* RECOGNITION.

REBUS SIC STANTIBUS: things as they are in a given situation; doctrine that a treaty is made in the context of a situation, and if the situation changes fundamentally then the treaty is no longer binding. *See* Art. 62 VIENNA CONVENTION ON THE LAW OF TREATIES.

RECALL OF DIPLOMATS: termination of a diplomatic envoy's mission by the receipt of a letter of recall, by the envoy which he presents to the state where he is stationed and receives his passport and a LETTRE DE RECREANCE (q.v.). The envoy enjoys his diplomatic privileges on his journey home. *See* LETTRE DE RAPPEL.

RECEIVED-FOR-SHIPMENT BILL OF LADING: document which evidences receipt of goods for transport, but does not indicate the actual date of loading. *See* BILL OF LADING.

RECEPTION OF DIPLOMATS: most states receive and send diplomatic envoys, but are under no obligation to do so. The mode of reception varies with the status of the envoy, ambassadors being received by the head of state while a charge d'affaires will be received by the foreign minister. *See also,* AGREATION.

RECIPROCITY: 1) The custom of exchanging diplomatic envoys of equal rank though it is not a rule of international law. 2) Any arrangement involving mutually agreed exchange between two or more countries.

RECLAME (F): the name and official designation of the person to whom a NOTE (q.v.) is sent.

RECLAMATION OF TIDELANDS: there are no specific restrictions placed by international law on the extension of territory out into the territorial sea by draining that land. *See* WETLANDS OF INTERNATIONAL IMPORTANCE CONVENTION (1971).

RECOGNITION: the act of acknowledging the existence of a new state, a new government, a state of war, etc. *See* CONSTITUTIVE THEORY OF RECOGNITION, DECLARATIVE THEORY OF RECOGNITION, RELATIONS OFFICIEUSES and 30 Am.J.Int.L.Supp. 185.

RECOGNITION AND ENFORCEMENT OF FOREIGN ARBITRAL AWARDS CONVENTION (1958) (New York Convention): uniform rules for recognition and enforcement of arbitral awards from foreign jurisdictions. *See* 21 U.S.T. 2517, 330 U.N.T.S. 3.

RECOMMENDATION OF THE UNITED NATIONS: except where specifically empowered to take binding action, the General Assembly of the United Nations has only the power to make recommendations. *See* VOTING PROCEDURES CASE.

RECONDUCTION OF ALIENS: the arrest and physical placement of an unwanted alien outside the border of a state without the formalities that would be observed in the case of deportation or expulsion.

RECONNAISSANCE SATELLITE: space objects used to gain militarily useful information. Even though space is to be used for peaceful purposes only this use of space for a military purpose is sanctioned, in a way, because of its role in the verification of arms limitation agreements, see the NATIONAL TECHNICAL MEANS (q.v.) of verification. *See also*, REMOTE SENSING SATELLITES.

RECONQUEST: the taking back of territory that has previously been conquered by another state.

RECREDENTIAL: *see* LETTRE DE RECREANCE.

RECUSATION: the challenge of a judge or arbitrator by one of the parties requesting disqualification due to bias.

RED CRESCENT: equivalent of the RED CROSS (q.v.) adopted by some Moslem countries.

RED CROSS: umbrella and symbol for a number of humanitarian organizations operating both nationally and internationally to relieve the suffering of victims of war and natural disasters under the protection of the Red Cross emblem. *See* 129 C.T.S. 361.

RED CROSS CONVENTION (1864): *See* GENEVA CONVENTION (1864).

RED CROSS CONVENTIONS: *see* GENEVA CONVENTIONS (1949).

RED CRUSADER INCIDENT: a British vessel, the Red Crusader, was arrested by Danish authorities for illegal fishing. *See* 35 I.L.R. 485.

RED LION AND SUN: emblem of Iran adopted by the Shah. Its use was discontinued by the Khomeni government.

RED SHIELD OF DAVID: Israel's attempted substitute for the Red Cross as an internationally recognized sign for a hospital, medic, etc. It was proposed and rejected at diplomatic conferences in 1949 and 1977.

REDINTEGRATION: mode of reacquiring nationality for a natural-born subject of a state who has lost that nationality through naturalization abroad or for some other reason.

REDINTEGRATION OF TREATIES: by mutual consent of the parties, a treaty which has lost its binding force through expiration or cancellation may be renewed, e.g., a treaty of peace may redintegrate those treaties which were cancelled because of war between the parties.

RE-EDUCATION: euphemism for "brain-washing" or forced political indoctrination used by ideological regimes to try to control their populations.

REEFS: a chain of rocks, coral, etc., which if detached from the adjacent land and submerged at high tide, are not used to determine the extent of the territorial sea.

RE-EXPORT: the purchase of foreign made goods by a concern in a country for resale in other foreign markets. This becomes a problem when it is used to evade trade restrictions on such items as weapons or sophisticated computers.

REFLAGGING OF KUWAITI SHIPS: in 1987, eleven Kuwaiti tankers were transferred to the United States registry to protect them against Iranian attack. *See* 26 I.L.M. 1429 and TRANSFER OF FLAG.

REFOULEMENT (F): the return of a person who has entered a country illegally to the border; a less formal procedure than expulsion or deportation. *See* 18 I.L.R. 301.

REFUGEE: person displaced from the permanent residence due to war, political oppression, etc. *See* 189 U.N.T.S. 150 and 19 U.S.T. 6223, 606 U.N.T.S. 267.

REFUGEE SEAMAN: a sailor who is a refugee according to the CONVENTION RELATING TO THE STATUS OF REFUGEES (q.v.). *See* Hague Agreement Relating To Refugee Seamen, 506 U.N.T.S. 125.

REGENT: person who acts on behalf of an infant or incapacitated monarch. While acting as such, he acquires all the privileges of the MONARCH (q.v.).

REGIME: 1) The current government of a territory. 2) A set of rules which apply to a particular place or activity, e.g., the OUTER SPACE TREATY (q.v.) establishes a basic legal regime for outer space.

REGION OF WAR: area where belligerent activities may be conducted legally, e.g., territory occupied by enemy troops.

REGIONAL ADMINISTRATIVE RADIO CONFERENCE (RARC): part of the INTERNATIONAL TELECOMMUNICATIONS UNION (q.v.) which deals with regional issues such as allocating short range radio frequencies within the region and general structure of the ITU allocations scheme.

REGIONAL ARRANGEMENTS: *see* REGIONAL SECURITY.

REGIONAL COOPERATION: efforts by countries in the same geographic region to act in their common interest. *See e.g.,* ORGANIZATION OF AMERICAN STATES or ORGANIZATION OF AFRICAN UNITY. Their operation is sanctioned by the UNITED NATIONS CHARTER, Arts. 52-54 (q.v.).

REGIONAL DEVELOPMENT BANK: institutions which supplement the work of the INTERNATIONAL BANK FOR RECONSTRUCTION AND DEVELOPMENT (q.v.) with an emphasis on special regional needs. *See* INTER-AMERICAN DEVELOPMENT BANK.

REGIONAL INTERNATIONAL LAW: international law which applies only to the countries in a particular geographic region, e.g., EUROPEAN COMMUNITY LAW (q.v.). *See* 12 Colum.J.Transnat'l.L. 415.

REGIONAL INTERNATIONAL ORGANIZATION: an organization among the countries of a region, examples are the EUROPEAN CIVIL AVIATION COMMISSION and the SOUTHEAST ASIA TREATY ORGANIZATION (qq.v.).

REGIONAL SECURITY: Art. 52 of the UNITED NATIONS CHARTER (q.v.) provides that regional arrangements may be made to maintain peace and security. *See e.g.,* the ORGANIZATION OF AMERICAN STATES.

REGISTRATION OF AGREEMENTS (treaties): a facet of OPEN DIPLOMACY (q.v.), all international agreements made by United Nations members are to be registered with the Secretary General as soon as possible under Art. 102 of the UNITED NATIONS CHARTER (q.v.). *See* 65 Am.J.Int.L. 771.

REGISTRATION OF OBJECTS LAUNCHED INTO OUTER SPACE: subject of a United Nations treaty which is widely adopted under which nations provide minimal information about all objects they launch into space including identification, orbital parameters, date of launch, and purpose. *See* 14 I.L.M. 43.

REGISTRATION OF SHIPS CONVENTION (1986): United Nations sponsored agreement making rules for the registration of ocean-going vessels. *See* 26 I.L.M. 1236.

REGISTRY: a record of the ships, airplanes, space objects, etc., kept by a nation which identifies those objects as being under the jurisdiction and protection of that state, and for which that state bears responsibility in international law.

REGLE DE DROIT POSITIF (F): a rule of applicable law.

REICHSGERICHTS: the German Supreme Court; its decisions are reported in *Entscheidungen des Bundesgerichtshofes.*

REINHEITGEBOT (G): German standard for the purity of beer; subject of a challenge as a TECHNICAL BARRIER TO TRADE (q.v.) in a case before the Court of Justice of the European Community, Dec. 1978/84, March 12, 1987.

REICHSTAG FIRE: arson of the German Parliament Building on Feb. 27, 1933, which provided the excuse for Hitler's assumption of dictatorial powers.

REJECTION OF A DIPLOMATIC NOTE: usually refers to a rejection of the contents of a NOTE (q.v.), but may refer to the actual refusal to accept delivery in which case it is a serious offense to the sender. *See* Satow, *A Guide to Diplomatic Practice* 76.

REJOINDER: response of the defendant to the REPLY (q.v.) of the PETITIONER (q.v.). For International Court practice *see* Rosenne, *Law and Practice of the International Court* 554.

RELATIONS OFFICIEUSES (F): unofficial relations; diplomatic intercourse with a state which is not officially recognized. *See* 34 Am.J.Int.L. 47.

RELATIVE RIGHT: a right which is only available to a state where other rights would not be prejudiced by its exercise. *See* ABSOLUTE RIGHT.

RELIEF ACTION: efforts to aid victims of disasters such as earthquakes or military bombardment. *See* 4 *Encyclopedia of Public International Law* 173.

RELIEF SOUGHT: the remedy which the instigator of a judicial procedure is requesting, e.g., monetary compensation or RESTITUTION (q.v.).

RELIGIOUS EDIFICE: efforts must be made to spare religious buildings when an area is under attack. *See* Art. 27 of the HAGUE CONVENTION RESPECTING THE LAW AND CUSTOMS OF WAR ON LAND.

RELIGIOUS FREEDOM: the United Nations has failed to adopt a convention protecting freedom of religion but has adopted the Declaration on the Elimination of All Forms of Intolerance and Discrimination Based on Religion or Beliefs, General Assembly Res. 55, U.N. Doc. A/Res/36/55 (XX) (1981).

RELIGIOUS INTOLERANCE: subject of a United Nations Declaration, *see* 82 Am.J.Int.L. 487.

REMOTE DAMAGES: damages which are not directly the result of an illegal act. *See* 2 I.L.R. 195 and 203.

REMOTE SENSING SATELLITES: civilian counterpart to spy satellites, i.e., surveying the surface of the earth for purposes such as estimating crop size, detecting mineral deposits, etc. It is the subject of negotiation for control measures in the COMMITTEE ON PEACEFUL USES OF OUTER SPACE (q.v.). *See* 25 I.L.M. 1331.

RENAMO: NATIONAL RESISTANCE MOVEMENT (Mozambique) (q.v.).

RENDITION OF CRIMINALS: the return of a fugitive, to the state from which he has fled, by the authorities of the capturing state, usually under the terms of an EXTRADITION TREATY (q.v.).

RENONCIATION (F): WAIVER (q.v.).

RENUNCIATION OF RIGHTS: under the GENEVA CONVENTIONS (1949) (q.v.), Common Art. 7, PROTECTED PERSONS (q.v.) cannot renounce their right to be treated in the manner specified in the Conventions.

RENUNCIATION OF WAR: *see* KELLOGG-BRIAND PACT (1928).

RENVERSEMENTS DES ALLIANCES (F): reversal of alliances, i.e., renouncing an alliance with one country to enter into an alliance with a former adversary.

REPARATIONS: payment to a victor, by a defeated party to a war, of sums to cover the victor's cost of prosecuting the war. Such payments have been exacted for centuries. Reparations posed particular problems as levied against Germany after World War I. *See* YOUNG PLAN and DAWES PLAN.

REPATRIATION: personal right extended to a civilian or prisoner of war to return to his country of nationality, usually under certain conditions. *See* HAGUE CONVENTION IV (1907).

REPLY: petitioner's response to the answer of the defendant to the petitioner's original complaint. The reply is countered with a REJOINDER (q.v.).

REPORTS OF INTERNATIONAL ARBITRAL AWARDS (R.I.A.A.): publication of the United Nations printing the decisions of international arbitration cases. Note that these decisions are a subsidiary means of determining international law under Art. 38 of the STATUTE OF THE INTERNATIONAL COURT OF JUSTICE (q.v.).

REPRESENTANTS PLENIPOTENTIAIRE (F): early attempt at egalitarian diplomatic titles for Soviet diplomats which was, shortly after its adoption, breached by the addition of traditional diplomatic titles, e.g., *Representants plenipotentiaire a titre d'ambassadeur extraordinaire.*

REPRESENTATIVES TO THE UNITED NATIONS: persons sent to the meetings of the United Nations by their respective countries to represent those countries in the deliberations of the organization. *See* 16 International Organization 483.

REPRISAL: act of self-help by an injured state. To be acceptable in international law (if at all) reprisals may be used only to redress a breach of international law, a demand for redress must have gone unanswered, and the reprisal must be reasonably proportional to the injury suffered. *See* NAULILAA INCIDENT and 12 Whiteman, *Digest of International Law* 148.

REPUDIATION OF AWARDS: a party to an international dispute may only repudiate an adverse award if it can be treated as a nullity, e.g., the award was outside the jurisdiction of the body awarding it. *See* 5 Am.J.Int.L. 782.

REPULSION DOCTRINE (1950): United States foreign policy aimed at halting the spread of Communism in Eastern Europe and isolating the Soviet Union; it failed.

REQUEST FOR AN ADVISORY OPINION: many international organizations are empowered, by the agreement creating them, to ask the International Court of Justice for an advisory opinion regarding the correctness of a proposed action under international law. *See* ADVISORY OPINION.

REQUISITION: the demand for supplies for a military force from the inhabitants of an occupied territory. *See* Art. 52 of the HAGUE CONVENTION RESPECTING THE LAW AND CUSTOMS OF WAR ON LAND (1907).

RES ALICUJUS (L): things owned by someone.

RES COMMUNIS (L): things that are owned by no one, but available for the use of all.

RES CONTROVERSA (L): the object of a dispute.

RES DERELICTAE (L): things which have been abandoned by their former owners and belong to no one.

RES EXTRA COMMERCIUM (L): things outside the stream of commerce, things not subject to trade.

RES FURTIVAE (L): stolen goods.

RES IN TRANSITU (L): goods being transported.

RES INTEGRA (L): area where law has not yet reached or developed; no legal precedent. *See* LACUNAE.

RES INTER ALIOS ACTA (L): an agreement only has force and effect as between the parties. It cannot give rights to or require action of one who is not party to the agreement.

RES JUDICATA(L): a judicially decided issue.

RES JUDICATA PRO VERITATE HABETUR (L): the issues decided are those which were placed before the court by the parties.

RES NOVITER VENIENS(L): new things have come about, formerly cited as grounds for not ratifying a treaty that had previously been signed.

RES NULLIUS(L): things which are not owned but which are subject to appropriation, e.g., a new island in the midst of the high seas would be subject to a claim by a nation occupying it.

RES PETITA(L): thing which is the object of a claim.

RES PERIT DOMINO (L): the loss falls on the owner.

RES TRANSIT CUM SUO ONERE(L): thing transferred with its burdens, i.e., territory cannot be ceded by one state to another unless the receiving state accepts the SERVITUDES (q.v.) which have been placed on the territory in the past.

RESCUE OF ASTRONAUTS CONVENTION (1968): widely adopted regime defining the status of personnel traveling in outer space, including the obligation of states to rescue and return such personnel to the LAUNCHING STATE (q.v.). *See* 19 U.S.T. 7570, 672 U.N.T.S. 119.

RESERVATION: a formal declaration by a state becoming party to a treaty, specifying a certain condition on which its acceptance of the treaty is based, e.g., it does not recognize a certain other party to the treaty as a party. *See* Art. 2, VIENNA CONVENTION ON THE LAW OF TREATIES.

RESIDENT: archaic designation for a diplomatic agent of inferior rank residing in a foreign capital, now a CHARGE D'AFFAIRES (q.v.).

RESISTANCE MOVEMENTS: military force made up of inhabitants of an occupied territory fighting an insurgency against the occupiers. They are to be treated as belligerents if they have a system of command, distinctive uniforms, carry arms openly, and obey the LAWS OF WAR (q.v.). *See* Art. 4, GENEVA CONVENTION III (1949).

RESOLUTION OF THE GENERAL ASSEMBLY: primary legislative product of the United Nations General Assembly. Generally, they are not binding, but serve as evidence of CUSTOMARY INTERNATIONAL LAW (q.v.) and are authoritative when they interpret the UNITED NATIONS CHARTER (q.v.).

RESOLUTIVE CONDITION: a future event which triggers the extinction of a right.

RESPONSA PRUDENTIUM(L): the opinions of jurists. *See* Art. 38 of the STATUTE OF THE INTERNATIONAL COURT OF JUSTICE.

RESPONDENT: the party-defendant in a proceeding before the INTERNATIONAL COURT OF JUSTICE (q.v.). The PETITIONER (q.v.) makes a claim against the respondent who then files an ANSWER (q.v.).

RESPONSIBILITY OF STATES: states must conduct themselves within the rules of international law and are to maintain law and order within their territory. *See* 16 Netherlands Y.B. Int'l L. 81.

RESSORTISSANT (F): a NATIONAL (q.v.), those in whom a sovereign has a legitimate interest.

RESTATEMENT OF THE FOREIGN RELATIONS OF THE UNITED STATES: product of the American Law Institute (a nongovernmental organization) which attempts to organize the common law of the United States concerned with intergovernmental relations. The third version was published in 1987.

RESTITUTIO AD INTEGRUM (L): restoring of the whole thing, e.g., when a ship is requisitioned in time of war it must be returned in the same condition.

RESTITUTIO IN INTEGRUM (L): *see* RESTITUTIO AD INTEGRUM.

RESTITUTION: remedy sometimes available to an international claimant where property which has been taken is returned to its original owner. *See e.g.,* the Settlement Convention, 332 U.N.T.S. 219 and 48 Brit.Y.B.Int'l.L. 1.

RESTORATION: placing a deposed monarch (or HEAD OF STATE (q.v.)) back on the throne (or in the office) from which he or she was deposed.

RESTRAINT OF INJURIOUS AGENTS: obligation of nations not to use or allow the use of their territory in such a manner as to cause harmful effects in other adjacent states. *See* TRAIL SMELTER ARBITRATION and 6 Whiteman, *Digest of International Law* 253.

RESTRICTIVE BUSINESS PRACTICES: subject of bilateral agreements on the application of antitrust and fair trade laws. *See e.g.,* the United States-West Germany agreement at 15 I.L.M. 1282.

RESTRICTIVE INTERPRETATION: the interpretation of a treaty such that it imposes the least restraint on a state party's freedom of action. *See* MOSUL DISPUTE (1925). The Reagan Administration has favored a restrictive interpretation of the ANTI-BALLISTIC MISSILE SYSTEM TREATY (q.v.), although the terminology is reversed and their interpretation, which allows anything not specifically banned by the treaty to be done is referred to as "a permissive interpretation." *See* 80 Am.J.Int.L. 854.

RESTRICTIVE PRACTICES: activities by business which violate the principles of free trade; acts which violate such laws as the United States antitrust laws.

RETALIATION: form of REPRISAL (q.v.) often taken against an innocent bystander, e.g., expelling all the nationals of a particular country for some action that country took which the expelling country found offensive. *See* 8 Whiteman, *Digest of International Law* 377.

RETINUE OF DIPLOMATIC ENVOYS: individuals accompanying an envoy including official members of the LEGATION (q.v.), private employees, family members, and couriers.

RETORSION: an unfriendly act which though legal is in the nature of a REPRISAL (q.v.), for a similar act by another state. *See* 5 Whiteman, *Digest of International Law* 268.

RETROACTIVE EFFECT: the making of a law which effects acts which took place prior to the time the law was made, e.g., an *ex post facto* criminal law making acts committed in the past criminal.

REUS IN EXCIPIENDO ACTOR EST (L): the defendant and the plaintiff switch places in the procedural order for a particular purpose.

REVENUE: the state has the right to levy taxes, and this power extends into the contiguous sea for enforcement purposes. *See* 9 I.L.R. 123.

REVERE COPPER ARBITRATION: dispute which arose between Jamaica, the OVERSEAS PRIVATE INVESTMENT CORPORATION (q.v.), and Revere Copper and Brass, Inc. over the purported expropriation of Revere's operations in Jamaica which Overseas Private Investment Corporation insured. *See* 56 I.L.R. 258 (1980).

REVERSALES (F): a declaration by a state that it will abide by a certain order or condition.

REVISIO IN JURE (L): describes a judicial body which hears appeals of law, but not of facts, a *cours de cassation*.

REVISION: a change in the terms of an international agreement accepted by the parties to the agreement. Most international agreements now provide a procedure for revisions.

REVISIONIST: one who places a new interpretation or presents newly gained knowledge changing the way in which a subject or event is perceived.

REVIVAL OF TREATIES: as a general rule treaties, unless specified otherwise or because of their nature, are suspended or abrogated by a state of war between the parties. When the war ends the parties may consider these treaties revived or may continue to consider them abrogated requiring the negotiation of new treaties. See *Argento v. Horn*, 241 F.2d 258 (1957).

REVOCATION OF EXEQUATUR: withdrawal of the acceptance by a state of a CONSUL (q.v.). See 4 Hackworth, *Digest of International Law* 673.

REVOLUTION: the overthrow or attempted overthrow of a government by some of its citizens, usually by force of arms. The status of revolutionaries usually depends on their success or failure.

REVOLUTION OF RISING EXPECTATIONS: the change in world outlook of individuals as their standard of living improves.

REVOLUTIONARY STATE: a state where the government is committed to changing the current social, economic, and legal regime and often espousing radical change through violence such as in Maoist China. Many states which claim to be "revolutionary" are, in fact, the most conservative in the sense that they permit no change at all, e.g., the Soviet Union under Brezhnev.

RHEE LINE: South Korean claim to its territorial sea and continental shelf. See 4 Whiteman, *Digest of International Law* 531 and Oda and Dwada, *The Practice of Japan in International Laws 1961-1970*, at 150.

RHINE CHEMICAL POLLUTION CONVENTION: provides for the control of chemical pollutants including those in the surface water which flow into the Rhine River Basin. See 16 I.L.M. 242 and 265.

RHINE POLLUTION COMMISSION: intergovernmental body to monitor and control pollution conditions of the Rhine River. *See* 1965 Recueil des Traites et Accords de la France 54.

RHINE RIVER COMMISSION: Central Commission for the Navigation of the Rhine, governs the free international navigation of the Rhine providing for navigational aids, locks, etc. *See* 138 C.T.S. 167.

RHINELAND OCCUPATION: at the end of World War I, the allies occupied parts of Germany along the Rhine River to guarantee German compliance with the armistice. This occupation became a bone of contention among the allies. *See* Allen, *The Rhineland Occupation*, Indianapolis, 1927.

RHODESIA: name of the former British Colony north of South Africa where the white settlers put up a long struggle against turning over political power to the black majority, defying the entire international community which imposed sanctions against the white regime. In 1980, blacks took power and the country became Zimbabwe. *See* 17 I.L.M. 261. For the original U.N. Resolution *see* 60 Am.J.Int.L. 921.

RHODIAN LAWS: a collection of maritime laws dating from the seventh to the ninth centuries; the source of the modern law of GENERAL AVERAGE (q.v.).

RHUMB LINES: straight line drawn on a MERCANTORIAL CHART (q.v.), which inaccurately represents a "straight line" on the surface of the earth. (All lines on the surface of the Earth are curved.) *See* 2 O'Connell, *The International Law of the Sea* 639-43.

R.I.A.A.: REPORTS OF INTERNATIONAL ARBITRAL AWARDS (q.v.).

RICE: *see* INTERNATIONAL RICE COMMISSION.

RIGHTS: 1) Qualities of states protected by international law. 2) Qualities of individuals protected by law, especially HUMAN RIGHTS (q.v.). *See also* ABUSE OF RIGHTS.

RIGHT OF ASYLUM: the power of a sovereign to admit nationals of other states to its territory, and because the sovereign has exclusive control over the individuals on its territory, it can protect those individuals from the wishes of other states. *See* 1949 Brit.Y.B.Int'l.L. 327.

RIGHT OF CHAPEL: *see* DROIT DE CHAPELLE (F).

RIGHT OF INNOCENT PASSAGE: *see* INNOCENT PASSAGE.

RIGHT OF LEGATION: the sovereign's ability (rather than a true right) to send diplomatic envoys and to accept diplomatic delegations form other sovereigns. *See* VIENNA CONVENTION ON CONSULAR RELATIONS (1963).

RIGHT OF PASSAGE OVER INDIAN TERRITORY CASE. Portugal's right to transit over Indian territory to garrison its colonial enclaves on the subcontinent was not recognized by the International Court of Justice. *See* 1960 I.C.J. Reports 6.

RIGHT OF PRESCRIPTION: acquisition of sovereignty over territory by long-standing, undisturbed possession even though the original taking of possession was wrongful or illegal. *See* 4 Am.J.Int.L. 133. *See also*, ACQUISITIVE PRESCRIPTION and EXTINCTIVE PRESCRIPTION.

RIGHTS AND DUTIES OF STATES: the privileges and requirements placed generally on states by international law. *See* Draft Declaration on the Rights and Duties of States, UNGA Res. 375(IV), 1951 UN Yearbook 846.

RIGHTS OF MANKIND: early expression by some publicists of the view that international law gave to individuals certain fundamental rights such as the right to life, liberty, and freedom of religion. This view is inconsistent with state practice in many cases, and contrary to the general principle that only states are subjects of international law.

RINALDI AFFAIR: an Italian court held that the private acts of a diplomatic agent (e.g., a contract for sale of personal property) are subject to local jurisdiction in the host country. *See* 4 Hackworth, *Digest of International Law* 550.

RINCON MURDER: a French Ambassador to the Porte was murdered while in transit by order of the Governor of Milan. *See* 2 Ward, *The Law of Nations* 557.

RINGEISEN CASE: suit in the European Court of Human Rights alleging that Austria had violated Art. 5b of the EUROPEAN CONVENTION ON HUMAN RIGHTS (q.v.) by keeping the plaintiff in detention longer than a "reasonable time." The Court found against Austria and awarded to Mr. Ringeisen 20,000 German Marks. *See* 11 I.L.M. 1062.

RIO TREATY (1947): INTERAMERICAN TREATY OF RECIP-ROCAL ASSISTANCE (q.v.), the collective defense treaty of the Western Hemisphere. Cuba withdrew in 1960.

RIOT: mob violence. States have a duty to maintain internal order, and may be held liable for injury to aliens injured if such order is not maintained. *See* 8 Whiteman, *Digest of International Law* 830 and 23 Am.J.Int.L. Special Supp. 134/188 (Art. 11).

RIVERS: rivers play three important roles in international law; as borders (*see*, e.g., CHAMIZAL TRACT), as means of navigation (*see* RHINE RIVER COMMISSION), and as sources of water (*see* HELSINKI RULES ON THE USE OF WATERS OF INTERNA-TIONAL RIVERS).

ROAD SIGNALS CONVENTION (1931): effort to minimize the number of different road signals in use and to standardize the inscriptions and signs thereon. *See* 150 L.N.T.S. 247.

ROADSTEADS: a place of anchorage off shore without a protective HARBOR (q.v.). *See* 4 Whiteman, *Digest of International Law* 263.

ROBE D'ENNEMI CONFISQUE CELLE D'AMY (F): neutral goods on enemy ships or enemy goods on neutral ships are subject to seizure. Outmoded rule as to personal property on the high seas in time of war.

ROCKS: where does one draw the line between a rock and an island? Rocks not submerged at low tide and located in the territorial waters are said to have their own territorial water. *See* NORWEGIAN FISHERIES CASE.

ROERICH PACT (1935): multilateral agreement to protect artistic and scientific institutions and historic monuments. It attempted to strengthen Art. 56(2) of the HAGUE REGULATIONS (q.v.), which prohibits the destruction or willful damage of such by military forces. *See* 49 Stat. 3267, 167 L.N.T.S. 289.

ROGERS PLAN (1969): attempt by United States Secretary of State, William P. Rogers, to end the state of war between Israel and Egypt and Israel and Jordan. *See* 64 Am.J.Int.L. 344.

ROMAN CATHOLIC CHURCH: *see* HOLY SEE and VATICAN.

ROMAN LAW: legal system developed by the citizens of Rome roughly between 200 B.C. and 400 A.D., which continues to have great influence on the development of law, particularly the CIVIL LAW (q.v.).

ROME CONVENTION (1933): created rules to determine liability for damage to surface objects by activities of foreign aircraft. Replaced by the ROME CONVENTION (1952) (q.v.).

ROME CONVENTION (1952): modernizes rules for determining liability to surface objects by activities of foreign aircraft. *See* 52 Am.J.Int.L. 593.

ROME TREATY (1957): treaty which established the EURO-PEAN ECONOMIC COMMUNITY (q.v.). *See* 298 U.N.T.S. 3.

ROOSEVELT COROLLARY TO THE MONROE DOCTRINE: the MONROE DOCTRINE (q.v.) will not be used to justify the acquisition of new territory to be incorporated into the United States, but to maintain peace and stability in the Western Hemisphere. *See* 5 Whiteman *Digest of International Law* at 410.

ROSS SECTOR: claim by the British government to all lands situated between 160 and 150 degrees west longitude which were at the time of the claim undiscovered, i.e., islands in the Arctic region north of the British Isles. *See* 28 Am.J.Int.L. 117.

ROUSSEAU-PORTALIS DOCTRINE: idea from Jean Jacque Rousseau adopted by Portalis that "... War is conceived as an exclusive relation between belligerent states and, therefore, ought to affect private citizens as little as possible." This idea is incorporated into the HAGUE REGULATIONS (q.v.).

ROYAL PERSONAGE: as used in the VERSAILLES PEACE TREATY (1919) (q.v.), it means only the person who is sovereign and does not include members of the royal family. *See* 4 I.L.R. 33.

RUHR OCCUPATION (1923): French and allied troops occupied the German territory along the Ruhr River, ostensibly to enforce the VERSAILLES PEACE TREATY (1919) (q.v.). *See* 17 Am.J.Int.L. 724.

RUHR RIVER AUTHORITY: *see* 43 AmJ.Int.L.Supp. 140.

RULE OF 1756: a neutral merchant ship which in time of war undertakes voyages closed to her in time of peace, such as, trade between ports of one of the belligerents may be treated as a belligerent merchant ship.

RULES OF THE ROAD AT SEA: basic rules for the operation of ships at sea; they are part of customary international law. *See*

Sears v. The Scotia, 81 U.S. 170 (1870), and TRINITY HOUSE RULES.

RULES OF WARSAW AND OXFORD: standard trade terms proposed through the INTERNATIONAL LAW ASSOCIATION (q.v.), particularly regarding C.I.F. (q.v.) contracts. *See* I.L.A. Reports of the 37th Conference, Oxford at 419 (1932).

RUPTURE OF DIPLOMATIC RELATIONS: means of termination of a diplomatic mission where the countries break diplomatic relations and withdraw their representatives, e.g., India broke off relations with Portugal over Goa in 1954. *See* BREAK IN DIPLOMATIC RELATIONS.

RUSE: the use of deception as part of a military operation. Proper use of ruses are allowed by the law of war; PERFIDY (q.v.) is not. *See* Art. 24, HAGUE REGULATIONS (1907).

RUSH-BAGOT TREATY (1817): between the United States and Great Britain, it limited the size, number, and equipping of warships on the Great Lakes; an often cited example of an early arms limitation agreement. *See* 8 Stat. 231, 12 Bevans 54.

RUSSELL-EINSTEIN MANIFESTO (1955): statement by Bertrand Russell, signed by Albert Einstein and several other noted scientists, urging that war was no longer a suitable instrument of national policy. It got the PUGWASH CONFERENCE (q.v.) started.

RUSSIAN INDEMNITY ARBITRATION: Russian claim for reparations based on the CONSTANTINOPLE TREATY (1879) (q.v.) was upheld, but a claim for interest was rejected. *See* 7 Am.J.Int.L. 178 and 11 R.I.A.A. 421.

RUSSO-FINNISH WAR (1939): invasion of Finland for which Russia was the first country expelled from the League of Nations. *See* 34 Am.J.Int.L.Supp. 127.

RUSSO-JAPANESE WAR (1904-5): military action in which the Japanese drove the Russians out of Manchuria and Korea. It may be considered an act of intervention since both of these territories belonged to neutrals (China and Korea), but were occupied by the Russians. At the conclusion of the war, Japans status as a power was recognized. *See* PORTSMOUTH TREATY (1905).

RUTILI CASE: ruling by the European Court involving the extent to which a member country to the European Community can restrict the movement of workers, 1975 E.C.R. 1219 and 9 Vand.J.Transnat'l.L. 651.

RYMER'S FOEDERIS: twenty volume collection of TREATIES (q.v.), and other international materials published between 1727-1731 by Thomas Rymer.

[S]

SAAD-ABAD PACT (1937): treaty of non-aggression signed by Iran, Iraq, Afghanistan, and Turkey. *See* 190 L.N.T.S. 21.

SAAFA: SPECIAL ARAB AID FUND FOR AFRICA (q.v.).

SAAR REFERENDUM (1935): plebiscite under the auspices of the League of Nations to decide whether the Saar region should be part of France or Germany. Germany won by a 9 to 1 majority and League administration of the region ended. *See* Wambaugh, *The Saar Plebiscite* (1940).

SAAR REFERENDUM (1955): plebiscite, supervised by a Commission of the WESTERN EUROPEAN UNION (q.v.), to decide the question of sovereignty over the Saar region which had been disputed between France and Germany for centuries. The plebiscite rejected a plan for autonomy, and France agreed to allow the Saar to become the tenth *Lander* (state) of the Federal Republic of Germany.

SAAVEDRA LAMAS PACT (1933) (or the Antiwar Treaty of Non- aggression and Conciliation): treaty condemning wars of aggression and territorial acquisitions that may be obtained by armed conflict. Designed to support the KELLOGG-BRIAND TREATY (1928) (q.v.), the Saavedra Lamas Pact extended antiwar sentiment to Latin American members of the League of Nations that had not joined Kellogg-Briand. *See* 27 Am.J.Int.L. 109.

SABAH: territory on the northeast coast of Borneo subject to disputed claims between the Philippines and Malaysia. *See* 1967 Aust. Ybk. Int'l L. 103.

SABBATINO CASE (*Banco Nationale de Cuba v. Sabbatino*, 376 U.S. 398): in 1960, Cuba expropriated U.S. owned sugar properties in Cuba. Because of the ACT OF STATE DOCTRINE (q.v.) the U.S. Supreme Court refused to inquire into the validity of public acts of a recognized foreign sovereign committed within its own territory, except in the case of an unambiguous agreement, even if the complaint alleges that the act is a violation of customary international law. *See* HICKENLOOPER AMENDMENT.

SABOTAGE: acts intended to do damage to the materials of the military forces of another state. Also, acts intended to subvert a government.

SADCC: SOUTHERN AFRICAN DEVELOPMENT COORDINATING COMMITTEE (q.v.).

SADR: SAHRAWI ARAB DEMOCRATIC REPUBLIC (q.v.).

SAFE-CONDUCT: a written pass granted by a belligerent permitting a person (who may or may not be an enemy subject) to proceed to a specific place by a given route and, generally for a specific purpose.

SAFEGUARD: a written protection against the use of its forces granted by a belligerent party to persons or property of another belligerent party, such person or property being located within the territory being occupied by the issuing belligerent.

SAFETY OF LIFE AT SEA CONVENTIONS: multilateral conventions establishing rules and principles to promote safety of life at sea. The first such convention was drafted after the Titanic, a British passenger liner, sank. The 1960 Convention, 536 U.N.T.S. 27 was replaced as between contracting parties by the 1974 version, 32 U.S.T. 47.

SAFETY ZONE: areas of protection for a nonbelligerent civilian population. Art. 14 of the GENEVA CONVENTION IV (1949), provides that in times of peace, and after the outbreak of hostilities, the parties thereto may designate safety zones to protect wounded, sick and aged persons, children under the age of 15, expectant mothers, and mothers with children under 7 from the effects of war.

SAHRAWI ARAB DEMOCRATIC REPUBLIC (SADR): putative nation formed from the former colony of Spain, Western Sahara, whose existence has been recognized by the ORGANIZATION OF AFRICAN UNITY (q.v.), but is sustained only by the fight of the POLISARIO (q.v.).

SAINT GERMAIN PEACE TREATY (1919): treaty between the allies and Austria ending World War I. The obligation to pay war reparations was imposed upon Austria. The Covenant of the League of Nations and the Constitution of the International Labour Organization were incorporated into the Saint-Germain Peace Treaty. *See* 226 C.T.S. 9, 14 Am.J.Int.L.Supp. 1 (1920).

SAINT JAMES DECLARATION (1942): first allied declaration on WAR CRIMES (q.v.). *See* 11 Whiteman, *Digest of International Law* 874.

SAINT PETERSBURG DECLARATION (1868): instrument signed by 17 states renouncing the use of projectiles weighing less than 14 oz.(400 grams) which are either explosive or loaded with explosive or inflammable substance. *See* 138 C.T.S. 297, 1 Am.J.Int.L.Supp. 95.

SALE OF GOODS: international sales of goods are the subject of two general international agreements. The first made in 1955, attempts to settle rules on which law should apply in a specific instance. *See* 510 U.N.T.S. 147. The second convention, drafted by the UNITED NATIONS COMMISSION ON INTERNATIONAL TRADE LAW (q.v.), attempts to establish a set of simple substantive rules that are uniform throughout the world. *See* 19 I.L.M. 668. *See also,* CMEA GENERAL CONDITIONS and INCOTERMS.

SALE OF TERRITORY: a common manner by which a CESSION OF TERRITORY (q.v.) can be effected, e.g., in 1867 Russia sold her Alaskan territory to the United States for $7,200,000.

SALMON FISHERIES TREATY (1930): convention between the United States and Canada establishing the International Pacific Salmon Fisheries Commission which has power to control the taking of sockeye salmon. *See* 6 Bevans 41, 184 L.N.T.S. 305 (amended by 8 U.S.T.1057, 290 U.N.T.S. 103 (1956) and 32 U.S.T 2475 (1977)).

SALT I AND II: STRATEGIC ARMS LIMITATIONS TALKS (q.v.).

SALUTES: maritime ceremonial acts of courtesy between vessels recognizing the dignity of the state whose flag the ship is sailing under. Also, ceremonial act of courtesy extended to a dignitary such as a HEAD OF STATE (q.v.) who may receive a twenty-one gun salute.

SALUS POPULI SUPREME LEX (L): the good of all is the highest law.

SALVAGE: the act of aiding a vessel in peril. The salvor is generally rewarded for his services. This remuneration is commonly a combination of compensation for services rendered, and a reward designed to encourage such service.

SAN FRANCISCO CONFERENCE (1945): meeting of the United Nations International Organization. The states represented at the Conference adopted the CHARTER OF THE UNITED NATIONS (q.v.) as a formal international treaty. *See* U.N. Yearbook 1946-7.

SAN JOSE PACT: popular name for the INTER-AMERICAN CONVENTION ON HUMAN RIGHTS (q.v.).

SAN SALVADOR CHARTER: *see* ORGANIZATION OF CENTRAL AMERICAN STATES.

SAN STEFANO TREATY (1878): preliminary peace between Russia and a defeated Turkey. Great Britain protested against the treaty on the grounds that its provisions were inconsistent with the LONDON DECLARATION (1871) and the PARIS TREATY (1856) (q.q.v.). The terms of the treaty were subsequently changed. *See* 152 C.T.S. 395, 2 Toynbee, *Treaties* 959.

SANATRA DOCTRINE (1989): as stated by Soviet President Gorbachev, the countries of Eastern Europe will be allowed to "do it their way" (after the Sanatra song "I did it my way"). *See* N.Y. Times, Oct. 26, 1989 (late ed. final) at 1, col 3.

SANCTIONS: measures taken by other states when a state defaults in its obligations. They may range from name calling to military actions. Economic sanctions which have been tried in a number of instances (notably South Africa) have been a dismal failure. *See* 12 Whiteman, *Digest of International Law* 361.

SANCTUARY: *see* POLITICAL ASYLUM.

SANCTUARY MOVEMENT: effort by persons in the United States, particularly church groups, to provide aid and comfort to refugees from Central American countries suffering the scourge of civil wars. Such aid sometimes involves violations of U.S. immigration laws according to United States officials. *See U.S. v. Merkt*, 764 F.2d 266 (5th Cir. 1985).

SANITARY CONVENTION (1926): attempt to control the spread of communicable diseases. *See* 78 L.N.T.S. 229, amended 198 L.N.T.S. 205.

SANITARY REGULATIONS: the sanitary formalities related to the movement of people and goods by ship or aircraft internationally, e.g., the International Sanitary Regulations -World Health Organization Regulations No. 2, 175 U.N.T.S. 215, were designed to ensure the maximum security against the spread of disease with a minimum interference with world traffic.

SANNIQUELLIE DECLARATION (1959): agreement between the presidents of Liberia, Ghana, and Guinea which contained six principles considered necessary for the achievement of a community of independent African States. *See* Amate, *Inside the OAU* 40-41.

SANTA MARIA INCIDENT (1961): a Portuguese passenger ship was seized by a Portuguese rebel leader who had embarked as a passenger on the ship. The ship was surrendered to authorities in Brazil and returned to the Portuguese government. Art. 15 of the GENEVA CONVENTION ON THE REGIME OF THE HIGH SEAS (1958) was inapplicable to this incident since the ship was taken over by one of its own passengers and not another ship.

SANTIAGO CONVENTION (1923): the Treaty to Avoid or Prevent Conflict between the American States; it set up a procedure for appointing an investigative commission and a "cooling-off period" if diplomatic negotiations or arbitration could not settle disputes. *See* 44 Stat. 2527, 2 Bevans 413, 33 L.N.T.S. 25.

SAPOA AGREEMENT (1988): NICARAGUAN VERIFICATION CONVENTION (1988) (q.v.).

SATELLITE: an object in space which orbits another object, e.g., the moon is a natural satellite of the earth. The placing of man-made satellites into orbit is governed generally by the OUTER SPACE TREATY (1967) (q.v.).

SATISFACTION: nonmonetary form of reparation for damages which is *not* restitution in kind. Satisfaction is a means of repairing breaches of international obligations where such did not result in actual damages or where monetary compensation would be inadequate, e.g., in the CORFU CHANNEL CASE (q.v.) the I.C.J. considered the moral condemnation of the United Kingdom's act adequate to satisfy the wrong against Albania.

SAVAGE TROOPS: forces composed of individuals belonging to barbarous tribes. Such troops may be employed if they would or could comply with the laws of war.

SCANDINAVIAN AIRLINES SYSTEM (SAS): international airlines operated by Norway, Sweden, and Denmark; the most successful venture of its kind as authorized by Art. 77 of the CHICAGO CONVENTION (q.v.). *See* 18 J. Air L. and Com. 304.

SCANDINAVIAN NEUTRALITY RULES (1938): joint affirmation of the rules of neutrality adopted by the Scandinavian countries agreeing to apply similar rules in the event of war between foreign powers. The rules were adopted separately by each country. *See* 32 Am.J.Int.L. 789 (1938).

SCAPA FLOW INCIDENT (1919): World War I armistice agreement was violated by the SCUTTLING (q.v.) of German naval ships at Scapa Flow, a bay in the Orkney Islands, by their German crews. *See* 6 Hackworth, *Digest of International Law* 561.

SCHEDULED INTERNATIONAL AIR SERVICE: subject of strict control by BILATERAL AIR TRANSPORT AGREEMENTS (q.v.), through Art. 6 of the CHICAGO CONVENTION (1944) (q.v.). Such service is one that flies between the same two points according to a timetable or with such regularity as to constitute systematic service. *See* 6 Air Law 133.

SCHENGEN AGREEMENT (1990): agreement to eliminate all border checks between France, Germany, Netherlands, Belgium, and Luxembourg; signed in the Luxembourg town of Schengen. This free movement zone is the first step in eliminating all such checks within the EUROPEAN COMMUNITY (q.v.). The resulting five-nation zone is referred to as "Schengenland." *See* N.Y. Times, June 20, 1990 at 1, col.1.

SCHLUSS-PROTOKOLL (G): FINAL PROTOCOL (q.v.).

SCHUMAN PLAN: proposal that led to the establishment of the EUROPEAN COAL AND STEEL COMMUNITY (q.v.). *See* 47 Am.J.Int.L. 183.

SCREWDRIVER CASE (1991): dispute under the GENERAL AGREEMENT ON TARIFFS AND TRADE (q.v.) involving EUROPEAN COMMUNITY (q.v.) regulations on the import of parts and components. *See* 30 I.L.M. 1075.

SCUTTLING OF A SHIP: intentional sinking of a ship by its crew to prevent its capture. This may be a violation of an armistice agreement as in the case of the scuttling of German warships at SCAPA FLOW INCIDENT (1919) (q.v.). *See also* GRAF SPEE.

SDR: SPECIAL DRAWING RIGHTS (q.v.).

SEA POACHER INCIDENT (1960): the U.S.S. Sea Poacher, a submarine, was fired upon by a Cuban patrol boat. Although the U.S. State Department requested an explanation from Cuba, no response was received. *See* 4 Whiteman, *Digest of International Law* 515.

SEABED: the floor of the sea. The jurisdiction which a state may exercise over the seabed varies according to the distance from the coastline. Within the INTERNAL WATERS and TERRITORIAL WATERS (q.q.v.), the state has exclusive rights to use the seabed, but farther out to sea such rights are conditioned upon the rights of other states. *See also* OUTER CONTINENTAL SHELF, EXCLUSIVE ECONOMIC ZONE, and LUSAKA DECLARATION OF PEACE . . .

SEABED WEAPONS TREATY (1971): the treaty on the prohibition of the deployment of nuclear weapons and other weapons of mass destruction on the seabeds, the ocean floor, and in the subsoil thereof, by which the parties also agree to continue to negotiate to prevent the spread of the arms race to the seabed. *See* 23 U.S.T. 701, 10 I.L.M. 145 (1971).

SEAMAN: person who by national law or regulation is deemed competent to perform any duty which may be required of a member of the crew serving in the deck department. *See* convention concerning the certification of able seamen, adopted by the International Labour Organization, 94 U.N.T.S. 11 (1948).

SEAT RULE: doctrine of effective domicile of a corporation; effective place of business or site of principal administration of the business. *See* 24 Int'l.Lawyer 459.

SEATO: SOUTHEAST ASIA TREATY ORGANIZATION (q.v.).

SEAWORTHINESS: the fitness of a ship to sail the high seas. Subject of a Scandinavian treaty, *see* 51 L.N.T.S. 9.

S

SECRET DIPLOMACY: clandestine contact between agents of nations where such contacts would be provocative if they became public, or their purpose would be defeated by disclosure, e.g., contact of "moderate elements in the Iranian government by the Reagan Administration."

SECRET TREATY: international agreement which is not made public by the parties. Such agreements are contrary to the spirit and language of the UNITED NATIONS CHARTER (q.v.) which provides that all international agreements are to be registered with the UN as soon as possible. Failure to register an agreement in a timely fashion makes it unenforceable by any United Nations organ. Similar provisions applied to treaties under the League of Nations as well.

SECRETARIAT: a bureaucracy, the principal offices of which are titled secretary. Particularly, one of the principal organs of the UN composed of the Secretary-General and his staff. The Secretary-General is appointed by the General Assembly and acts as the chief administrative officer of the UN. *See* Arts. 97 to 102 of the UNITED NATIONS CHARTER (q.v.).

SECRETARY GENERAL: chief administration officer of an INTER-NATIONAL ORGANIZATION (q.v.) or political party. For the duties of the United Nations Secretary-General, *see* Arts. 97 et seq. of the UNITED NATIONS CHARTER.

SECRETARY OF STATE: United States government cabinet officer in charge of foreign policy under the direction of the President.

SECRETARY OF STATE FOR FOREIGN AFFAIRS: British cabinet official in charge of foreign relations.

SECTIONAL INSTITUTIONS: distinguished from REGIONAL INTERNATIONAL ORGANIZATIONS (q.v.) by provisions that close their membership to certain countries in a geographic region, e.g., the ARAB LEAGUE (q.v.) though representing most countries in a region is closed to membership by Israel, its primary "target."

SECTOR PRINCIPLE: devise used by states making claims on the Arctic, whereby a state claims all Arctic land located between lines drawn from its east and west coasts to the North Pole.

SECUESTRADOS (S): those kidnapped by left- and right-wing terrorists in Argentina in the 1970's. *See* DIRTY WAR.

SECUNDUM AEQUUM ET BONO (L): following that which is just and good.

SECURITY AND COOPERATION IN EUROPE: *see* HELSINKI ACCORDS.

SECURITY COMMUNITY: a geographic area in which the countries solve their problems peacefully and eventually work toward integration.

SECURITY COUNCIL: organ of the United Nations composed of five permanent members (China, France, United Kingdom, Union of Soviet Socialist Republics, and United States) and ten non-permanent members elected by the General Assembly for two year terms. The principal responsibility of the Security Council is the power to bring about a peaceful settlement of disputes and to undertake proceedings in the event of any threat to or violation of peace. *See* Arts. 23 *et seq.* of the UNITED NATIONS CHARTER.

SEDENTARY FISHERIES: fisheries containing oysters, sponge, coral, mussels, and other sedentary marine products. *See* Art. 2(4) of the GENEVA CONVENTION ON THE CONTINENTAL SHELF (1958).

SEDES MATERIAE (L): jurisdiction where a legal matter is settled; the court of last resort.

SEDITION: inciting revolution against a government.

SEISIN: the status of having possession; when applied to a court it means the status of having taken jurisdiction over a case.

SEIZURE: the taking control of a ship and its cargo during time of war subject to the law of PRIZE (q.v.).

SELA CONVENTION (1975): Convencion del Sistema Economico Latino-Americano, established the Latin American Economic System to promote regional development. *See* 15 I.L.M. 1081.

SELF-DEFENSE: the customary right of states to protect their territorial integrity and political independence from armed violation. The right also extends to the protection of aircraft and ships on the high seas. The means of self-defense employed are to be proportional to the violation that gave rise to the exercise of the right of self-defense. Under Art. 51 of the UNITED NATIONS CHARTER, self-defense is permissible only in the case of an "armed attack."

SELF-DEFENSE OBLIGATION: proposition that nature imposes a duty to act for self-preservation upon nations as well as individuals. *See* Vattel, *Law of Nations* (Fenwick translation of 1758 ed.) at 130.

SELF-DETERMINATION: principle that each state has the right to establish its own internal public order. The principle included the right of the people to freely determine their political status and freely pursue economic, social, and cultural development. *See* 78 Am.J.Int.L. 642.

SELF-EXECUTING TREATY: an international agreement that does not require legislative action on the part of the parties for it to perform its intended function, e.g., a treaty of friendship. *See* 82 Am.J.Int.L. 760.

SELF-GOVERNING DOMINION: unique status of the nations within the British Commonwealth in that they are fully sovereign but recognize the British monarch as their HEAD OF STATE (q.v.). They exchange high commissioners rather than ambassadors. *See* STATUTE OF WESTMINISTER.

SELF-HELP: actions of a state to remedy an injury by another state without resort to international legal institutions such as the International Court of Justice or international arbitration. Though self-help is a common practice it is frowned upon and limited by international law. *See* NAULILAA INCIDENT (1914).

SELF-JURISDICTION OF DIPLOMATIC ENVOYS: privilege of a diplomatic mission to exercise limited civil and criminal jurisdiction over persons assigned to the mission as a result of the extraterritoriality of a diplomatic mission. This is a matter for agreement between the sending and host countries. *See* Arts. 41-45, VIENNA CONVENTION ON CONSULAR RELATIONS.

SELF-PRESERVATION: a fundamental right of a state so that it may act to prevent violence against itself, to protect its citizens, and possessions. *See* 5 Whiteman, *Digest of International Law* 2.

SELF-PROTECTION: *see* PROTECTION OF NATIONALS.

SENSU HONESTO (L): in the true sense.

SEPARATE OPINION: a written opinion by a member of the International Court of Justice (or other judicial body) agreeing with the Court's decision but giving other reasons for the decision.

SEQUESTRATION: the seizure of property of individuals by a government, EXPROPRIATION (q.v.), e.g., the property of British and French nationals was seized by the Egyptian government after the SUEZ CRISIS (1956) (q.v.). *See* 12 Whiteman, *Digest of International Law* 320.

SERAJEVO: town in what is now Yugoslavia where Archduke Francis Ferdinand was assassinated precipitating World War I. *See* 9 Am.J.Int.L. Supp. 361.

SERBIAN LOANS CASE: dispute involving loans made to the Serbian government by French nationals to be repaid in either francs or gold with the creditors demanding gold. The Permanent Court of International Justice accepted jurisdiction over the case as presented by France on behalf of its nationals affirming the Court's ability to hear cases that involved questions of municipal law. *See* PCIJ, Series A, No. 20 (1929).

SERVANTS OF DIPLOMATIC AGENTS: formerly, it was customary to extend some diplomatic protection to the personal servants of a diplomat who accompanied him on a mission.

SERVICE COMMANDE (F): on a mission, e.g., a messenger sent by a military officer or ship's captain. For a strange case *see* 11 I.L.R. 165.

SERVICE OF LEGAL DOCUMENTS: *see* HAGUE CONVENTION ON THE SERVICE OF JUDICIAL AND EXTRAJUDICIAL DOCUMENTS.

SERVITUDES: a restriction on the exercise of sovereignty over territory; a binding obligation of a state to permit a specific use to be made of all or part of its territory by another state. *See North Atlantic Coast Fisheries Arbitration (U.S. v. Great Britain)*, 1932 P.C.I.J. (series A/B) No. 46.

SET-OFF: an amount claimed by a defendant to be credited against any award to the plaintiff. *See* 6 I.L.R. 234.

SETTLEMENT OF DISPUTES: *see* GENERAL ACT FOR THE PACIFIC SETTLEMENT OF INTERNATIONAL DISPUTES and Art. 33 et seq. of the UNITED NATIONS CHARTER.

SEVERANCE OF TREATY OBLIGATIONS: generally, treaties are considered an indivisible whole, but practice allows for the necessity of treating parts of treaties as separable so that, e.g., when one subsidiary obligation becomes impossible it does not destroy the entire agreement. *See* McNair, *Law of Treaties* 474 (1961).

SHANTUNG QUESTION: German interests in the Chinese Province of Shantung were ceded back to the Chinese by the VERSAILLES TREATY (q.v.). *See* 13 Am.J.Int.L. 687 and 16 Am.J.Int.L.Supp. 84.

SHARING OF INFORMATION: a number of international agreements call for the sharing of information on such matters as criminal activities (*see* 17 I.L.M. 801), scientific research (*see* OUTER SPACE TREATY), and military activities (*see* CONFIDENCE-BUILDING MEASURES).

SHARM-EL SHEIKH AREA: former territory of Egypt at the entrance of the Gulf of Aqaba occupied by Israel. *See* 4 Whiteman, *Digest of International Law* 465.

SHATT-AL-ARAB BOUNDARY QUESTION: dispute over the border between Iran and Iraq and possession of the narrow body of water at the north end of the Persian Gulf. *See* Kaikobad, *The Shatt-Al-Arab Boundry Question* 1988.

SHEREEFIAN EMPIRE: nineteenth century Morocco. *See* ALGECIRAS CONFERENCE (1906).

SHIP: ocean-going vessel with a juridical personality and the subject of *in rem* admiralty jurisdiction. *See* 1 Benedict, *Admiralty* sec. 162 (1985).

SHIPPING CONFERENCES: *See* LINER CONFERENCES.

SHIP'S FLAG: banner identifying a ship as being registered in a particular country, that state having jurisdiction over it and bearing responsibility for its acts. *See* BARCELONA DECLARATION and Art. 90 *et seq.* of the LAW OF THE SEA CONVENTION (1982).

SHIP'S PAPERS: merchant ships should carry a certificate of registry, muster-roll, log book, cargo manifest, bills of lading, and charter-party (if appropriate). If a ship is visited to check its neutrality missing papers may raise suspicion of its character, though they are not conclusive evidence of the ship's status. *See* Art. 92 of the LAW OF THE SEA CONVENTION (1982).

SHIP'S WARRANT: document issued by British authorities during World War II evidencing the ship owner's agreement not to carry CONTRABAND (q.v.) which facilitated the passage of the ship through the blockade of Germany. *See* 12 I.L.R. 532, 534. *See also* NAVICERT.

SHIPWRECKED: persons (in the law of war, combatants) who are in distress at sea or other waters, whether from loss or damage to a naval vessel or from an aircraft. *See* Art. 8(b) of GENEVA CONVENTION PROTOCOL I (1977).

SHUFELDT CLAIM (1930): arbitration of a claim by a United States citizen against the government of Guatemala over their withdrawal of a concession to harvest chicle. It was found that the government broke its agreement and Shufeldt was awarded damages. *See* 2 R.I.A.A. 1079.

SI OMNES CLAUSE: *see* GENERAL PARTICIPATION CLAUSE.

SIC SUBSCRIBITUR (L): in witness of this it is signed.

SIC UTERE JURE TUO UT ALIENUM NON LAEDAS (L): exercise your rights in a manner that does not injure another. *See* CORFU CHANNEL CASE.

SICK AND WOUNDED: *see* GENEVA CONVENTION I (1949).

SIEGE: the surrounding of a city or other locale for the purpose of cutting off supplies to the defenders and forcing their surrender. The GENEVA CONVENTIONS (1949) (q.v.) urge that the belligerents make local arrangements for the evacuation of non-combatants.

SIEGE SOCIAL (F): head office of a company, its location may be used to determine the nationality of the company in some legal systems.

SIGNAL: uniform maritime signals were set out by agreement found at 125 L.N.T.S. 95. *See also* ROAD SIGNALS CONVENTION.

SIGNATURE: mark (usually the handwritten name) of a representative of a state indicating the authenticity of the text of an agreement, and where ratification is not necessary it may also indicate the will of the party to be bound by the agreement. *See* Arts. 11 & 12, VIENNA CONVENTION ON THE LAW OF TREATIES.

SIMLA RULES (1931): addendum to the LOAD LINE CONVENTION (q.v.) replacing certain provisions *vis-a-vis* Moslem pilgrims who were carried unberthed in large numbers on ships bound for Arabia. *See* 5 Hudson, *International Legislation* 1003.

SINE DIE(L): with no date set for resumption, e.g., a legislature will adjorn *sine die*, without a date set for reconvening.

SINE QUA NON (L): a condition which must be accepted in order for the proposing party to accept the agreement.

SINGLE CONVENTION ON NARCOTIC DRUGS (1961): a unified convention controlling the cultivation, manufacture, and distribution of narcotic drugs. *See* 18 U.S.T. 1407, 520 U.N.T.S. 204, and protocol, 26 U.S.T. 1439, 11 I.L.M. 804.

SINGLE EUROPEAN ACT (1986): most recent step in the process of EUROPEAN INTEGRATION (q.v.) through the institution of the EUROPEAN COMMUNITY (q.v.). The integration process is to be completed in many respects by 1992. *See* 25 I.L.M. 506.

SINO-JAPANESE DISPUTE (1932): *see* LYTTON REPORT (1932).

SIPRI: STOCKHOLM INTERNATIONAL PEACE RESEARCH INSTITUTE (q.v.).

SKYJACKING: *see* AIR PIRACY.

SLAVE TRADE: the selling or transport of slaves outlawed by the SLAVERY CONVENTION (1926) (q.v.) among other international agreements.

SLAVERY CONVENTION (1926): parties undertook to prevent and suppress slave trade. *See* 46 Stat. 2183, 2 Bevans 607, 60 L.N.T.S. 253, Protocol 7 U.S.T. 479, 182 U.N.T.S. 51. *See also* ABOLITION OF SLAVERY CONVENTION (1956), 18 U.S.T. 3201, 266 U.N.T.S. 3.

SLOVENIJA INCIDENT (1958): a Yugoslav vessel was stopped by the French who claimed that arms were being smuggled to the Algerian rebels. The arms were seized, and the Yugoslavian government protested. *See* 4 Whiteman, *Digest of International Law* 513.

SMALL THREE: the Benelux countries; Belgium, the Netherlands, and Luxembourg.

SMITHSONIAN AGREEMENT (1971): International Monetary Fund agreement which sought appropriate measures for defending stable currency exchange rates. *See* 66 Am.J.Int.L. 737.

SMUGGLING: transfer of goods across borders in a manner to avoid customs laws; the first basis for national claims of jurisdiction beyond their territorial waters in order to protect their commerce against illicit traffic. *See* 40 Harvard L. Rev. 1.

SOCIALIST STATES: usually nations that have Marxist-Leninist governments. Countries with a democratic socialist government may be included. Theoretically, there is a natural struggle between capitalist and socialist states. *See* PEACEFUL COEXISTENCE.

SOCIEDAD ANOMIMA (S): a corporation.

SOCIETE COOPERATIVE (F): a cooperative; an organization with unlimited personal liability for its members. *See* 80 I.L.R. 139.

SOCIETE DE CAPITAUX (F): a corporation.

SOCIETE DES NATIONS (F): the LEAGUE OF NATIONS.

SOCIETE EN COMMANDITE PAR ACTIONS (F): a limited partnership with shared capital.

SOCIETE EN NOM COLLECTIF (F): general partnership

SOERING CASE (1989): EUROPEAN COURT OF HUMAN RIGHTS (q.v.) decision holding that EXTRADITION (q.v.) to a jurisdiction using the death penalty violates the EUROPEAN CONVENTION ON HUMAN RIGHTS (q.v.). *See* 28 I.L.M. 1063.

SOLAS: SAFETY OF LIFE AT SEA CONVENTION (q.v.).

SOLDIER: member of an armed force, usually applied to ground troops. *See* GENEVA CONVENTION I (1949).

SOLIDARITE NATIONALE (F): guarantees made by a state such as an undertaking to compensate repatriated persons for the loss of property when a colony is given independence. *See* 80 I.L.R. 438.

SON MY MASSACRE (1968): killing of about 500 innocent villagers by United States troops in Vietnam for which several officers, including Lt. William Calley, were court-martialed. *See* Hammer, *One Morning in War* (1970).

SOUND DUES: toll charged for passage through a strait. *See* DANISH SOUND DUES.

SOUNDING DOCTRINE: method of ascertaining the extent of the territorial sea by reference to the depth of the water; the territorial sea extending to a certain depth. It is a forerunner to the claim over the CONTINENTAL SHELF (q.v.).

SOURCES OF INTERNATIONAL LAW: that which may be consulted to determine the rules of international law, generally today, the STATUTE OF THE INTERNATIONAL COURT OF JUSTICE (q.v.) is said to set out in Art. 38 the sources to be consulted. They are TREATIES, CUSTOMARY INTERNATIONAL LAW, GENERAL PRINCIPLES OF LAW, decisions of the International Court of Justice, and other judicial bodies, and writings of PUBLICISTS (q.q.v.).

SOUTH PACIFIC COMMISSION: established among Australia, Netherlands, New Zealand, United Kingdom, and United States to advise the participants on economic and social development of the non-self-governing South Pacific Trust Territories. *See* 1948-9 U.N. Yearbook 702, 744 and 97 U.N.T.S. 227.

SOUTH POLE: *see* ANTARCTIC TREATY (1959).

SOUTHEAST ASIA TREATY ORGANIZATION (SEATO) (1954): collective defense treaty machinery set up by Australia, France, New Zealand, Pakistan, the Philippines, Thailand, the United Kingdom, and the United States. *See* 6 U.S.T. 81, 209 U.N.T.S. 28.

SOUTHERN AFRICAN DEVELOPMENT COORDINATING COMMITTEE (SADCC): regional organization of black, southern African states attempting to reduce their economic dependence on South Africa. Their headquarters is at 22 Coleman Fields, London N1 7AF, England.

SOUTH-WEST AFRICA: *see* NAMIBIA.

SOUTH-WEST AFRICA CASE: International Court of Justice Advisory Opinion on the status of Southwest Africa which was a League of Nations mandate administered by South Africa. The Court ruled that the mandate reporting requirements continued with the UN replacing the League in its supervisory capacity. *See* 1950 I.C.J. 128 and 1966 I.C.J. 6.

SOUTHWEST AFRICAN PEOPLES' ORGANIZATION (SWAPO): guerrilla organization fighting against the rule of Southwest Africa (Namibia) by South Africa which held the League of Nations Mandate over the territory, but whose recent occupation was condemned by the United Nations. *See* SOUTH-WEST AFRICA CASE.

SOVEREIGN: 1) The ruler of a state. 2) A state which exercises exclusive power over its territory having DOMINIUM and IMPE-RIUM (q.q.v.).

SOVEREIGN EQUALITY: all independent states have equal status in their ability to act without external control (sovereignty), thus Rwandi is just as much a sovereign nation as Japan.

SOVEREIGN IMMUNITY: legal doctrine that a sovereign cannot be sued without its consent. The modern version of this is that a state cannot be sued for its public acts, but may be sued with regard to its private acts (JURE GESTIONIS) such as operating a national airline.

SOVEREIGN MILITARY ORDER OF ST. JOHN OF JERUSA-LEM, OF RHODES AND OF MALTA: *see* ORDER OF MALTA.

SOVEREIGN STATE: political entity comprised of territory and a government exercising DOMINIUM and IMPERIUM (q.q.v.). Sovereign states are the principal subjects of international law.

SOVEREIGNTY: the ability of a state to act without external controls on the conduct of its affairs. *See* PALMAS ISLAND ARBI-TRATION and MAGALHAES DOCTRINE.

SOVEREIGNTY OVER NATURAL RESOURCES: principle adopted by the United Nations General Assembly that "people and nations [but mostly nations] have permanent sovereignty over their natural resources" and also approves of nationalization

S

and expropriation to enforce the right. *See* 1962 U.N. Yearbook 498.

SOVIET REPUBLICS: the several provinces that make up the Soviet Union. At the founding of the UN the Soviets claimed that each republic was an independent nation and should have a vote. In a compromise, several were given votes separate from the U.S.S.R.'s vote. The Republics are now demonstrating that the claim was true.

SOYUZ-APOLLO MISSION: *see* APOLLO-SOYUZ MISSION (1975).

SPACE: *see* OUTER SPACE.

SPACE ACTIVITIES: all of the man-created events and objects in outer space; they are governed generally by the OUTER SPACE TREATY (q.v.).

SPACE VEHICLE: *see* REGISTRATION OF OBJECTS LAUNCHED INTO SPACE.

SPACECRAFT: *see* REGISTRATION OF OBJECTS LAUNCHED INTO SPACE.

SPACE WARC: International Telecommunications Union Technical Conference to establish rules for telecommunications in outer space, especially the use of the GEOSTATIONARY ORBIT (q.v.) for communications satellites. *See* 13 J. Space L. 174 or 80 Am.J.Int.L. 699. For the second session *see* 83 Am.J.Int.L. 596.

SPANISH CIVIL WAR (1936-39): battle for control of Spain between fascist and republican forces. Gen. Franco's fascists won and he governed Spain until his death in 1975. *See* 31 Am.J.Int.L. 226, 578.

SPANISH ZONE OF MOROCCO CASE: arbitration of the claims of British citizens against Spain as the PROTECTING

POWER (q.v.) in Morocco for damages arising out of rebellion there. *See* 2 R.I.A.A. 615.

SPECIAL AGREEMENT: honorific title for an agreement.

SPECIAL ARAB AID FUND FOR AFRICA (SAAFA): fund established by eight Arab oil producing countries in January 1974, to provide emergency loans to African countries. *See* Amate, *Inside the OAU* 517.

SPECIAL DECLARATION: an ancillary agreement between some or all the parties to a treaty, e.g., agreement to interpret a certain term in the agreement in a particular way.

SPECIAL DRAWING RIGHT (SDR): monetary unit used in international transactions, especially by the International Monetary Fund; its value is calculated by reference to a "market basket" of hard currencies. *See* 4 Lowenfeld, *The International Monetary System* 99-112 and STOCKHOLM COMMUNIQUE (1968).

SPECIAL LATIN AMERICAN COORDINATING COMMITTEE (CECLA): antecedent to the LATIN AMERICAN ECONOMIC SYSTEM CONVENTION (q.v.).

SPECIAL MISSION: an ad hoc diplomatic mission such as sending a delegation to the funeral of a foreign head of state. *See* UN Convention on Special Missions, 1969 U.N. Yearbook 750.

SPECIAL PASSPORT: a passport issued to a government official (and his or her immediate family) who does not have diplomatic status.

SPECIAL POLITICAL COMMITTEE OF THE U.N. GENERAL ASSEMBLY: shares jurisdiction with the FIRST COMMITTEE OF THE UNITED NATIONS (q.v.) in reviewing resolutions of a political nature coming before the General Assembly.

SPECIAL PROTEGE: *see* PROTEGE SPECIAL (F).

SPECIAL RAPPORTEUR: official appointed to take minutes or compile information for the use of the group making the appointment, usually on a temporary basis.

SPECIAL RAPPORTEUR ON HUMAN RIGHTS: official appointed by the UN General Assembly to compute a list of those countries where a state of emergency or martial law is currently in force. These are possible sites of HUMAN RIGHTS (q.v.) abuses and deserve a close watch.

SPECIAL TRUCE: an ad hoc suspension of hostilities, e.g., an agreement to suspend fighting on a holiday.

SPECIALIZED AGENCIES OF THE UNITED NATIONS: institutions created by international agreement and related by agreement to the U.N., to carry on functions in a particular field, e.g., the WORLD HEALTH ORGANIZATION. *See* Art. 57 of the UNITED NATIONS CHARTER.

SPECIALITY RULE: provision sometimes included in an extradition treaty to the effect that the person extradited may be tried only for the crimes for which he is being extradited. *See U.S. v. Vreeken*, 803 F. 2d 1085 (1986).

SPHERES OF INFLUENCE: geographical areas in which a particular power (state) holds sway over the politics of the states of the region. *See* HEGEMONY, MONROE DOCTRINE, and EISENHOWER DOCTRINE.

SPILLOVER PROCESS: a factor in the functional theory of international integration which encompasses the effect of integration in one sector on other sectors, e.g., economic integration of two national systems will bring their political systems closer together.

SPIRITUAL HERITAGE: sites of importance to the religious history of a people or nation. *See* Art. 53 GENEVA PROTOCOL I (1977).

SPITZBERGEN: archipelago north of Norway, granted to Norway by the VERSAILLES PEACE TREATY (q.v.), with rights to certain uses reserved for the benefit of the other allied powers. *See* 4 Cal.West.Int'l L.J. 61.

SPOILS OF WAR: *see* UTI POSSIDETIS (L).

SPONSIO JUDICIALIS (L): the spurious prosecution of a case; a groundless legal case.

SPONSION: an undertaking by an official not empowered to do so, and therefore, requiring subsequent ratification by his government.

SPONSIONES (L): class of treaty in Roman law binding two nations with a promise that the stronger would defend the weaker, and solemnized by a religious ceremony.

SPY: one who acts clandestinely to obtain information and communicate it to a hostile party. *See* Art. 29-31 of the HAGUE CONVENTION RESPECTING THE LAWS AND CUSTOMS OF WAR ON LAND.

STANDARDS OF INTERNATIONAL LAW: *see* MINIMUM STANDARDS OF INTERNATIONAL LAW.

STAND-BY ARRANGEMENT: a drawing right issued to a country by the INTERNATIONAL MONETARY FUND (q.v.) giving it the ability to borrow a certain amount during the next six months to one year. *See* Gold, *Stand-by Arrangements of the International Monetary Fund* (1970).

STANDING BEFORE INTERNATIONAL TRIBUNALS: generally, individuals may not bring actions before international tribunals; only international persons, states, and international organizations may so appear.

STANDING CONSULTATIVE COMMISSION: regular meeting of representatives of the United States and Soviet Union to discuss problems arising out of the several arms limitations treaties in force between the two countries. *See* 24 U.S.T. 238.

STARK INCIDENT (1987): the U.S. Frigate Stark was hit by a missile launched by an Iraqi plane. *See* 26 I.L.M. 1422.

START TALKS: *see* STRATEGIC ARMS REDUCTIONS TALKS.

STAT PRO RATIONE VOLUNTA (L): one who makes a voluntary account (admission) must stand by it.

STATE: a group of people permanently occupying a fixed territory and having common laws, government, and capable of conducting international affairs. They may be SOVEREIGN, DEPENDENT, or a SUZERAINTY (q.q.v.). *See* 1 Hackworth, *Digest of International Law* 47.

STATE ACTIVITIES: those aspects of life in which the state (government) becomes involved, as opposed to private activities of individuals.

STATE AIRCRAFT: aircraft engaged in activities associated with governmental functions, e.g., military aircraft, police helicopters, mailplanes, Air Force One. These aircraft are not covered by the rules of the CHICAGO CONVENTION (1944) (q.v.) according to its Art. 3.

STATE CONTINUITY: a state retains its international identity even though it changes governments, or even political system, gains or loses territory, or changes names.

STATE CONTRACTS: agreements (usually commercial in nature) in which at least one party is a national government. *See* 37 Brit.Y.B.Int'l.L. 156.

STATE DEBTS: the fiscal obligations owed by a state's government, e.g., borrowing from International Monetary Fund or obligations to pay off bonds it has issued.

STATE EQUALITY: *see* SOVEREIGN EQUALITY.

STATE IMMUNITY: *see* SOVEREIGN IMMUNITY.

STATE JURISDICTION: the ability of a state to make and enforce law within its territory. *See* 111 Recueil des Cours 9.

STATE OF EMERGENCY: *see* MARTIAL LAW.

STATE OF INTERMEDIACY: *see* STATUS MIXTUS.

STATE OF SEIGE: *see* MARTIAL LAW.

STATE PRACTICE: the activities and conduct of states in carrying on their international affairs; state practice is one of the elements in proving a rule of CUSTOMARY INTERNATIONAL LAW (q.v.).

STATE PROPERTY: any tangible or intangible property owned by the state, formerly such property held immunity, but this status has deteriorated. *See* JURE GESTIONIS and JURE IMPERII.

STATE RESPONSIBILITY: for a state to be responsible in international law there must be a violation of international law imputable to the state which has resulted in injury to the claimant state.

STATE SHIPS: vessels which are used for governmental functions, such as police, coast guard patrol boats, or the presidential yacht.

STATE SUCCESSION: the question of which rights and obligations are continued when a territory changes governments or sovereigns, e.g., when a colony becomes independent is it obligated by the treaty commitments made by the former colonial power.

See 2 Whiteman, *Digest of International Law* 810 and VIENNA CONVENTION ON THE SUCCESSION OF STATES IN RESPECT TO TREATIES.

STATE TERRORISM: terrorist acts carried out under the auspices of a particular government, e.g., the alleged bombing of a West German discotheque by agents of the Libyan Government. *See* 80 Am.J.Int.L. 632.

STATE TRADING: a government conducting commercial activities. The problem of sovereign immunity arises when such dealings go wrong. *See* 25 Brit.Y.B.Int'l.L. 34.

STATEHOOD: a state should possess: 1) a permanent population; 2) a defined territory; 3) a government; and 4) the ability to deal with other nations. *See* 1 Whiteman, *Digest of International Law* 230.

STATELESS PERSON: a person who is not considered a national by any state. The Stateless Persons Convention, 360 U.N.T.S. 117, provides such persons with certain protections as well as the obligation to abide by the laws of the country where they reside.

STATUS DISCREPANCY THEORY OF WAR: an explanation of war which stresses the gap between the capability and prestige of a country rather than the gap between the two contesting countries, e.g., a country with high capabilities but low international prestige will cause trouble. *See* 1 Journal of Peace Research 95.

STATUS MIXTUS (L): state of relations between war and peace.

STATUS OF ALIENS CONVENTION (1928): this agreement recognizes the right of states to control the entrance and residence of foreigners. *See* 46 Stat. 2753.

STATUS OF FORCES AGREEMENT: treaties which control the stationing of foreign military forces in a friendly country. *See e.g.,*

NATO Status of Forces Agreement, 14 U.S.T. 531, 481 U.N.T.S. 262.

STATUS OF REFUGEES CONVENTION (1951): parties granted certain rights and undertook certain duties *vis-a-vis* refugees. *See* 189 U.N.T.S. 150.

STATUS OF WOMEN: the UN has made some efforts to improve the status of women. *See* 18 I.L.M. 550.

STATUS ORDER: a society organized with formally constituted social hierarchy of privileged class and unprivileged class.

STATUS QUO ANTE (L): the situation as it was before, e.g., as a remedy to an illegal seizure of territory, an arbitrator would rule that the boundary must be returned to its original location, i.e., the *status quo ante*.

STATUS QUO ANTE BELLUM (L): the state of affairs as they existed prior to the beginning of a war.

STATUS QUO POST BELLUM (L): the state of affairs after a war.

STATUTE OF THE INTERNATIONAL COURT OF JUSTICE: part of the UNITED NATIONS CHARTER (q.v.) which serves as organic document for the International Court of Justice. *See* 59 Stat. 1031, 3 Bevans 1153.

STATUTE OF THE PERMANENT COURT OF INTERNA-TIONAL JUSTICE: constitutive document of the P.C.I.J. *See* 1 Hudson, *International Legislation* 530.

STATUTE OF WESTMINISTER (1931): constituted the British Commonwealth in roughly its current form. *See* 7 Halsbury's Statutes 12 (4th ed.).

STGB: STRAFGESETZBUCH (q.v.).

STIMSON DOCTRINE (1932): formalized by a note from U.S. Secretary of State Stimson to Japan saying that the United States would not recognize Japan's claim to territory acquired through aggression against China. The Doctrine states the refusal of the United States to acquiesce to fruits of aggression. *See* Foreign Relations of the United States (1932), Vol. 3. at 8, and 14 Brit.Y.B.Int'l.L. 65.

STIPULATION POUR AUTRUI (F): provision of a treaty conferring a benefit on a third party. *See* 11 Brit.Y.B.Int'l.L. 12.

STOCKHOLM COMMUNIQUE (1968): statement by the GROUP OF TEN (q.v.) supporting amendments to the INTERNATIONAL MONETARY FUND (q.v.) including the adoption of the SPECIAL DRAWING RIGHTS (q.v.). *See* 7 I.L.M. 709.

STOCKHOLM CONFERENCE (1984-5): meeting to review progress on the HELSINKI ACCORDS (q.v.).

STOCKHOLM DECLARATION ON HUMAN ENVIRONMENT (1972): product of the United Nations Conference on the Environment (attended by 113 countries). It is often cited as a source of international environmental law, although its binding effect is questionable at best. *See* 1972 U.N. Yearbook 319.

STOCKHOLM INTERNATIONAL PEACE RESEARCH INSTITUTE (SIPRI): an independent institute for research into the problems of peace and conflict established in 1966 by the Swedish government. *See* SIPRI Yearbook (World Armament and Disarmament).

STOCKHOLM TRIBUNAL: mock war crimes trial charging the United States government with waging a war of aggression in Vietnam. *See* Duffett, *Against the Crime of Silence* (1968).

STOWAWAY: a person who hides aboard a ship and begins a voyage thereon; the subject of an international convention (not in force), *see* Singh, *International Conventions of Merchant Shipping* 1354 (2d ed. 1973).

STRAFGESETZBUCH (STGB) (G): Criminal Code of Germany.

STRAIGHT BASE-LINE: method of determining the extent of territorial waters by measuring out from a straight line drawn through points along the coast. *See* 1951 I.C.J./JUL 15.

STRAITS: narrow sea lanes between two land masses which are both part of the territorial sea of the littoral states and very important to international shipping and, therefore, the main object of the right of INNOCENT PASSAGE (q.v.). *See* 4 Whiteman, *Digest of International Law* 176.

STRASBOURG DECLARATION ON THE RIGHT TO LEAVE AND RETURN (1986): adopted to attempt to overcome the impediment to the exercise of an individual right to leave and return to one's country, placed on that right by many municipal jurisdictions. *See* 81 Am.J.Int.L. 434.

STRATEGIC ARMS LIMITATIONS AGREEMENTS (SALT I and II): between the United States and Soviet Union, SALT I includes the ANTI-BALLISTIC MISSILE SYSTEM TREATY and the INTERIM OFFENSIVE ARMS AGREEMENT (q.q.v.). SALT II refers to an unratified (but both parties have complied generally with its provisions) limit on strategic weapons. *See* 18 I.L.M. 1112.

STRATEGIC ARMS LIMITATIONS TALK: series of negotiations between the United States and Soviet Union aimed at ending the strategic arms race, and particularly in limiting the development and deployment of powerful long-range nuclear weapons.

STRATEGIC ARMS REDUCTION TALKS (START): ongoing successor to the SALT talks under the Reagan administration. So far, they have concluded the ELIMINATION OF INTERMEDIATE-RANGE AND SHORTER-RANGE NUCLEAR MISSILES CONVENTION (q.v.).

STRATEGIC BALANCE: the weighing of the strategic capabilities (e.g., number of weapons stockpiled, trained personnel, industrial infrastructure) of rival countries as a means of gauging security.

STRENGBEWEISVERFAHREN (G): rules of evidence surrounding the establishment of criminal acts. *See* 80 I.R.L. 412.

STRUCTURAL POWER: the power not only to influence the outcome of a particular dispute, but to frame the dispute, establish the rules, and manipulate the other actors.

STUTTGART DECLARATION (1946): statement by U.S. Secretary of State Byrnes of the U.S. policy toward the administration of postwar Germany and its economic recovery. *See* 1946 Dept. State Bull. 496.

SUB JUDICE (L): that which is under consideration by a judicial body.

SUB POTESTATE (L): under the protection of.

SUB SPE RATI (L): in hopes that it will be ratified; an agreement made by one without proper authority and thus requiring later ratification. *See* Satow, *A Guide to Diplomatic Practice* 110 (1957).

SUBIC BAY: United States Naval Base in the Philippines; the subject of much political tension in that country. *See* 61 Stat. 4019.

SUBJECTIVE IMPOSSIBILITY: a state may rely on equitable principles and not fulfill an obligation when that fulfillment requires an act which it believes to be impossible, e.g., the repayment of a debt when the country is bankrupt.

SUBJECTIVE RESPONSIBILITY: element of placing blame for an illegal act requiring that the guilty party must have comprehended the illegality of its act.

SUBJECTS OF INTERNATIONAL LAW: traditionally only nation states were subjects of international law. Recently international law has developed branches which include international organizations and even individuals as subjects, *see e.g*, HUMAN RIGHTS.

SUBJUGATION: the permanent occupation, annexation, and extermination of an enemy state. *See* DEBALLATIO.

SUBMARINE: rules for the operation of submarines with regard to merchant vessels are found in the LONDON SUBMARINE PROTOCOL (q.v.).

SUBMARINE CABLES: wires laid on the ocean floor for the transmission of telecommunications across the ocean. *See* 24 Stat. 989 and 25 Stat. 1424.

SUBMERGED LAND: privately owned land adjacent to navigable or public waters which are subject to reasonable use by boatmen, e.g., for anchorage in an emergency. *See Scranton v. Wheeler*, 179 U.S. 141 (1900).

SUBSIDIARY AGENCY: organizations under the European Community such as the EUROPEAN INVESTMENT BANK (q.v.).

SUBSTANTIAL NATIONAL OWNERSHIP CLAUSE: in BILATERAL AIR TRANSPORT AGREEMENTS (q.v.) there is often a requirement that the airline designated to provide service must be substantially owned by nationals of the designating country. *See* Art. 6 of the BERMUDA AGREEMENT I.

SUCCESSION OF STATES WITH RESPECT TO TREATIES: *see* VIENNA CONVENTION ON THE SUCCESSION OF STATES IN RESPECT TO TREATIES and STATE SUCCESSION.

SUCCESSOR STATE: a government which has replaced another government with regard to the responsibility for the international relations of a particular territory, e.g., a colony which becomes in-

dependent and, thus, a new state. *See* VIENNA CONVENTION
ON THE SUCCESSION OF STATES IN RESPECT TO TREATIES.

SUDETENLAND: part of the territory of Czechoslovakia an-
nexed by Germany in 1938, pursuant to the MUNICH AGREE-
MENT (q.v.) between Hitler and English Prime Minister Neville
Chamberlain. The Germans shortly, thereafter, invaded all of
Czechoslovakia which was rendered defenseless by the loss of the
Sudetenland where all of its fortifications were located. *See* 3
Whiteman, *Digest of International Law* 157.

SUEZ CANAL: manmade canal between the Gulf of Suez and
the Mediterranean Sea declared neutral and open to all ships by
the CONSTANTINOPLE CONVENTION (1888) (q.v.). *See* SUEZ
CRISIS (1956).

SUEZ CRISIS (1956): Anglo-French intervention into the war between Israel and Egypt, ostensibly to protect their nationals and
to keep the Suez Canal open. They were slightly bloodied and
withdrew, as did Israel from most of the territory it had seized,
but Israel retained the GAZA STRIP and SHARM-EL SHEIKH
(q.q.v.). *See* 51 Am.J.Int.L. 277.

SUJETS MIXTUS (F): individuals who are DUAL NATIONALS
(q.v.).

SULLIVAN PRINCIPLES: guidelines named after Reverend
Leon Sullivan for the conduct of American companies doing business in South Africa which are to insure equal treatment of employees of all races and to support an end to APARTHEID (q.v.).
See 24 I.L.M. 1485.

SUMATRA-TIMOR PASSAGE: the longest of important international sea lanes passing through the territorial waters of the Indonesian Archipelago for over 2500 miles. *See* 4 Whiteman, *Digest
of International Law* 322.

SUMMARY INTERPRETATION: technique for interpretation of a treaty when it is found that the text has a clear meaning and no further elaboration is necessary.

SUMMARY PROCEDURE: an expedited judicial process, e.g., the hearing of a case by a few judges rather than the entire membership of a court.

SUMMIT MEETING: direct, face-to-face meeting of heads of state or heads of governments. *See e.g.*, MOSCOW SUMMIT (1988).

SUPER FUND EXCISE TAX DISPUTE: a G.A.T.T. (q.v.) dispute settlement panel investigated the legality of United States excise taxes to fund hazardous waste cleanup. *See* 27 I.L.M. 1596.

SUPER POWERS: until recently, the United States and the Soviet Union were the two or so countries among the more powerful nations that stand above the rest. The United States now stands alone as the superpower.

SUPER 301: designation by the United States Trade Representative of countries whose unfair trade practices are to be challenged with particular vigor. *See* 19 U.S.C. Sec. 2420 (1988).

SUPERIOR ORDERS DEFENSE: defense offered by those on trial for war crimes that they were only following orders given them by the chain of military command which they were obliged to follow. The defense is usually unsuccessful. *See* 63 Jurid.Rev. 234.

SUPPRESSION AND PUNISHMENT OF THE CRIME OF APARTHEID CONVENTION (1973): United Nations sponsored convention making APARTHEID (q.v.) an international crime. *See* 13 I.L.M. 50, 11 I.L.M. 212.

SUPRA-NATIONAL INSTITUTIONS: international organizations which take on some of the powers of the member states, e.g., the European Community which has been given a great deal of power to regulate commerce by the member governments which thus give up some of that power.

SUPRA-NATIONAL PROFESSIONAL: members of the world's scientific and technical elite who through multinational contacts become somewhat independent of their national viewpoint. International civil servants might also be included in this group.

SURFACE DAMAGE: *see* LIABILITY FOR DAMAGE CAUSED BY SPACE OBJECTS CONVENTION (1973), and the ROME CONVENTION (1952).

SURRENDER: the turning over of a body of troops or a locale to the enemy; such as, part of a CAPITULATION (q.v.); it would include agreement on the terms of surrender and be more than one-sided. *See* 10 Whiteman, *Digest of International Law* 517.

SUSPENSION CONDITION: an occurrence in the future which will give rise to a right, e.g., nonpayment of a portion of a loan on schedule may (by the terms of the agreement) cause the entire loan repayment to be due immediately.

SUSPENSION FROM THE UNITED NATIONS: the Security Council may suspend the rights of a member when it takes enforcement action though the members' obligations continue. *See* Art. 5 of the UNITED NATIONS CHARTER.

SUSPENSION OF A TREATY: a temporary abeyance of an international agreement, e.g., during time of war.

SUSPENSION OF HOSTILITIES: a truce, cease-fire, or armistice which may be temporary or may lead to a permanent end to the conflict by a peace treaty. *See* 71 Am.J.Int.L. 461.

SUUM CUIQUE: in the law of PRIZE (q.v.), the severing of a cargo from the vessel carrying it, e.g., hostile goods may be taken from a neutral ship. *See The Nereides*, 13 U.S. 388.

SUZERAINTY: quasi-sovereign status of certain territories where the local sovereign is a subject (vassal) of another sovereign, and yet exercises most of the powers of government internally. The terms of the status may vary. *See* 1 Whiteman, *Digest of International Law* 430.

SWAPO: SOUTHWEST AFRICAN PEOPLES' ORGANIZATION (q.v.).

SWEDISH RESOLUTION: UNGA Res. 1665 (XVI) Dec. 4, 1961, requesting the secretary general to investigate the possibility of a nuclear nonproliferation treaty. *See* 1961 U.N. Yearbook 31.

SWISS BANKS: financial institutions located in Switzerland and favored by many throughout the world because of the strict bank secrecy laws of Switzerland. *See* 16 I.L.M. 767.

SWISS COAT OF ARMS: a white cross on a red background. It has been the subject of conflict between the United States and Switzerland over its use, especially by U.S. commercial concerns which view it as a trademark or advertising. *See* 5 Whiteman, *Digest of International Law* 175.

SYKES-PICOT TREATY (1916): secret agreement between England and France to divide-up spheres of influence in the Middle East. *See* 221 C.T.S. 323.

SYNALLAGMATIC: reciprocal.

SYRIAN CRISIS (1860-61): intervention by the European Powers to protect human rights. Brownlie cites this as the only real example of HUMANITARIAN INTERVENTION (q.v.) in history. *See* 23 Can.Y.B.Int'l L. 246.

SYSTEMATIC INTERPRETATION: the interpretation or construction of the meaning of a document by reference to its context rather than to a strict or literal interpretation.

[T - U]

TABA ARBITRATION (1988): settlement of a boundary dispute between Egypt and Israel over the resort community of Taba located on the Red Sea. *See* 27 I.L.M. 1421.

TABULA AMALFITANA: collection of maritime laws from the town of Amalfi, Italy dating from the tenth century.

TABULA RASA CONCEPT: "blank slate;" principle from the VIENNA CONVENTION ON SUCCESSION OF STATES IN RESPECT TO TREATIES (q.v.). Newly formed states are not burdened by the obligations made by their predecessors *vis-a-vis* other states.

TACIT AGREEMENT: an agreement which is implied through action or lack of objection, though not stated explicitly. A very useful tool of international relations where later deniability of involvement for political reasons may be very important.

TACIT CONSENT: an assumption in international law that a subject of international law which does not object to a rule that is being formulated by common practice is, in fact, agreeing with the rule's adoption without the giving of explicit consent to its adoption. *See* Art. 45 of the VIENNA CONVENTION ON THE LAW OF TREATIES (1969).

TACITO CONSENSU (L): TACIT CONSENT (q.v.).

TACNA-ARICA CONTROVERSY: dispute between Chile and Peru arising out of the unfulfilled provisions of the ANCON TREATY (q.v.) which ended the WAR OF THE PACIFIC (q.v.). President Hoover who exercised good offices at the request of the parties made a proposal accepted by both countries and put into a formal treaty, 23 Am.J.Int.L. 605 (1929).

TAFT ARBITRATION TREATIES: two treaties signed by the United States and Great Britain and by the United States and France, but never ratified. The treaties were intended to preserve the peace between the parties by the submission of all disputes to arbitration (if it could not be settled by diplomacy). These treaties served as a model for the BRYAN TREATIES (q.v.). *See* 5 Am.J.Int.L.Supp. 249 and 253 (1911).

TAKING OF EVIDENCE ABROAD: *see* HAGUE CONVENTION ON THE TAKING OF EVIDENCE ABROAD.

TAKING OF HOSTAGES CONVENTION (1979): United Nations sponsored convention whereby the parties agree to make hostage taking a criminal offense and to prosecute hostage takers. *See* 74 Am.J.Int.L. 277.

TAKING OF PROPERTY: *see* EXPROPRIATION.

TAMPICO INCIDENT (1914): Mexican soldiers arrested three United States seamen and released them shortly thereafter. The United States used the Incident as an excuse for the VERA CRUZ OCCUPATION (q.v.). *See* 2 Hyde, *Digest of International Law* 420.

TAMUZ I: Iraqi nuclear reactor destroyed by an Israeli air raid in 1981. The raid was justified by the Israelis by a claim that nuclear weapons were about to be manufactured there for use against Israel, and thus, it was an act of SELF-DEFENSE (q.v.). *See* 13 Cal.West.Int'l L.J. 86.

TANKER OWNERS VOLUNTARY AGREEMENT CONCERNING LIABILITY FOR OIL POLLUTION (TOVALOP): system created by private tanker owners agreeing to accept liability for oil spills from their vessels in return for a limitation on the amount of their liability. *See* 8 I.L.M. 497. *See also* CRISTAL.

TARIFFS: taxes on goods as they enter or leave a country; normally designed to protect local industry. *See* 14 Whiteman, *Digest of International Law* 823.

TASHKENT DECLARATION (1966): agreement ending hostilities which had erupted in 1965, between India and Pakistan. *See* 5 I.L.M. 320.

TATE LETTER: letter from the United States State Department to the Justice Department suggesting the immunity of the Soviet government from suits involving their bonds. *See* 26 Dept. State Bull. 984 (1952) and 54 Am.J.Int.L. 790.

TATTOOING: tattooing or marking of the body of CIVILIAN (q.v.) internees is prohibited by Art. 100 of the GENEVA CONVENTION IV (1949).

TAXATION: levy on the citizens to fund the operation of the government. In international law the problem of double taxation arises where two states tax the same individual for the same transaction, *see* 1985 Intertax 145-157. The levy of taxes in occupied territory is governed by Art. 48, HAGUE CONVENTION RESPECTING LAWS AND CUSTOMS OF WAR ON LAND (1907) (q.v.).

TAXIS OF THE MARNE EPISODE: distinction between combatants and noncombatants is often difficult as in this case where the Military Governor of Paris commandeered cabs and drivers to take troops to the front in 1914.

T.C.: TRUSTEE'S COUNCIL OF THE UNITED NATIONS (q.v.).

TECHNICAL ASSISTANCE: activities of many United Nations specialized agencies providing expertise to developing countries in such areas as agriculture, health, and telecommunications. Many developed countries also provide technical assistance to lesser developed countries on a bilateral basis.

TECHNICAL BARRIERS TO TRADE: subject of a GATT (q.v.) agreement, 18 I.L.M. 1098. Technical barriers are regulations which effectively bar foreign goods by the imposition of standards or requirements that serve no other purpose though couched in terms of health, safety, etc. *See e.g.*, REINHEITGEBOT.

TECHNOLOGY TRANSFER: *see* TRANSFER OF TECHNOL-OGY.

TEGUCIGULPA DECLARATION (1982): product of a meeting of the CENTRAL AMERICAN DEMOCRATIC COMMUNITY (q.v.) urging *inter alia* development and a halt to the arms race in Central America. *See* 1982 American Foreign Policy 1369.

TEHERAN CONFERENCE (1943): meeting of Churchill, Roosevelt, and Stalin where a common policy against Hitler was established. *See* 38 Am.J.Int.L.Supp. 9

TEHERAN CONFERENCE ON HUMAN RIGHTS (1968): a run-of-the-mill United Nations Human Rights Conference. *See* 1968 U.N. Yearbook 104.

TELECOMMUNICATIONS: any transmission, emission, or reception of signals of an intelligent nature by wire, radio, optical, or electronic means. *See* 9 Whiteman, *Digest of International Law* 690.

TELEGRAPHS: early form of telecommunications using long and short electrical impulses sent by wire. *See* 9 Whiteman, *Digest of International Law* 717.

TELEVISION: *See* DIRECT BROADCAST SERVICE and INTERNATIONAL TELECOMMUNICATIONS UNION.

TEMPLE OF PREAH VIHEAR (*Cambodia v. Thailand*): dispute over the location of the boundary was settled in Cambodia's favor. *See* 1962 I.C.J. 6.

TEN DOWNING STREET: official residence of the British prime minister and, therefore, slang for the British government.

TEN NATION COMMITTEE ON DISARMAMENT: established in 1959, by the United States, United Kingdom, France, Soviet Union, Canada, Italy, Bulgaria, and Czechoslovakia. The

Soviet Bloc withdrew after the U-2 INCIDENT (q.v.) and was later replaced by the EIGHTEEN NATION COMMITTEE ON DISARMAMENT (q.v.).

TERCEIRA AFFAIR (1828): Portuguese rebels attempted to launch a military expedition from England which took questionable action to stop them. This is an early example of the principle that a nation should not let its territory be used as a base for attacks on the territory of another nation.

TERMINATION OF A MISSION: a diplomat's mission may end by *inter alia*, expiration of his appointment, RECALL OF DIPLOMATS (q.v.), the outbreak of war, or the extinction of one of the states involved. *See* Satow, *A Guide to Diplomatic Practice* 274 (1957).

TERMINATION OF A TREATY: the effect of a treaty may end by EXPIRATION, DISSOLUTION, VOIDANCE (e.g., impossibility of execution), or CANCELLATION (qq.v.) (e.g., by war). *See* McNair, *Law of Treaties* 493-535.

TERMINATION OF PROCEEDINGS: discontinuance of a judicial proceeding by agreement of the parties and with the approval of the tribunal hearing the case.

TERRA FIRMA: solid land; the nearest continent or major island. *See* PALMAS ISLAND ARBITRATION (1928).

TERRA NULLIUS: land of no one; land which has not been claimed by a nation, but may be subject to such a claim, e.g., a newly formed island in the midst of the high seas.

TERRAE DOMINIUM FINITUR, UBI FINITUR ARMORUM VIS: one's territory ends where the effective force of one's arms ends. *See* CANNON SHOT RULE.

TERRAE POTESTAS FINITUR, UBI FINITUR ARMORUM VIS: the dominion over land reaches only as far as the range of one's guns. That is the CANNON SHOT RULE (q.v.).

TERRITET AWARD (1933): arbitral decision which laid down the governing principles with respect to the exchange of goods between the Free Zones of Upper Savoy and Gex and Switzerland. *See* 1933 P.C.I.J. (series E) no. 10.

TERRITORIAL AIR SPACE: atmosphere above a nation's territory and territorial waters; outer limits which is unsettled, i.e., line between territorial air space and outer space has yet to be drawn. *See* Arts. 1 and 2 of the CHICAGO CONVENTION (1944).

TERRITORIAL ASYLUM: *see* POLITICAL ASYLUM.

TERRITORIAL BAY: BAY (q.v.); part of the TERRITORIAL WATERS (q.v.) of a state.

TERRITORIAL INTEGRITY: a state has a right to retain the territory over which it rightly has dominion. An existing state should not have part of its territory taken from it. *See* 5 I.L.R. 8.

TERRITORIAL JURISDICTION: competence of a state to act within its own territory; e.g., a state may declare a certain act done within its territory to be a crime. *See* 26 I.L.R. 513.

TERRITORIAL PRINCIPLE: basis of jurisdiction often invoked by states. All states claim jurisdiction over crimes committed within their territory. Common law countries generally claim criminal jurisdiction only over acts committed within their territory. *See* 6 Whiteman, *Digest of International Law* 889.

TERRITORIAL SEA: *see* TERRITORIAL WATERS.

TERRITORIAL SOVEREIGNTY: authority a state exercises over persons and things found within its territory to the exclusion of the jurisdiction of other states, and subject to the limitations imposed by international law. *See* 31 I.L.R. 120.

TERRITORIAL WATERS: strip of sea along the coast of a state (LITTORAL STATE); defined as a certain distance out from a BASE-LINE (q.v.) drawn along the coast. The extent of the territorial waters is the subject of some dispute, and claims of states vary from 3 to 200 miles. *See* Arts. 2-4 of the LAW OF THE SEA CONVENTION (1982). The United States recently extended its territorial sea to 12 miles. *See* 28 I.L.M. 284.

TERRITORIUM NULLIUS: territory not under the jurisdiction of a sovereign.

TERRITORIUM SERVIENS (L): state servitude; a territory of a sovereign which is subject to a right to its use by another party, e.g., the UNITED NATIONS HEADQUARTERS AGREEMENT (q.v.) grants such a right in United States territory to the United Nations.

TERRITORY: any portion of the earth's surface within a state's boundaries which is subject to the state's sovereign rights and interests.

TERROR BOMBING: most widely used means of terrorizing civilian populations during recent wars has been aerial bombardment, but such bombardment is forbidden by Art. 22 of the HAGUE RULES OF AIR WARFARE (1923) (q.v.).

TERRORISM: the use of arbitrary violence against a defenseless population; it is often difficult to draw the line between terrorism and "legitimate struggle." *See* TAKING OF HOSTAGES CONVENTION, HIJACKING, and EUROPEAN CONVENTION ON TERRORISM.

TEST-BAN TREATY (1963): treaty banning tests of nuclear explosives in the atmosphere, in outer space, and under water should the explosion cause radioactive debris to be present outside the territory of the state conducting the test. The treaty is in force in over 100 countries including the United States and the Soviet Union. *See* 14 U.S.T. 1313, 480 U.N.T.S. 43.

TFCN: Treaty of Friendship, Commerce, and Navigation. *See* FRIENDSHIP, COMMERCE AND NAVIGATION TREATIES.

THAI CIGARETTE CASE (1991): dispute under the GENERAL AGREEMENT ON TARIFFS AND TRADE (q.v.) involving Thailand's restrictions on the importation of cigarettes and taxes thereon. *See* 30 I.L.M. 1122.

THALWEG: main channel of a river.

THEATER OF WAR: the area in which a war is actually occurring. In World War II, the term was used to describe the area of war in Europe, e.g., the European Theater of Operation.

THEOLOGY OF LIBERATION: *see* LIBERATION THEOLOGY.

THERMO-NUCLEAR WEAPONS: weapons providing most of their explosive force from a fusion reaction (hydrogen splitting). Thermonuclear explosions are usually measured in megatons of TNT.

THIRD BASKET: miscellaneous agenda items, specifically, group of problems for the agenda of the CONFERENCE ON SECURITY AND COOPERATION IN EUROPE (q.v.) that were neither political nor economic in nature, most importantly, human rights.

THIRD STATE: a state not party to a treaty. *See* Art. 2 of the VIENNA CONVENTION ON THE LAW OF TREATIES (1969).

THIRD WORLD: general reference to those countries which are neither prosperously industrialized (the First World, *see* GROUP OF TEN), nor part of the SOVIET BLOC (q.v.). The least developed countries are sometimes referred to as the FOURTH WORLD (q.v.). May also refer to the NONALIGNED MOVEMENT (q.v.).

THREE-MILE ZONE: the minimum claim made to TERRITO-RIAL WATERS (q.v.). Until recently the United States claimed only a three mile zone though effectively controlling much more, *see* CONTINENTAL SHELF and CANNON SHOT RULE.

THREE RULES OF WASHINGTON: rules for deciding the issue of liability in the arbitration between the United States and Great Britain over claims of the United States arising from Great Britain's aid to the Confederacy during the Civil War. *See* 17 Stat. 863, 12 Bevans 170.

THRESHOLD NUCLEAR TEST BAN TREATY (1974): *see* LIMITED NUCLEAR TEST BAN TREATY (1974).

THROUGH BILL OF LADING: document issued for goods to be transported in several stages by more than one shipping line or by more than one mode of transport, e.g., by truck to Port A; by ship to Port B; and by truck to destination. *See* BILL OF LADING.

TIANANMEN SQUARE MASSACRE: killing of large numbers of prodemocracy demonstrators in Tiananmen Square in Beijing, China on June 4, 1989. *See* 8 Dick. J. Int'l L, 245.

TIBET: autonomous region of Western China; it has been the subject of calls for a United Nations protectorate and the site of alleged human rights abuses. *See* Van Praag, *The Status of Tibet* (1986).

TIDE WATERS: the setting of maritime boundaries is problematic because of the effects of weather and tides on the location of the shoreline. *See* 2 O'Connell, *The International Law of the Sea* 635.

T.I.A.S.: TREATIES AND OTHER INTERNATIONAL AGREEMENTS (q.v.).

TIENTSIN TREATY (1858): between Great Britain and China; opening diplomatic and consular relations, and granting to the British the right to carry on trade. *See* 119 C.T.S. 163.

TIGRE PEOPLE'S LIBERATION FRONT: group fighting for the independence of the Tigre region of Ethiopia. *See* N.Y. Times, Jan. 6, 1985, p.1.

TILSIT TREATY (1807): armistice agreement between France and Russia in the Napoleanic Wars. *See* Toynbee, 1 *Treaties* 469.

TIME-LIMITS: the time-limits on the various stages of proceedings before the INTERNATIONAL COURT OF JUSTICE (q.v.) are set by formal order of the Court for each case. *See* 2 Rosenne, *The Law and Practice of the International Court* 559.

TIMOR ISLAND ARBITRATION: dispute between Portugal and the Netherlands resulting from a mistake in the designation in the border treaty of a river intended to serve as part of the boundary between these countries' holdings on Timor Island. The Permanent Court of Arbitration Arbitors held, *inter alia*, that treaties are not to be interpreted literally, but rather according to the true intentions of the parties involved. Therefore, the river shown on the map annexed and not the river named was the boundary. *See* 11 R.I.A.A. 481 (1961).

TIN AGREEMENT: *see* INTERNATIONAL TIN AGREEMENT.

TINOCO CONCESSIONS ARBITRATION: a dispute arose between Great Britain and Costa Rica as to the validity of a Costa Rican law invalidating all contracts made during the regime of Frederico Tinoco, a revolutionary in power for three years before constitutional government was restored. United States President Taft serving as sole arbitrator found in favor of Costa Rica because the contracts could not have been validly entered into under Costa Rican law in force during Tinoco's Regime. *See* 18 Am.J.Int.L. 147.

TIR CARNETS: customs document for expedited road transport through countries without lengthy customs inspection. *See* U.N. DOC ECE/TRANS/17 (14 Nov. 1975) or Evans and Standford Transport Law of the World at I/H/1.2.

TITLE: the honorific designation of a SOVEREIGN or other noble, e.g., Elizabeth II, by the Grace of God, of Great Britain, Ireland (GRAND-TITRE), and the British Dominions beyond the Seas, Queen (TITRE-MOYEN), Defender of the Faith (PETIT-TITRE).

TITLE OF DISCOVERY: right of a state to occupy and develop sovereignty over previously undiscovered territory within a reasonable time after the discovery. If sovereignty is not perfected the right will lapse. *See* 4 I.L.R. 103 and 108.

TITLES OF STATES: presently few states have titles although such titles did exist in the past, e.g., the former Republic of Venice was addressed as "Serene Republic."

TITRE (F): TITLE (q.v.).

TLATELOLCO DECLARATION (1974): product of a conference of most of the nations of the Western Hemisphere's foreign ministers. They agreed to the necessity of the spirit of inter-American solidarity, and that their relations should be based on effective equality between states, nonintervention, renunciation of the use of force, and respect for free choice of political, economic, and social systems. *See* 13 I.L.M. 465.

TLATELOLCO TREATY (1967): Treaty for the Prohibition of Nuclear Weapons in Latin America. *See* 64 Am.J.Int.L. 282 and Documents on Disarmament (1967), at 69-83.

TOBAR DOCTRINE: expressed in two Central American treaties. The doctrine states that the governments of the contracting parties shall not recognize any other government which may come into power in one of the five Central American republics as a consequence of a coup d'etat, or of a revolution against the recognized government as long as the freely elected representatives of the people thereof have not constitutionally reorganized the country. *See* Art. 2 of the Central American Convention of 1907, 206 C.T.S. 73. *See also* 28 Am.J.Int.L. 325 (1934).

TOKYO INTERNATIONAL MILITARY TRIBUNAL: established to try Far Eastern war criminals after World War II. Its jurisdiction and the law it applied were substantially the same as the NUREMBERG TRIBUNAL (q.v.).

TOKYO ROUND (1979): meeting, under the GENERAL AGREEMENT ON TARIFFS AND TRADE (q.v.), resulting in a series of agreements on agriculture and nontariff trade barriers. *See* 18 I.L.M. 1052 and 75 Am.J.Int.L. 131.

TOKYO TRIALS: *see* TOKYO INTERNATIONAL MILITARY TRIBUNAL.

TOLLS: generally states do not have the right to impose fees for passage through their TERRITORIAL WATERS (q.v.), *but see* DANISH SOUND DUES.

TONKIN GULF INCIDENT (1964): an alleged attack on the United States destroyer Maddox, in international waters in the Gulf of Tonkin off the North Vietnamese coast, by North Vietnamese gunboats. This action was used to justify expansion of the United States' role in the war in Vietnam. *See* 4 Whiteman, *Digest of International Law* 529.

TONKIN GULF RESOLUTION: congressional approval of an expanded United States role in the war in Vietnam based on the TONKIN GULF INCIDENT (1964) (q.v.). *See* 78 Stat. 384, 51 Dept. State Bull. 268.

TONNAGE MEASUREMENT: states have different means of calculating a ship's tonnage. Tonnage is the measure by which port fees are calculated, therefore, agreements exist to rectify the differences. *See e.g.,* 208 U.N.T.S. 3.

TORDESILLAS TREATY (1494): treaty between Portugal and Spain dividing up the Western Hemisphere. They drew a line 100 leagues west and south of the Azores and Cape Verde from the North Pole to the South Pole. Portugal received everything in the new world east of the line; Spain received everything to the west. *See* 1 De Martens, *Supplement en Recueil* (1801).

TORPEDOES: THE HAGUE CONVENTION ON SUBMARINE MINES (1907) (q.v.), Art. 1(3) requires that torpedoes be designed to become harmless after they miss their target. In older usage, underwater mines were called torpedoes.

TORREY CANYON INCIDENT: grounding of the oil tanker Torrey Canyon did large scale damage to the coasts of France and England and led to the adoption of the International Convention Relating to Intervention on the High Seas in Cases of Oil Pollution Casualties. *See* 9 I.L.M. 633 and 6 I.L.M. 480.

TORRES STRAITS TREATY: settlement of the question of sovereignty over islands in the Torres Straits between Australian and Papua, New Guinea. *See* 7 Aust. Ybk. Int'l L. 87.

TORTURE: acts, usually, to elicit information causing unnecessary pain and suffering either physically, mentally, or emotionally to prisoners. Torture is outlawed by a United Nations treaty, 25 I.L.M. 519. *See also* 16 Int'l J.Legal Information 267 and the European Convention for the Prevention of Torture and Inhuman or Degrading Treatment or Punishment, 27 I.L.M. 1152.

TOTAL BLOCKADE: cutting off all sea trade through an enemy port, and making no distinction between legitimate OBJECTS OF WAR (q.v.) and neutral goods as is required by customary international law.

TOTAL WAR: war pursued in an all-out manner involving the entire population and territory of the belligerents. This is a violation of the traditional LAWS OF WAR (q.v.) where only targets of military significance are legitimate targets.

TOTALITARIANISM: system of government where the state attempts to control the lives of its citizens completely, using all means available to it including mass murder. Stalinist Russia and Nazi Germany are the principal examples of such states.

TOVALOP: TANKER OWNERS VOLUNTARY AGREEMENT CONCERNING LIABILITY FOR OIL POLLUTION (q.v.).

TPLF: TIGRE PEOPLE'S LIBERATION FRONT (q.v.).

TRADE: *see* GENERAL AGREEMENT ON TARIFFS AND TRADE.

TRADE IN ENDANGERED SPECIES OF WILD FLORA AND FAUNA CONVENTION (1975): attempt to help conserve endangered species. The convention is found at 27 U.S.T. 1087, 12 I.L.M. 1085, with the United States implementing regulations at 50 C.F.R. part 17 *et seq.* (or 16 I.L.M. 390).

TRADE IN WORKS OF ART: *see* the United Nations Convention In the Means of Prohibiting the Illicit Import, Export, or Transfer of Ownership of Cultural Property, 249 U.N.T.S. 242.

TRADE MISSION: an informal representation of one country in another with status less than that of a consulate. A trade mission may perform certain functions that are normally done by a consulate. This forum may be used to carry on relations where there is no formal recognition of one country by the other.

TRADE UNIONS: various groups of organized labor and the subject of several international agreements and organizations. *See* INTERNATIONAL LABOUR ORGANIZATION and WORLD FEDERATION OF TRADE UNIONS.

TRADING WITH THE ENEMY: essentially a matter of municipal law in most countries trading with alien enemies becomes, ipso facto, illegal upon the outbreak of war, unless allowed by special license. *See e.g.,* Trading with the Enemy Act of 1917, 40 Stat. 411, 50 U.C.S. App. sec.1 and IRAN-CONTRA AFFAIR (1986).

TRADEMARK REGISTRATION AGREEMENT (1968): current regime for international recognition and control of trademarks under the auspices of the WORLD INTELLECTUAL PROPERTY ORGANIZATION (q.v.). *See* 828 U.N.T.S. 389.

TRADITION OF TERRITORY: the formal transfer of possession of ceded territory from one sovereign to another. Tradition is not necessary to complete the transfer. *See* 1 I.L.R. 84.

TRAFFIC a wildlife trade monitoring group affiliated with the World Wildfife Fund. *See* 8 Dick. J. Int'l L. 218.

TRAFFIC ACCIDENT CONVENTION (1968): sponsored by the Hague Conference on Private International Law to establish common provisions on the law applicable to civil noncontractual liability arising out of traffic accidents. *See* 8 I.L.M. 34.

TRAFFIC IN WHITE SLAVES: *see* WHITE SLAVE TRAFFIC.

TRAFFIC IN SLAVES: *see* SLAVE TRADE.

TRAFFIC SEPARATION: routing of ships in shipping lanes to avoid collisions (or aircraft in air ways). *See* 28 U.S.T. 3459.

TRAGEDY OF THE COMMONS: problem which arises when the whole community has the right to unlimited use of a limited resource, and it is in no individual's interest to conserve the resource. The resource is eventually destroyed, e.g., the community has a common pasture, everyone tries to graze as many cattle as possible on it and the pasture is trampled to dust. The phrase may be applied to many environmental problems facing the world.

TRAIL SMELTER ARBITRATION: a Canadian smelting plant discharged sulfur dioxide which was carried by winds into the United States causing extensive damage to crops, timber, and livestock. An arbitral tribunal, held Canada responsible for the present as well as the future activities of the smelter, stated "under the principles of international law . . . no state has the right to use or permit the use of its territory in such manner as to cause injury by fumes in or to the territory of another . . . when the case is of serious consequences and the injury is established by clear and convincing evidence," 3 R.I.A.A. 1903, 1965 (1949).

TRAITE-CONTRATS (F): treaties that are contractual in nature, e.g., a bilateral air transport agreement exchanging rights to conduct scheduled air service between the two countries, sometimes distinguished from TRAITE-LOIS (q.v.). *See* 13 R.I.A.A. 396.

TRAITE DES BLANCHES (F): WHITE SLAVE TRAFFIC (q.v.).

TRAITE-LOIS (F): law-making treaties, e.g., the Geneva Conventions on the Laws of War, sometimes distinguished from TRAITE-CONTRATS (q.v.).

TRAITEMENT: the mention of the addressee's title of courtesy at the beginning of a note.

TRANSBORDER DATA FLOW: a subject of concern on two fronts; the closed societies wish to control the flow of news from their countries (*see* New International Information Order), and the western industrial nations are concerned with the loss of valuable technical information and the invasion of privacy of the individuals by the use of computers and telecommunications. *See* 6 Boston College Int'l and Comp. L.R. 591.

TRANSBOUNDARY MOVEMENT OF HAZARDOUS WASTE CONVENTION (1989): United Nations sponsored agreement to control the international transport of hazardous waste. *See* 28 I.L.M. 649.

TRANSFER OF FLAG: changing the state of registry of a ship so that it then flies the flag of another country. The Reagan administration transferred the registry of several Kuwaiti oil tankers to the United States registry and, thus provided them with the protection of the United States' flag. *See* 29 Va.J.Int'l.L. 387.

TRANSFER OF NUCLEAR MATERIALS: basic rules of the international transport of nuclear materials are found in the Convention on the Physical Protection of Nuclear Materials, 18 I.L.M. 1419.

TRANSFER OF POPULATIONS: evacuations of civilians may be made for military necessity or for the civilians protection. *See* Art. 49 of the GENEVA CONVENTION IV (1949).

TRANSFER OF TECHNOLOGY: passage of industrial know-how to another country as part of a sale or a development program. The transfer sometimes takes place illegally in contravention of patent laws or national security measures. *See* 14 I.L.M. 1329 and 3 Inter-American Legal Materials 356.

TRANSFRONTIER COOPERATION: joint action between councils, counties, intercommunity units, or other local authorities of neighboring states directed at strengthening the relations between the respective states.

TRANSFRONTIER POLLUTION: generally, industrial pollutants that cross national boundaries and cause harm beyond the jurisdiction where they are created. The problem is the subject of several treaties, *see* 18 I.L.M. 1442 and 30 I.L.M. 800. *See also* TRAIL SMELTER ARBITRATION.

TRANSFRONTIER TELEVISION CONVENTION (1989): attempt by the COUNCIL OF EUROPE (q.v.) to expand the availability of television programs for the populations of member states. *See* 28 I.L.M. 857.

TRANSJORDAN: the portion of Palestine on the East Bank of the Jordan River.

TRANSNATIONAL CORPORATION: business organization which conducts business in more than one country on a regular basis. *See Transnational Corporations in World Development:* Trends and Prospects (1988).

TRANSNATIONAL ENTERPRISE: general term for commercial ventures involving parties and activities in more than one country. *See* CODES OF CONDUCT.

TRANSNATIONAL GOVERNMENT OF NATIONAL UNITY (GUNT): established by the efforts of the ORGANIZATION OF AFRICAN UNITY (q.v.) in 1979, to end the CHADIAN CIVIL WAR (q.v.), it quickly broke down and became another faction in the renewed civil war.

TRAVEL CONTRACTS CONVENTION (CCV): UNIDROIT (q.v.) sponsored convention to unify the law of travel contracts among the parties. *See* 9 I.L.M. 699.

TRAVEL DOCUMENTS: documents that are issued by governments to permit or facilitate travel. *See* PASSPORT, VISA, LAISSEZ-PASSER, and MILITARY PASSPORT.

TRAVAUX PREPARATOIRES (F): preparatory works; the documents and proceedings of the meetings where a treaty is drafted. Some courts allow their use as tools for interpretation of treaty language. *See Fothergill v. Monarch Airlines*, (1980) 2 All.E.R. 696.

TREACHERY: an act of PERFIDY (q.v.).

TREASON: breach of a subjects allegiance to his sovereign. *See* 16 I.L.R. 239. *See also*, PERDUELLIO, CRIMEN LAESAE MAJESTATIS, and HIGH TREASON.

TREATIES AND OTHER INTERNATIONAL ACTS (T.A.I.S.): United States Department of State publication of treaties in pamphlet form. Prior to being compiled into United States Treaties and Other International Agreements the pamphlets are referred to by a T.A.I.S. number.

TREATY: formal agreement entered into between states in order to define or modify their mutual duties and obligations. Although, there are no technical rules in international law as to treaty form, generally a treaty consists of a preamble, the body, final clauses, and concludes with a testimonium and signatures. Ratification by each of the signatory states is usually required. *See*, VIENNA CONVENTION ON THE LAW OF TREATIES.

TREUGA DEI (L): peace of God; custom of war to suspend fighting for religious holidays, especially Christmas.

TREVES PERCHERESSES (F): fishing truce under which fishing vessels are left unmolested during a war. This was a common practice between Great Britain and France during their many wars.

TRIAD: the United States nuclear weapons policy which states that land, naval, and air based weapons should be deployed giving deterrence as broad a base as possible so that an enemy attacking the United States would have a very difficult time successfully attacking all three types of weapons, and thus, the threat of retaliation is insured.

TRIAGE: system for allocating medical care or other aid by dividing the needy into three groups - slightly needy, needy, and hopelessly needy - and concentrating aid on the middle group who will benefit most from the aid. *See* 8 Psychology Today 40 (Sept. 1974).

TRIAL IN ABSENTIA: trial of a criminal defendant who is not present. A number of war criminals were tried in this manner.

TRIANON PEACE TREATY (1920): ended World War I as between the allied powers and Hungary. The treaty reduced Hungary's territory by two-thirds and its population by three-fifths. Although, Hungary was obligated to pay proportionate war reparations to the allies, an exact amount was not specified. *See* 3 Toynbee, *Major Peace Treaties of Modern History* at 1863.

TRIBAL POPULATION: *see* INDIGENOUS POPULATION.

TRIESTE: port in northeastern Italy which was a free city claimed by both Italy and Yugoslavia after World War II. *See* 4 Stanford L.Rev. 112 and 45 Am.J.Int.L. 541.

TRIGGER PRICE MECHANISM: United States policy to stem the flow of low cost steel into the United States which was wiping out the United States steel industry. When imported steel was sold below a "trigger price," fast track anti-dumping procedures were followed. *See* 17 I.L.M. 952.

TRILATERAL COMMISSION: a private international group founded by David Rockefeller to promote cooperation among the United States, Western Europe, and Japan. They publish a journal, *Trialog*. The yahoos believe they control the world. *See* 35 Stanford L.Rev. 633 and 647.

TRINITY HOUSE RULES: code of regulation of seamanship (e.g., rules of the road) which were enforced by English Courts of Admiralty. *See e.g., The Duke of Sussex*, 1 Wm. Rob. 274 (1841).

TRIOKA: a dictatorship of three; executive power exercised by a group of three.

TRIPOLI DECLARATION (August 1982): at an informal meeting of thirty-five Organization of African Unity members, after the failure of the organization to meet because of the walkout of some states after the admission of SADR (q.v.), this declaration by those present attempted to continue the work of the organization and to reconvene a summit at Tripoli at a later date.

TRIPOLI DECLARATION (November 1982): final document of the second attempt of 1982, to hold an Organization of African Unity Summit. It made provisions for the continuance of the work of the organization.

TRIPOLAR SYSTEM: world order in which there would be a third force sufficient to counter the influence of the two superpowers. No such force has yet arisen.

TROPICAL TIMBER AGREEMENT (1983): United Nations effort to regulate the harvesting and consumption of tropical forest wood. *.See* 23 I.L.M. 1195.

TRUCE: agreement between belligerents to discontinue military operations. *See* SPECIAL TRUCE and GENERAL TRUCE.

TRUCE ENVOY: one bearing a message about a truce. *See* Art. 32 of the Annex to the HAGUE CONVENTION RESPECTING LAWS AND CUSTOMS OF WAR ON LAND (1907).

TRUCE FLAG: historically, the means for initiating truce negotiations between belligerents has been the display of a white flag by the party who wishes to surrender or open communications with a view to concluding a truce. A white flag has no other significance in international law.

TRUCE SYSTEM: United Nations operations to arrange cease fires and establish UN forces to patrol the separation of the belligerents. *See e.g.*, UNITED NATIONS FORCES IN CYPRUS.

TRUMAN DOCTRINE (1947): package of economic assistance and U.S. personel sent to Greece and Turkey to stabilize the situation there. It was the beginning of the policy of containment of Soviet expansionism into western and southern Europe. *See* 61 Stat. 103.

TRUMAN PROCLAMATION: policy statement by the United States President that the seabed and subsurface resources of the continental shelf were under the jurisdiction of the United States. *See* 40 Am.J.Int.L.Supp. 45, 47.

TRUMAN'S TWELVE POINTS: restatement of principles of United States foreign policy. *See* N.Y. Times, Oct.28, 1945.

TRUST TERRITORY: non-self-governing territory under the United Nations' international trusteeship system. These territories are administered by one or more of the member states or the UN for political, economic, educational, and social advancement of the inhabitants. It is a matter of agreement as to which territories will be brought under the trusteeship system and upon what terms. *See* UNITED NATIONS CHARTER, Chapters XI, XII, and XIII.

TRUSTEE'S COUNCIL OF THE UNITED NATIONS: *See* UNITED NATIONS TRUSTEESHIP SYSTEM.

TRUSTEESHIP: international rule over a territory under the UNITED NATIONS TRUSTEESHIP SYSTEM (q.v.). *See* TRUST TERRITORY.

TRYGVE LIE PLAN (1950): proposed 20 year plan for UN efforts to strengthen peace formulated by UN Secretary General Trygve Lie. *See* U.N. Bulletin, April 1, 1950.

TUNISIA-LIBYA CONTINENTAL SHELF CASE: the International Court of Justice settled the boundary between Tunisia and Libya, and has been criticized for not applying law but merely compromising the claims of the two states. *See* 77 Am.J.Int.L. 219.

TWENTY-FOUR HOUR RULE: a warship at the outbreak of war must leave a neutral port within twenty-four hours. *See* Arts. 12-14, HAGUE CONVENTION RESPECTING THE RIGHTS AND DUTIES OF NEUTRALS IN CASE OF NAVAL WARFARE.

TWINNINGS: association of local communities belonging to different states. These alliances are usually formed without use of legally binding instruments of cooperation. They are often called sister cities.

TWO BLOCK SYSTEM: community structure where the population divides rather evenly into two parties giving a balance of power, and the ability to make yes-no decisions. The world followed a two block system for a short while, before the THIRD WORLD (q.v.) became independent of the east and west.

TWO FREEDOMS AGREEMENT: *see* INTERNATIONAL AIR SERVICE TRANSIT AGREEMENT.

U-2 INCIDENT: when the Soviet Union shot down a U-2 (U.S. spy plane) over their territory, the United States refused to apologize for the violation of Soviet airspace, and the summit meeting then scheduled was cancelled. The pilot, Francis Gary Powers, was tried by the Soviets and later released. *See* 54 Am.J.Int.L. 836.

UAM: UNION OF AFRICAN AND MALAGASY STATES (q.v.).

UAS: UNION OF AFRICAN STATES (q.v.).

UBI JUS, IBI REMEDIUM: where there is a right, there is a remedy.

UBIQUITAT (G): concurrent jurisdiction. *See* 80 I.L.R. 383.

ULTIMATE DESTINATION: the nature of goods as contraband is determined by the place where they will end their journey, not by an intervening neutral port. *See* CONTINUOUS VOYAGE.

ULTIMA RATIO (L): the final or best argument; the use of force as one's final argument.

ULTIMATUM: a communications containing final and categorical terms with respect to a dispute between states; rejection which may break diplomatic relations or even lead to war. *See* 26 I.L.R. 647.

ULTRA PETITA (L): more than the petitioner requested. A judicial doctrine that the court will not make an award greater than the relief that the petitioner sought, even though the court may feel more is justified.

ULTRA POSSE NEMO TENETUR (L): what is not possible cannot exist.

UN: UNITED NATIONS (q.v.).

UN DOC: UNITED NATIONS DOCUMENT (q.v.).

UNANCHORED MINE: mines which are not fixed in place and, therefore, pose a threat to all shipping and are illegal in that their use does not discriminate between belligerent and neutral shipping.

UNANIMITY RULE: typical rule for decision-making in many international organizations where all members must agree on a decision before it comes into effect. *See* CONSENSUS.

UNAT: UNITED NATIONS ADMINISTRATIVE TRIBUNAL (q.v.).

UNAVM: UNITED NATIONS ANGOLA VERIFICATION MISSION (q.v.).

UNCITRAL: UNITED NATIONS COMMISSION ON INTERNATIONAL TRADE LAW (q.v.).

UNCITRAL ARBITRATION RULES: widely used procedure for dispute settlement in international dealings. *See* 15 I.L.M. 701.

UNCLOS: UNITED NATIONS CONFERENCE ON THE LAW OF THE SEA (q.v.).

UNCONDITIONAL SURRENDER: SURRENDER (q.v.) without any assurances of the treatment which will be had by the defeated party. *See* CAPITULATION.

UNCTAD: UNITED NATIONS CONFERENCE ON TRADE AND DEVELOPMENT (q.v.).

UNCTAD II ACTION PLAN: *see* CHARTER OF ALGIERS.

UNCTAD CODE OF CONDUCT FOR MULTINATIONAL CORPORATIONS: a failed effort of the NEW INTERNATIONAL ECONOMIC ORDER (q.v.). *See* 30 Am.U.L.Rev. 941.

UNCURK: UNITED NATIONS COMMISSION FOR THE UNIFICATION AND REHABILITATION OF KOREA (q.v.).

UNDEFENDED LOCALITIES: *see* OPEN PLACES or OPEN CITIES.

UNDEN PLAN (1961): proposal by Swedish Foreign Minister Unden calling for agreement among non-nuclear nations to agree to not acquire nuclear weapons. *See* SWEDISH RESOLUTION.

UNDERSTANDING: an informal agreement between states usually involving a minor matter, or a sensitive matter to which they do not wish to call attention.

UNDOF: UNITED NATIONS DISENGAGEMENT OBSERVER FORCE (q.v.).

UNDP: UNITED NATIONS DEVELOPMENT PROGRAM (q.v.).

UNEF: UNITED NATIONS EMERGENCY FORCE (q.v.).

UNEP: UNITED NATIONS ENVIRONMENT PROGRAM (q.v.).

UNEQUAL TREATY: international agreement where the bargaining power of the two sides is so unequal that the agreement lacks mutuality and is, therefore, unenforceable against the weaker party.

UNESCO: UNITED NATIONS EDUCATIONAL, SCIENTIFIC, AND CULTURAL ORGANIZATION (q.v.).

UNFICYP: UNITED NATIONS FORCES IN CYPRUS (q.v.).

UNFRIENDLY ACT: act that is declared to be unfriendly by the parties involved, e.g., state A says to state B, "if you sell arms to state C, we will consider that an unfriendly act and proceed accordingly."

UNGA: UNITED NATIONS GENERAL ASSEMBLY (q.v.).

UNICEF: UNITED NATIONS CHILDREN'S FUND (q.v.).

UNICUM (L): dispute which is unique and thus cannot be decided on the basis of general rules or principles. *See* 84 Am.J.Int.L. 838.

UNIDO: UNITED NATIONS INDUSTRIAL DEVELOPMENT ORGANIZATION (q.v.).

UNIDROIT: INTERNATIONAL INSTITUTE FOR THE UNIFICATION OF PRIVATE LAW (q.v.).

UNIFICATION OF LAWS: efforts by a number of international organizations to make the municipal laws of the countries of a region or the entire world as uniform as possible, thus, eliminating conflicts of laws problems. *See e.g., INTERNATIONAL INSTITUTE FOR THE UNIFICATION OF PRIVATE LAW.*

UNIFIL: UNITED NATIONS INTERIM FORCES IN LEBANON (q.v.).

UNIFORM CUSTOMS AND PRACTICES FOR DOCUMENTARY CREDITS: widely accepted rules published by the International Chamber of Commerce (q.v.) governing the use of letters of credit in international trade.

UNILATERAL ACT: acts done by an individual state within its capacity, e.g., the recognition of another state or the sending of a note of protest.

UNION DE PAISES EXPORTADORES DE BANANAS (UPEB): ineffective attempt to establish an international banana producers' cartel. *See* U.N.T.S. Series I/21294.

UNION OF AFRICAN AND MALAGASY STATES: organization of the Congo, Ivory Coast, Senegal, Mauritania, Burkino

Faso, Benin, Niger, Chad, Central African Republic, Gabon, Cameroon, and Malagasy formed Dec. 19, 1960, at the BRAZ-ZAVILLE CONFERENCE (q.v.).

UNION OF AFRICAN STATES: established by Ghana, Guinea, and Mali in 1961, in hopes of eventually becoming the United States of Africa. *See* 1 Whiteman, *Digest of International Law* 429.

UNION OF AMERICAN REPUBLICS: *see* PAN-AMERICAN UNION.

UNION OF INDEPENDENT AFRICAN STATES: failed attempt at African unity begun as the Ghana-Guinea Union in 1959. *See* 1 Whiteman, *Digest of International Law* 428.

UNIPOM: United Nations India-Pakistan Observation Mission, *see* KASHMIR QUESTION (1947).

UNISPACE '82: Second UN Conference on the Exploration and Peaceful Uses of Outerspace. *See* 7 Annals of Air and Space Law 510.

UNITA: Uniao Nacionial par la Independencia Total de Angola, western supported faction in the ANGOLAN CIVIL WAR (q.v.).

UNITAR: UNITED NATIONS INSTITUTE FOR TRAINING AND RESEARCH (q.v.).

UNITED ARAB REPUBLIC: name of an abortive union between Egypt and Syria (1958-1961) and retained by Egypt.

UNITED INTERNATIONAL BUREAU FOR THE PROTECTION OF INTELLECTUAL PROPERTY (BIRPI): international organization to promote cooperation, and unify the law of patents among its members. It has been superseded by the WORLD INTELLECTUAL PROPERTY ORGANIZATION (q.v.). *See e.g.,* 7 I.L.M. 981 and 9 I.L.M. 978.

UNITED KINGDOM V. NORWAY: *see* NORWEGIAN FISHER-IES CASE.

UNITED NATIONS: 1) Name for the allied nations in World War II (United States, Soviet Union, Great Britain, Australia, etc.) *See* 55 Stat. 1600, 3 Bevans 697. 2) World organization formed after World War II to replace the LEAGUE OF NATIONS (q.v.), its charter was adopted at the San Francisco Conference in 1945. *See* 59 Stat. 1031, 3 Bevans 1153.

UNITED NATIONS ADMINISTRATIVE TRIBUNAL (UNAT): nine-member body elected by the General Assembly to review complaints and issues related to the conditions of employment of UN staff members.

UNITED NATIONS ANGOLA VERIFICATION MISSION (UNAVM): groups established to supervise the withdrawal of Cuban troops from Angola. *See* 28 I.L.M. 961.

UNITED NATIONS CAPITAL DEVELOPMENT FUND: rather unsuccessful attempt at development. The money was not forthcoming, and the administration of the "fund" was turned over to the UNITED NATIONS DEVELOPMENT PROGRAM (q.v.). *See* 13 Whiteman, *Digest of International Law* 617.

UNITED NATIONS CHARTER: the organic document of the United Nations adopted by the San Francisco Conference in 1945. *See* 59 Stat. 1031, 3 Bevans 1153.

UNITED NATIONS CHILDREN'S FUND (UNICEF): special body of the UNITED NATIONS ECONOMIC AND SOCIAL COUNCIL (q.v.), to aid children who are war victims and to help support child health activities in general.

UNITED NATIONS COMMISSION FOR THE UNIFICATION AND REHABILITATION OF KOREA (UNCURK): a seven-nation body, established by UNGA Res. 376 (V), to advise the Unified Command in Korea on relief measures.

UNITED NATIONS COMMISSION ON INTERNATIONAL TRADE LAW (UNCITRAL): body charged with the development of trade law conventions. They drafted UNCITRAL ARBITRATION RULES, the HAMBURG RULES, and the INTERNATIONAL SALE OF GOODS CONVENTION (qq.v.). *See* 27 Am.J.Comp.L. 201.

UNITED NATIONS CONFERENCE ON CONSULAR RELATIONS (1963): meeting which drafted the VIENNA CONVENTION ON CONSULAR RELATIONS (q.v.).

UNITED NATIONS CONFERENCE ON DIPLOMATIC INTERCOURSE AND IMMUNITY (1961): meeting in Vienna, Austria which drafted the VIENNA CONVENTION ON DIPLOMATIC RELATIONS (q.v.).

UNITED NATIONS CONFERENCE ON DISARMAMENT (1969): *see* 1969 U.N. Yearbook 3-12.

UNITED NATIONS CONFERENCE ON FOOD AND AGRICULTURE (1943): *see* 37 Am.J.Int.L.Supp. 159.

UNITED NATIONS CONFERENCE ON FREEDOM OF INFORMATION (1948): drafted three conventions, and draft articles on freedom of information for the DECLARATION OF HUMAN RIGHTS and the COVENANT ON HUMAN RIGHTS (q.q.v.). *See* 1947-48 U.N. Yearbook 588. *Contra see* NEW INTERNATIONAL INFORMATION ORDER.

UNITED NATIONS CONFERENCE ON THE LAW OF THE SEA III: meeting convened in 1973, to rewrite the law of the sea; they drafted the LAW OF THE SEA CONVENTION (1982) (q.v.). Two previous United Nations Conferences on the Law of the Sea were held in 1958 and 1960.

UNITED NATIONS CONFERENCE ON TRADE AND DEVELOPMENT (UNCTAD): hybrid in the United Nations organization - a cross between the Economic and Social Council and a specialized agency - its work has been primarily to promote the

NEW INTERNATIONAL ECONOMIC ORDER (q.v.). *See* 7 J.W.T.L. 527.

UNITED NATIONS DECLARATION (1942): originally signed by 26 allies fighting against the axis states in World War II. They declared that they would cooperate in winning the war and not make a separate peace. *See* 55 Stat. 1600, 3 Bevans 697.

UNITED NATIONS DEVELOPMENT PROGRAM: central co-ordinating agency for United Nations efforts at assisting developing countries. *See* 1965 U.N. Yearbook 270.

UNITED NATIONS DISARMAMENT COMMISSION: consultative organ of the General Assembly to make recommendations on disarmament issues. *See* 1952 U.N. Yearbook 312.

UNITED NATIONS DISENGAGEMENT OBSERVER FORCE (UNDOF): military force established to provide a buffer between Israeli and Syrian forces along their border after the end of the YOM KIPPUR WAR (q.v.). *See United Nations Chronicle,* Jan. 1984, p. 80.

UNITED NATIONS DOCUMENT (U.N. DOC): an official publication of the UN including official records of proceedings, draft conventions, reports, and studies. *See Catalog of United Nations Publications.*

UNITED NATIONS DOCUMENT NUMBER: alphanumeric designator used to arrange UN documents by UN organ and subject.

UNITED NATIONS ECONOMIC AND SOCIAL COUNCIL (ECOSOC): body with main responsibility for United Nations activities involving economic and social development. It coordinates the activities of the specialized agencies. *See* W.R. Sharp, *The United Nations Economic and Social Council* (1969).

UNITED NATIONS ECONOMIC COMMISSION: *see* ECONOMIC COMMISSION FOR ASIA AND THE FAR EAST, ECO-

NOMIC COMMISSION FOR AFRICA and ECONOMIC COM-
MISSION FOR LATIN AMERICA.

**UNITED NATIONS EDUCATIONAL, SCIENTIFIC AND CUL-
TURAL ORGANIZATION (UNESCO):** specialized agency to
promote education, scientific and cultural exchanges; and to develop respect for justice, the rule of law, human rights, and fundamental freedoms. Recently, it has so worked against its stated
program that several countries, including the United States, have
withdrawn. *See* 12 Brooklyn J. Int'l L. 161.

UNITED NATIONS EMERGENCY FORCE (UNEF): attempt by
the General Assembly to establish a multinational armed force to
intervene in the SUEZ CRISIS (1956) (q.v.). The Soviet Union objected that this was a violation of the prerogatives of the Security
Council. *See* Rosner, *The United Nations Emergency Forces* (1963).

UNITED NATIONS ENVIRONMENT PROGRAM (UNEP): established to follow-up and implement the recommendations of
the STOCKHOLM DECLARATION ON HUMAN ENVIRON-
MENT (1972) (q.v.). *See* 14 I.L.M. 1070.

UNITED NATIONS FORCES: a number of United Nations military operations have been carried out by multinational forces under the United Nations command. *See e.g.*, UNITED NATIONS
FORCES IN CYPRUS and 52 Am.J.Int.L. 229.

UNITED NATIONS FORCES IN CYPRUS (UNFICYP): established in 1964, to separate the Greek and Turkish communities on
Cyprus which had been engaged in a civil war. *See* 11 U.N. Review (April 1964) p.14.

UNITED NATIONS GENERAL ASSEMBLY: meeting of representatives of all members of the UN which may discuss and make
recommendations to other UN organs and decide questions involving the UN's internal organization, e.g., admission of new
members. *See* (1959) II Recueil des Cours 207-92.

UNITED NATIONS HABITAT AND HUMAN SETTLEMENT FOUNDATION: part of the UNITED NATIONS ENVIRON-MENT PROGRAM (q.v.) which collects voluntary contributions to improve human habitation. *See* 2 Environmental Policy and the Law 114.

UNITED NATIONS HEADQUARTERS AGREEMENT: between the United States and the United Nations establishing the UN headquarters in New York. *See* 61 Stat. 3416, 11 U.N.T.S. II, 43 Am.J.Int.L.Supp. 8.

UNITED NATIONS HIGH COMMISSIONER FOR REFU-GEES: principal United Nations official responsible for refugee problems. *See* 78 Am.J.Int.L. 480-84 and 57 Brit. Y.B.Int'l.L. 317-36.

UNITED NATIONS INDUSTRIAL DEVELOPMENT ORGANI-ZATION: agency established by UNGA Res 2152 (XXI) (Nov. 17,1966) to promote industrial development. *See* 18 I.L.M. 667 and 18 J.W.T.L. 553-55.

UNITED NATIONS INSTITUTE FOR TRAINING AND RE-SEARCH (UNITAR): autonomous institution organizing seminars and sponsoring studies aimed at improving the effectiveness of the United Nations. *See* 30 Int'l Org. 163-71 and UNITAR News.

UNITED NATIONS INTERIM FORCES IN LEBANON (UNI-FIL): after the Israeli invasion of Lebanon in 1978, to expel the PLO forces there, this force was established to confirm the withdrawal of the Israelis and to provide a buffer force between them and the Lebanese. *See* U.N. Chronicle, Ap. 1982, at 13.

UNITED NATIONS IRAQ-KUWAIT OBSERVATION MIS-SION: see 30 I.L.M. 843.

UNITED NATIONS KOREAN RECONSTRUCTION AGENCY (UNKRA): *see* UNGA Res. A/1567.

UNITED NATIONS MARITIME CONFERENCE: *see* GENEVA CONFERENCE ON THE LAW OF THE SEA (1958).

UNITED NATIONS MONETARY AND FINANCIAL CONFERENCE (1944): *see* BRETTON WOODS AGREEMENT (1944).

UNITED NATIONS NATIONALS: any individual, corporation, or association that is a national of one of the United Nations, i.e., the allies during World War II. *See* 22 I.L.R. 443.

UNITED NATIONS MILITARY OBSERVER GROUP IN INDIA AND PAKISTAN (UNMOGIP): *see* KASHMIR QUESTION and 1955 Int'l Org. 19.

UNITED NATIONS OBSERVER GROUP IN YEMEN (UNYOM): force to monitor the withdrawal of Great Britain from its former territory in 1963.

UNITED NATIONS OBSERVATION GROUP IN LEBANON (UNOGIL): sent to Lebanon during the crisis that led to the BEIRUT INVASION (1958) (q.v.) by United States forces.

UNITED NATIONS OFFICE OF PUBLIC INFORMATION: office of the United Nations Secretariat responsible for public relations.

UNITED NATIONS PARTICIPATION ACT: United States legislation implementing participation in UNITED NATIONS (q.v.) activities. *See* 59 Stat. 619 (1945), 22 U.S.C. Sec. 287.

UNITED NATIONS PEACEKEEPING SYSTEM: efforts voted by the Security Council under the provisions of Chapter VII of the UNITED NATIONS CHARTER (q.v.), including the establishment of observer and peacekeeping forces. *See* 64 Am.J.Int.L. 241.

UNITED NATIONS PREPARATORY COMMISSION: interim group to carry out the program established for the United Nations at the SAN FRANCISCO CONFERENCE (1945) until the formal structure of the organization could be put in place. *See* 14 Whiteman, *Digest of International Law* 327.

UNITED NATIONS RACIAL CONVENTION: *see* ELIMINATION OF ALL FORMS OF RACIAL DISCRIMINATION CONVENTION (1965).

UNITED NATIONS RELIEF AND REHABILITATION ADMINISTRATION (UNRRA): founded in 1943, by 44 countries to provide relief to those in countries liberated by the allied forces in World War II. Its operations were taken over by various United Nations agencies in 1947. *See* Woodbridge, *UNRRA:* the History (1950), and 38 Am.J.Int.L. 650.

UNITED NATIONS RELIEF AND WORKS AGENCY FOR PALESTINIAN REFUGEES IN THE MIDDLE EAST (UNRWA): *see* 1966 U.N. Yearbook 179.

UNITED NATIONS SCIENTIFIC COMMITTEE ON THE EFFECTS OF ATOMIC RADIATION (UNSCEAR): *See* International Atomic Energy Agency Bulletin (Dec. 1982).

UNITED NATIONS SECRETARIAT: established by Arts. 7, 12 and 97-101 of the UNITED NATIONS CHARTER (q.v.), it is the executive branch of the United Nations conducting the day-to-day administration of the organization. *See* 49 Am.J.Int.L. 295.

UNITED NATIONS SECRETARY GENERAL: chief operating officer of the UNITED NATIONS (q.v.). *See* UNITED NATIONS SECRETARIAT.

UNITED NATIONS SECURITY COUNCIL: *see* SECURITY COUNCIL.

UNITED NATIONS SPECIAL COMMITTEE ON THE BALKANS: first dispatch of military observers by the U.N. Security Council. *See* UNGA Res. 109 (II).

UNITED NATIONS SPECIAL FUND: fund made up of voluntary monetary contributions for social and economic projects of the United Nations. *See* 13 Whiteman, *Digest of International Law* 305.

UNITED NATIONS SPECIALIZED AGENCIES: *see* SPECIALIZED AGENCIES OF THE UNITED NATIONS.

UNITED NATIONS TEMPORARY AUXILIARY GROUP (UNTAG): group established to supervise elections in the process of freeing Namabia from South African colonial rule. *See* 28 I.L.M. 952.

UNITED NATIONS TEMPORARY EXECUTIVE AUTHORITY IN WEST GUINEA (UNTEA): group which supervised the withdrawal of the Dutch from Indonesia. *See* A.M. Taylor, *Indonesian Independence and the United Nations* (1960).

UNITED NATIONS TREATY SERIES (UNTS): publication containing the text of treaties registered with the UN Secretary General pursuant to Art. 102 of the UNITED NATIONS CHARTER (q.v.), it continues such publication in the League of Nations Treaty Series.

UNITED NATIONS TRUCE SUPERVISORY ORGANIZATION (UNTSO): the UN force to supervise the truce between Arabs and Jews in 1947, after the declaration of Israeli statehood and the ensuing war. *See* 3 Whiteman, *Digest of International Law* 523-561.

UNITED NATIONS TRUSTEESHIP SYSTEM: system to govern non-self governing territories liberated after World War II. *See* 27 Brit.Y.B.Int'l.L. 164.

UNITED NATIONS UNIVERSITY: established in Tokyo by UNGA Res. 2951 (XXVII), it is really an umbrella organization for national and UN sponsored research institutions. *See* U.N. Chronicle, Sept. 1983, p. 80.

UNITED STATES COURT OF INTERNATIONAL TRADE: federal court with jurisdiction over cases involving United States trade law, especially cases of anti-dumping and countervailing duties. *See* 10 Boston College Int'l and Comp. L.R. 173-274.

UNITED STATES DIPLOMATIC AND CONSULAR STAFF IN TEHERAN CASE: action brought by the United States before the International Court of Justice to try to free hostages held by the revolutionary government in Iran after the fall of the Shah. *See* 1979 I.C.J. Report 7 and 1980 I.C.J. Report 3 and 74 Am.J.Int.L. 395.

UNITED STATES INTERNATIONAL TRADE COMMISSION: an independent regulatory agency of the United States government which studies international trade issues and administers the import relief laws of the United States. *See* 12 Canada-U.S.L.J. 187.

UNITED STATES-IRAN CLAIMS TRIBUNAL: judicial body established in 1981, by an agreement between the United States and Iran to settle claims arising out of the conflict between the two countries after the fall of the Shah. Reports of their decisions are published by Grotius Publications as the United States-Iran Claims Tribunal Reports. *See* 20 I.L.M. 224 and Dames and Moore v. Regan, 453 U.S. 654 (1981).

UNITED STATES-MEXICO INTERNATIONAL BOUNDARY AND WATER COMMISSION: group to solve problems concerning the United States-Mexico border, and the waters of the rivers forming it. *See* 7 I.L.M. 320.

UNITED STATES NATIONALS IN MOROCCO CASE: the International Court of Justice dealt with the rights of United States nationals *vis-a-vis* the French colonial government which discriminated in favor of French nationals. See 2 Int'l.& Comp.L.Q. 354-367.

UNITED STATES TRADE REPRESENTATIVE: United States government official watchdog of foreign trade, GATT complainers, etc. *See* 14 I.L.M. 181.

UNITED STATES-U.S.S.R FISHERIES CLAIMS BOARD: judicial body to settle fishing disputes between the United States and the Soviet Union. *See* 14 I.L.M. 447.

UNITING FOR PEACE RESOLUTION: United Nations General Assembly Resolution urging the Security Council to act to maintain peace. *See* 45 Am.J.Int.L.Supp. 1 and 20 Colum.J.Transnatat'l.L 1.

UNIVERSAL COPYRIGHT CONVENTION (1952): each contracting state undertakes to protect the literary property of copyright holders through their own legal systems. *See* 6 U.S.T. 2731, 216 U.N.T.S. 132, 49 Am.J.Int.L.Supp. 149.

UNIVERSAL DECLARATION OF HUMAN RIGHTS (1948): United Nations General Assembly Resolution stating, *inter alia*, that all human beings are born free and equal and have the right to life, liberty, and security in their persons. *See* 43 Am.J.Int.L.Supp. 127.

UNIVERSAL POSTAL CONVENTION: international agreement to facilitate postal services, *see* UNIVERSAL POSTAL UNION.

UNIVERSAL POSTAL UNION (UPU): established in 1875, to set rates for international mail, and to improve postal service and international cooperation. The current version of the organization is governed by a constitution adopted in 1974, 16 U.S.T. 1291.

UNIVERSAL SUCCESSION: takes place when one state completely absorbs another and the latter is extinguished.

UNIVERSALIST INSTITUTIONS: organization open to all relevant interested parties, e.g., the United Nations is open to all nations (under certain conditions).

UNIVERSALITY: including all the relevant members.

UNIVERSITATES SUPERIOREM RECOGNOSCUNT (L): a community which acknowledges a superior division of communities, in the theory of Bartolus concerning sovereignty.

UNIVERSITY ENTRANCE REQUIREMENTS CONVENTION (1965): parties agreed to eliminate obstacles for admission to Universities and to recognize degrees granted. *See* 218 U.N.T.S. 125 and 514 U.N.T.S. 270.

UNIVERSITY FOR PEACE: international center for post graduate studies established by the United Nations in Costa Rica. *See* UNGA Res 35/55 (XIV) (5 Dec. 1980).

UNJUST ENRICHMENT: gain of wealth which is not produced by legal activities or is a result of an ABUSE OF RIGHT (q.v.).

UNJUST WAR: a war which is not preceded by a legitimate cause upon which the instigator may act; now called an ILLEGAL WAR (q.v.).

UNKRA: UNITED NATIONS KOREAN RECONSTRUCTION AGENCY (q.v.).

UNMOGIP: UNITED NATIONS MILITARY OBSERVER GROUP IN INDIA AND PAKISTAN (q.v.).

UNNEUTRAL SERVICE: activities of a neutral ship which expose it to liability as a belligerent, e.g., carrying CONTRABAND (q.v.).

UNOGIL: UNITED NATIONS OBSERVATION GROUP IN LEBANON (q.v.).

UNPA: *see* UNITED NATIONS PARTICIPATION ACT.

UNPRIVILEGED BELLIGERENCY: acts of persons participating in war-making which are outside the protection offered by the LAWS OF WAR (q.v.), e.g., a SPY (q.v.).

UNRRA: UNITED NATIONS RELIEF AND REHABILITATION ADMINISTRATION (q.v.).

UNRWA: UNITED NATIONS RELIEF AND WORKS AGENCY FOR PALESTINIAN REFUGEES IN THE MIDDLE EAST (q.v.).

UNSCEAR: UNITED NATIONS SCIENTIFIC COMMITTEE ON THE EFFECTS OF ATOMIC RADIATION (q.v.).

UNSCOB: UNITED NATIONS SPECIAL COMMITTEE ON THE BALKANS (q.v.).

UNSC: UNITED NATIONS SECRETARY GENERAL (q.v.).

UNTAG: UNITED NATIONS TEMPORARY AUXILIARY GROUP (q.v.).

UNTEA: UNITED NATIONS TEMPORARY EXECUTIVE AUTHORITY IN WEST GUINEA (q.v.).

UNTS: UNITED NATIONS TREATY SERIES (q.v.).

UNTSO: UNITED NATIONS TRUCE SUPERVISORY ORGANIZATION (q.v.).

UNYOM: UNITED NATIONS OBSERVER GROUP IN YEMEN (q.v.).

UPEB: UNION DE PAISE EXPORTADORE DE BANANAS (q.v.).

UPU: UNIVERSAL POSTAL UNION (q.v.).

URBI ET ORBI (L): to the city and the world; a papal decree for general publication and acceptance.

URUGUAY ROUND: session in September 1986, of the on-going negotiations that are part of the GENERAL AGREEMENT ON TARIFFS AND TRADE (q.v.) focusing on trade in goods and services. *See* 25 I.L.M. 1623 AND 28 I.L.M. 1023.

USAGE: the practice which is commonly followed; an element of the development of a customary rule of law.

USE OF FORCE: the use of force in international law is prohibited by the United Nations Charter Art. 2(4), except where specifically permitted, *see e.g.*, COLLECTIVE SELF DEFENSE. *See* 64 Am.J.Int.L. 809. *See also* 27 I.L.M. 1672.

USTR: UNITED STATES TRADE REPRESENTATIVE (q.v.).

USUCAPIO (L): use (e.g. settlement) of land; one of the means of establishing possession of territory (TERRA NULLIUS) by a sovereign.

USUFRUCT: principle in civil law similar to trust in common law. An occupying power (in time of war) must treat occupied territory as a usufruct, thus maintaining and safeguarding it as much as possible. *See* Art.55, HAGUE CONVENTION RESPECTING THE LAWS AND CUSTOMES OF WAR ON LAND (1907).

USUS ANCIPITUS (L): articles which are of ambiguous use; may be considered contraband if used in relation to a war effort.

USUS IN BELLO (L): customs of warfare, pre-19th century "laws of war."

UT RES MAGIS VALEAT QUAM PEREAT (L): it is better to give effect to a thing than to render it void.

UTI POSSIDETIS (L): rule that leaves, in the hands of the winner of a war, that which has been captured. *See* 2 Whiteman, *Digest of International Law* 1079.

V-1 AND V-2: first modern weapons based on rocket technology. The V-1 was a form of cruise missile having wings for aerodynamic flight, while the V-2 was a traditional rocket. Both were produced by Germany during World War II and used against Britain.

VALEUR D'ACHAT (F): purchase price.

VALEUR DE FAIT (F): of mature value. *See* 80 I.L.R. 501.

VALEUR EN DOUANE (F): value placed on goods for purpose of customs, *see e.g.,* AMERICAN SELLING PRICE.

VALEURS EXIGIBLE (F): realizable security interest. *See* 15 I.L.R. 599 (case 199).

VALIDITY OF ILLEGAL ACTS: acts contrary to international law may be acceptable in municipal law, and acts contrary to municipal law may be valid in international law. *See* 1 O'Connell, *International Law* 44 (1970).

VALIDITY OF MARRIAGE CONVENTION (1971): product of the HAGUE CONFERENCE ON PRIVATE INTERNATIONAL LAW (q.v.); it makes uniform rules for the law governing the celebration and validity of marriages. *See* 16 I.L.M. 18.

VALISE: *see* DIPLOMATIC BAG.

VALUATION OF PROPERTY: as arises in international disputes; market value is often cited as an appropriate guide for tribunals with the proviso that abnormal economic conditions such as high rates of inflation should be considered. *See Ferenc Claim* 26 I.L.R. 296.

VALUE-ADDED TAX: tax incurred at each step of the manufacturing process, and calculated as a percent of the increase in the value of the product due to the process it has undergone, e.g., wheat is harvested and taxed, milled into flour and taxed, and finally, baked into bread and taxed.

VAN GEND EN LOOS CASE: case before the European Court of Justice concerning the elimination of custom duties among members of the EUROPEAN ECONOMIC COMMUNITY (q.v.), and the standing of individuals to bring actions in the Court under terms of the EEC Convention. *See* 2 I.L.M. 505 and 58 Am.J.Int.L. 152.

VANDENBERG RESERVATION: United States reservation to the compulsory jurisdiction of the International Court of Justice where the dispute arises under a multilateral treaty, and not all parties to the treaty have accepted the compulsory jurisdiction of the I.C.J. This reservation was pleaded by the United States in the NICARAGUA JURISDICTION CASE, 25 I.L.M. 1032, 1107, 1124.

VANDENBERG RESOLUTION (1948): senate resolution sponsored by Sen. Vandenberg reaffirming United States' commitment to the UN and the concept of COLLECTIVE SECURITY (q.v.). This led to the framing of the NORTH ATLANTIC TREATY (q.v.). *See* 43 Am.J.Int.L. 634.

VASSAL STATE: state which owes feudal obligations to a superior state. There are no true vassal states extant, but the term is sometimes applied to emphasize the subservient status of one state to another, such as the landlocked countries surrounded by South Africa. *See* 3 I.L.R. 38.

VAT: VALUE ADDED TAX (q.v.).

VATICAN: territory in the center of Rome and the seat of the Pope, who acts as a HEAD OF STATE (q.v.). However, some of the other aspects of sovereignty for the Vatican are delegated to the Italian government by the LATERAN TREATY (1929) (q.v.). *See* 8 I.L.R. 151.

VATTEL DOCTRINE (1758): pre-positivist formulation of international law, dividing it into necessary (or natural) law and contractual obligations. The latter being the only rules that could be enforced among nations. *See* 42 Am.J.Int.L. 36-38.

VENEZIA GUILIA: part of the territory in dispute between Italy and Yugoslavia after World War II. *See* 3 Whiteman, *Digest of International Law* 50.

VENEZUELA BLOCKADE (1902): to force settlement of claims Germany, Great Britain and Italy established a BLOCKADE (q.v.) against Venezuela. The United States mediated a settlement. *See* D'Amato, *International Law Process and Prospective* at 46.

VENEZUELA BOUNDARY ARBITRATION: to settle boundary dispute between Venezuela and the territory of British Guiana. It was agreed that adverse holding for fifty years would make good title. The United States had earlier intervened in the dispute asserting the MONROE DOCTRINE (q.v.). *See* 1 Hyde, *International Law* 143.

VENIA AETATIS (L): granting of majority (adulthood) before the age specified by law, common in the Germanic civil law system.

VENIRE CONTRA FACTUM PROPRIUM (L): act which is incompatible with previous acts.

VERA CRUZ OCCUPATION (1914): Vera Cruz had been in the hands of the Huerta faction in the ongoing civil war. United States troops occupied the Mexican city of Vera Cruz, in order to punish that faction for purported wrongs to American citizens. *See* 1914 Foreign Relations 483.

VERBAL NOTE: *see* NOTE VERBAL (F).

VERBIS EXPRESSIS (L): express language, e.g., what is not prohibited, *verbis expressis*, is permitted.

VEREENIGING TREATY (1902): capitulation of the Dutch settlers, in what is now South Africa, to the British Colonial Forces. *See* 191 C.T.S. 232, II Toynbee, *Treaties* 1145.

VEREINBARUNG (G): term for a contract where both parties have the same goal. It is applied to treaties having law-making characteristics such as those forming international organizations. *See* 4 I.L.R. 8. *See Contra,* VERTRAG *(G).*

VEREINTEN NATIONEN (G): the UNITED NATIONS.

VERIFICATION: methods of self-assurance for the parties to a treaty to determine if the other parties are in compliance. Recent superpower arms limitation treaties have relied on "national technical means of verifications" which translates as "spy satellites." *See* LIMITED NUCLEAR TEST-BAND TREATY (1974).

VERIFICATION DU PAVILLION (F): or Droit d'Enquete (F), power vested in men-of-war (capital naval vessels) to require suspicious private vessels on the open sea to show their flag. The home state is responsible for any damage done in enforcing this right.

VERSAILLES ECONOMIC SUMMIT (1982): meeting of the leaders of the GROUP OF SEVEN (q.v.). They pledged to coordinate intervention by their central banks to stabilize their currencies. *See* N.Y. Times, June 7, 1982, p. D6, col. 1-6.

VERSAILLES PEACE TREATY (1919): formal end to World War I as between Germany and Britain, France, Italy, Japan, and United States. It redrew the borders of Europe, established the League of Nations, and exacted war reparations from Germany. *See* 225 C.T.S. 188. The United States did not ratify the Versailles Treaty and signed a separate peace treaty, the BERLIN TREATY (1921) (q.v.).

VERTICAL FUSION: feature of international organizations where, because delegates are appointed by their national government, they follow instructions from that government rather than developing an independent voice.

VERTRAG (G): term for a contract where parties agree to perform different obligations to further their individual goals. It is applied to describe treaties having a contract-like function, e.g., agreeing to cede territory for a cash payment. *See Contra*, VEREINBARUNG (G).

VESSEL: general term for any water-borne craft including war ships, barges, and dredging equipment. For a discussion of marking and identification of vessels on the high seas *see* 4 Whiteman, *Digest of International Law* 535.

VESTED RIGHT: a right based on treaty which cannot be lost by the subsequent termination of the treaty such as the ceding of a territory by nation A to nation B. Nation B retains sovereignty over the land despite subsequent termination of the treaty.

VETO: the power vested in a single member or officer to void a legislative act, e.g., the individual permanent members of the United Nations Security Council have a veto over Security Council resolutions. *See* Art. 27 of the UNITED NATIONS CHARTER.

VICARIOUS PERFORMANCE: the fulfillment of a state's obligation under a treaty by an act of another state. This may be done only with the permission of the state to which performance is owed or in cases where it cannot have any consequences as to who performs the obligation.

VICARIOUS RESPONSIBILITY: as opposed to ORIGINAL RESPONSIBILITY (q.v.). The responsibility a state has to police its nationals as they conduct themselves in ways that effect other countries, e.g., a state bears vicarious liability for an aircraft on its registry that violates the airspace of another country, and it has a duty to apologize for the violation and to punish the wrongdoer.

VICTIM STATE: state which is the object of aggressive acts by another state or states whether political, economic, or by the use of force. *See e.g.,* Art. 93 of the CHICAGO CONVENTION (1944).

VIENNA CONFERENCE ON SECURITY AND COOPERA-TION IN EUROPE (1986): third of the scheduled review conferences to examine compliance with the HELSINKI ACCORDS (q.v.). *See* 87 Dept. of State Bull. 34 (April 1987).

VIENNA CONGRESS (1815): meeting of the great powers and representatives of many other countries to reshape the international scene at the conclusion of the Napoleanic Wars. The final act of the Congress dealt with many subjects including the neutrality of Switzerland, free navigation on certain rivers, and rules for diplomatic relations. *See* 64 C.T.S. 453 (in French) or 1 Toynbee, *Treaties 519.*

VIENNA CONVENTION ON CIVIL LIABILITY FOR NU-CLEAR DAMAGE (1963): agreement which would make operators of nuclear reactors absolutely liable for "nuclear damage" caused by their reactors, but it would allow states to limit the amount of liability to as little as $5 million. *See* 2 I.L.M. 727.

VIENNA CONVENTION ON CONSULAR RELATIONS (1963): codification of the rules for the establishment and conduct of CONSULAR RELATIONS (q.v.), including the functions and privileges of consular missions. *See* 21 U.S.T. 77, 596 U.N.T.S. 261.

VIENNA CONVENTION ON DIPLOMATIC RELATIONS (1961): codifies the rules for sending and receiving diplomatic representatives between countries. It also enumerates the rights and duties of those representatives. *See* 23 U.S.T. 3227, 500 U.N.T.S. 95.

VIENNA CONVENTION ON SUCCESSION OF STATES IN RESPECT OF TREATIES (1978): codifies international law with respect to the application of treaty obligations. These obligations may be carried on by a newly independent territory, even though the obligations were incurred by the former sovereign of the territory. *See* 17 I.L.M. 1488. For a case involving the problem of succession *see, Burdell v. CP Air,* 11 Avi. Cases 17, 352.

VIENNA CONVENTION ON THE LAW OF TREATIES (1969): codification of the basic rules for the conclusion and application of international agreements among states. *See* 8 I.L.M. 679.

VIENNA CONVENTION ON THE LAW OF TREATIES BE-TWEEN STATES AND INTERNATIONAL ORGANIZA-TIONS (1986): sets forth substantive and procedural rules for agreements between states and international organizations, or between international organizations. It includes rules for the acceptance, modification, and revocation of such agreements. *See* 25 I.L.M. 543.

VIENNA CONVENTION ON THE REPRESENTATION OF STATES IN THEIR RELATIONS WITH INTERNATIONAL ORGANIZATIONS OF A UNIVERSAL CHARACTER: *see* 69 Am.J.Int.L. 730.

VIENNA DECLARATION (1989): CONFERENCE ON SECURITY AND COOPERATION IN EUROPE (q.v.) document recognizing the economic, social and cultural rights of individuals. *See* 28 L.L.M. 527, 534.

VIENNA RULES: International Law Association draft rules on the payment of debts in foreign money. *See* International Law Association Report, 34th Conference, Vienna, 1926 at 718.

VIENNA RULES (1815): diplomatic code adopted by the CONGRESS OF VIENNA (1815) (q.v.). It was replaced by the VIENNA CONVENTION ON DIPLOMATIC RELATIONS (1961) (q.v.).

VIENNA TREATY (1815): *See* VIENNA CONGRESS (1815).

VIET-CONG: insurgent forces fighting the government of South Vietnam and its United States ally from the early 1960's to the VIETNAM AGREEMENT (1973) (q.v.).

VIET-MIEN: insurgent forces fighting the French colonial administration in Vietnam in the early 1950's leading to the GENEVA CONFERENCE (1954) (q.v.), the withdrawal of the French, and the start of United States involvement leading to the VIETNAM WAR (q.v.).

VIETNAM AGREEMENT (1973): between the United States, South Vietnam, and North Vietnam and providing for the cessation of hostilities and the withdrawal of United States troops. This led to the complete victory of North Vietnam and first significant United States military defeat in history. *See* 24 U.S.T. 485, 935 U.N.T.S. 6, or 12 I.L.M. 48.

VIETNAM WAR: civil war between communist insurgents and the government of South Vietnam created in 1954, when the Geneva Conference (1954) (q.v.) divided the country as the French colonial administration pulled out. Things went to hell from there! *See* 60 Am.J.Int.L. 629.

VIETNAMIZATION: 1) Turning the fight against communist guerrillas over to the indigenous population (one of President Nixon's failed policies in Vietnam). 2) The term may now be applied to any policy which might result in the involvement of the United States in a foreign civil war.

VIGILANTIBUS JURA SUNT SCRIPTA (L): the laws of the vigilant are written; an agreement should state its specific terms in writing.

VILLAFRANCA PRELIMINARIES (1859): meeting (in person) of the Emperors of Austria and France after the defeat of the Austrians at the Battle of Solferino. At this meeting, a preliminary peace was concluded. It was unusual in that heads of state usually act through authorized representatives rather than in person.

VILNA DISPUTE (1919-23): question of Polish and Lithuanian claims to the city of Vilna. This city changed hands several times after World War I. *See* 20 Am.J.Int.L. 483.

VINCULUM JURIS (L): a bond of law; an obligation created by law for one party to perform an act for another.

VIOLACION DE DOMICILIO (S): trespass; unlawful entry onto private property.

VIOLACION DE TERRITORIO (S): unlawful entry into a sovereign territory, or a diplomatic premises.

VIOLATION: *see* BREACH OF TREATY.

VIS MAJOR (F): FORCE MAJEURE (q.v.).

VISA: a travel document; usually a stamp and validation on a page of the passport, allowing entry or exit from a country. *See* 9 Whiteman, *Digest of International Law* 1197.

VISBY RULES (1968): (the Brussels Protocol of Amendments to the Hague Rules) agreement to, *inter alia*, raise the liability limitations available to those engaged in CARRIAGE OF GOODS BY SEA CONVENTION (q.v.). *See* 1974 Lloyd's Mar. & Comm. L.Q. 225.

VISIT AND SEARCH: the right of a belligerent man-of-war to stop and search suspicious vessels on the high seas for contraband or to investigate the possibility of unneutral activity. *See* 10 I.L.R. 594.

VISITATION: *see* VISIT AND SEARCH.

VISITING FORCES: the entry into the territory of another sovereign of armed forces with the consent of the host sovereign, usually by formal agreement. *See* STATUS OF FORCES AGREEMENTS.

VITAL BAY: *see* HISTORIC BAY.

VITAL INTEREST CLAUSE: a clause in arbitration treaties relieving parties from the duty to submit a dispute to binding arbitration (especially if the clause involves their honor, independence, or vital interests).

VITAL INTERESTS: those aspects of a nation's foreign relations that are seen by that nation as most important. When a problem involves the vital interests of a country, it is seldom left to be decided in an international judicial forum.

VITIANU CASE: involved the question of the status of Mr. Vitianu and his wife as consular representatives of Romania in Switzerland. He was eventually convicted of spying and bribery. *See* 16 I.L.R. 281.

VOEUX (F): statements by individuals in a summary of proceedings or a final act of a conference, etc. They have no binding effect on the other participants. *See* Satow, *Guide to Diplomatic Practice* (4th ed.) 345.

VOIDANCE OF TREATIES: the loss of binding force of a treaty because of factors other than expiration or renunciation, such as the extinction of one of the contracting parties, the extinction of its object, or the fulfillment or impossibility of its object, e.g., a treaty of alliance between three nations would become void if two of the nations went to war against each other thus making the agreement of the third nation impossible to fulfill. *See* 5 I.L.R. 350.

VOIE DE FAIT (F): abuse of power. *See* 77 I.L.R. 535.

VOLKERBUND (G): LEAGUE OF NATIONS (q.v.).

VOLKERRECHT (G): INTERNATIONAL LAW (q.v.).

VOLTAIRE DOCTRINE (1713): proposal to treat those who prosecute wars in the same manner as ordinary criminals.

VOLUNTARY CONTRIBUTION: funds provided by individual nations to an international organization over and above the amounts they are obligated to pay as members, e.g., a country might pay its annual assessment to the United Nations and contribute an additional $10 million to UNICEF.

VOLUNTARY EXPATRIATION: the willful abandonment of one's country, possibly including the loss or renunciation of one's citizenship. *See* 28 I.L.R. 287.

VOLUNTARY JURISDICTION: the appearance of a nation before, and the acceptance of the authority of an international judicial body is a free choice for that nation to make. *See* COMPULSORY JURISDICTION.

VON IGEL CASE: criminal case against a German military attache involving his diplomatic immunity, and the inviolability of documents in his possession at the time of his arrest. *See* 4 Hackworth, *Digest of International Law* 517.

VOTING: means of decision-making where each participant voices his or her opinion. The opinion supported by the most participants wins. *See also,* WEIGHTED VOTING AND CONSENSUS.

VOTING PROCEDURES CASE: International Court of Justice ADVISORY OPINION (q.v.) review the power of the UNITED NATIONS GENERAL ASSEMBLY (q.v.) to supervise South African administration of NAMIBIA (q.v.). *See* 1959 I.C.J. 47.

VOTUM SEPARATUM (L): separate vote, the practice of a court in which each judge issues a separate opinion.

WAITANGI TREATY: treaty by which the Maoris (indigenous population) ceded New Zealand to the British Crown. For the dispute over its validity *see, Hoani Te Heu Heu Tukino v. Aotea District Maori Land Board*, (1941) A.C. 308.

WAIVER: the voluntary unilateral renunciation of a right or claim by a state. *See* 71 Am.J.Int.L. 1, 15.

WAL WAL ARBITRATION: a skirmish between Italian and Ethiopian troops at the oasis of Wal Wal. This skirmish led to an arbitration that illustrates the ineffectiveness of that procedure where the dispute is part of a much larger disagreement, and the ground rules for the specifics of the arbitration are not agreed upon in advance. *See* 8 I.L.R. 268.

WAR: formal state of hostilities between nations governed by the rules of war and neutrality. *See e.g.*, the HAGUE CONVENTION RESPECTING LAWS AND CUSTOMS OF WAR ON LAND.

WAR CRIMES: breaches of the laws of war (e.g., the mistreatment of prisoners of war) and CRIMES AGAINST PEACE and CRIMES AGAINST HUMANITY (q.v.). *See* NUREMBURG TRIBUNAL and TOKYO INTERNATIONAL MILITARY TRIBUNAL.

WAR EXCLUSION CLAUSE: reservation attached to an acceptance of compulsory jurisdiction of an international juridical body to the effect that jurisdiction is not accepted in cases where the dispute arises out of war, hostilities, or some other national security interest. *See* 1 Rosenne, *The Law and Practice of the International Court* 400.

WAR MATERIALS: resources directly relating to the prosecution of war such as weapons, ammunition, and combat vehicles. *See* 32 Brit.Y.B.Int'l.L.

WAR OF AGGRESSION: the use of armed forces against the territory of another sovereign in contradiction to the principles of the UNITED NATIONS CHARTER (q.v.), i.e., for purposes other than self-defense. *See* CRIMES AGAINST PEACE.

WAR OF THE PACIFIC (1879): war between Chile on one side and Bolivia and Peru on the other. Chile won the war which ended with the ANCON TREATY (q.v.), but a further dispute arose over provinces (*see* TACNA-ARICA DISPUTE). *See* 23 Am.J.Int.L. 605.

WAR PROPAGANDA: false or distorted information published in a manner which tends to incite war. *See* 34 Am.J.Int.L. 58.

WAR RISK CLAUSE: term in an insurance policy or CHARTER-PARTY (q.v.) defining the effect of the outbreak of war on the policy or lease. *See e.g.*, [1939] 2 K.B. 544.

WAR ZONE: an area on the HIGH SEAS (q.v.) declared off-limits to neutral shipping by a belligerent.

WARC: WORLD ADMINISTRATIVE RADIO CONFERENCE (q.v.).

WARC 1985: International Telecommunications Union meeting to revise the rules governing the use of the GEOSTATIONARY ORBIT (q.v.). *See* 80 Am.J.Int.L. 699.

WARNING ZONE AT SEA: area of the HIGH SEAS (q.v.) where a state is conducting activities pursuant to the freedom of the high seas and which might prove a danger to others. Thus, they are warned away.

WARS OF NATIONAL LIBERATION: insurrections aimed at enforcing a repressed people's right of SELF-DETERMINATION (q.v.), a popular third world propaganda term. *See* 1 Italian Y.B.Int'l.L. 192.

WARSAW AND OXFORD RULES: *see* RULES OF WARSAW AND OXFORD.

WARSAW CONFERENCE (1955): produced the Treaty of Friendship, Cooperation, and Mutual Assistance among Albania, Bulgaria, Czechoslovakia, German Democratic Republic, Hungary, Poland, Romania, and the Soviet Union, the basic agreement of the Warsaw Pact. *See* 49 Am.J.Int.L.Supp. 194.

WARSAW CONFERENCE ON CARRIAGE BY AIR (1929):
meeting at which the WARSAW CONVENTION (1929) (q.v.) was
finalized and signed.

WARSAW CONVENTION (1929): private international law
treaty creating certain uniform rules for the liability of international air transport operators. These include limitations on their
liability for injury to passengers or cargo. The Warsaw Convention has remained in force throughout most of the world as modified by the HAGUE PROTOCOL (1955) (q.v.). *See* 49 Stat. 3000, 2
Bevans 983, 137 L.N.T.S. 11 (Hague Protocol not in force in the
United States).

WARSAW PACT ORGANIZATION: former military alliance
among the eastern European countries under the leadership of
the Soviet Union as a "balance" to the NORTH ATLANTIC
TREATY ORGANIZATION (q.v.). *See* 49 Am.J.Int.L.Supp. 198.

WARSAW TREATY ORGANIZATION (WTO): *See* WARSAW
PACT ORGANIZATION.

WARSHIP: vessel designed for the conduct of naval warfare.
When damaged they may seek a neutral port for repairs. *See*
HAGUE CONVENTION RESPECTING THE RIGHTS AND DU-
TIES OF NEUTRALS IN THE CASE OF NAVAL WARFARE
(1907) and the WASHINGTON TREATY (1922).

WASHINGTON AGREEMENT (1957): provisions for submit-
ting the border dispute between Nicaragua and Honduras for judicial settlement. *See 1* Rosenne, *The Law and Practice of the
International Court* 81.

**WASHINGTON CONFERENCE ON THE LIMITATION OF
ARMAMENTS (1922):** *see* WASHINGTON TREATY (1922) and
16 Am.J.Int.L. 159.

WASHINGTON COMMITTEE OF JURISTS (1945): meeting,
called by the United States, of representatives of the United Nations to draft a STATUTE OF THE INTERNATIONAL COURT

OF JUSTICE (q.v.). Its proceedings are reported in 14 *Documents of the United Nations Conference on International Organization* (1945).

WASHINGTON DECLARATION (1954): a joint statement by President Eisenhower and Prime Minister Churchill reaffirming the close bond between the United States and the United Kingdom. *See* 31 Dept. State Bull. (July 12, 1954) 49.

WASHINGTON DECLARATION OF THE UNITED NATIONS (1942): established certain principles for a system of an international organization after the conclusion of World War II. *See* 204 L.N.T.S. 381, 36 Am.J.Int.L.Supp. 191.

WASHINGTON ENERGY CONFERENCE (1974): meeting called in reaction to the energy crisis of the early 1970's by the western industrial countries. They agreed to measures including conservation, research, and exploration for additional energy sources. *See* 13 I.L.M. 462.

WASHINGTON RULES: *see* WASHINGTON TREATY (1871).

WASHINGTON TREATY (1871): established rules for neutral powers to observe in sea warfare and included the COMPROMIS (q.v.) for the **ALABAMA ARBITRATION (q.v.).** Also, referred to as the Washington Rules. *See* 17 Stat. 863, 12 Bevans 170.

WASHINGTON TREATY (1903): agreement governing the rights and duties of the United States *vis-a-vis* the Panama Canal. *See* 33 Stat. 2234, 10 Bevans 663.

WASHINGTON TREATY (1922): short-lived naval disarmament treaty between the United States, Great Britain, France, Italy, and Japan limiting the size of each party's navy. Japan withdrew in 1936 terminating the treaty. *See* 43 Stat. 1655, 2 Bevans 351.

WATER POLLUTION: some international controls have been established for pollution of the seas, *see* POLLUTION FROM SHIPS CONVENTION (1973). INTERNATIONAL RIVERS (q.v.) have been subject to some pollution controls by treaty, but the general application of controls has been weak. *See* 186 Recueil de Cours 117 or 60 International Law Assignment Reports 533.

WATERFOWL: *see* WETLANDS OF INTERNATIONAL IMPORTANCE CONVENTION (1971).

WATERSHED DOCTRINE: claim of sovereignty over an entire river system based upon control of the territory around the mouth of the river. This was the basis of the United States' claim in the OREGON BOUNDARY DISPUTE (1827) (q.v.).

WEATHER MODIFICATION: subject of a United Nations Convention banning its use for military purposes, e.g., as causing it to rain in Moscow on May Day. *See* 16 I.L.M. 88.

WEATHER SATELLITES: system of orbiting observer satellites designed to gather meteorological data. This system is an early example of United States-Soviet cooperation in outer space. *See* 2 I.L.M. 902.

WEBSTER-ASHBURTON TREATY (1842): settled the boundary between the United States and Canada (the British Dominion in North America) and also addressed slave-trade and extradition. *See* 8 Stat. 572 and 1 Malloy, Treaties, Conventions, International Acts, Protocols, and Agreements Between the United States of America and Other Powers, 1909 (9110) 650.

WEIGHTED VOTING: voting where rather than follow the principle of one-man-one-vote or one-country-one-vote, the vote of each participant has more or less value based on a factor such as size, population, and financial contribution. The United States has proposed weighted voting on budget matters in the United Nations based on financial contribution to the organization. *See* 80 Am.J.Int.L. 973, 975.

WEIGHTS AND MEASURES: *See* INTERNATIONAL BUREAU OF WEIGHTS AND MEASURES.

WEST AFRICAN COMMON MARKET: *see* ABIDJAN TREATY (1973).

WEST AFRICAN ECONOMIC COMMUNITY: the abortive West African Common Market. *See* 595 U.N.T.S. 288.

WEST BANK OF JORDAN: territory which Israel occupied during the YOM KIPPUR WAR (q.v.), including the city of East Jerusalem. The occupation continues despite United Nations protest. *See* 8 Loyola of Los Angeles International and Comparative Law Journal 551.

WEST NEW GUINEA CASE: dispute between the Netherlands and Indonesia over the status of West New Guinea which was eventually turned over to Indonesia. *See* 24 I.L.R. 87.

WESTERN EUROPEAN UNION (1948): a treaty (BRUSSELS TREATY (1948)) of economic, social and cultural collaboration, and collective self-defense between Belgium, France, Luxembourg, Netherlands, and United Kingdom. *See* 19 U.N.T.S. 51.

WESTERN SAHARA ADVISORY OPINION: International Court of Justice's thoughts on the process for decolonialization of the Spanish Sahara, and the position of Morocco and Mauritania in that process. *See* 1975 I.C.J. 12 and 28 Int'l & Comp. L.Q. 296.

WESTMINISTER STATUTE (1931): gave full autonomous statehood and equal status to the Dominions of the British Crown (e.g. Canada); separating the Dominion parliaments powers from any control by the British Parliament. *See* 22 7 Halsbury's Statutes (4th ed.) 12.

WESTMINISTER TREATY (1674): the Netherlands recognized British sovereignty over "British Seas." *See* 13 C.T.S. 355 (in French).

WESTPHALIA PEACE TREATY (1648): treaty which ended the Thirty Years War; this was the first European great power's attempt to establish a world order. *See* 1 C.T.S. 119. *See also* 42 Am.J.Int.L. 20.

WET LEASE: the rental of a boat or plane with the owner providing the crew and supplies.

WETLANDS OF INTERNATIONAL IMPORTANCE CONVENTION (1971): also known as the Ramsar Convention. The parties undertake to protect wetlands, especially those important to migratory birds. *See* 11 I.L.M. 963.

WFTU: WORLD FEDERATION OF TRADE UNIONS (q.v.).

WHALING REGIME: series of international agreements first limiting then banning the hunting of whales. *See* 62 Stat. 1716, 161 U.N.T.S. 72 and 10 U.S.T. 952, 338 U.N.T.S. 366.

WHITE SLAVE TRAFFIC: procuring persons (usually women or children) for transport across boundaries for immoral purposes, e.g., kidnapping women to supply brothels in another country. *See* 9 L.N.T.S. 415 and 96 U.N.T.S. 271.

WHO: WORLD HEALTH ORGANIZATION (q.v.).

WILLFUL MISCONDUCT: imprecise translation of the French *dol* used in Art. 25 of the WARSAW CONVENTION (1929)(q.v.); it is more than negligence, but less than gross negligence. *See KLM v. Tuller*, 292 F. 2d 775.

WILHELMINA AFFAIR (1915): the British took capture (*see* PRIZE) of an American cargo ship carrying foodstuffs to Germany. *See* 7 Hackworth, *Digest of International Law* 69.

WILHELMSTRASSE: site of the German Foreign Ministry (until 1945) and, thus a synonym for German foreign policy.

WILSON DOCTRINE (1913): policy statement supporting United States intervention in Mexico and the VERA CRUZ OCCU-

PATION (q.v.), because the Mexican Government was said to be corrupt. *See* 7 Am.J.Int.L.Supp. 279.

WILSON'S FOURTEEN POINTS: in a speech to the United States Congress, January 8, 1918, President Wilson set forth principles for establishing peace at the end of World War I. These included public treaties of peace, efforts at disarmament, and the establishment of the League of Nations. *See* 1 Foreign Relations, Supp.1 (1933).

WIMBLEDON CASE: concerning the status of the Kiel Canal stated, ". . . when an artificial water way connecting two open seas has been permanently dedicated to the use of the whole world, such waterway is assimilated to natural straits in the sense that even the passage of a belligerent man-of-war does not compromise the neutrality of the sovereign state under whose jurisdiction the waters in question lie." 1923 P.C.I.J. (ser. A) No.1 at 28.

WINE: an international wine office was created in 1924. It is now called the International Vine and Wine Office. *See* 80 L.N.T.S. 293.

WIPO: WORLD INTELLECTUAL PROPERTY ORGANIZATION (q.v.).

WITNESS: one giving evidence, in person, before a judicial body. Before the International Court of Justice, both the parties and the Court may call witnesses. *See* 1 Rosenne, *Law and Practice of the International Court* 216.

WOMEN'S DECADE: United Nations effort to promote the rights of women. *See* 18 I.L.M. 550.

WORKING LANGUAGE: the language or languages chosen by an international organization in which to conduct their work, e.g., the working languages of the United Nations are English, French, Russian, Spanish, Chinese, and Arabic.

WORLD ADMINISTRATIVE RADIO CONFERENCE (WARC): a working group of the INTERNATIONAL TELECOM-

MUNICATIONS UNION (q.v.), where such items as the allocation of radio frequencies among various uses are determined. *See e.g.*, SPACE WARC.

WORLD BANK: *see* INTERNATIONAL BANK FOR RECONSTRUCTION AND DEVELOPMENT.

WORLD COURT: popular name for the PERMANENT COURT OF INTERNATIONAL JUSTICE and the INTERNATIONAL COURT OF JUSTICE (qq.v.).

WORLD EVENTS INTERACTION SURVEY (WEIS): a statistical analysis of the interactions between states, e.g., the number of diplomatic protests lodged by each country. *See* 5 International Interaction 199 (1978).

WORLD FAIR: *see* EXHIBITIONS.

WORLD FEDERAL GOVERNMENT CONFERENCE (1953): meeting in Norway to develop the structure of the international community.

WORLD FEDERATION OF TRADE UNIONS (WFTU): a non-governmental international organization of trade unions. *See* 13 Whiteman, *Digest of International Law* 82, 85.

WORLD FOOD CONFERENCE (1974): United Nations meeting which, *inter alia*, recommended the establishment of the WORLD FOOD COUNCIL (q.v.). *See* 14 I.L.M. 266

WORLD FOOD COUNCIL: organization established by the United Nations at the suggestion of the WORLD FOOD CONFERENCE (1974) (q.v.). Except for the establishment of the INTERNATIONAL FUND FOR AGRICULTURAL DEVELOPMENT (q.v.), its efforts at developing international political support for food assistance have met with little success. *See* UNGA Res. 3348 (XXIX) (December 17, 1974).

WORLD FOOD PROGRAMME: under the Food and Agricultural Organization of the United Nations, this effort distributes voluntary contributions of food to developing countries. *See* UNGA Res. 1714 (XVI) (December 19, 1961).

WORLD GOVERNMENT: aim of internationalists particularly in the mid-twentith century to create an effective supranational governing organization for the world. Both attempts, the LEAGUE OF NATIONS and the UNITED NATIONS (qq.v.), have failed to develop into such.

WORLD HEALTH ORGANIZATION (WHO): United Nations organization to promote world health through medical cooperation and assistance to less developed countries. Its achievements have included the immunization of most of the children in the world against several major diseases and the eradication of small pox. *See* 14 U.N.T.S. 185.

WORLD INTELLECTUAL PROPERTY ORGANIZATION (WIPO): United Nations affiliated organization which promotes the international protection of copyrights, patents, and trademarks. WIPO Convention, 21 U.S.T. 1749, 828 U.N.T.S. 3. *See also*, the BERNE UNION and the PARIS UNION, and PATENT COOPERATION TREATY (1970).

WORLD METEOROLOGICAL ORGANIZATION (WMO): intergovernmental organization, affiliated with the United Nations, to study world weather and to cooperate on the exchange of weather information. *See* the World Meteorological Convention, 1 U.S.T. 281, 77 UNTS 143.

WORLD ORDER: the system of international law and international organization in operation or an idealized version of the same.

WORLD PEACE THROUGH LAW: non-governmental organization to promote the development of law with the belief that this will promote peace.

WORLD TOURISM ORGANIZATION (WTO): United Nations affiliated organization to promote tourism. *See* 27 U.S.T. 2211.

WORLD WAR I: documents concerning the start of hostilities are found in 9 Am.J.Int.L.Supp. and Special Supp. Documents concerning the end of hostilities are compiled in *Foreign Relations of the United States 1919*.

WORLD WAR II (1939-1946): war began by German's invasion of Poland with France and Great Britain coming to Poland's defense. Italy joined Germany. In 1941, Japan attached Pearl Harbor and the United States declared war (see 36 Am.J.Int.L.Supp. 2, 24). The war with Germany is only recently coming to a formal conclusion. *See* 30 I.L.M. 570. Japan and the Soviet Union have not concluded a peace treaty. *See* 263 U.N.T.S. 100.

WOUNDED, SICK AND SHIPWRECKED: subject of humanitarian efforts in the development of international law especially the founding of the RED CROSS (q.v.), for the care of wounded on the battle field and rules for the protection of hospitals and hospitalships. *See* HAGUE CONVENTIONS I,II,III, and IV and the SAFETY OF LIFE AT SEA CONVENTIONS.

WRECK RIGHT: the law surrounding the salvage of wrecked and derelict ships. *See* 2 O'Connell, *The International Law of the Sea* 908-918.

WRITINGS OF PUBLICISTS: scholarly articles written by professors of international law, or other highly qualified persons examining points of international law. Writings of publicists is a source of international law according to the STATUTE OF THE INTERNATIONAL COURT OF JUSTICE (q.v.).

WRITTEN PLEADINGS: documents submitted to a judicial body stating one's side of the case. Basic pleading before the International Court of Justice is called a MEMORIAL (q.v.).

WSS: WOUNDED, SICK, AND SHIPWRECKED (q.v.).

WTO: WARSAW TREATY ORGANIZATION (q.v.).

WTO: WORLD TOURISM ORGANIZATION (q.v.).

[X - Z]

XENOPHOBIA: fear of foreigners. *See* United Nations High Commissioner on Refugees Round Table on Refugees, Victims of Xenophobia (Geneva, 1984), and PROTECTION OF THE RIGHTS OF MIGRANT WORKERS AND THEIR FAMILIES CONVENTION (1979).

X-RAY LASER: possible component of a space based strategic defense system. X-ray lasers require a nuclear explosion for their energy requirements and thus violate the OUTER SPACE TREATY (1967) (q.v.).

YACHT: privately owned pleasure boat; usually large enough to navigate on the high seas. Regarding yachts as the subject of the law of PRIZE (q.v.) *see* 12 I.L.R. 481-86.

YACHT CLUBS: formerly vessels belonging to yacht clubs and having charters from their sovereigns. These vessels were sometimes afforded the privileges of public vessels when arriving in foreign territorial waters. *See* Ferguson, *Manual of International Law* 440.

YAKIMETZ CASE (1986): a request for an International Court of Justice advisory opinion concerning the status of a Soviet citizen working at the United Nations in New York. Yakimetz defected to the United States after receiving a recall notice to the Soviet Union. *See* 26 I.L.M. 1264.

YALTA CONFERENCE (1945): second meeting of Churchill, Roosevelt, and Stalin to discuss, *inter alia*, allied policy toward the defeated states after World War II, and the establishment of the United Nations. *See Foreign Relations of the United States, the Conferences at Malta and Yalta* (GPO, 1955).

YAOUNDE CONVENTIONS: two agreements linking the European Economic Community with a number of African states. The agreements are published at 2 I.L.M. 971 and 9 I.L.M. 489. They were replaced by the LOME CONVENTION (q.v.).

YEARBOOK OF INTERNATIONAL LAW: a common type of publication by a department of a government charged with a state's foreign policy. They typically contain scholarly articles by persons connected with the government and may reflect the governments positions on the questions discussed.

YEMEN CONFLICT: civil war between royalists and republican forces in Yemen on the southern coast of the Arabian Peninsula. United Nations efforts to end the conflict are documented in 2 I.L.M. 644.

YOM KIPPUR WAR (1967): a surprise attack on Israel by her neighbors. They were quickly defeated by the Israeli forces which occupied the Sinai and even crossed the Nile. The Israeli forces occupied the Golan Heights in Syria and the whole of the West Bank in Jordan, including Jerusalem. *See* 62 Am.J.Int.L., 303 (U.N. Doc. involved), and 12 I.L.M. 1312 (cease-fire agreement).

YORK-ANTWERP RULES: adopted by the International Law Association to promote uniformity in the law of GENERAL AVERAGE (q.v.). *See* 3 American Maritime Cases Supp. (1925).

YOUNG PLAN: last effort to settle German reparation payments problems after World War I. It attempted to shift the obligations to pay reparations from the political to the commercial sector. The Plan included the selling of bonds and the creation of the BANK FOR INTERNATIONAL SETTLEMENT (q.v.). *See* 24 Am.J.Int.L.Supp. 81.

YOUNG PLAN LOANS ARBITRATION: dispute between Germany and several western countries over the terms concerning currency valuation in the YOUNG PLAN (q.v.). *See* GERMAN EXTERNAL DEBT ARBITRATION (1980).

YOUNIS REPORT: detailed study of the ORGANIZATION OF AFRICAN UNITY (q.v.) bureaucracy. *See* Amate, *Inside the OAU* 105-108.

ZANU: Zimbabwe African National Union, *see* ZANU-ZAPU PATRIOTIC FRONT.

ZANU-ZAPU PATRIOTIC FRONT: rival black guerrilla organizations joined forces to topple the white minority rule government of Ian Smith in what was then RHODESIA (q.v.) (*see* LANCASTER HOUSE AGREEMENT). This organization has been close to civil war ever since. They represent the two principal ethnic groups in the country.

ZAPU: Zimbabwe African People's Union, *see* ZANU-ZAPU PATRIOTIC FRONT.

ZEISS CASES: involved the right to use the trade name Zeiss, the domicile of the group claiming to own the trade name, and the position of the Soviet Union *vis-a-vis* an action against East German defendants. *See* 1967 A.C. 853.

ZIMBABWE: see LANCASTER HOUSE AGREEMENT and RHODESIA.

ZIMMERMAN NOTE (1917): NOTE (q.v.) from the German Foreign Minister to his Mexican Embassy proposing an alliance between Mexico and Germany against the United States. *See* Tuchman, *The Zimmerman Telegram* (1958).

ZIONISM: movement among some of the world's Jewish population to reclaim their biblical homeland in what had become Palestine (now Israel). *See* BALFOUR DECLARATION (1917) and BASIL PROGRAM (1897).

ZIPA FRONT (early 1975): attempt at establishment of a unified guerrilla force to overthrow the white minority government of Ian Smith in Northern RHODESIA (q.v.), now Zimbabwe, which later succeeded as the ZANU-ZAPU PATRIOTIC FRONT (q.v.).

ZIVILPROZESSORDNUNG (ZPO) (G): the Code of Civil Procedure of Germany.

ZOLLVEREIN (G): German customs union, effort by the thirty or so German states before the unification of Germany to act in a concerted manner to protect themselves against the economic power of their unified neighbors, especially Great Britain and France.

ZONE FOR REVENUE AND SANITARY LAW: extension of a coastal state's authority beyond the territorial sea by municipal laws which attempt to control vessels approaching the state's ports with regards to matters of customs and health regulations.

ZONE FRANC (F): countries where the French franc is the legal tender.

ZONE OF OPERATION: during war an area somewhat bigger than the CONTACT ZONE (q.v.), but probably not including all of the belligerent's territory.

ZONE OF PROTECTIVE JURISDICTION: claim of littoral states to the right to take defensive actions beyond the limits of their territorial waters. *See* AIR DEFENSE IDENTIFICATION ZONE.

ZPO: ZIVILPROZESSORDNUNG (q.v.).

ZUIDER ZEE: former HISTORIC BAY (q.v.), now most of the submerged land has been reclaimed and a small inland sea has been formed of the remaining water.

ZURICH TREATY (1859): peace treaty between France and Sardinia and Austria after Austria's defeat in Italy. *See* 121 C.T.S. 145 et seq. or 1 Toynbee, *Treaties* 603 (English transl.)

ZUSICHERUNG (G): an assurance of administrative promise; usually either to carry out or refrain from a particular administrative act. *See* 24 Int'l.Lawyer 411.

ZWANGSKURS (G): compulsory currency; the only money circulating legally.

ZWECKVERMOGEN (G): special purpose fund which may act as a legal entity. *See* 77 I.L.R. 450.